The Beatles a diary

Copyright ©1998 Omnibus Press
(A Division of Book Sales Limited)

Edited by Chris Charlesworth
Cover and book designed by
Stephen Coates and Jason Beard
Picture research by Nikki Russell

ISBN: 0.7119.6315.0
Order No: OP 47880

Exclusive Distributors:
Book Sales Limited
8/9 Frith Street
London, W1V 5TZ, UK

Music Sales Corporation
257 Park Avenue South
New York, NY 10010, USA

Music Sales Pty Limited
120 Rothschild Avenue, Rosebery
NSW 2018, Australia

To the Music Trade only:
Music Sales Limited
8/9, Frith Street
London, W1V 5TZ, UK

Printed and bound in Great Britain

A catalogue record for this book is
available from the British Library.

Visit Omnibus Press at
http://www.musicsales.co.uk

The Beatles a diary

An intimate day by day history by Barry Miles

 OMNIBUS PRESS

Introduction

The Beatles were a Sixties band, the only band to encompass the entire decade, literally beginning in 1960, when they went to Hamburg, and ending in 1970, when Paul sued to end their partnership. Other bands, like The Shadows, lived through it, but they were a Fifties group who managed to hang on indefinitely. The Beatles both reflected the enormous changes in society through the decade and were themselves catalysts for that change. They came together during the era of 'How Much Is That Doggie In The Window?' and 'The Deadwood Stage', and went professional at the time of The Avons' 'Three Little Girls Sitting In The Back Seat' and Ricky Valence's 'Tell Laura I Love Her'. By the time they broke up, Jimi Hendrix, The Doors, Brian Jones' Rolling Stones and Syd Barrett's Pink Floyd had been and gone. The Beatles were both precursors and survivors.

They started it all, entering the music business when the BBC had a monopoly on radio, and the industry giants EMI and Decca dominated the record charts. Before The Beatles, an American would have been hard pressed to name one British singer or group; after The Beatles, British acts occupied a large percentage of the American charts. They paved the way for The Rolling Stones, The Who, The Kinks, The Yardbirds, The Animals, Herman's Hermits and the scores of other bands that constituted "The British Invasion".

Pop music, as it was known in the days before "rock", was seen as part of show business: to their bosses at EMI, there was little difference between The Beatles and Alma Cogan. They were on the cusp between music hall and MTV, playing variety shows along with hoofers, jugglers and comedians, though there is no recorded instance of them following a performing dog act. It is unlikely that Oasis would consider sharing top billing on a TV show with a glove puppet, but The Beatles did. Pop groups were regarded as variety acts, and in these pages The Beatles can be seen playing *Saturday Night At The London Palladium*, and *Mike and Bernie Winters' Big Night Out*, along with Arthur Askey, Bruce Forsyth, Morecambe and Wise and the like, where they were expected to take part in skits as well as play their latest single. (In fact, as pop music has become more of a packaged commodity, new bands can be seen doing much the same thing in the Nineties, but in the heady days of "rock" it was a point of principle for Led Zeppelin never to appear on television, regardless of the show.)

Live performance was more important to The Beatles than to many present day acts because that was how they made their money, at least in the early years. Their royalties from EMI were so derisory that the greatest benefit of having a record in the charts came from the ability to charge more for live performances. No-one expected to make serious money from record sales, but with records in the charts you could play a lucrative summer season in a seaside resort and a sold-out Christmas panto. The Beatles did all of this after their initial success. Of course, all that would change. Indeed,

they sold so many records that even on a farthing per record each they were able to get rich, and when it came time to renew their contract with EMI they got their own back by driving an incredibly hard bargain.

Their work-load was astonishing: more than 800 hours on stage in Hamburg, 275 performances at The Cavern alone. On top of that, Brian Epstein experimented with bookings, trying out new markets, booking them into a public school here, a débutante dance there, three weeks at The Paris Olympia, Carnegie Hall. Brian was determined to present them as a class act. Looking through the chronology it is fascinating to see who else was on the bill, particularly in the early days. At The Cavern, with its origins as a jazz club, they were often as not sharing the bill with one or two traditional jazz bands. Trad jazz enjoyed a period of popularity just as The Beatles were getting going. It was a peculiar business, bearing little relationship to its supposed origins in Twenties' New Orleans. All its original practitioners were either dead or in their seventies and eighties. Acker Bilk headlined in bowler hat and striped waistcoat and The Temperance Seven were cool and languid in a smooth flapper style that owed little to a New Orleans street band. This was what The Beatles were up against. Not great competition admittedly, but their energy and belief in themselves and their music saw them through, blowing their rivals off the stage one by one, first in Hamburg, then Liverpool, London and then the world.

Why The Beatles and not, say, Rory Storm and The Hurricanes who already featured Ringo Starr? The answer lies in their extraordinary ability as composers. It was fortuitous that Lennon and McCartney should meet because not only were they rock'n'roll fanatics, but they were also both already writing songs. The chemistry between them worked perfectly and together they composed an extraordinary body of work. The Beatles recorded 184 original songs (some of which were by George) without which they would almost certainly not have enjoyed such world-wide success. It was remarkable that they wrote songs at all, coming from their background, but what made The Beatles unstoppable was the momentum they created in their work, striving to make each album and single different, relying not on a tried and tested blues format or a series of traditional pop hooks, but experimenting with harmonies and rhythms, changing tempos and even tagging on whole new melodies. Songs poured out of them, so many that they didn't need to use singles on albums to fill the space. In the modern era, up to three years or more often elapse between album releases by top recording acts, but The Beatles – the top act in the world – managed to release 12 original albums, including one double, in the eight years between 1963 and 1970, not to mention around 30 non-album tracks, including many of their biggest and best loved hit singles. Astonishingly, the third member of the group, George Harrison, also flowered as a songwriter. To his chagrin, Frank Sinatra always

introduced 'Something' as "a Lennon and McCartney composition" and George didn't get his full due until after the band split up. Even Ringo wrote the odd song, such as 'Octopus's Garden', but his best songs came later: 'It Don't Come Easy', 'Back Off Boogaloo'.

They heralded the singer-songwriter, hastening the collapse of the Brill Building and its commercial song writing teams. Before The Beatles it was rare to sing your own material: Elvis never wrote a song. After The Beatles it was seen as a sign of weakness if you didn't sing your own stuff. As old time rocker Jerry Lee Lewis said, referring to the demise of Bobby Vee, Bobby Darin, Bobbie Vinton and all the other Bobbies as The Beatles wiped the board clean: "Thank God for The Beatles, they cut 'em down like wheat before the sickle".

They turned touring upside down too. Before The Beatles there were no stadium concerts: after they filled Shea Stadium to its 55,000 capacity – the biggest rock'n'roll audience ever assembled at that time – the American stadium tour became the norm for a world-class act. The Beatles toured America with two roadies and a driver, playing hockey arenas and baseball stadiums, using whatever existing PA there was and with no foldback speakers on stage. Modern groups tour with an entourage of 150 crew and have more volume in their stage monitors than The Beatles had for a whole stadium, but once again, it was The Beatles that led the way.

As if all this wasn't enough, during the

Beatlemania years of non-stop touring and recording they also somehow found the time to make two full-length feature films, scores of live radio and TV appearances and give more media interviews in a day than today's superstars are inclined to give in a year. Somehow, amidst all this, they also coped with being the most famous and sought after people on the planet.

No other group developed so much. It would have been easy to retire, or at least settle back into comfortable celebrity after Beatlemania, but instead the Four Moptops transformed themselves into the Princes of Psychedelia and began a whole new life and a whole new series of experiments, dragging pop music forever out of Denmark Street and Tin Pan Alley and into the realm of art. *Revolver* had been a landmark album, filled with beautifully crafted songs and yet using experimental studio techniques that had other groups consulting with their studio managers. It was hard to see how they could better it. Everyone was waiting to see what they did next.

Sgt Pepper was the world's first "concept" album, the first to print the lyrics on the sleeve (another blow to Denmark Street), and musically, it blew everyone's minds. It had the huge iconic chord on 'A Day In The Life' and it even had an iconic sleeve that was much parodied and copied over the years. It was their "masterpiece" in the traditional Renaisssance sense of a piece of work to prove you knew your craft.

Drugs certainly helped this transformation and, because LSD and marijuana were illegal, The Beatles found themselves

assigned yet another pioneering role as spokesmen for the newly emerging drug culture: they signed (and paid for) the "pot ad" in *The Times*, they recorded psychedelic music that was banned by the BBC and were interviewed about LSD by serious newspapers. Naturally they were also busted. Having abandoned their identity as the Fab Four, the nation's favourite boys, they were fair game for the drugs squad.

The strain of it all took its toll. They were tired to their bones, stressed and taking too many drugs. John, perhaps, felt it most keenly. Once again they both mirrored and led the direction of Sixties' popular culture when they became involved in meditation and the Maharishi Mahesh Yogi. The Maharishi might have been a passing interest had Brian Epstein not died when The Beatles were on one of his meditation courses. His words helped them deal with their grief and the next year they set off to India, in John and George's case with no clear idea of when, if ever, they might come back.

In the event, they did not become yogis, but their period of enforced sobriety allowed scores of songs to come flowing from them, many of which appeared on the double *White Album* and *Abbey Road*. Ultimately it all came to an end: first Ringo, then George left the group and both returned. Then John left and they told no-one. When Paul got fed up with waiting around instead of getting on with a solo career, he revealed that The Beatles were no more in a press release that accompanied his first solo album. The press misunderstood the story and thought that he

was the one who had left. They soon found out the truth, and in looking for someone to blame, picked on Yoko Ono. Yoko certainly played a role in the break-up by sticking close to John in the studio, inhibiting the close-knit working relationship they had previously enjoyed, something that the other Beatles' wives and girlfriends did not do – and something that John would have objected to strenuously if anyone else had done it. But the band had run its course. They had grown apart. It was a marriage approaching divorce, and, as with many divorces, it was acrimonious, doubly so because it attracted the media spotlight. With so much money at stake there were powerful conflicting forces at work, one of which was their last "manager" Allen Klein, who later went to jail for financial skulduggery.

The Beatles have become icons: just as the Eiffel Tower is for Paris, Big Ben for London, The Empire State Building for New York, a clip of Hitler ranting locates us at the beginning of the World War II. For the Sixties we have Harold Wilson puffing his pipe, Christine Keeler sitting astride her famous chair, and there, jigging their guitars on some forgotten stage, their fringes covering their foreheads, screaming girls drowning out their words: The Beatles – the last great band in black and white.
Miles

Acknowledgements

I first met The Beatles in 1965: George and John at Allen Ginsberg's 39th birthday party in London, Paul at Peter Asher's house and Ringo at a recording session at Abbey Road. Together with John Dunbar and Peter Asher, I founded a company called Miles Asher and Dunbar Limited (M.A.D. Ltd) and opened Indica Books and Gallery. Paul McCartney was then living in the Asher household and quickly became involved in the project: putting up shelves, plastering holes in walls and designing and printing the wrapping paper. In 1966 it was at Indica that John met Yoko Ono when we gave her her first European show.

That same year I co-founded *International Times* (*IT*) and once again Paul was the first Beatle to get involved. He suggested I interview him, and that on the strength of that we would be able to get record company advertising. I did, and he was right. It was my first interview.
I followed it up with one with George, then Mick Jagger and many years of rock journalism followed. Paul and John came to Indica quite regularly, and I often hung out at their recording sessions, particularly when they were making Sgt Pepper. When Apple was started, Paul made me the label manager for Zapple, the spoken word and experimental label. John and Yoko were very involved with Zapple and it was in 1969 that I did a two-day interview with them – once again for the underground press – this time for *Oz*.

Throughout the period I kept journal notes, as well as bulging clipping files and these have been the basis of much of this book. As the years went by, I also accumulated an enormous library of Beatles books and related trivia, always assuming they would come in useful one day. Well, that day finally came. As we were putting this book together new books on The Beatles were appearing at the rate of one or two a month, literally one every three weeks. I have details of more than 350, though many of these are little more than picture books, and I cannot claim to have referred to more than 150 of them. In the end there were a dozen or so essential source books that I found myself pulling from the shelf time and time again, the primary one of which was of course Mark Lewisohn's *The Complete Beatles Chronicle* (London, Pyramid, 1992). Anyone wishing to know the full details of every Beatles recording session will find Mark's book indispensable. Another key book was Kevin Howlett's *The Beatles At The BEEB*, the story of their radio career (London, BBC, 1982).

For early dates and addresses of homes and schools I used Hunter Davies' authorised *The Beatles* (London, Heinemann, 1968, revised and updated several times since then), and of course, another indispensable source of information was *The Beatles Book Monthly* 1-77 (August 1963 – December 1969).

For John, by far the best for facts was Albert Goldman's *The Lives of John Lennon*, which added new information to the story (the name and dates of John's first school, for instance) even though the book is ungenerous in spirit. John's murder provoked about 100 "tribute" books of one sort or another, which I'll not list here. The following books proved useful in assembling this chronology: Baird, Julia, with Giuliano, Geoffrey: *John Lennon, My Brother* (London, Grafton, 1988); The editors of *Rolling Stone*: *The Ballad of John and Yoko* (London, Michael Joseph, 1982); Fawcett, Anthony: *John Lennon, One Day At A Time* (New York, Grove, 1976); Harry, Bill: *The Book of Lennon* (London, Aurum, 1984); [eds] Herzogenrath, Wulf and Hansen, Dorothee: *John Lennon: Drawings Performances Films* (Stuttgart, Cantz Verlag, 1995); Lennon, Cynthia: *A Twist Of Lennon* (London, Star, 1978) [also updated and rewritten in Hello! magazine]; Lennon, Pauline: *Daddy Come Home* (London, Harper Collins, 1990); Miles, [Barry], ed: *John Lennon In His Own Words* (London, Omnibus Press, 1980); Peebles, Andy: *The Lennon Tapes* (London, BBC, 1981); Sheff, David: *The Playboy Interviews with John Lennon* (London, NEL, 1982); Shotton, Pete and Schaffner, Nicholas: *John Lennon In My Life* (London, Coronet, 1983); Wenner, Jan, ed: *Lennon Remembers* (Harmondsworth, Penguin, 1973).

For Paul I used his brother's three books: McCartney, Michael: *Mike Mac's White and Blacks* (London, Aurum, 1986); *Remember, The Recollections and Photographs of Michael McCartney* (London, Merehurst, 1992) and *Thank U Very Much, Mike McCartney's Family Album* (London, Arthur Barker, 1981). I also looked at the following and found the odd date or two among them: Benson, Ross: *Paul McCartney, Behind The Myth* (London, Victor Gollancz, 1992); Coleman, Ray: *McCartney, Yesterday and Today* (London, Boxtree, 1995); [duNoyer, Paul][Ed]: *The Paul McCartney World Tour* (London, MPL/EMAP, 1989); Elson, Howard: *McCartney, Songwriter* (London, W.H.Allen, 1986); Flippo, Chet: *McCartney, The Biography* (London, Sidgwick & Jackson, 1988); Gambaccini, Paul: *Paul McCartney In His Own Words* (London, Omnibus Press, 1976); Giuliano, Geoffrey: *Blackbird, the Life and Times of Paul McCartney* (New York, Dutton 1991.); Harry, Bill: *The McCartney File* (London, Virgin, 1986); Salewicz, Chris: *McCartney: The Biography* (London, Macdonald, 1986); Schwartz, Francie: *Body Count* (San Francisco, Straight Arrow, 1972); Welch, Chris: *Paul McCartney, the Definitive Biography* (London, Proteus, 1984) and Paul's fan club magazine: *Club Sandwich*.

For George I used his autobiography: *I Me Mine* (New York, Simon & Schuster, 1980); Giuliano, Geoffrey: *Dark Horse* (London, Bloomsbury, 1989), and Taylor, Derek: *As Time Goes By, Living In The Sixties* (San Francisco, Straight Arrow, 1973).

For Ringo I checked my dates and addresses against Clayson, Alan: *Ringo Starr, Straight Man or Joker?* (London, Sidgwick & Jackson, 1991).

As far as record releases went, I found Harry Castleman and Walter Podrazik's 1976 discography *All Together Now* to be the most accurate and complete of the dozens of Beatles' discographies I have seen, though I also consulted Campbell, Colin and Murphy, Allan: *Things We Said Today*, (songs concordance) (Ann Arbor, Michigan, Pierian Press, 1980); Carr, Roy and Tyler, Tony: *The Beatles: An Illustrated Record* (London, Triune, 1978); Dowlding, William: Beatlesongs (New York, Simon & Schuster, 1989); Guzek, Arno: *Beatles Discography* (Hvidovre, Denmark, 1976); McGeary, Mitchell: *The Beatles Discography* (Olympia, Washington, Ticket To Ride, 1975); Reinhart, Charles: *You Can't Do That! Beatles Bootlegs & Novelty Records* (Ann Arbor, Michigan, Pierian Press, 1981); Russell, Jeff: *The Beatles: Album File and Complete Discography* (Poole, Dorset, Blandford, 1982); Stannard, Neville: *The Long And Winding Road, A History of The Beatles On Record* (London, Virgin, 1982); Turner, Steve: *A Hard Day's Write, the Stories Behind Every Beatles Song* (London, Carlton, 1994); Wallgren, Mark: *The Beatles On Record* (New York, Simon & Schuster, 1982); Wiener, Allen: *The Beatles: The Ultimate Recording Guide* (London, Aurum, 1993) and *The Beatles For The Record* (Knutsford, Cheshire, 1981).

I think Tom Schultheiss's *A Day In The Life: The Beatles Day-By-Day, 1960 – 1970* (Ann Arbor, Michigan, Pierian Press, 1980) was the first day-by-day chronology though there have been many since and I have taken dates from all of them, in particular: *Beatles Diary for 1965* (Glasgow, Beat Publications, 1964); *Beatles Press Book* (London, Apple Records, 1969); Benson, Harry: *The Beatles In The Beginning* (Edinburgh, Mainstream, 1993); Bunt, Jan Van De: *The Beatles Concert-ed Efforts* (The Netherlands, 1979); Fulpen, H.V.: *The Beatles, An Illustrated Diary* (London, Plexus, 1982); Lewisohn, Mark: *The Beatles Live!* (London, Pavilion, 1986) and Pawlowski, Gareth: *How They Became The Beatles* (London, Macdonald, 1990). The source of many of the above books has been the (virtually identical) chronologies given in George Tremlett's two individual Beatle biographies: *The John Lennon Story* (London, Futura, 1976) and *The Paul McCartney Story* (London, Futura, 1975), an idea picked up by Ray Coleman in his useful *John Lennon* (London, Futura, 1985).

There have been books about most of The Beatles' tours and sometimes about individual concerts, and I have used them all. For their days in Hamburg, the following were useful: Williams, Allan: *The Man Who Gave The Beatles Away* (London, Coronet, 1976); Jürgs, Michael, Ziemann, Hans Heinrich and Meyer, Dietmar: *Das Album Der Beatles* (Hamburg, Stern, 1981); Rehwagen, Thomas and Schmidt, Thorsten: *Mach Schau! Die Beatles In Hamburg* (Braunschweig, EinfallReich, 1992); Zint, Günter: *Große Freiheit 39* (Munich, Wilhelm Heyne Verlag) and Vollmer, Jürgen: *Rock 'n' Roll Times* (New York, Google Plex, 1981).

There are two essential books about Liverpool: Thompson, Phil: *The Best of Cellars, the Story of the World Famous Cavern Club* (Liverpool, Bluecoat, 1994) and Harry, Bill, ed: *Mersey Beat, The Beginnings of The Beatles* (London, Omnibus Press, 1977) [Facsimiles from *Mersey Beat* magazine]. Evans, Mike and Jones, Ron: *In The Footsteps of The Beatles* (Liverpool, Merseyide Council guidebook, 1981) was also valuable.

The Beatles In Sweden (London, City Magazines, 1963) was about just that and Glenn Baker's *The Beatles Down Under, the 1964 Australia and New Zealand Tour* (Glebe, Wild and Woolley, 1982) is the standard work on The Beatles in Australia, with so many facts and anecdotes your head spins. The Beatles in the USA were, naturally, very well covered. I made particular use of *26 Days That Rocked The World* (Los Angeles, O'Brien, 1978) which consisted entirely of facsimile newspaper clips of The Beatles' first US tour, and also found data in Leach, Sam: *The Beatles On Broadway* (Manchester, World Distributors, 1964), a souvenir of The Beatles' first visit to the USA; Cosham, Ralph: *The Beatles At Carnegie Hall* (London, Panther Pictorial, 1964); Freeman, Robert: *The Beatles In America* (London, Daily Mirror Publications, 1964); Freeman, Robert: *Yesterday, Photographs of The Beatles* (London, Weidenfeld & Nicolson, 1983); Rayl, A.J.S.: *Beatles '64. A Hard Day's Night In America* (London, Sidgwick & Jackson, 1989); Harrison, George [of the *Liverpool Echo*]: *Around The World With The Beatles* (Liverpool, *Liverpool Echo*, 1964). Alf Bicknell with Gary Marsh: *"Baby You Can Drive My Car"* [np] (Number 9 Books, 1989) provided a few hotel names.

There are only a few books about Apple. The most useful were: DiLello, Richard: *The Longest Cocktail Party* (London, Charisma, 1972); Martin, George: *Summer of Love, The Making of Sgt. Pepper* (London, Macmillan, 1994); McCabe, Peter and Schonfeld, Robert: *Apple To The Core, the Unmaking of The Beatles* (London, Martin Brian & O'Keeffe, 1972) and Taylor, Alistair: *Yesterday, The Beatles Remembered* (London, Sidgwick & Jackson, 1988).

For the three films I consulted: Dellar, Fred: *NME Guide to Rock Cinema* (London, Hamlyn, 1981); Yule, Andrew: *The Man Who "Framed" The Beatles, A Biography of Richard Lester* (New York, Donald Fine, 1994); Matahira, Toru: *Beatles Movie Catalog* (Japan, 1979) and Cott, Jonathan and Dalton, David: *The Beatles Get Back* (London, Apple, 1969).

I should also mention: Black, Johnny: *The Beatles Complete* (London, HMV, 1988); Blake, John: *All You Needed Was Love* (London, Hamlyn, 1981); Braun, Michael: *Love Me Do! The Beatles Progress* (Harmondsworth, Penguin, 1964); Brown, Peter and Gaines, Steven: *The Love You Make* (London, Macmillan, 1983); Castleman, Harry & Podrazik, Walter: *The Beatles Again?* (Ann Arbor, Michigan Pierian Press, 1977); Castleman, Harry & Podrazik, Walter: *The End Of The Beatles?* (Ann Arbor, Michigan Pierian Press, 1985); Friede, Goldie, Titone, Robin and Weiner, Sue: *The Beatles A To Z* (New York, Methuen, 1980); Harry, Bill: *The Ultimate Beatles Encyclopedia* (London, Virgin, 1992); Hoffmann, Dezo: *With The Beatles* (London, Omnibus Press, 1982); Schreuders, Piet and Smith, Adam: *The Beatles London*, (London, Hamlyn, 1994); Miles [Barry], ed: *Beatles In Their Own Words* (London, W.H. Allen, 1978); Schaffner, Nicholas: *The British Invasion* (New York, McGraw-Hill, 1982); Schaffner, Nicholas: *The Beatles Forever* (New York, McGraw-Hill, 1977); Southall, Brian: *Abbey Road, The Story of the World's Most Famous Recording Studios* (Cambridge, Stevens, 1982); Taylor, Derek: *It Was Twenty Years Ago Today* (London, Bantam, 1987).

Finally, I used the following Beatles internet sites, some of which will probably not still be up, but any search engine will take you to a site with links:

Dave Haber's Beatles page:
http://www.primenet.com/~dhaber/beatles.html

The Official rec.music.beatles Home Page:
http://kiwi.imgen.bcm.tmc.edu:8088/public/rmb.html

Troni's Beatles Page:
http://nobile.wirtschaft.tuilmenau.de/~weigmann/beatles.html

Alan Braverman's Beatles Page:
http://turtle.ncsa.uiuc.edu/alan/beatles.html

Mike Markowski's Beatles Page:
http://www.eecis.udel.edu/~markowsk/beatles/

Aaron Gill's Paul McCartney page:
http://www.halcyon.com/marieg/paul.html

Harald Gernhardt's Paul McCartney Home Page:
http://131.188.139.62:8080/hyplan/gernhard/macca.html and on usenet: rec.music.beatles

As this is the acknowledgments page, it is the correct place to thank my assistant Polly Timberlake for working so long and hard on this book as well and to give a nod to Chris Charlesworth and Bob Wise for commissioning it in the first place.

John: "I met **Paul** and said 'Do you **wanna**'

Then **George** joined and then **Ringo** joined.
We were **just** a band who **made it**

join me band?'

very, very very

That's all."

1934-59

1934
February 18
– Yoko Ono was born in Tokyo, Japan.
September 19
– Brian Epstein was born in Liverpool.
1938
December 3
– Julia Stanley married Alfred Lennon.
1939
September 10
– Cynthia Powell was born in Blackpool, Lancashire.
September 15
– John's Aunt Mimi married George Smith.
1940
June 23
– Stuart Sutcliffe was born in Edinburgh, Scotland.
July 7
– Richard Starkey was born at 9 Madryn Street, Liverpool 8, in the Dingle.
October 9
– John Winston Lennon born at Oxford Street Maternity Hospital, Liverpool, to Alfred Lennon and Julia Lennon, née Stanley. Contrary to other reports, there was no Luftwaffe raid that night. The previous raid had been on the night of September 21 – 22, and the next was on October 16, when the Walton and Everton districts were hit, causing 30

casualties. John lived at 9 Newcastle Road, Liverpool 15, with his mother, his Aunt Mimi and his grandparents. His father was away at sea.
1941
April 15
– James McCartney married Mary Mohin in Liverpool and they went to live in furnished rooms in Sunbury Road, Anfield.

Paul McCartney, aged 6, with his younger brother Michael. Opposite: Primary school John Lennon.

1942
June 18
– James Paul McCartney was born at Walton Hospital, Liverpool, to James McCartney, cotton salesman, and Mary Patricia McCartney, née Mohan, midwife. Because Mary had previously been a matron at the hospital she was entitled to a bed in a private ward. Jim's job at Napiers aircraft factory was classifed as war work, so they were able to get a small house in Wallasey, at 92 Broadway, across the Mersey.
September 24
– Linda Louise Eastman was born in Scarsdale, New York.
1943
February 24
– (not the 25th, as many publications state) George Harrison was born at 11:42 pm to Louise Harrison, née French, a Liverpool shopgirl, and Harold Hargreaves Harrison, bus conductor since 1937 and for ten years before that a ship's steward on the Liverpool White Star Line. George was their fourth and last child, and grew up in a little two-up-two-down redbrick terraced house at 12 Arnold Grove, Wavertree, Liverpool 15.
1944
– Julia Lennon found another man, John Dykins.
January
– The McCartney family moved to a bungalow in Roach Avenue, Knowsley Estate, Liverpool.
1945
March 17
– Patricia Boyd was born.
November 12
– John went to his first school: Mosspits County Primary School on Mosspits Lane.

Freddie Lennon

Freddie Lennon was a ship's steward on the liners, and had been in New York when the war broke out. He was transferred to a Liberty Boat, but demoted from head waiter to assistant steward. He purposely missed the boat and wound up spending three months in jail. His cheques to Julia stopped, and his marriage more or less ended because of it.

Aunt Mimi moved into "Mendips" when her husband George, returned home from the war. She suggested that Julia and baby John move into a cottage owned by her husband at 120A Allerton Road, Woolton, which she did. Julia thought that her husband Freddie had deserted both her and the Navy. Free from the watchful eyes of her parents, she went out on the town, frequently leaving baby John alone in the cottage.

1946
March
– Freddie Lennon and John Dykins came to blows when Julia announced that she was going to live with Dykins. She moved in with him at 1 Blomfield Road, Liverpool 18. John was sent to live with Julia's sister Mimi and her husband George at "Mendips", 251 Menlove Avenue, Liverpool 25 because Dykins didn't want to bring up another man's son.
April 5
– Jane Asher was born in London.
– John was expelled from Mosspits County Primary School for misbehaviour. He was five and a half.
– John was enrolled in Dovedale Road Primary School.

August 4
– Maureen Cox was born in Liverpool.
– The McCartney family moved to a ground-floor flat in Sir Thomas White Gardens, Liverpool city centre, and not long afterwards to a new council house at 72 Western Avenue, Speke.
1947
September
– Paul started at Stockton Wood Road Primary School, Speke.
1948
September
– George went to Dovedale Road Primary School. John Lennon was still there but three years ahead so they never met.
1949
– George's family moved to a new

two-up-two-down council house at 25 Upton Green, Speke. They had been on the council housing list for 18 years, ever since George's eldest sister, Louise, was born.
1952
– Paul's family moved to 12 Ardwick Road, Speke.
September
– John started at Quarry Bank High School.
1953
June
– John's Uncle George, Aunt Mimi's husband, had a haemorrhage and died. John had been very close to him and was deeply shocked.
September
– Paul entered the Liverpool Institute. The Institute was the best known of Liverpool's grammar schools and had an impressive list of old boys, including High Court judges, politicians, even a Nobel Prizewinner. Exceptional 11-Plus results enabled the brightest children in Liverpool to be sent to the Institute. Paul was offered a place and went even though it was a long ride from Speke.
1954
September
– George started at the Liverpool Institute. Paul was already there, in the year above. **George: "It took from four o'clock to five to get home in the evening to the outskirts of the Speke estate and it was on that bus journey that I met Paul McCartney, because he, being at the same school, had the same uniform and was going the same way as I was so I started hanging out with him.**
1955
– Paul's family moved to Forthlin Road, Allerton, Liverpool 18.

His **mother** was a **midwife** and he had a **trumpet."**

John's upbringing

Freddie Lennon returned to Liverpool and took his five-year-old son to Blackpool for a holiday. Freddie was planning to emigrate to New Zealand, along with the man he was staying with in Blackpool, and intended to take John with him. After several weeks, Julia arrived at the door, wanting John back. Freddie invited her to come with them, but she declined. She just wanted John. Five-year-old John had to decide which parent he wanted, and inevitably chose his mother. But Julia did not intend to bring him up. He was delivered back to Aunt Mimi and Uncle George, this time for good.

we **thought** we made a **pretty** good **sound** **but** so did about **four million** other **groups."**

September

– John was now in the C stream at school because his marks were so poor. By the final term, he was 20th in the class: the bottom of the bottom class.

1956

September

– A new headmaster Mr. Pobjoy, took over Quarry Bank High School. He recognised that John's poor marks were due to personal problems and that John was capable of much better work.

October 31

– Mary Patricia McCartney died of breast cancer, aged 47. From then on, Jim McCartney brought up Paul and his brother Michael single-handedly, as well as holding down a full-time job.

1957

– George's mother bought him a guitar from a boy at school who was selling it for £3. It soon became obvious that he needed something better and his mother saved up her housekeeping money until she could buy him a £30 model with a cut-away neck.

Summer

– George and his brother Pete, together with Pete's school friend Arthur Kelly, played a gig at the British Legion Club in Speke calling themselves The Rebels. Since no other band scheduled to play had turned up, they were forced to play all through the evening.

George: "I remember The Rebels had a tea chest with a lot of gnomes around it. One of my brothers had a five shilling guitar which had the back off it. Apart from that it was all fine. Just my brother, some mates and me. I tried to lay down the law a bit, but they weren't having any of that.

The next morning on the bus to school, George told Paul about the gig. After that, Paul began to join George in the Harrison's front room, where they played their way through his chord books.

George: "Paul was very good with the harder chords, I must admit. After a time though, we actually began playing real songs together, like 'Don't You Rock Me

Daddy-O' and 'Besame Mucho'. Paul knocked me out with his singing especially, although I remember him being a little embarrassed to really sing out, seeing as we were stuck right in the middle of my parents' place with the whole family walking about. He said he felt funny singing about love and such around my dad. We must have both been really a sight. I bet the others were just about pissing themselves trying not to laugh."**

Paul: "I knew George long before John and any of the others. They were all from Woolton, the posh district, and we hailed from the Allerton set which was more working class. George and I had got together to learn the guitar and we were chums, despite his tender years as it seemed to me then. In fact George was only nine months younger than I was but to me George was always my little mate. But he could really play the guitar, particularly a piece called 'Raunchy' which we all loved. If anyone could do something as good as that, it was generally good enough to get them in the group."

March

– Inspired by Lonnie Donegan and fired up by Elvis Presley's 'Heartbreak Hotel', John and his school friend Pete Shotton started a skiffle group which they called The Blackjacks. John played guitar, bought for him for £17 from Hessy's Music Shop on Stanley Street and "guaranteed not to split". He played it with only four strings and used banjo chords taught to him by his mother. Pete played washboard. The traditional skiffle-group line-up was completed shortly afterwards by the addition of Bill Smith on tea-chest bass.

May

– John was a difficult and argumentative band leader and the line-up changed rapidly. Since they

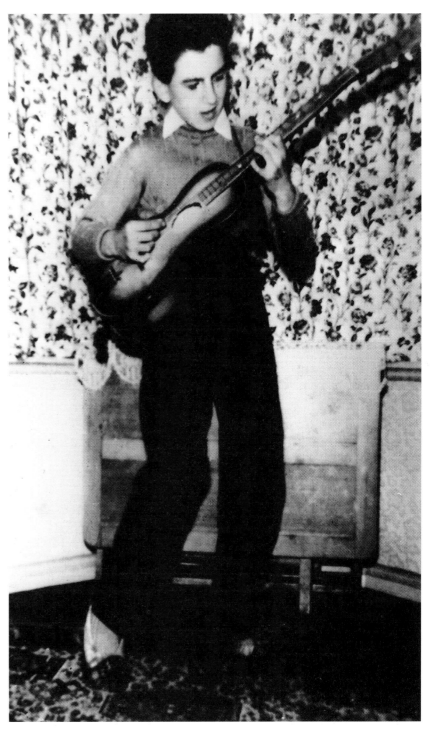

George Harrison, aged 12 with his first guitar.

were all from Quarry Bank High School, The Blackjacks changed their name to The Quarrymen whose initial line-up was John on vocals and guitar; Eric Griffiths on guitar; Colin Hanton on drums; Len Garry on tea-chest bass; Pete Shotton on washboard; and Rod Davis on banjo.

May 24
– The Quarrymen played their first gig:

John: "Our first appearance was in Rose Street, it was their Empire Day celebrations. They all had this party out in the street."

June 9
– The Quarrymen entered the *ABC TV* TV Star Search talent contest organised by "Mr Star Maker" Carroll Levis, held at the Empire Theatre, Liverpool. The contest was performed before a live audience and the winners of the audition went on to appear on television. It was a cheap way of producing a variety show, but sadly, the Quarrymen didn't pass the audition and the winners were The Sunnyside Skiffle from Speke fronted by a midget, Nicky Cuff, on vocals and tea-chest bass (he literally played it standing on top).

June 22
– The Quarrymen played at an outdoor street party at Roseberry Street, Liverpool, to celebrate the 750th anniversary of King John granting a charter to Liverpool making it a free borough. They played their sets from the back of a coal lorry, with the power leads running through the front window of number 76.

July 2
– John and his friend Nigel Whalley signed on the seamen's unemployment register at the Merchant Navy Establishment at the Pier Head. They telephoned Mimi who was horrified at the idea that John might follow in his father's footsteps, and ordered him home at once.

July 6
– **Paul:** "At Woolton village fête I met him. I was a fat schoolboy and, as he leaned an arm on my shoulder, I realised that he was drunk. We were 12 then, but, in spite of his sideboards, we went on to become teenage pals."

John: "The day I met Paul I was singing 'Be-Bop-A-Lula' for the first time on stage. There's a picture of me with a checked shirt on, holding a little acoustic guitar – and I am singing 'Be-Bop-A-Lula'."

we **played** from the back of a **lorry.** we **didn't** get **paid** or anything."

That **alone** made me resolve **never** to **become** a **lead** guitarist."

Paul: "A mate of mine at school, Ivy Vaughan, had said, 'Come along and see this group, they're great.' We used to go to the fair together with these great jackets with flaps here, light blue with flecks in them... Sharp!... I went to see the group and loved it – it was a young group, instead of dance music. John was obviously leading this thing – he had an acoustic guitar; brown wood with a hole, and a bit of a crew cut, with a little quiff. He didn't know the words for anything, he'd obviously only heard the records and not bought them, but I was pretty impressed. I met up with John backstage in this little church hall, and just picked up his guitar (which I had to play upside down, because I'm left handed), and played 'Twenty Flight Rock'. They were all impressed 'cos I knew all the words, then somebody played the piano, somebody sang 'Long Tall Sally', and later they asked me to join."

John: "Shortly after that we started to do big beat numbers like 'Twenty Flight Rock' – funny really because we were meant to be a skiffle group. 'Let's Have A Party' used to be my big number."

Aunt Mimi: "When Paul first came to Mendips he had a buckle on his shoe. John had never seen anything like it."

July 29
– Paul and his brother Michael went to Scout camp at Hathersage in Derbyshire.

August 7
– *The Cavern*, with Ron McKay's Skiffle Group, Dark Town Skiffle Group and The Deltones Skiffle Group. The Cavern in those days was a jazz club but skiffle was then seen as an offshoot of jazz and so was acceptable, and the evening was billed as a "Skiffle Session". The Quarrymen Skiffle Group began with 'Come Go

With Me' which was okay but John blasted straight into 'Hound Dog' followed by 'Blue Suede Shoes', prompting club owner Alan Sytner to send a note on-stage reading "Cut out the bloody rock!"

Though Paul had been invited to join the group he was away at Scout camp with his brother Michael and did not play this gig which marked John Lennon's début at The Cavern.

Summer
– Paul and George took their guitars and hitchhiked to the south coast.

George: "When I was 14 Paul and I went to Paignton in Devon on a hitchhiking holiday. It was a bit of a laugh, too, because we ran out of money and had nowhere to sleep. So Paul suggested we sleep on the beach. Sand, however, is as hard as concrete when you lie on it all night."

September
– The McCartney family went to the Butlin's Holiday Camp at Filey in Yorkshire, where Paul and Michael entered *The People* National Talent Contest and, appearing as The McCartney Brothers, did a rendition of the Everly Brothers' 'Bye Bye Love' and Little Richard's 'Long Tall Sally'. As they were both under 16 they didn't qualify. It was Paul's first time on stage.

– John began attending Liverpool Art School.

October 18
– *Conservative Club, New Clubmoor Hall, Liverpool.* Paul's first gig with The Quarrymen.

Paul: "That night was a disaster because I got sticky fingers and blew the solo in 'Guitar Boogie Shuffle', which is one of the easiest things in the world to play.

Autumn
– Paul and John began to practise their guitars together. **Paul:** "We never played our guitars indoors at Mimi's house. If we didn't go round to Julia's and we stayed there, then we

Woolton Parish Church
Garden Fete
and
Crowning of Rose Queen
Saturday, July 6th, 1957

To be opened at 3p.m. by Dr. Thelwall Jones

PROCESSION AT 2p.m.

LIVERPOOL POLICE DOGS DISPLAY
FANCY DRESS PARADE
SIDESHOWS   REFRESHMENTS
BAND OF THE CHESHIRE YEOMANRY
THE QUARRY MEN SKIFFLE GROUP

ADULTS 6d., CHILDREN 3d.   OR BY PROGRAMME

GRAND DANCE

at 8p.m. in the Church Hall
GEORGE EDWARDS' BAND
THE QUARRY MEN SKIFFLE GROUP
Tickets 2/-

He was a terribly **sarcastic** bugger **right** from day **one,** but I never **dared** back **down** from him.

Holly was a **big thing** then, an **inspiration,** sort of.

practised outside the front door in the glass porch. John told me Mimi banished him out there from the first day he brought home his guitar on account of all the noise. He didn't mind, though. He liked it out on the porch as the echo of the guitars bounced nicely off the glass and the tiles."

By the end of the year they had begun to write songs together.

John: "When Paul and I started writing stuff, we did it in the key of A because we thought that was the key Buddy Holly did all his songs in. Anyway, later on I found out he played in C and other keys but it was too late and it didn't worry us anyway. It all sounded okay in A so that's the way we played out stuff. Oh yeah, we keep up with all the keys – C, D, G, F but we keep out of B flat and that. It doesn't give you an artistic sound."

November 7
– Wilson Hall, Garston. A notorious teddy boy hangout. The Quarrymen played there four times on Charlie Mac's Thursday "Rhythm Nights".
November 16
– Stanley Abattoir Social Club, Liverpool. Good acoustics.
November 23
– New Clubmoor Hall, Conservative Club, Liverpool. The line-up at this point consisted of John, guitar and vocals; Paul, guitar and vocals; Eric Griffiths, guitar; Colin Hanton, drums; Len Garry, tea-chest bass.
– Late in the year Nigel Whalley resigned as the group's manager because he developed tuberculosis. Rod Davis also quit the group.
December 7
– Wilson Hall, Garston, Liverpool. A Saturday night hop.
– Late in the year George saw The Quarrymen play for the first time.
George: "I'd been invited to see them play several times by Paul but for some reason never got round to it before.

'**Yeah,** man, he'd be **great.**' And **that** was that. George was **in** and we **were** on our way."

The Quarrymen on stage at the Walton Village Fete, July 6, 1957 – the day John met Paul for the first time.

I remember being very impressed with John's big thick sideboards and trendy teddyboy clothes. In a way, all that emotional rough stuff was simply a way for him to help separate the men from the boys, I think. I was never intimidated by him. Whenever he had a go at me I just gave him a little bit of his own right back."
1958
January 10
– New Clubmoor Hall, Garston, Liverpool.
January 24
– The Cavern (evening), with the Merseysippi Jazz Band. They were billed as "The Quarrymen Skiffle Group". This was Paul's Cavern début.
February 6
– Wilson Hall, Garston, Liverpool. After the gig, John accompanied Paul and George part of the way home.
Paul: "George slipped quietly into one of the seats on this almost empty bus we were on, took out his guitar and went right into 'Raunchy'. Some days later I asked John, 'Well, what do you think about George?' He gave it a second or two and then he replied,
– The Quarrymen line-up now consisted of: John, Paul, George, Len Garry, Eric Griffiths and sometimes John "Duff" Lowe on piano.
Paul: "We had a bloke called Duff as pianist for some time, but his dad wouldn't let him stay out late. He'd be playing away one minute, and the next he would have disappeared, gone home in the middle of a number."
December 15
– John's mother, Julia, was killed in a road accident, hit by a policeman who was driving illegally alone on "L"-plates, speeding because he was late for work.
Paul: "When I look back on Julia's death, all I can see is the word TRAGEDY written in big black letters. The only way I could help John was

to empathise, as I'd had the same thing happen to me. There wasn't anything I could say that would magically patch him up.

Julia's death affected John very deeply. His work at art college - poor at the best of times – suffered badly and he virtually lost interest in the group. The Quarrymen played very few gigs during 1958.

March 13
– *The Morgue Skiffle Cellar, Broadgreen, Liverpool.* The first of several appearances at this illegal club held in the cellar of a Victorian mansion. The police closed it down a month later.

Summer
– Paul and George made another hitchhiking trip, this time to Wales.

George: "We ran out of cash again, and Paul had the idea that we could sleep at the police station in one of the cells. Unfortunately the police refused but did suggest we could kip in the grandstand of the local football club. With great difficulty we climbed the wall surrounding the football ground, and with even greater difficulty got to sleep on the concrete steps of the grandstand. Just as day was breaking, I woke to see the caretaker standing over us.

"'What are you doing in my grandstand?' he demanded.

"'S-sleeping,' Paul croaked. We didn't need telling twice."

– That summer John Lennon arranged for a recording of the Quarrymen to be made at a small studio in the back room of a house at 53 Kensington, Liverpool, where Percy Phillips would record two sides for 17 shillings and sixpence. Only one copy of the single was cut and the tape itself was destroyed 24 hours later. The A-side featured John singing Buddy Holly's 'That'll Be The Day' and on the B-side was a love song credited to Paul and George (the only known example of them writing as a team) entitled 'In Spite Of All The Danger'. The line-up on the recording was John, Paul, George and John "Duff" Lowe.

December 20
– Group played at the wedding

That kind of **hurt** goes **far** too deep for **words."**

"Well, you're not **anymore!'**

reception of George's brother Harry to Irene McCann, in Speke.
– Late in the year The Quarrymen failed an audition for ABC Television in Manchester.

1959
January 1
– *Wilson Hall, Garston, Liverpool. Speke Bus Depot Social Club.* George's father was chairman of the club so naturally The Quarrymen got the gig.

January 24
– *Woolton Village Club, Woolton, Liverpool.*

Summer
– Because The Quarrymen were doing very little in the way of gigs, George began playing with other groups, particularly The Les Stewart Quartet.

August 29
– *Casbah Coffee Club, West Derby, Liverpool.* The Les Stewart Quartet (featuring George on guitar) was booked for the opening night of Mona Best's new club, held in the basement of her house, but that afternoon Les Stewart had a terrific row with his bass player, Ken Brown, resigned from the group and stalked off. Ken Brown asked George if he knew anyone who could help out and John and Paul were called in. The Quarrymen played the gig and every Saturday night for the next seven weeks. The Quarrymen line-up for these gigs had been reduced to John, Paul, George and Ken Brown. No drummer, but as they always told promoters, "The rhythm's in the guitars".

September 5
– *Casbah Coffee Club, West Derby, Liverpool.*
September 12
– *Casbah Coffee Club, West Derby, Liverpool.*
September 19
– *Casbah Coffee Club, West Derby, Liverpool.*
September 26
– *Casbah Coffee Club, West Derby, Liverpool.*
October 3
– *Casbah Coffee Club, West Derby, Liverpool.*
October 10
– *Casbah Coffee Club, West*

Derby, Liverpool.
Ken Brown left the group and the group left the Casbah over an argument about wages. Paul objected when Mona Best paid Brown his 15 shillings even though he had not played that evening because of a heavy cold. The future Beatles closed ranks and walked away.

Mid-October
– The group changed their name to Johnny and The Moondogs for another audition for Carroll Levis's *TV Star Search* at the Empire Theatre (held on the 11th, 18th and 25th – they appeared at only one). This time The Moondogs qualified for the final round which was held at the Empire Theatre between the 26th and 31st. They appeared twice during the week and qualified for the next round.

November 15
– *Hippodrome Theatre, Ardwick, Manchester.* This was the final round of *TV Star Search*. If they qualified here they would have made it on to the TV show itself. Unfortunately they had nowhere to stay, and as the voting was based on a "clapometer" which measured the volume of the audience applause when the group made a brief reappearance, The Moondogs lost out because they had already caught the last train back to Liverpool, and weren't there to be clapped.

November 17
– The Second Biennial John Moores Exhibition was held in Liverpool at the Walker Gallery. John's friend from art school, Stuart Sutcliffe, submitted the remains of a large canvas entitled "Summer Painting". It had begun life as a large abstract expressionist painting on two six-feet-by-four-feet panels, with a highly textured surface made from sand and wax. One panel had gone missing when Stuart was evicted from his flat in Percy Street, but his friend Rod Murray helped him to carry the other half to the gallery to submit it for the show. Not only was the painting accepted for the show (Stuart's work showed the influence of Peter Lanyon, the British abstract expressionist who happened to be on the selection panel), but John Moores himself bought it for £65 when the show ended in January.

19'60

'The **beetles** missed yuh, all the beetles **missed** yuh. **C'mon** Johnny, let's **you** and I ...'

January 17

– The John Moores Exhibition ended and John persuaded Stuart that what he really wanted to do with this large sum of money was buy a bass guitar and join Johnny and The Moondogs. He bought a Hofner President, more for its looks than for its sound, since he was unable to play it.

April 23

– John and Paul hitchhiked down to Caversham in Berkshire, to stay with Paul's older cousin, Bett Robbins, who, together with her husband Mike, ran a pub called The Fox and Hounds. Prior to this they had been redcoats at Butlin's, and Mike had a small amount of showbusiness experience – appearing on the radio and being interviewed by local newspapers – which their visitors were delighted to hear about. John and Paul worked behind the bar and on Saturday night performed in the tap room as The Nerk Twins (they were advertised on the door of the saloon bar as such). They sat on high barstools with their acoustic guitars and opened with an old Butlin's favourite 'The World Is Waiting For The Sunrise' before moving on to their usual repertoire.

April 24

– *The Fox and Hounds, Caversham.* The Nerk Twins performed in the tap room again this lunchtime before hitchhiking back to Liverpool.

May

– Allan Williams was asked by John to be the band's manager. Williams owned the Jacaranda Coffee Bar on Slater Street, a regular meeting place for Liverpool groups such as Rory Storm & The Hurricanes and Derry

Wilkie & The Seniors. The Jac featured live shows in the tiny basement which Williams had converted into a tiny dance floor. His friends, The Royal Caribbean Steel Band were the residents. Williams was not too impressed by The Moondogs but agreed to manage them.

The Moondogs were unhappy with their name. One night at Stuart's Gambier Street flat, John and Stuart came up with a new name for the group, taken from Marlon Brando's film *The Wild One*:

Lee Marvin to Marlon Brando: 'You know I've missed you. Ever since the club split up I've missed you. Did you miss him?'

Motorcycle gang: 'Yeah.'

Lee Marvin, Robert Keith and Marlon Brando in The Wild One.
Opposite: George, Stuart Sutcliffe and John pose for Astrid Kirchherr at der Dom, the Hamburg park, October 1960.

Lee Marvin: 'We all missed you,' points to the girls in the gang.

Stuart suggested The Beetles because it was like Buddy Holly's Crickets. John then modified the name by changing an "e" to an "a" to make a pun on beat. Allan Williams didn't like it and suggested Long John and The Silver Beatles. Other names considered at that time were The Silver Beats, Silver Beetles and Beatals.

May 5

– Through Cass of Cass and The Cassanovas, Allan Williams found the group a drummer called Tommy Moore and allowed them to practise at the Jacaranda in return for doing odd jobs. Sometimes they filled in on The Royal Caribbean Steel Band's day off.

May 10

– *Wyvern Social Club.* Looking for musicians who would play for low wages, London promoter Larry Parnes came to Liverpool to audition groups to back Billy Fury on a tour of northern England and Scotland (Billy Fury was from Liverpool). Fury himself attended the auditions, as did every hopeful group in Liverpool. John dropped the "Long John" and they attended Parnes' audition as The Silver Beatles. Drummer Johnny "Hutch" Hutchinson of Cass and The Cassanovas stood in at

Royston Ellis

The London "Beat" poet, 19-year-old Royston Ellis, author of *Jiving To Gyp: A Sequence of Poems* (Scorpion Press, London, 1959), was booked to read his poems at the University of Liverpool. He met The Beatles and convinced them to back him for a reading at the Jacaranda. At this time reading poetry to a jazz backing had been popularised in the US by Jack Kerouac, Kenneth Patchen and Lawrence Ferlinghetti, and in Britain by Christopher Logue.

After the reading Ellis visited Gambier Terrace, where John and Stuart were then living, and showed them how to unscrew a Vick's inhaler to get the Benzedrine out. Years later it was Ellis who inspired John by introducing him to Polythene Pam.

the audition as Tommy Moore arrived late. Larry Parnes considered that the group, except for Tommy, had some potential, and a few days later he contacted Williams with a job offer.

May 14
– *Lathom Hall, Liverpool,* as The Silver Beats, promoted by Brian Kelly ("Beekay"). Also on bill were Cliff Roberts & The Rockers, The Deltones and King Size Taylor & The Dominoes. The Silver Beats had not been advertised to play but were allowed to do a few numbers in the interval while Brian Kelly sized them up. He booked them for the following Saturday.

May 18
– The group were offered a job by Larry Parnes as Johnny Gentle's backing group on a nine-day tour of Scotland and they decided to change their names for the occasion; Paul changed his to Paul Ramon, George changed to Carl Harrison (after Carl Perkins) and Stu changed Sutcliffe to de Stael (after the then-fashionable painter). They chose as their name The Silver Beetles. Tommy and George arranged time off work, John and Stuart skipped college and Paul somehow managed to persuade his father that the trip would enable him to study for his A-levels.

May 20
– *Town Hall, Alloa, Clackmannanshire* (Johnny Gentle tour).

May 21
– *Northern Meeting Ballroom, Inverness.* "The Beat Ballad Show" with Ronnie Watt and The Chekkers Rock Dance Band. While they rocked upstairs Lindsay Ross and his Famous Broadcasting Band led the old-tyme dancing downstairs. (Johnny Gentle tour). Brian Kelly had advertised them as headliners at the Lathom Hall but they neglected to inform him that they were out of town.

May 23
– *Dalrymple Hall, Aberdeen.* On the way to the venue, Johnny Gentle crashed the car. Tommy Moore was concussed and lost several teeth. He was taken to hospital but the manager of Dalrymple Hall was outraged that the group had no drummer and

stormed into the hospital and dragged Tommy from his bed to take his place on stage (Johnny Gentle tour).

May 25
– *St Thomas' Hall, Deith, Banffshire* (Johnny Gentle tour).

May 26
– *Town Hall, Forres, Morayshire* (Johnny Gentle tour). The tour was not going well and The Silver Beetles did a runner from their hotel, The Royal Station, without paying the bill.

May 27
– *Regal Ballroom, Nairne, Nairnshire* (Johnny Gentle tour).

May 28
– *Rescue Hall, Peterhead, Aberdeenshire* (final concert of the Johnny Gentle tour).

May 29
– The Silver Beetles arrived back in Liverpool, tired, exhausted and just as poor as the day they left but having clocked up their first road experience as a rock'n'roll band.

May 30
– *Jacaranda Coffee Bar, Liverpool.* Allan Williams engaged The Silver Beetles to play Monday night "fill-in" performances (when not otherwise engaged) on the evenings that the house band, The Royal Caribbean Steel Band, took the night off. Their fee was Coca-Cola and beans on toast.

Opposite: John, on stage in Hamburg with Stuart (left) and George, autumn 1960.
Below: Stuart, George, John and Tony Sheridan on stage in Hamburg.

June 2
– *The Institute, Neston, Wirral.* An event promoted by Les Dodd's Paramount Enterprises arranged by Williams while the group had been away in Scotland. This was the first of their Thursday night sessions at this notoriously rough venue. During one Silver Beetles set at The Institute, a 16-year-old boy was nearly kicked to death.

June 4
– *Grosvenor Ballroom, Liscard.* Les Dodd's other, even rougher, venue where he promoted his Saturday "Big Beat" nights.

June 6
– *Grosvenor Ballroom, Liscard,* a special Whitsun bank holiday, Jive and Rock session. The Silver Beetles shared a bill with Gerry and The Pacemakers for the first time.

June 9
– *The Institute, Neston, Wirral.*

June 11
– *The Grosvenor Ballroom, Liscard.* Another rowdy Saturday night. The group had no drummer since Tommy Moore had resigned, having had enough of John's malicious wit, and of the pressure from his girlfriend to "get a proper job". John asked if anyone in the audience could play drums and "Ronnie", the drunk grinning leader of a local gang of teddy boys, settled himself behind Moore's kit (still on hire-purchase). Though Ronnie had obviously never played drums before, no-one dared take them off him. In the interval John managed to phone Allan Williams who drove over to the Grosvenor and saved them.

June 13
– *The Jacaranda* as The Silver Beetles. This was Tommy Moore's last gig with the group before he went back to being a fork-lift truck-driver at the Garston bottle works. They were now a beat group without a drummer.

June 16
– *The Institute, Neston, Wirral.*

June 18
– *Grosvenor Ballroom, Liscard.*

June 23
– *The Institute, Neston, Wirral.*

June 25
– *Grosvenor Ballroom, Liscard.*

'We can't **read** music, sorry, we can **play** the Harry Lime **Cha-Cha** which we've **arranged** ourselves,

June 30
– *The Institute, Neston, Wirral.*
July
– With no drummer The Silver Beatles (as they were now called) were reduced to playing at Williams' strip club. In early July Allan Williams and his friend "Lord Woodbine" opened an illegal strip club in Upper Parliament Street called the "New Cabaret Artists Club". He offered the group 10 shillings (50p) each every night to provide the music for a stripper called Janice.

Paul: "John, George and Stu and I used to play at a strip club in Upper Parliament Street, backing Janice the Stripper. At the time we wore little lilac jackets... or purple jackets or something. Well we played behind Janice and naturally we looked at her... the audience looked at her, everybody looked at her, just sort of normal. At the end of the act she would turn round and... well we were all young lads, we'd never seen anything like it before, and all blushed... four blushing red faced lads.

"Janice brought sheets of music for us to play all her arrangements. She gave us a bit of Beethoven and the Spanish Fire Dance. So in the end we said, and instead of Beethoven you can have 'Moonglow' or 'September Song' – take your pick... and instead of the 'Sabre Dance' we'll give you 'Ramrod'. So that's what she got. She seemed quite satisfied anyway. The strip

club wasn't an important chapter in our lives, but it was an interesting one."
– According to Williams they played two sets each night for a week, with Paul on drums.
July 2
– *The Grosvenor Ballroom, Liscard.* Johnny Gentle, visiting his home in Liverpool on a weekend off, stopped by the Jacaranda to look up his old backing group. Williams told him where The Silver Beatles were playing and Gentle and his father went over to the Grosvenor where Gentle leaped up and joined the group on stage for a few numbers.
July 7
– *The Institute, Wirral.*
July 9
– *Grosvenor Ballroom, Liscard.*
July 16
– *Grosvenor Ballroom, Liscard.*
July 23
– *Grosvenor Ballroom, Liscard.*
July 30
– *Grosvenor Ballroom, Liscard.* Drummer Norman Chapman worked across the street from the Jacaranda as a picture framer, and would practise in his office after everyone had gone home. One night Allan Williams followed the sound and persuaded him to play with The Silver Beatles. After playing three gigs with them at The Grosvenor he was conscripted for his two years' National Service.
– By the end of July the violence at The Grosvenor had become so bad that the local residents complained to Wallasey Council who owned it. They cancelled the rest of the season and reintroduced the Ballroom's "strict tempo" dances.
    It was probably at one of these Grosvenor Ballroom gigs that Stuart Sutcliffe was beaten unconscious

by teddy boy thugs in a fight. His injuries caused the blood clot on his brain which eventually killed him. He was rescued from his attackers by Pete Best and John Lennon.
August 2
– Things were going so well for Bruno Koschmider at the Kaiserkeller in Hamburg that he decided to open another music venue in a nearby strip club he owned. He wrote to Allan Williams asking if he could supply another group, and Williams in turn offered the engagement to The Silver Beatles, provided they could find a drummer.
August 6
– With their usual Saturday night engagement at the Grosvenor cancelled, the group went over to Mona Best's Casbah Coffee Club where they found The Blackjacks playing, with Mona's son, Pete, playing a brand new drum kit. The Blackjacks were about to split up, so The Beatles shrewdly asked Pete if he wanted to come to Hamburg with them and arranged for Pete to audition for them the following Saturday.
August 12
– Pete Best was auditioned by John, Paul and George to be their permanent drummer and go with them to Hamburg. Since he was their only hope of getting a drummer and therefore getting the gig, he passed the audition. It was just before the Hamburg tour that the group changed their name to The Beatles.
    Pete Best: **"A few years ago I used to sit in with various groups at The Casbah, Heyman's Green, and also had a trio called The Blackjacks. The Beatles used to play at the club and I got to know them there. They were auditioning for a drummer at the Wyvern Club, Seel Street (now the Blue Angel) and asked me to come along. They desperately needed a drummer at the time as they had to go to Germany within a few days' time.**

They **asked** me to **join** the **group** and two days later I was in **Hamburg** with them..."

The Hamburg Connection

Without bothering to inform Allan Williams, his resident group at the Jacaranda, The Royal Caribbean Steel Band, had accepted an engagement at a club in Hamburg in late June and simply failed to turn up one night. They happily wrote to Williams telling him there was a good market for British bands in Hamburg and urging him to visit. Williams, always looking for a new angle, visited the city with his friend Lord Woodbine and met Bruno Koschmider, owner of the Kaiserkeller. Since American rock'n'roll bands would have been too expensive to bring over, Koschmider was delighted to find that cheap rock groups were available in Britain, and at the end of July Williams sent one of his groups, Derry & The Seniors, to Hamburg to play at the Kaiserkeller.

'Hamburg Stamp and Yell' music might be more accurate. It was all that work on various club stages in Germany that built up our beat."

August 16
– The Beatles, accompanied by Allan Williams, his wife, her brother and Lord Woodbine, left Liverpool for Hamburg in Williams' old Austin van. They stopped off in London for a further passenger, Herr Steiner, an Austrian then working at the Heaven & Hell coffee bar on Old Compton Street, who was to act as Koschmider's interpreter. They took the ferry from Harwich to the Hook of Holland.

August 17
– The Beatles and company arrived in Hamburg in the early evening.
– Contract signed between Alan Williams' Jacaranda Enterprises and Bruno Koschmider to provide a five-piece band called The Beatles who were to be paid DM 30 per day of work.

They began work right away at the Indra, at 58 Grosse Freiheit. They were to play seven days a week from 8 until 9; from 10 until 11; 11 until 12 and from 1 until 2. On Saturdays they began work at 7, playing until 8. Then from 9 until 10; 10 until 11; 12 until 1 and 1 until 3 am. On Sundays began even earlier: 5 until 6, 6:30 until 7:30, 8 until 9, 9:30 until 10:30, 11 until 12 and 12:30 until 1:30.

Paul: Like at Hamburg we often played an eight-hour day! Playing like that, you get

Laden with The Beatles' equipment, Allan Williams' green and cream Austin minibus is hoisted aboard the Harwich to Hook of Holland ferry en route for their first Hamburg season, August 16, 1960. Below: At Arnhem, en route to Hamburg, The Beatles party break their journey to pose by the memorial to the dead of World War II. Left to right: Allan Williams, his wife Beryl, his friend 'Lord Woodbine', Stuart Sutcliffe, Paul, George and Pete Best. John stayed in the van.

"You **revved** your **engines** up so **much** that when you let them **go**, you just **coasted.**

to have a lot of tunes, if nothing else. So what we used to do, even on our eight-hour stint, was to try not to repeat any numbers. That was our own little ambition to stop us going round the bend. That gave us millions of songs, though some we could only just get away with – 'Dum-da-dum-da-dum-da-dum!' for half-an-hour! We'd shout out a title the Germans wouldn't understand to keep ourselves amused, like 'Knickers', but eventually we built up quite a programme."

George: "When you think about it sensibly, our sound really stems from Germany. That's where we learned to work for hours and hours on end, and keep on working at full peak even though we reckoned our legs and arms were about ready to drop off.

"Sure we come from Liverpool. There are hundreds of groups there, many on an R & B kick. But you won't hear us shouting about a Liverpool Sound, or Merseybeat, simply because it's been dreamed up as an easy way to describe what's going on with our music.

Only John and Paul did vocals before the first Hamburg trip, but the eight-hour sessions meant that George had to share the work, and by the time they returned to Liverpool they had three vocalists.

Paul: "Hamburg was a good exercise really in commercialism – a couple of students would stick their heads round the door, and we'd suddenly go into a piece of music that we thought might attract them. If we got people in, they might pay us better. That club was called the Indra – which is German for India. We were nicking left, right and centre off other bands there; we'd see something that we'd like, and after they left Hamburg, we'd put it in our set. Well you've got to, haven't you? We used to like going up and watching Tony Sheridan, 'cos he was a little bit of the generation above us; he used to play some blues, real moody stuff."

JGO HAA
HANNOVE

20 km

In this, the most memorable image of the early Beatles, Pete Best, George, John, Paul and Stuart Sutcliffe pose for Astrid by the funfair in der Dom, the Hamburg Park.

The Beatles got on well with Tony Sheridan and his group, The Jets. Paul and Iain Hines, the keyboard player with The Jets, used to double date two Hamburg barmaids: Paul's was called Liane. Iain: **"Every evening, when we'd finished working, Liane used to pick us up in her tiny Volkswagon and take us to her flat for coffee and a record session. Paul and I used to play Elvis and Everly records while Liane prepared a supper of Deutsch Beefsteak (hamburgers) and coffee."** It was already 4 when she picked them up from the club.

When The Beatles arrived at the Indra they were completely broke. Rosa, the cleaning lady, gave them a few marks so they could go across the street to Harold's café for a meal of potato fritters, cornflakes and chicken soup. Rosa washed their shirts and socks, gave them chocolate bars, and for a time, Paul lived in her small bungalow down on the docks.

Rosa: **"I remember when young Paul used to practise guitar on the roof of my little place. They shouted out things in German, but Paul didn't understand them. We used to get crowds of burly old Hamburg dockers hanging around, just listening. It's odd. They were a very hard audience who didn't really know what Paul was playing, but somehow they took to him."**

The Beatles' accommodation was two shared rooms behind the screen of the Bambi-Filmkunsttheater where they had to use the cinema bathrooms to wash. There were no cooking facilities and the group used to frequent the British Sailors' Society where the manager, Mr Hawk, would feed them cornflakes and pints of milk.

September 1 – 30
– Indra Club, Grosse Freiheit, Hamburg.

Paul at the piano, Pete Best on drums, Stuart Sutcliffe on his Hofner President bass guitar, George on his Futurama III guitar, John with his first Rickenbacker: the leather jacketed Beatles in Hamburg.

"Clap your **hands, you fuckin' Nazis."**

Paul: "The first time we went to Hamburg we stayed four-and-a-half months. It's a sort of blown up Blackpool, but with strip clubs instead of waxworks; thousands of strip clubs, bars and pick-up joints, not very picturesque. The first time it was pretty rough but we all had a gear time. The pay wasn't too fab, the digs weren't much good, and we had to play for quite a long time."

October 1 – 3
– Indra, Grosse Freiheit, Hamburg.

October 4
– Police pressure caused by noise complaints – mostly from the old woman who lived above the club – caused Bruno Koschmider to stop using the Indra as a music club and bring back the strippers. So after 48 nights on stage, The Beatles moved to the much larger Kaiserkeller, at 36 Grosse Freiheit. Here they alternated with Rory Storm & The Hurricanes who had arrived in Hamburg three days before, after playing a summer season at Butlin's. The drummer with The Hurricanes was Ringo Starr.

October 10
– Allan Williams returned to Hamburg on a visit. The Beatles had a problem with the stage at the Kaiserkeller which was much larger than they were used to and made them appear like frozen wax works. Koschmider complained to Williams who yelled "Make a show, boys!" and encouraged them to move around. Koschmider, who spoke no English, took up the chant: "Mach schau!" In future, every time they slowed down or looked tired, Koschmider would exhort them to "Mach shau!"

Their act was transformed: first John and then the others began to throw microphones and instruments about the stage. They smoked, drank and sometimes even fought on stage. John once performed wearing only his underwear and a toilet seat around his neck. They painted swastikas on old Afrikka Corps caps, and goose-stepped around the stage giving illegal Seig Heil salutes and yelling at the audience

The thing that **concerned** me was the **music,** and that we get on **musically,** and we **didn't.** Same with **Pete Best."**

The audience loved it. Insulting the customers not only went down well but also began to attract large crowds. Half the time the band were drunk or - with the exception of Pete – on Benzedrine; there was no other way they could get through the two final sets. The gangsters in the audience would send up crates of beer and hand them preludin; it was sensible not to refuse gifts from these people. The Beatles and Rory Storm had a competition to see which group could demolish the club's unstable and potentially dangerous stage. Rory Storm won the bet during an enthusiastic version of "Blue Suede Shoes". The outraged Koschmider fined him DM65 to pay for the damage.

October 15
– The Beatles' contract was extended until December 31. They were making good money for Koschmider.

The audience was composed mostly of gangsters, people in the sex industry, rockers and visiting sailors. Then one day, an art student happened by, attracted by the sound of Rory Storm & The Hurricanes. Klaus Voorman was an "exi" – an existentialist – the sworn enemies of the rockers, and felt a certain trepidation at venturing into their territory, but having seen The Beatles do their set he was so excited that he returned the next day, and the one after, this time bringing with him his girlfriend, the photographer Astrid Kirchherr. Astrid and Stuart Sutcliffe soon became a couple, leading Astrid to take some of the best-known photographs of the group from that time.

Though Stuart was regarded as the most attractive member of the group, he had still not learned how to play his bass guitar, preferring to pose with it and look moody. This caused a tremendous friction in the group with Paul complaining to John, and both John and Paul complaining to Stuart. John was torn between friendship and his desire for the group to make it. He knew that Paul was right and The Beatles could never be any good musically as long as Stuart remained in the group.

Paul: "The problem with Stu was that he couldn't play bass guitar. We had to turn him away in photographs because he'd be doing F-sharp and we'd be holding G. Stu and I had a fight once on stage in Hamburg but we were virtually holding each other up. We couldn't move, couldn't do it.

October 16
– Walter Eymond, the singer and bass player with The Hurricanes, made an amateur recording of 'Summertime' at the small Akustik studio by the railway station – a place where messages to family and friends could be recorded on 78rpm discs. Eymond's stage name was Lou Walters but everyone knew him as Wally. Backing him were Ringo, also in The Hurricanes, and John, Paul and George from The Beatles. Stuart was there as an observer as he couldn't play well enough for recording, so for the first time on record, John, Paul, George and Ringo played together. Wally and Ringo also made recordings of 'Fever' and 'September Song'. Nine copies of the 'Summertime' 78 were cut, but only one copy has surfaced.

November 1 – 30
– *Kaiserkeller, Grosse Freiheit, Hamburg.*

Paul: "One night we played at the Top Ten Club and all the customers from the Kaiserkeller came along. Since the Top Ten was a much better club, we decided to accept the manager's offer and play there. Naturally the manager of the Kaiserkeller didn't like it. One night prior to leaving his place, we accidentally singed a bit of cord on an old stone wall in the corridor and he had the police on us.

"'Leave please, thanks very much, but we don't want you to burn our German houses.' Funny really because we couldn't have burnt the place if we had gallons of petrol - it was made of stone.

"There was an article on

the group in a German magazine. I didn't understand the article, but there was a large photograph of us in the middle page. In the same article there was a photograph of a South African negro pushing the jungle down. I still don't quite know what he has to do with us, but I suppose it has some significance."

November 1
– Bruno Koschmider terminated The Beatles' contract. His notice to quit read: "I the undersigned hereby give notice to Mr George Harrison and to Beatles' Band to leave on November 30th, 1960. The notice is given to the above by order of the Public Authorities who have discovered that Mr George Harrison is only 17 (seventeen) years of age."

November 21
– George was deported from Germany for being too young to work in nightclubs.

November 22
– Despite the loss of their lead guitarist The Beatles were expected to continue playing at the Kaiserkeller normally. The work sheet for this date gives the exact times they were expected on stage: 7:30 pm until 9; 9:30 until 11; 11:30 until 1; 1:30 until 2:30 am:

John in Hamburg.

when we came back, suddenly we were a **WOW.** Mind you, 70 per cent of the **audience thought** we were a **German** wow,

five and half hours of playing time, seven days a week.

November 29
– During a change of digs from the Bambi-Filmkunsttheater to quarters provided by Peter Eckhorn, Pete and Paul accidentally set their old room on fire: there was no light and they set fire to a condom in order to see to pack. Though no damage was done except a singe mark on the wall, Koschmider had them arrested and deported for arson.

Peter Eckhorn: **"They were working at the Kaiserkeller in Hamburg at the time, but they didn't like it there and so they came to see me and ask if there was any work to be had at the Top Ten. To show what they could do they played a couple of numbers for me. I liked them. I said OK, I'd give them a job. But before I could hire them, the owners of the Kaiserkeller made a complaint about the boys to the police, saying they'd tried to set fire to the club! It wasn't true, of course, but the complaint had the desired effect: The Beatles were deported. It took seven months to get them back again. They stayed three months and were very popular, not so much for their music (which wasn't so different from the other groups), but for their personalities. Nobody in particular shone out – they were all well liked."**

November 30
– The Beatles made a verbal agreement with Peter Eckhorn to play the Top Ten Club in April provided that he sort out their immigration problems.
– Tony Sheridan and Iain Hines joined The Beatles on-stage at the Top Ten for a jam session which ended with a 70-minute version of 'What'd I Say'.

December 1
– Paul and Pete arrived back in England after being deported from Germany.

December 10
– John set off for England by train. Stuart stayed on in Hamburg with Astrid, conveniently solving the problem of how to remove him from the group.
December 15
– John finally contacted Paul, George and Pete, having arrived home broke and depressed four days earlier.
December 17
– *Casbah Coffee Club, West Derby, Liverpool.* With Stuart still in Hamburg, Pete Best contacted Chas Newby, the former rhythm guitarist with his group The Blackjacks, to play bass.
December 24
– *Grosvenor Ballroom, Liscard,* with Derry & The Seniors. Rock dances had been resumed under

Above: The Beatles at The Top Ten Club. Opposite: John, photographed in 1960 in a Hamburg doorway. This image was later used on the album of rock and roll classics he would release in February, 1975.

the supervision of Wallasey Corporation itself.
December 27
– *Litherland Town Hall* where they were advertised as "Direct from Hamburg". This "Welcome Home" engagement had been booked for them by Bob Wooler with Brian Kelly (who had forgiven them for letting him down on the May 21 booking). The Beatles played their normal Hamburg set which had an electrifying effect on the young audience. Immediately after the show Brian Kelly booked them for another 36 dances – at £6 to £8 a gig – before any other promoter could get to them.

John: **"We'd been playing round Liverpool for a bit without getting anywhere, trying to get work, and the other groups kept telling us, 'You'll do all right, you'll get work someday.' And off we went to Hamburg, but we didn't care about that... In Liverpool, people didn't even know we were from Liverpool. They thought we were from Hamburg. They said, 'Christ, they speak good English!' Which we did of course, being English. But that's when we first stood there being cheered for the first time."**
December 31
– *Casbah Coffee Club, West Derby, Liverpool.* Chas Newby's final engagement with the group before returning to college.

Neil Aspinall

When Brian Kelly booked them for 36 gigs over the next three months, The Beatles decided that they needed a full time roadie. Neil Aspinall, who was studying to become a chartered accountant, lived in Pete Best's parents' house and helped to run the Casbah Club in the basement while Pete was in Hamburg. He had helped with the gear at the Litherland Town Hall and the

Casbah to augment his fifty shilling a week salary. When they asked if he would work for them full time, Neil gave up his studies, bought an £80 Commer van and has been with them ever since.

Neil was born on October 13 1941 in Prestatyn where his mother had been evacuated at the height of the blitz on Liverpool. His father was in the navy. In 1942, with the end

of the bombing, they returned to Liverpool. He passed his 11 Plus at West Derby School and went to the Liverpool Institute where he took art and English lessons alongside Paul. George was one year below them, but they soon met.

Neil: "My first encounter with George was behind the school's air-raid shelters. This great mass of shaggy hair loomed up and an

out-of-breath voice requested a quick drag of my Woodbine. It was one of the first cigarettes either of us had smoked. We spluttered our way through it bravely but gleefully. After that the three of us did lots of ridiculous things together. By the time we were ready to take the GCE exams we'd added John Lennon to our 'Mad Lad' gang. He was doing his first term at Liverpool

College of Art which overlooks the Institute playground and we all got together in a students' coffee bar at lunchtime."

Neil took nine GCEs and passed them all except for French. He stayed on at the Institute until July 1959, when he joined a firm of chartered accountants. He started working for The Beatles in December 1960.

1961

January

– When Chas Newby returned to college the group were left without a bass player. John tried to get George to play bass but this met with a solid refusal and so Paul, who had been playing both rhythm guitar and piano, got the job. He put together a bass out of a Solid 7 model and three piano strings. It was not very satisfactory, but it sounded better than Stuart had done.

– After the "Welcome Home" Concert Bob Wooler began to promote the group and to encourage other promoters to book them. He was often the MC at their gigs, making the performance as dramatic as possible by playing the *William Tell Overture* for their entrance or getting them to start playing before the curtain went up. Girls would start screaming and rushing the stage, mostly for Pete Best who on one occasion was nearly pulled into the audience. Beatlemania was beginning.

January 5
– *Litherland Town Hall.* The first of the engagements booked by Brian Kelly (Beekay). Ringo Starr, who had just returned from Hamburg, was in the audience.

January 6
– *St John's Hall, Bootle in Lancashire.*

January 7
– *Aintree Institute, Liverpool.*
– *Lathom Hall, Seaforth, Liverpool* (both events were Brian Kelly promotions).

January 13
– *Aintree Institute, Liverpool.*

January 14
– *Aintree Institute, Liverpool.*

January 15
– *Casbah Coffee Club, West Derby, Liverpool.*

January 18
– *Aintree Institute, Liverpool.*

January 19
– *Alexandra Hall, Crosby, Liverpool.*

January 20
– *Lathom Hall, Seaforth.*

January 21
– *Lathom Hall, Seaforth.*
– *Aintree Institute, Liverpool.*

January 25
– *Hambleton Hall, Huyton, Liverpool,* with Derry & The Seniors and Faron & The Tempest Tornadoes.

January 26
– *Litherland Town Hall.*

January 27
– *Aintree Institute, Liverpool.*

January 28
– *Lathom Hall, Seaforth.*
– *Aintree Institute, Liverpool.*

January 29
– *Casbah Coffee Club, West Derby, Liverpool.*

January 30
– *Lathom Hall, Seaforth.*

February 1
– *Hambleton Hall, Huyton, Liverpool.*

February 2
– *Litherland Town Hall.*

February 3
– *St. John's Hall, Bootle in Lancashire.*

February 4
– *Lathom Hall, Seaford.*

February 5
– *Blair Hall, Walton, Liverpool.*

February 6
– *Lathom Hall, Seaforth.*

February 7
– *Merseyside Civil Services Club, Liverpool.*

February 8
– *Aintree Institute, Liverpool.*
– *Hambleton Hall, Huyton, Liverpool.*

February 9
– *The Cavern* (lunchtime).

February 10
– *Aintree Institute, Liverpool.*
– *Lathom Hall, Seaforth.*

February 11
– *Lathom Hall, Seaforth.*
– *Cassanova Club, Sampson & Barlow's New Ballroom, Liverpool.* This was the first booking for the group from promoter Sam Leach.

February 12
– *Casbah Coffee Club, West Derby, Liverpool.*

February 14
– *Cassanova Club, Sampson & Barlow's New Ballroom, Liverpool.*
– *Litherland Town Hall,* with Ray & The Del Rena's with Joan. A St Valentine's Day Special. Paul sang Elvis's 'Wooden Heart' wearing a red satin heart bearing the names of the group pinned to his jacket. The heart was raffled but when the winner climbed up on stage to receive her prize and a kiss from Paul, the stage was inundated with squealing girls and the group had to be rescued by bouncers.

February 15
– *Aintree Institute, Liverpool.*
– *Hambleton Hall, Huyton, Liverpool.*

February 16
– *Cassanova Club, Sampson & Barlow's New Ballroom, Liverpool.*
– *Litherland Town Hall.*

February 17
– *St John's Hall, Tuebrook, Liverpool.* Promoted by Pete Best's mother, Mona, who negotiated a number of The Beatles' bookings at this stage in their career. It was thought that she also had ideas of managing them.

February 18
– *Aintree Institute, Liverpool.*

February 19
– *Casbah Coffee Club, West Derby, Liverpool.*

February 21
– *The Cavern* (lunchtime).
– *Cassanova Club, Sampson & Barlow's New Ballroom, Liverpool.*
– *Litherland Town Hall.*

February 22
– *Aintree Institute, Liverpool.*
– *Hambleton Hall, Huyton, Liverpool.*

The Cavern

February 9 was the first time the group played The Cavern under the name of The Beatles. The club would become forever associated with the group. As this was an unadvertised lunchtime session, George arrived in blue jeans, which were banned from the club, but fortunately the bouncer, Paddy Delaney, recognised him as being part of the act. The club was small - each of the three vaulted arches was only five chairs wide - and airless, but it was free of violence despite the tightly packed audiences. John had first played The Cavern in August 1957 when The Quarrymen were a skiffle band, and skiffle was seen as an adjunct of jazz.

February 24
– Grosvenor Ballroom, Liscard.
February 25
– Aintree Institute, Liverpool.
– Latham Hall, Seaforth.
February 26
– Casbah Coffee Club, West Derby, Liverpool.
February 28
– The Cavern (lunchtime).
– Cassanova Club, Sampson & Barlow's New Ballroom, Liverpool.
– Litherland Town Hall.
– In late February, Stuart Sutcliffe returned to Liverpool to see his parents but only stayed for a couple of weeks.
March 1
– Aintree Institute, Liverpool.
March 2
– Litherland Town Hall.
– Date of the contract signed between Alan Williams' Jacaranda Enterprises and Peter Eckhorn of the Top Ten Club, Hamburg. The Beatles were contracted to play seven nights a week at DM40 per person per night. Williams was to receive £10 a week that the Top Ten management was supposed to deduct from the band's wages and pay into Williams' account at the Commerz Bank in Hamburg. From Monday to Friday The Beatles were to play from 7 pm until 2 am, on Saturday they were to play from 7 pm until 3 am and on Sunday from 6 pm until 1 am. "After each hour of playing, there shall be a break of not less than 15 minutes."
March 3
– St John's Hall, Bootle in Lancashire.
March 4
– Aintree Institute, Liverpool.
March 5
– Casbah Coffee Club, West Derby, Liverpool.
March 6
– The Cavern (lunchtime).
– The Liverpool Jazz Society, (the previously named and later to be renamed Old Iron Door Club), with Gerry & The Pacemakers, Rory Storm & The Hurricanes, The Big Three, Derry & The Seniors and Kingsize Taylor & The Dominoes.

Ringo, with Rory Storm and The Hurricanes, at Butlins in Skegness. Left to right: Bobby Thompson, Ringo, Rory Storm, a Butlins Redcoat, and Johnny Guitar.

March 7
– Cassanova Club, Sampson & Barlow's New Ballroom, Liverpool, with Derry & The Seniors.
March 8
– The Cavern (lunchtime).
– Aintree Institute, Liverpool.
– Hambleton Hall, Huyton, Liverpool, with Rory Storm & The Hurricanes and Derry & The Seniors.
March 10
– The Cavern (lunchtime).
– Grosvenor Ballroom, Liscard.
– St. John's Hall, Tuebrook, Liverpool.
March 11
– Aintree Institute, Liverpool.
– Liverpool Jazz Society, (Old Iron Door Club). A 12-hour concert billed by adventurous promoter Sam Leach as "An All Night Rock Ball". Also on the bill were Rory Storm & The Hurricanes, Gerry & The Pacemakers, The Remo Four, Kingsize Taylor & The Dominoes, The Big Three, Dale Roberts & The Jaywalkers, Derry & The Seniors, Ray & The Del Renas, The Pressmen, Johnny Rocco & The Jets and Faron & The Tempest Tornadoes.

March 12
– Casbah Coffee Club, West Derby, Liverpool.
– Cassanova Club, Sampson & Barlow's New Ballroom, Liverpool, with Kingsize Taylor & The Dominoes.
March 13
– The Cavern (lunchtime).
– Liverpool Jazz Society, Old Iron Door Club, with Kingsize Taylor & The Dominoes.
March 14
– The Cavern (lunchtime).
March 15
– The Cavern (lunchtime).
– Liverpool Jazz Society (afternoon), with Gerry & The Pacemakers and Rory Storm & The Wild Ones. This was a "Swinging Lunchtime Rock Session" running from 12 midday until 5 pm which they went to straight after their lunchtime date at the Cavern.
– Stuart Sutcliffe returned to Hamburg to his girlfriend, Astrid Kirchherr, and the State College of Art where he was studying painting.
March 16
– The Cavern (lunchtime).
March 17
– Mossway Hall, Croxteth.
– Liverpool Jazz Society, Old Iron Door Club.
March 19
– Casbah Coffee Club, West Derby, Liverpool.
March 20
– The Cavern (lunchtime).
– Hambleton Hall, Huyton, Liverpool, with The Rockin' Ravens.
March 21
– The Cavern (evening) with The Remo Four, Dale Roberts & The Jaywalkers and The Swinging Blue Genes, on a Blue Genes guest night. This was their first evening gig at the Cavern.
March 22
– The Cavern (lunchtime).
March 24
The Cavern (lunchtime).
March 26
– Casbah Coffee Club, West Derby, Liverpool.
March 27
– The Beatles returned to Hamburg

by train to play at the Top Ten. They received DM35 per man per day and accommodation: the fourth-floor attic above the club.

April 1 – 30
– Top Ten Club, Reeperbahn, Hamburg.
April 1
– The Beatles began a three-month, 13 week season at the Top Ten Club, at Reeperbahn 136; a venue of about the same size as the Kaiserkeller, with a couple of dozen small tables surrounding a square dance floor by the stage. Their residency at the Top Ten Club lasted from April 1 until July 1, playing seven-hour sessions on week nights and eight hours at weekends with a 15-minute break every hour. They alternated first with The Jaybirds and later with Rory Storm & The Hurricanes. Mark Lewisohn has calculated that they spent 503 hours on stage over 92 nights.

In Hamburg they were reunited with Stuart Sutcliffe, who had returned there two weeks before and sometimes sat in with them. Stuart's decision not to remain in the band was now final. It was during this Hamburg visit that Astrid dressed Stuart in black leather, an outfit which the rest of the group then had copied by a tailor on the Reeperbahn. She also brushed Stu's hair forward, to look like her "exi" friends. The other Beatles did not go for this – yet.

June 1 – 30
– Top Ten Club, Reeperbahn, Hamburg.
– John's girlfriend, Cynthia Powell,

Paul at the Cavern, with his first violin bass.

and Paul's Liverpool girlfriend, Dot Rohne, came to Hamburg on a visit. John and Cynthia stayed with Astrid while Paul and Dot stayed with Rosa down in the docks. John and Paul bought them black leather skirts to make them look like Brigitte Bardot.

June 22
– Friedrich-Ebert-Halle, Hamburg-Harburg. The Beatles, with Paul on bass and Stuart Sutcliffe watching but not playing, backed Tony Sheridan on a recording session for German producer and orchestra leader Bert Kaempfert. For some reason the sessions spread over three days. However, since the equipment consisted of nothing more than a portable tape recorder set up on the stage of an infant school hall with the curtains drawn, it was not as expensive or time consuming as real studio time would have been.

They recorded four tracks backing Sheridan: 'My Bonnie Lies Over The

Ocean', 'When The Saints Go Marching In', 'Why (Can't You Love Me Again)', 'Nobody's Child' and then did two of their own, 'Ain't She Sweet', with John on vocals, and 'Cry For A Shadow', an instrumental credited to John Lennon and George Harrison.

The single 'My Bonnie'/'The Saints' was released in Germany as POLYDOR 24 673 in June. The Beatles were called "The Beat Brothers" because their name sounded too much like "Peedles", a German slang term for male genitalia. Bert Kaempfert made the recordings as an independent producer and licensed the tapes to Polydor.

June 24
– Studio Rahlstedt, Hamburg. A further track with Tony Sheridan was recorded: Jimmy Reed's 'Take Out Some Insurance On Me Baby'.

June 28
– The publishing contract with Bert Kaempfert for 'Cry For A Shadow' was signed by John and George.

Paul's Violin Bass

Paul: "I'd gone out there (to Hamburg) with a red Rosetti Solid 7, which was a real crappy guitar, but looked quite good. Stuart Sutcliffe was leaving the band and he wanted to stay in Hamburg, so we had to have a bass player. So I got elected bass player, or lumbered as the case may be. Stuart lent me his bass, so I got off the piano then and came up on the front line again to play

it, but I actually played it upside down. I kind of wangled my way round that.

"I got my Hofner violin bass at the Steinway shop in the town centre. I remember going along and there was this bass which was quite cheap, it cost the German mark equivalent of £30 or so – my dad had always hammered into us never to get into debt because we weren't that rich. John and

George went easily into debt and got beautiful guitars: John got a Club 40 and George had a Futurama – which is like a Fender copy – and then later Gretsches. Then John got Rickenbackers. They were prepared to use hire purchase credit, but it had been so battered into me I wouldn't risk it. So I bought a cheap guitar. And once I bought it I fell in love with it."

July 2
– The Beatles set off for Liverpool from Hamburg, with the exception of Stuart, who had decided definitely to quit the group and remain in Hamburg with Astrid Kirchherr and to study at the State College of Art.

July 3
– The Beatles arrived back in Liverpool.

July 6
– Bill Harry published the first issue of his fortnightly beat music paper *Mersey Beat* which included "Being a Short Diversion on the Dubious Origins of The Beatles translated from the John Lennon:

"Once upon a time there were three little boys called John, George and Paul, by name christened. They decided to get together because they were the getting together type. When they were together they wondered what for after all, what for? So all of a sudden they all grew guitars and formed a noise. Funnily enough, no one was interested, least of all the three little men. So-o-o-o on discovering a fourth little even littler man called Stuart Sutcliffe running about them they said, quote, 'Sonny get a bass guitar and you will be alright' and he did – but he wasn't alright because he couldn't play it. So they sat on him with comfort 'til he could play. Still there was no beat, and a kindly old aged man said, quote 'Thou hast not drums!' We had no drums! they coffed. So a series of drums came and went and came.

"Suddenly, in Scotland, touring with Johnny Gentle, the group (called The Beatles called) discovered they had not a very nice sound – because they had no amplifiers. They got some. Many people ask what are Beatles? Why Beatles? Ugh, Beatles, how did the name arrive? So we will tell you. It came in a vision – a man appeared on a flaming pie and said unto them 'From this day on you are Beatles with an A'. Thank you, Mister Man, they said, thanking him.

"And then a man with a beard cut off said – will you go to Germany (Hamburg) and play mighty rock for the peasants for money? And we said we would play mighty anything for money.

"But before we could go we had to grow a drummer, so we grew one in West Derby in a club called Some Casbah and his trouble was Pete Best. We called 'Hello,

Opposite: The Beatles' image evolved in Hamburg under the direction of Astrid Kirchherr; John and George in Astrid's loft. Above: Stuart Sutcliffe.

Pete, come off to Germany!' 'Yes!' Zooooom. After a few months, Peter and Paul (who is called McArtrey, son of Jim McArtrey, his father) lit a Kino (cinema) and the German police said 'Bad Beatles, you must go home and light your English cinemas'. Zooooom, half a group. But even before this, the Gestapo had taken my friend little George Harrison (of Speke) away because he was only twelve and too young to vote in Germany; but after two months in England he grew eighteen, and the Gestapoes said 'you can come'. So suddenly all back in Liverpool Village were many groups playing in grey suits and Jim said 'Why have you no grey suits?' 'We don't like them, Jim' we said speaking to Jim. After playing in the clubs a bit, everyone said 'Go to Germany!' So we are, Zooooom. Stuart gone. Zoom zoom John (of Woolton) George (of Speke) Peter and Paul zoom zoom. All of them gone.

Thank you club members, from John and George (what are friends)."

July 13
– St John's Hall, Tuebrook, Liverpool.

July 14
– The Cavern (lunchtime)
– The Cavern (evening) "Welcome Home Night", with Ian & The Zodiacs and The White Eagles Jazz Band.

July 15
– Holyoake Hall, Wavertree, Liverpool.

July 16
– Blair Hall, Walton, Liverpool.

July 17
– The Cavern (lunchtime)
– Litherland Town Hall.

July 19
– The Cavern (lunchtime).
– The Cavern (evening), with The Remo Four and The Pressmen.

July 20
– St John's Hall, Tuebrook.
– The second issue of *Mersey Beat* featured a picture of The Beatles on the cover with a report on their recording session with Tony Sheridan. Brian Epstein ordered 12 dozen copies for his record shop, NEMS.

July 21
– The Cavern (lunchtime).
– Aintree Institute, Liverpool, with Cy & The Cimarrons.

July 22
– Holyoake Hall, Wavertree, Liverpool.

July 23
– Blair Hall, Walton, Liverpool.

July 24
– Litherland Town Hall.

July 25
– The Cavern (lunchtime).
– The Cavern (evening), with the Remo Four and Gerry & The Pacemakers on the Blue Genes Guest Night.

July 26
– The Cavern (evening), with Johnny Sandon & The Searchers and The Four Jays.

July 27
– The Cavern (lunchtime).
– St John's Hall, Tuebrook, with The Big Three, Cass & the Cassanovas and Cilla White, whom The Beatles backed. Brian Epstein later changed her name to the funkier sounding Cilla Black.

July 28
– Aintree Institute, Liverpool.

July 29
– Blair Hall, Walton, Liverpool.

July 30
– Blair Hall, Walton, Liverpool,

July 31
– The Cavern (lunchtime).
– Litherland Town Hall.

August 2
– The Cavern (lunchtime).
– The Cavern (evening), with Karl Kerry & The Cruisers and Dale Roberts & The Jaywalkers.

August 3
– Brian Epstein began his record review column for *Mersey Beat* magazine called "Stop the World – And Listen to Everything In It" by "Brian Epstein Of NEMS".

August 4
– The Cavern (lunchtime).
– Aintree Institute, Liverpool.

August 5
– The Cavern (evening), an all-night session with The Cimmerons, The Panama Jazz Band, The Mike Cotten Jazz Band, The Kenny Ball Jazzmen and The Remo Four.

August 6
– Casbah Coffee Club, West Derby, Liverpool.

George, on stage at the Cavern.

August 7
– Town Hall, Litherland.
August 8
– The Cavern (lunchtime).
August 9
– The Cavern (evening).
August 10
– The Cavern (lunchtime).
– St. John's Hall, Tuebrook, Liverpool.
August 11
– The Cavern (evening) with Alan Elsdon's Jazz Band.
August 12
– Aintree Institute, Liverpool.
August 13
– Casbah Coffee Club, West Derby, Liverpool.
August 14
– The Cavern (lunchtime).
August 16
– The Cavern (evening) with The Pressmen.

August 17
– St John's Hall, Tuebrook, Liverpool, with The Big Three. Johnny Gustafson, bassist from The Big Three, sat in with them that night.
– The first Beatles fan letters were printed in *Mersey Beat*.
August 18
– The Cavern (lunchtime).
– Aintree Institute, Liverpool.
August 19
– Aintree Institute, Liverpool.
August 20
– Hambleton Hall, Huyton, Liverpool.
August 21
– The Cavern (lunchtime).
August 23
– The Cavern (lunchtime).
– The Cavern (evening) with The Rockin' Blackcats and Kingsize Taylor & The Dominoes.
August 24
– St John's Hall, Tuebrook, Liverpool.
August 25
– The Cavern (lunchtime).
– M.V. Royal Iris, River Mersey, with Acker Bilk and his Paramount Jazz Band. A "Riverboat Shuffle" promoted by Ray McFall, owner of The Cavern, who closed the club for the event. The Royal Iris was a Liverpool institution, known as the "Fish & Chip Boat", which hosted dances and cruises for 40 years, until she was mothballed in January 1991. The Beatles were to play there a number of times.
August 26
– Aintree Institute, Liverpool.
August 27
– Casbah Coffee Club, West Derby, Liverpool.
August 28
– The Cavern (lunchtime).
August 29
– The Cavern (lunchtime).
August 30
– The Cavern (evening) with The Strangers.
August 31
– St John's Hall, Tuebrook, Liverpool.
– *Mersey Beat* reported that a "Beatles" fan club had been started with Bernard Boyd as President, Jennifer Dawes the Treasurer and Maureen O'Shea the

Secretary. "The club will open officially in September ..."
September
– The EP **My Bonnie** by Tony Sheridan and The Beat Brothers was released in Germany on Polydor:
  SIDE A: **'My Bonnie', 'Why';**
  SIDE B: **'Cry For A Shadow', 'The Saints'.**
September 1
– The Cavern (lunchtime) with Karl Terry & The Cruisers.
– The Cavern (evening) with Dizzy Burton's Jazz Band.
September 2
– Aintree Institute, Liverpool.
September 3
– Hambleton Hall, Huyton, Liverpool.
September 6
– The Cavern (evening) with Johnny Sandon & The Searchers and Ian & The Zodiacs.
September 7
– The Cavern (lunchtime).
September 8
– St John's Hall, Tuebrook, Liverpool.
September 9
– Aintree Institute, Liverpool.
September 10
– Casbah Coffee Club, West Derby, Liverpool.
September 11
– The Cavern (lunchtime).
September 13
– The Cavern (lunchtime).
– The Cavern (evening), with The Remo Four and The Pressmen.
September 14
– Litherland Town Hall.
– John's column "Around and About", written under the pseudonym Beatcomber, first appeared in *Mersey Beat* magazine.
September 15
– The Cavern (lunchtime).
– Grosvenor Ballroom, Liscard.
– Village Hall, Knotty Ash. This second gig of the evening was promoted by Pete Best's mother, Mona, who was still interested in managing the group.
September 16
– Aintree Institute, Liverpool.
September 17
– Hambleton Hall, Huyton, Liverpool.

We didn't **know** much about him
but he seemed very **interested** in us
and **also** a little bit **baffled.**

The origins of the 'Beatle Cut'

John: "Paris has always been the object of English romanticism, hasn't it? I fell for Paris first of all, even before Hamburg. I remember spending my 21st birthday there with Paul in 1961..."

In Paris they visited Jürgen Vollmer, their friend from the Reeperbahn, who had moved there to study photography. He wore his hair brushed forward which was a fashion among some French youths, a style he had been introduced to by Astrid Kirchherr, who cut Stuart Sutcliffe's hair that way when they were all in Hamburg. John and Paul decided they wanted their hair like Jürgen's and asked him to do it. Jürgen Vollmer: "I gave both of them their first Beatles haircut in my hotel room on the Left Bank."

Paul: "Jürgen was in Paris on that trip, and we said, 'Do us a favour, cut our hair like you've cut yours.' So he did it, and it turned out different, 'cos his wasn't exactly a Beatle cut, but ours fell into The Beatles thing. We didn't really start that. The impression that got over was that it was just us, that we'd started it all. We kept saying, 'But there's millions of people in art schools who look like this. We're just the spokesmen for it.'"

Astrid had copied the style from a Jean Cocteau movie. Cocteau's favourite actor, Jean Marais, wore his hair brushed forward to play Oedipus in Cocteau's 1959 *Le Testament d'Orphée* which is the ultimate origin of the famous Beatles haircut.

Aunt Mimi told the *Liverpool Echo* that she remembered the time that John slipped off to Paris to "sell his paintings" and that some unsuspecting Frenchman has a Lennon original on his wall.

September 19
– *The Cavern* (afternoon).
September 20
– *The Cavern* (evening) with Karl Terry & The Cruisers and Ian & The Zodiacs.
September 21
– *The Cavern* (lunchtime).
– *Litherland town Hall,* with Gerry & The Pacemakers and Rory Storm & The Hurricanes.
September 22
– *Village Hall, Knotty Ash.*
September 23
– *Aintree Institute, Liverpool.*
September 24
– *Casbah Coffee Club, West Derby, Liverpool.*
September 25
– *The Cavern* (lunchtime).
September 27
– *The Cavern* (lunchtime).
– *The Cavern* (evening) with Gerry & The Pacemakers and Mark Peters & The Cyclones.
September 28
– *Litherland Town Hall.*
September 29
– *The Cavern* (lunchtime).
– *Village Hall, Knotty Ash.*
September 30
– Paul and John set off to hitchhike to Paris.
October 9
– John spent his 21st birthday in Paris with Paul.
October 15
– *Albany Cinema, Northway* (lunchtime). A charity concert promoted by Jim Getty (who sold John his first guitar) in aid of local St John's Ambulance Brigade.

There were 16 acts on a three-hour bill headed by local comedian Ken Dodd and ending with a ten-minute Beatles set.
– *Hambleton Hall, Huyton.*
October 16
– *The Cavern* (lunchtime).
October 17
– *David Lewis Club, Liverpool.* Promoted by The Beatles' newly formed fan club.
October 18
– *The Cavern* (lunchtime).
– *The Cavern* (evening) with Ian & The Zodiacs and The Four Jays.
October 19
– *Litherland Town Hall* with Gerry & The Pacemakers and Karl Terry & The Cruisers. Halfway through the evening, The Beatles and The Pacemakers combined to form a "supergroup": George, lead guitar; Paul, rhythm guitar; John, piano; Pete Best and Freddy Marsden, drums; Les Maguire, saxophone; Les Chadwick, bass; Gerry Marsden, lead guitar and vocals; Karl Terry, vocals. Among the numbers they performed were 'Whole Lotta Shakin' Goin' On', 'What'd I Say?', 'Red Sails in the Sunset' and 'Hit the Road Jack'.
October 20
– *The Cavern* (lunchtime).
– *Village Hall, Knotty Ash.*
October 21
– *The Cavern* (all night session) with The Panama Jazz Band, The Remo Four, Gerry & The Pacemakers, The Yorkshire Jazz Band and The Collegians Jazz Band.

October 22
– *Casbah Coffee Club, West Derby, Liverpool.*
October 24
– *The Cavern* (lunchtime).
October 25
– *The Cavern* (evening) with Gerry & The Pacemakers and The Strangers.
October 26
– *The Cavern* (lunchtime).
October 27
– *Village Hall, Knotty Ash.*
October 28
– *Aintree Institute, Liverpool.*
– This is the legendary day that Raymond Jones asked Brian Epstein for 'My Bonnie' by The Beatles at NEMS record store. The record was released only in Germany at that time and was by Tony Sheridan and The Beat Brothers, not The Beatles, so it took him a little while to track it down.
October 29
– *Hambleton Hall, Huyton, Liverpool.*
October 30
– *The Cavern* (lunchtime).
– Two girls asked for 'My Bonnie' at NEMS, causing Brian Epstein to search foreign record importers' lists for this elusive record. Since he had sold 12 dozen copies of *Mersey Beat* and even wrote a column for it, it is virtually impossible that he didn't know who The Beatles were.
October 31
– *Litherland Town Hall.*
November 1
– *The Cavern* (lunchtime).
– *The Cavern* (evening) with The Strangers and Gerry & The Pacemakers.

November 3
– *The Cavern* (lunchtime).
November 4
– *The Cavern* (evening) with The Collegians Jazz Band.
November 7
– *The Cavern* (lunchtime).
– *Merseyside Civil Service Club.*
– *The Cavern* (evening), with Gerry & The Pacemakers and The Strangers on a Blue Genes guest night.
November 8
– *The Cavern* (evening) with The Remo Four and Ian & The Zodiacs.
November 9
– *The Cavern* (lunchtime). Brian Epstein, accompanied by his assistant, Alistair Taylor, and wearing a pinstriped suit, visited the club for the first time. His presence was announced by DJ Bob Wooler over the PA: "We have someone rather famous in the audience today." It is a measure of how small-town Liverpool was that a record shop owner could be regarded as famous.

Brian was intrigued by all the publicity attending The Beatles, particularly by the coverage that the band had been receiving in *Mersey Beat*, and had come to see what the fuss was about. He began to visit the club regularly to see The Beatles, always taking time to have a few words with them.

George: "He started talking to us about the record that had created the demand. He came back several times and talked to us."

"It seemed there was something he wanted to say, but he wouldn't come out with it. He just kind of watched us and studied what we were doing. One day he took us to the store and introduced us. We thought he looked rather red and embarrassed about it all."
– *Litherland Town Hall.* This was the group's last appearance at this venue.
November 10
– *Tower Ballroom, New Brighton, Wallasey,* with Roy Storm & The

Quite **frankly,** I was **excited** about their **prospects,** provided **some** things could be **changed."**

Hurricanes, Gerry & The Pacemakers, The Remo Four, Kingsize Taylor & The Dominoes. The first of promoter Sam Leach's "Operation Big Beat" concerts. The Beatles played two sets, the first at 8 and the second at 11:30. In between sets they drove to Knotty Ash where they played another gig.
– *Village Hall Knotty Ash.*
November 11
– *Aintree Institute, Liverpool.*
To celebrate the success of "Operation Big Beat" the previous night, Sam Leach gave a late-night party at the Liverpool Jazz Centre which The Beatles all attended.
November 12
– *Hambleton Hall, Huyton, Liverpool.*
November 13
– *The Cavern* (lunchtime).
November 14
– *Merseyside Civil Service Club.*
– *The Cavern* with The Remo Four and Gerry & The Pacemakers on a Blue Genes guest night.
November 15
– *The Cavern* (lunchtime).
– *The Cavern* (evening) with The Four Jays and Johnny Sandon & The Searchers.
November 17
– *The Cavern* (lunchtime).
– *Village Hall, Knotty Ash.*
November 18
– *The Cavern* (evening) with The White Eagles Jazz Band.
November 19
– *Casbah Coffee Club, West Derby, Liverpool.*
November 21
– *The Cavern* (lunchtime).
– *Merseyside Civil Service Club.*
November 22
– *The Cavern* (evening) with Gerry & The Pacemakers and Earl Preston & The TT's
November 23
– *The Cavern* (lunchtime).
November 24
– *Casbah Coffee Club, West Derby, Liverpool.*
– *Tower Ballroom, New Brighton, Wallasey* with Rory Storm & The Hurricanes, Gerry & The Pacemakers, The Reno Four, Earl Preston & The Tempest Tornadoes and Faron Young

ONE WEEK TO GO FOR OPERATION BIG BEAT
TOWER BALLROOM, NEW BRIGHTON.
FRIDAY, NOVEMBER 10, 7.30-1 A.M.
Merseyside's Top 5 Bands Starring
THE BEATLES
(By kind permission of Mrs. Best)
RORY STORM & THE HURRICANES
GERRY & THE PACEMAKERS
THE REMO FOUR (After 11 p.m.)
KINGSIZE TAYLOR & THE DOMINOES
Two licensed bars (until 11.30 p.m.). Buffet. Late transport (Liverpool, Wirral and Cheshire). Transport details from Agencies and Crown Coachways. Tickets 5/- from Rushworth's, Lewis's, Crane's, Nems, Top-Hat, Hessy's, Strother's, Tower and Mersey Beat. Details in to-day's "Mersey Beat."

& The Flamingos. The evening was Sam Leach's "Operation Big Beat II". The Beatles arrived for an 11 pm set, and there were surprise appearances by Emile Ford, who performed with Rory Storm and The Hurricanes, and Davy Jones who did two numbers backed by The Beatles.
November 26
– *Hambleton Hall, Huyton, Liverpool.*
November 27
– *The Cavern* (lunchtime).
November 28
– *Merseyside Civil Service Club.*
November 29
– *The Cavern* (lunchtime).
– *The Cavern* (evening) with Ian & The Zodiacs and The Remo Four.
December 1
– *The Cavern* (lunchtime).
– *Tower Ballroom, New Brighton, Wallasey.* Another of Sam Leach's "Operation Big Beat" sessions with The Beatles heading the bill of six groups.

December 2
– *The Cavern* (evening) with The Zenith Six Jazz Band.
December 3
– *Casbah Coffee Club, West Derby, Liverpool.*
– The first meeting between the group and Brian Epstein to discuss his becoming their manager was held at Epstein's office at NEMS. Paul was late because he was having a bath, but once the full complement had gathered they retired to a milk bar for Brian to put his proposals to them.
George: "Eventually he started talking about becoming our manager. Well, we hadn't really had anybody actually volunteer in that sense. At the same time, he was very honest about it, like saying he didn't really know anything about managing a group like us. He sort of hinted that he was keen if we'd go along with him."
Brian: "There was something enormously attractive about them. I liked the way they worked and the obvious enthusiasm they put into their numbers... It was the boys themselves though who really swung it. Each had something which I could see would be highly commercial if only someone could push it to the top. They were different characters but they were so obviously part of the whole.
The Beatles were not sure and went away to think about it. Meanwhile, a second meeting was arranged.
December 5
– *The Cavern* (lunchtime).
December 6
– *The Cavern* (evening) with The Remo Four and The Strangers.
– The Beatles' second meeting with Brian Epstein. John, acting as the spokesman for the group, accepted Brian's proposal but no documents were drawn up.
December 8
– *The Cavern* (lunchtime). They also backed Davy Jones whom Ray

McFall had booked for the lunchtime session as well.

– *Tower Ballroom, New Brighton, Wallasey,* with Danny Williams and Davy Jones who headed the bill and for whom The Beatles again provided backing.

December 9

– *Palais Ballroom, Aldershot,* with Ivor Jay and The Jaywalkers. Sam Leach's first attempt at promoting in southern England ended in disaster. As he was not known to them, the local newspaper refused to accept his cheque for an advertisement, and as he neglected to leave his telephone number with them, his ad was not run. The Beatles arrived at an empty hall; no one knew the "Battle of the Bands" was happening. A quick run round the local coffee bars asking people to come to a free dance resulted in an audience of 18 people.

They had nowhere to stay so they drove into London to visit the Blue Gardenia, a Soho drinking club run by their old friend Brian Cassar, formerly of Cass and The Cassanovas. They jammed on stage (minus George) to an even smaller audience than in Aldershot.

December 10

– *Hambleton Hall, Huyton, Liverpool.*

December 11

– *The Cavern* (lunchtime).

December 13

– *The Cavern* (lunchtime).
– *The Cavern* (evening) with Gerry

& The Pacemakers and The Four Jays. Brian Epstein used his influence as a major record dealer to persuade the A&R manager of Decca Records, Mike Smith, to visit Liverpool to see them play The Cavern. After watching them play he agreed to audition them in London.

December 15

– *The Cavern* (lunchtime).
– *Tower Ballroom, New Brighton, Wallasey,* with a reformed Cass & The Cassanovas and The Big Three.
– The Beatles signed a management contract with Brian Epstein. The four of them wrote their signatures over four of the five sixpenny stamps attached to the document as was required in those days to make it legally binding. Then Brian announced that he was not going to sign, saying that he did not want The Beatles to feel tied to him in any way. Alistair Taylor was asked to witness his non-signing. Since Brian's original agreement with the band was that he would get them a recording contract, which he had not yet done, his decision not to sign was not that surprising.

December 16

– *The Cavern* (evening) with The White Eagles Jazz band.

December 17

– *Casbah Coffee Club, West Derby.*

December 18

– *The Cavern* (lunchtime).

December 19

– *The Cavern* (lunchtime).

December 20

– *The Cavern* (evening) with The

Strangers and Mark Peters & The Cyclones.

December 21

– *The Cavern* (lunchtime).

December 23

– *The Cavern,* all-night session with The Micky Ashman Jazz Band, The Remo Four, Gerry & The Pacemakers, The Saints Jazz Band and The Searchers.

December 26

– *Tower Ballroom, New Brighton, Wallasey.* "The Beetles" with Rory Storm & The

Hurricanes and Tony Osborne & His Band for a "Boxing Night Big Beat Ball".

December 27

– *The Cavern* (evening) with Gerry & The Pacemakers and Kingsize Taylor & The Dominoes. Advertised as "The Beatles' Xmas Party".

December 29

– *The Cavern* (evening) with the Yorkshire Jazz Band.

December 30

– *The Cavern* (evening) with The White Eagles Jazz Band.

Brian Epstein

The group came to an informal agreement with Brian Epstein, making him their manager providing he could get them a recording contract. He also promised to release them from their contract with Bert Kaempfert in Hamburg. Brian had studied acting at RADA and had very specific ideas about stage presentation. There was to be no eating, drinking or fighting on stage, nor were they to shout at the audience. Brian wanted them to be punctual and to plan their set in advance. His biggest change was to take them out of their black leathers and put them all into neat suits. The group assumed that he knew what he was doing and went along with it.

John: "We were in a daydream 'till he came along. We'd no idea what we were doing. Seeing our marching orders on paper made it all official. Brian was trying to clean our image up. He said we'd never get past the door of a good place. He'd tell us that jeans were not particularly smart and could we possibly manage to wear proper trousers. But he didn't want us suddenly looking square. He let us have our own sense of individuality. We respected his views. We stopped chomping at cheese rolls and jam butties on stage. We paid a lot more attention to what we were doing. Did our best to be on time. And we smartened up, in the sense that we wore suits instead of any sloppy old clothes."

Ringo, at New Brighton Tower Ballroom before he joined The Beatles, with George.

19'62

January 1

– The Beatles auditioned for Mike Smith, an A&R manager at Decca Records, at Decca's studios in Broadhurst Gardens, West Hampstead, north London. They arrived in London after a ten-hour drive through stormy conditions on New Year's Eve with the group and roadie Aspinall squashed into a van with all their equipment. Tony Meehan, the former drummer for The Shadows, had joined Decca as a producer the year before and was present in the control room, and the group were impressed to meet him. The Beatles were nervous and Mike Smith was late after an all-night party. When Smith saw the state of their amps he insisted that they use the unfamiliar studio equipment. The group recorded 15 songs chosen by Brian Epstein. They got started at 11 am and finished about an hour later. They recorded a mixtures of oldies, some of their own compositions and a selection of recent chart hits, intending to show all sides of their ability: 'Like Dreamers Do' (Lennon/McCartney), 'Money (That's What I Want)', 'Till there Was You', 'The Sheik Of Araby', 'To Know Her is to Love Her', 'Take Good Care of My Baby', 'Memphis, Tennessee', 'Sure to Fall (In Love With You)', 'Hello Little Girl' (Lennon/McCartney), 'Three Cool Cats', 'Crying, Waiting, Hoping', 'Love Of The Loved' (Lennon/McCartney), 'September In The Rain', 'Besame Mucho' and 'Searchin'.

Smith said he would let Epstein know and hurried them out of the studio because he was running late and had another appointment to see Brian Poole and The Tremeloes. He had been enthusiastic and the group left feeling optimistic. The Beatles and Brian Epstein stayed at the Royal Hotel (27 shillings a night plus breakfast) and celebrated with Rum and Scotch-and-Cokes.

Mike Smith cut a number of acetates for his boss Dick Rowe, the head of "Pop" A&R at Decca, to hear when he returned from America. But Rowe turned the group down, famously telling Brian Epstein: "Groups of guitars are on the way out, Mr Epstein. You really should stick to selling records in Liverpool." Electric guitars, he told him, were now "old hat". He became known as "The man who turned down The Beatles" but quickly made up for it by signing The Rolling Stones to Decca – on George Harrison's advice.

January 3

– *The Cavern* (lunchtime).

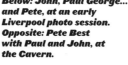

Below: John, Paul George... and Pete, at an early Liverpool photo session. Opposite: Pete Best with Paul and John, at the Cavern.

– *The Cavern* (evening) with Johnny Sandon & The Searchers and Kingsize Taylor & The Dominoes.

January 4

– A poll of 5,000 readers of *Mersey Beat* magazine to find Liverpool's most popular group showed The Beatles at number one with Gerry & The Pacemakers in second place.

January 5

– *The Cavern* (lunchtime).
– The single **'My Bonnie'/'The Saints'** was released in the UK as Polydor NH 66833 by Tony Sheridan and The (now-correctly-named) Beatles: an Epstein promotional plan which meant that "Polydor Recording Artists" could be now added to posters and advertisements even though there was little chance of the record getting into the charts.

January 6

– *The Cavern* (evening) with The Collegians Jazz Band.

January 7

– *Casbah Coffee Club, West Derby, Liverpool.*

January 9

– *The Cavern* (lunchtime).

January 10

– *The Cavern* (evening) with Gerry & The Pacemakers.

January 11

– *The Cavern* (lunchtime).

January 12

– *The Cavern* (evening) with The Mike Cotten Jazzmen.
– *Tower Ballroom, New Brighton, Wallasey,* with Mel (King of Twist) Turner & The Bandits, Rory Storm & The Hurricanes, The Strangers. When Screaming Lord Sutch and His Horde of Savages didn't arrive, The Beatles took over the 11.30 headline spot.

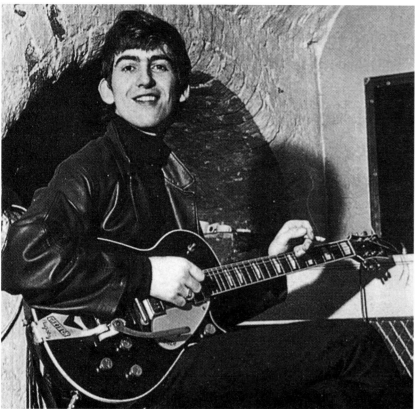

George, at the Cavern.

January 13
– *Hambleton Hall, Huyton.* This was
their last performance at this venue.
January 14
– *Casbah Coffee Club, West
Derby, Liverpool.*
January 15
– *The Cavern* (lunchtime).
January 17
– *The Cavern* (lunchtime).
– *The Cavern* (evening) with Ian
& The Zodiacs and The Remo Four.
January 19
– *The Cavern* (lunchtime).
– *Tower Ballroom, New
Brighton, Wallasey.*
January 20
– *The Cavern* (evening) with The
Yorkshire Jazz Band.
January 21
– *Casbah Coffee Club, West
Derby, Liverpool.*
January 22
– *The Cavern* (lunchtime). First of
The Cavern's five experimental one-
hour lunchtime sessions (instead of
two hours). Admission one shilling
(five pence).
– *Kingsway Club, Southport.*

January 24
– *The Cavern* (lunchtime).
– *The Cavern* (evening) with The Four
Jays and Gerry & The Pacemakers.
– That afternoon The Beatles signed
a management contract with Brian
Epstein, witnessed by his assistant
Alistair Taylor, at Brian's NEMS office.
Brian Epstein hedged his bets by again
not actually putting his own signature
to the document. He was to receive 25
per cent of their gross earnings. The
four Beatles divided what was left after
their expenses had been deducted.
This meant that Brian always received
more money than any individual Beatle,
and, when their expenses became
enormous, he received considerably
more. The normal management
percentage in those days was ten
per cent
January 26
– *The Cavern* (lunchtime).
– *The Cavern* (evening) with The
Yorkshire Jazz Band.
– *Tower Ballroom, New
Brighton, Wallasey.*
January 27
– *Aintree Institute, Liverpool.* This
was the last time that the group played
for promoter Brian "Beekay" Kelly.
Brian Epstein was insulted when Kelly
paid the group their £15 fee in loose
change and ensured they never worked
for him again.
– The Liverpool Echo published an
account of the group's audition with
Decca written by Tony Barrow who
was later to become their publicist.
January 28
– *Casbah Coffee Club, West
Derby, Liverpool.*
January 29
– *Kingsway Club, Southport.*
January 30
– *The Cavern* (lunchtime).
January 31
– *The Cavern* (evening) with The
Remo Four and Kingsize Taylor &
The Dominoes.
February 1
– *The Cavern* (lunchtime).
– *Thistle Café, West Kirby,* with
Steve Day & The Drifters. Billed as
"The Grand Opening of The Beatle
Club" this was the first booking where
Brian Epstein took a commission.

(The Beatles never played there again).
February 2
– *Oasis Club, Manchester,* with
The Allan Dent Jazz Band and Tony
Smith's Jazzmen. This was their first
professionally organised gig
outside Liverpool.
February 3
– *The Cavern* (evening) with
The Saints Jazz Band and Gerry &
The Pacemakers.
February 4
– *Casbah Coffee Club, West
Derby, Liverpool.*
February 5
– *The Cavern* (lunchtime).
– *The Kingsway Club, Southport,*
with The Quiet Ones. Pete Best was
ill and couldn't make these two gigs.
Since Rory Storm and The Hurricanes
had no bookings this day, Ringo stood
in as The Beatles' drummer for
both performances.
February 7
– *The Cavern* (lunchtime).
– *The Cavern* (evening) with Dale
Roberts & The Jaywalkers and Gerry
& The Pacemakers.
February 8
– Brian Epstein had the Decca audition
tape made into acetates at EMI's His
Master's Voice record shop at 363
Oxford Street, London, which was
managed by a friend of his called Bob
Boast. Jim Foy, the disc-cutter, was
impressed by their performance and
when Brian told him that John and
Paul wrote some of their own material,
he suggested that Brian should meet
Sid Coleman, the head of EMI's record
publishing company, Ardmore and
Beechwood, whose offices were on the
top floor. Coleman eventually published
two of John and Paul's songs, 'Love
Me Do' and 'P.S. I Love You', which
are now owned by Paul McCartney, the
only Beatles songs in the MPL
catalogue. It was Sid Coleman who sent
Brian to see George Martin, head of
A&R at another of EMI's companies,
Parlophone Records.
February 9
– *The Cavern* (lunchtime).
– *The Cavern* (evening), with Gerry &
The Pacemakers and The Collegians
Jazz Band.
– *Technical College Hall,*

Birkenhead. This was the first of three consecutive Friday-night sessions at the Tech.

February 10
– *Youth Club, St. Paul's Presbyterian Church Hall, Tranmere, Birkenhead.*

February 11
– *Casbah Coffee Club, West Derby, Liverpool.*

February 12
– The Beatles were auditioned by Peter Pilbeam who produced BBC Radio programmes for teenage audiences made in the North of England. The Beatles did two numbers with Paul on vocals: 'Like Dreamers Do', which was his own composition, and Peggy Lee's 'Till There Was You'; and two with John singing: his own 'Hello Little Girl' and Chuck Berry's 'Memphis, Tennessee'. Pilbeam's notes read "Yes" for John and "No" for Paul. He booked them to record a session for *Teenagers' Turn* on March 7. It was their first radio broadcast.

February 13
– *The Cavern* (lunchtime).

February 14
– *The Cavern* (evening), with Johnny Sandon & The Searchers and The Strangers.

February 15
– *The Cavern* (lunchtime).
– *Tower Ballroom, New Brighton, Wallasey,* with Terry Lightfoot and his New Orleans Jazz Band. Billed as the "Pre-Panto Ball" as there was to be a "Panto Ball" at the Tower the next night. Between them they drew a large audience of 3,500 people.

February 16
– *Technical College, Birkenhead.*
– *Tower Ballroom, New Brighton, Wallasey.*

February 17
– *The Cavern* (evening) with Cyril Preston's Excelsior Jazz Band and The Zenith Six Jazz Band.

February 18
– *Casbah Coffee Club, West Derby, Liverpool.*

February 19
– *The Cavern* (lunchtime).

February 20
– A contract was sent by BBC Manchester for The Beatles to record

the *Teenager's Turn* radio show on March 7.
– *Floral Hall, Southport,* with Gerry & The Pacemakers, Rory Storm & The Hurricanes and The Chris Hamilton Jazzmen. "A Rock 'n' Trad Spectacular" and their biggest venue booked by Brian Epstein to date.
– Brian Epstein wrote to Bert Kaempfert in Hamburg asking him to release The Beatles from their recording contract of May 1961.

February 21
– *The Cavern* (lunchtime).
– *The Cavern* (evening) with Ken Dallas & The Silhouettes and Steve Day & The Drifters.

February 23
– *The Cavern* (lunchtime).
– *Tower Ballroom, New Brighton, Wallasey.* Sets at 9 pm and 10.45 pm sets.
– The group just had time between

"An unusual group, not as rocky as most, more C&W with a tendency to play music."

Pete Best's refusal to adopt a 'Beatle' haircut estranged him from the other three.

sets at the Tower to squeeze in this half-hour appearance.

February 24
– *YMCA Wirral.* The audience were bored by the group's long introductions between songs and booed them off the stage.
– *The Cavern.* An all-night session which also featured The Red River Jazzmen, Tony Smith's Jazz Band, Ken Sim's Jazz Band, Gerry & The Pacemakers and Ken Dallas & The Silhouettes.

February 26
– *Kingsway Club, Southport.*

February 27
– *The Cavern* (lunchtime).

February 28
– *The Cavern* (evening) with Gerry & The Pacemakers and The Searchers.

March 1
– *The Cavern* (lunchtime).
– *Storyville Jazz Club, Liverpool.*

March 2
– *St John's Hall, Bootle.*
– *Tower Ballroom, New Brighton, Wallasey,* with Johnny Sandon's Searchers and The Tenabeats. Billed as the "Mad March Rock Ball".

March 3
– *The Cavern* (evening) with Jim McHarg's Storeyville Jazzmen.
– Replying to Brian Epstein's request, Bert Kaempfert agreed to release the group from their May 1961 recording contract but asked that they agree to record for Polydor during their spring engagement in Hamburg.

March 4
– *Casbah Coffee Club, West Derby, Liverpool.*

March 5
– *The Cavern* (lunchtime).
– *Kingsway Club, Southport.*

March 6
– *The Cavern* (evening) with Gerry & The Pacemakers on the Blue Genes' Guest Night.

March 7
– The group drove to the Playhouse Theatre in Manchester to record their set for the BBC Light Programme show *Teenagers' Turn – Here We Go.* They did three numbers before a teenage audience: 'Dream Baby (How Long Must I Dream)', 'Memphis, Tennessee' and 'Please Mister Postman'.

March 8
– *Storyville Jazz Club.*
– The BBC Light Programme broadcast The Beatles' appearance on *Teenagers' Turn – Here We Go.*

March 9
– *The Cavern* (lunchtime).
– *The Cavern* (evening) with The Saints Jazz Band.

March 10
– *St Paul's Presbyterian Church Youth Club, Church Hall, Tranmere, Birkenhead.* Also on the bill were The Country Four with Brian Newman.

March 11
– *Casbah Coffee Club, West Derby, Liverpool.*

March 12
– *The Cavern* (lunchtime).

March 13
– *The Cavern* (lunchtime).

March 14
– *The Cavern* (evening) with Gerry

& The Pacemakers and Clay Ellis & The Raiders.

March 15
– *The Cavern* (lunchtime).
– *Storyville Jazz Club, Liverpool.*

March 16
– *The Cavern* (evening) with The Collegians Jazz Band.

March 17
– *Village Hall, Knotty Ash.* A "St Patrick's Night Rock Gala" which also featured Rory Storm & The Hurricanes. Afterwards the promoter, Sam Leach, held a memorable party to celebrate his engagement to be married, which did not end until the following afternoon.

March 18
– *Casbah Coffee Club, West Derby, Liverpool.*

March 19
– *Kingsway Club, Southport.*

March 20
– *The Cavern* (evening) with The Remo Four, The Zodiacs and Johnny Sandon on a Blue Genes Guest Night.

March 21
– *The Cavern* (lunchtime).

March 22
– *The Cavern* (evening) with Peppy & The New York Twisters.

March 23
– *The Cavern* (lunchtime).
– *The Cavern* (evening) with Pete Hartigan's Jazzmen and Gerry & The Pacemakers.

March 24
– *Heswall Jazz Club, Barnston Women's Institute, Heswall, Wirral,* with The Pasadena Jazzmen. The Beatles wore suits as stage costumes for this prestigious event.

March 25
– *Casbah Coffee Club, West Derby, Liverpool.*

March 26
– *The Cavern* (lunchtime).

March 28
– *The Cavern (lunchtime).*
– *The Cavern* (evening) with Gerry & The Pacemakers and The Remo Four with Johnny Sandon.

March 29
– *Odd Spot Club, Liverpool,* with The Mersey Beats.

March 30
– *The Cavern* (lunchtime).

Below: Stuart Sutcliffe. Opposite: George, John and Paul, outside Paul's family home in Liverpool.

– *The Cavern* (evening) with the Dallas Jazz Band.

March 31
– *Subscription Rooms, Stroud in Gloucestershire* with The Rebel Rousers. Punters warned: "At the request of the Council – No Teddy Boys and Ladies please do not wear stilleto heels."

April 1
– *Casbah Coffee Club, West Derby, Liverpool.*

April 2
– *The Cavern* (lunchtime).
– *Liverpool Pavilion* with "Ireland's Pride", the Royal Show Band from Waterford.

April 4
– *The Cavern* (lunchtime).
– *The Cavern* (evening) with The Searchers and Earl Preston & The TTs.

April 5
– *The Cavern* (evening). Presented by The Beatles' Fan Club, called "The Beatles for their Fans, or an Evening with John, Paul, George and Pete." The compere was Bob Wooler, and The Four Jays were also on the bill. Ticket holders received a free photograph of the group. The Beatles played the first half in their old Hamburg black leathers before changing into their new Epstein suits and ties for the second half.

April 6
– *The Cavern* (lunchtime).
– *Tower Ballroom, New Brighton, Wallasey.* The Beatles (spelled "Beetles" on the poster) played support to Emile Ford & The Checkmates. Also on the bill were Gerry & The Pacemakers, Howey Casey & The Seniors, Rory Storm & The Hurricanes, The Big Three and The Original King Twisters. All for six shillings.

April 7
– *The Cavern* (evening) with The Saints Jazz Band. Advertised as "The Beatles Farewell Show" before they left for Hamburg.
– *Casbah Coffee Club, West Derby, Liverpool.* George was ill and couldn't play these two gigs.

April 10
– Stuart Sutcliff, who had remained in Hamburg, was rushed to hospital with a brain haemorrhage, but died in the ambulance. He was 22.

April 11
– The Beatles, except <u>George</u>, flew to Hamburg from Ringway Airport, Manchester.

April 13 – 30
– *Star-Club, Grosse-Freiheit, Hamburg.* The Beatles played a seven-week season at the Star-Club ending on May 31, with only one day off: April 20, when the club closed for Good Friday. For the first two weeks they were on the same bill as Gene Vincent.

Mersey Beat described the club: "There are two bars, a refreshment counter and a small 'twistin' base' situated in the balcony. Over the ground floor and beneath the balcony a suspended trellis ceiling has been slung from which hang attractive lanterns which give the club an exciting and intimate atmosphere."

April 23
– The single **'My Bonnie'/'The Saints'** was released in the US as DECCA 31382, by Tony Sheridan and The Beat Brothers.

May 1 – 31
– *Star-Club, Grosse Freiheit, Hamburg.*

May 9
– George Martin met with Brian Epstein at Abbey Road at the suggestion of Sid Coleman of Ardmore and Beechwood, EMI's music publishing division. On the strength of the Decca audition tapes, Martin offered Brian a recording contract before he had even seen the group play. The paperwork was processed and Brian's signature added. All that remained was for George to audition the group at Abbey Road, and if he liked them, EMI's official signature could be added and the contract would be legally binding. A date was set of June 6 for The Beatles to make their first visit to Abbey Road. Brian sent a telegram to The Beatles in Hamburg which read, "Congratulations boys. EMI request recording session. Please rehearse new material."

May 28
– The Beatles opened what the Star-Club billed as their "Rockin'-Twist Festival 62 mit Gene Vincent, King of Rock '61 in USA, Davy Jones, Tony Sheridan, The Batchelors, Tanya Day, Roy Young, Tex Roberg und den Rock-

"Well I **don't** like your tie for a **start!**"

und-Twist-Bands: The Beatles, The Graduates, Gerry & The Pacemakers, The Starlioners, Roy & Tony's Star Inc." which ran from May 28 until June 11.

June 6
– *Abbey Road.* The Beatles recorded four numbers in studio three: 'Besame Mucho', 'Love Me Do', 'P.S. I Love You' and 'Ask Me Why'. The session was produced by Ron Richards. George Martin was not at the session from the beginning, and only showed up when the balance engineer, Norman Smith, liked their first Lennon and McCartney composition and sent the tape operator, Chris Neal, to fetch him. George Martin saw the potential in what he heard, but he did not like Pete Best's drumming and said they could use a session drummer for the recording sessions. George Martin ordered the final signature to be placed on the contract. The Beatles were on EMI.

George Martin: **"If there's anything you don't like, just tell me."**

George Harrison:

June 9
– *The Cavern* (evening): "The Beatles' Welcome Home Show" also featuring The Red River Jazzmen, The Spidermen, The Four Jays and Ken Dallas & The Silhouettes. Nine hundred fans managed to squeeze into the airless basement for this gig, breaking The Cavern's attendance record.

June 11
– The group recorded another set for the BBC Light Programme's *Teenagers' Turn – Here We Go*, at the BBC's Playhouse Theatre, Manchester. They played 'Ask Me Why', 'Besamo Mucho' and 'A Picture of You'.

June 12
– *The Cavern* (lunchtime).
– *The Cavern* (evening) with no support.

June 13
– *The Cavern* (lunchtime).
– *The Cavern* (evening) with The Dakotas and The Dennisons.

June 15
– *The Cavern* (lunchtime).
– *The Cavern* (evening) with Group One and The Spidermen.

– The Beatles' appearance on *Teenagers' Turn – Here We Go* was broadcast by the BBC Light Programme.

June 16
– *The Cavern* (evening) with Tony Smith's Jazzmen.

June 19
– *The Cavern* (lunchtime).
– *The Cavern* (evening) with The Mersey Beats and The Swinging Blue Genes.

June 20
– *The Cavern* (lunchtime).
– *The Cavern* (evening) with The Sorrals and Kingsize Taylor & The Dominoes.

June 21
– *Tower Ballroom, New Brighton, Wallasey.* Bruce Channel topped the bill with Delbert McLinton and The Barons as his backing group. Also on the bill were Howie Casey & The

Paul in Liverpool, with his father Jim and brother Mike.

Seniors, The Big Three and The Four Jays.

June 22
– *The Cavern* (lunchtime).
– *The Cavern* (evening) with Clay Ellis & The Raiders and The Olympics.

June 23
– *The Victory Memorial Hall, Northwich in Cheshire.*
– Brian Epstein formed NEMS Enterprises Limited to deal with Beatles affairs.

June 24
– *Casbah Club, West Derby, Liverpool.* The Beatles' final appearance at Mona Best's club.

June 25
– *The Cavern* (lunchtime).
– *Plaza Ballroom, St Helens in Lancashire,* with The Big Three "Big Beat Bargain Night".

June 27
– *The Cavern* (lunchtime).
– *The Cavern* (evening) with The Swinging Blue Genes.

June 28
– *Majestic Ballroom, Birkenhead,* "Merseyside's luxury ballroom". The Beatles' first booking with the Top Rank Organisation.

June 29
– *The Cavern* (lunchtime).
– *Tower Ballroom, New Brighton, Wallasey.* "Operation Big Beat III", a five-and-a-half hour "Cavalcade of Rock 'n' Twist".

June 30
– *Heswall Jazz Club at the Barnston Women's Institute in Heswall,* with The Big Three.

July 1
– *The Cavern* (evening) with Gene Vincent & Sounds Incorporated. A bootlegged recording of Gene Vincent playing 'What'd I Say' is said to feature The Beatles sitting in with Sounds Incorporated.

July 2
– *Plaza Ballroom, St Helens in Lancashire.*

July 3
– *The Cavern* (lunchtime).

July 4
– *The Cavern* (evening) with Group One and The Spidermen.

July 5
– *Majestic Ballroom, Birkenhead.*

July 6
– Riverboat Shuffle on board the M.V. Royal Iris, organised by The Cavern. Also on the bill were Acker Bilk's Paramount Jazz Band.

July 7
– *Golf Club Dance, Hulme Hall, Port Sunlight, Birkenhead.*

July 8
– *The Cavern* (evening) with The Swinging Blue Genes and Tony Smith's Jazzmen.

July 9
– *Plaza Ballroom, St Helens.*

July 10
– *The Cavern* (lunchtime).

July 11
– *The Cavern* (evening) with The Statesmen and The Morockans.

July 12
– *The Cavern* (lunchtime).
– *Majestic Ballroom, Birkenhead.*

July 13
– *Tower Ballroom, New Brighton, Wallasey.*

July 14
– *Regent Dansett, Rhyl, Wales,* with The Strangers.

July 15
– *The Cavern* (evening) with The Saints Jazz Band, The Swinging Blue Genes and The Four Jays.

July 16
– *The Cavern* (lunchtime).
– *Plaza Ballroom, St Helens in Lancashire.*

July 17
– McIlroy's Ballroom, Swindon.

July 18
– *The Cavern* (lunchtime).
– *The Cavern* (evening) with Ken Dallas & The Silhouettes and The Spidermen.

July 19
– *Majestic Ballroom, Birkenhead.*

July 20
– *The Cavern* (lunchtime).
– *The Bell Hall, Warrington.*

July 21
– *Tower Ballroom, New Brighton, Wallasey.*

July 22
– *The Cavern* (evening) with The Swinging Blue Genes, The Red River Jazzmen and Ken Dallas & The Silhouettes.

July 23
– *Kingsway Club, Southport.*

July 24
– *The Cavern* (lunchtime).

July 25
– *The Cavern* (lunchtime) with Gerry & The Pacemakers.
– *The Cavern* (evening) with The Dakotas, Ian & The Zodiacs and The Dennisons.
– *Cabaret Club, Liverpool.* A failed attempt by Brian Epstein to get The Beatles into the lounge band circuit. The audience hated The Beatles. The Beatles hated the audience.

July 26
– *Cambridge Hall, Southport,* supporting Joe Brown & The Bruvvers. A NEMS Enterprises promotion.

July 27
– *Tower Ballroom, New Brighton, Wallasey,* supporting Joe Brown & The Bruvvers. Also on the bill were The Statesmen, The Big Three, The Four Jays and Steve Day & The Drifters. A NEMS Enterprises promotion.

July 28
– *The Cavern* (evening), with The Red River Jazzmen and Dee Fenton & The Silhouettes.
– *Majestic Ballroom, Birkenhead, Cheshire,* with The Swinging Blue Genes and Billy Kramer & The Coasters.

July 30
– *The Cavern* (lunchtime).
– *Blue Penguin Club, St John's Hall, Bootle in Lancashire,* with The Mersey Beats and The Sensational Sinners.

August 1
– *The Cavern* (lunchtime).
– *The Cavern* (evening) with Gerry & The Pacemakers and The Mersey Beats.

August 3
– *Grafton Ballroom, Liverpool,* with The Big Three and Gerry & the Pacemakers. A "Holiday Spectacular!!"; the first time a rock concert was held here.

August 4
– *Victoria Hall, Higher Bebington in the Wirral.*

August 5
– *The Cavern* (evening) with The Saints Jazz Band and The Swinging Blue Genes.

August 7
– *The Cavern* (lunchtime).

– *The Cavern* (evening), with Wayne Stevens & The Vikings, Ken Dallas & The Silhouettes and The Swinging Blue Genes.

August 8
– *Co-op Ballroom, Doncaster.*

August 9
– *The Cavern* (lunchtime).

August 10
– Riverboat Shuffle held on the M.V. Royal Iris, with Johnny Kidd & the Pirates and The Dakotas.

August 11
– *Odd Spot Club, Liverpool.*

August 12
– *The Cavern* (evening) with The Swinging Bluegenes and The Red River Jazzmen.

August 13
– *The Cavern* (lunchtime).
– *Majestic Ballroom, Crewe.* "The Biggest Rock Since Blackpool Rock".

August 15
– *The Cavern* (lunchtime).
– *The Cavern* (evening). This was Pete Best's last performance with the group before he was unceremoniously fired.
– John Lennon telephoned Ringo Starr in Skegness, where he was about to complete a summer season with Rory Storm & The Hurricanes at Butlin's Holiday Camp, and confirmed that he was to become The Beatles' new drummer, something that Ringo and

Below: Gerry and The Pacemakers.

"Pete left the group by mutual agreement. There were no arguments or difficulties, and this has been an entirely amicable decision."

The Beatles had already had several clandestine meetings about.

August 16

– John, Paul and George asked Brian to tell Pete that he was no longer in the group. The Beatles' roadie, Neil Aspinall, who lived in Pete's house and was a close friend of his was going to quit in disgust but Pete insisted that he change his mind.

The Beatles' official comment was: They had decided that he did not fit the image of the group they wanted: he was too moody, and would not wear his hair in the distinctive Beatle cut.

In 1963 Pete Best gave his version of what happened: **"On our third trip to Hamburg we became the first group to play at a new venue, The Star Club. Whilst over there we received a telegram saying we'd got a Parlophone contract. Just before the first release I was told that I would have to leave the group. The news came as a complete surprise to me as I had no hint that it would happen and didn't even have the opportunity of discussing it with the rest of the group."**

– *Riverpark Ballroom, Chester.* Johnny "Hutch" Hutchinson, drummer with The Big Three, filled the empty drum stool.

August 17

– *Majestic Ballroom, Birkenhead.*
– *Tower Ballroom, New Brighton, Wallasey.* Again "Hutch" Hutchinson played drums with The Beatles even though his own group had a date this night and had to find someone to replace him.

August 18

– *Horticulture Society Dance, Hulme Hall, Port Sunlight, Birkenhead,* with The Four Jays. This was Ringo's debut as a Beatle. They managed a two-hour rehearsal together before the 10 pm gig.

August 19

– *The Cavern* (evening) with The Zenith Six Jazz Band, The Swinging Blue Genes and Peppy & The New York Twisters. This was Ringo's Cavern debut as a Beatle. Pete Best had a lot of

Below: Ringo signs up: unlike Pete Best, he had no qualms about combing his hair forward.

fans who were aggrieved at his dismissal, and the group were attacked as they entered the club. George got a black eye.

August 20

– *Majestic Ballroom, Crewe.*

August 22

– *The Cavern* (lunchtime). Granada Television filmed the group playing 'Some Other Guy' and 'Kansas City'/'Hey-Hey-Hey-Hey!' for their *Know The North* programme. It was scheduled to be shown on November 7 but the film never actually went out. The film clips survived but the sound on 'Kansas City' was lost.
– *The Cavern* (evening) with Gerry & The Pacemakers and Dee Fenton & The Silhouettes.

August 23

– *Riverpark Ballroom, Chester.*
– John and Cynthia got married at the Mount Pleasant Register Office with Paul as best man. George, Brian Epstein, Cynthia's brother Tony and his wife Marjorie were the only guests. John's harridan Aunt Mimi boycotted the event. Most of the ceremony was

drowned by the noise of a nearby pneumatic drill, making the party hysterical. Afterwards Brian Epstein took them all to Reece's cafe for a set lunch of roast chicken with all the trimmings followed by fruit salad. The cafe did not sell alcohol so they toasted each other with water. Brian allowed the couple to move into a small bachelor flat he maintained near the art college. (Cynthia was pregnant and John did the decent thing.) John spent his wedding night on stage.
– *Mersey Beat* announced the change in The Beatles' line-up.

August 24

– *The Cavern* (lunchtime).
– *Majestic Ballroom, Birkenhead, Wirral.*

August 25

– *Marine Hall Ballroom, Fleetwood in Lancashire.*

August 26

– *The Cavern* (evening) with Mike Berry & The Phantoms, The Red River Jazzmen and The Swinging Blue Genes.

Below Left: Though badly short-sighted, John refused to be seen wearing spectacles in public. Throughout Beatlemania he would never have a clear view of a frenzied Beatles audience. Opposite: Paul and John, at Paul's Liverpool home.

August 28
– *The Cavern* (evening) with The Swinging Blue Genes and Gerry Levine & The Avengers.
August 29
– *Floral Hall Ballroom, Morecambe.*
August 30
– *The Cavern* (lunchtime).
– *Riverpark Ballroom, Chester,* with Gerry & The Pacemakers, compared by Bob Wooler.
August 31
– *Town Hall, Lydney* in Gloucestershire.
September 1
– *Subscription Rooms, Stroud* in Gloucestershire.
September 2
– *The Cavern* (evening) with Kingsize Taylor & The Dominoes and The Zenith Six Jazz Band.
September 3
– *The Cavern* (lunchtime).
– *Queen's Hall, Widnes in Cheshire,* with Billy Kramer & The Coasters, Rory Storm & The Hurricanes, Sonny Kaye & The Reds. The first of three Monday evening gigs.
September 4
– *Abbey Road.* The Beatles flew from Liverpool Airport to London, where they checked into a small hotel in Chelsea. Neil Aspinall had already driven their equipment down and was waiting with it at the studio. They rehearsed until 5 pm, then George Martin took the group to his favourite Italian restaurant for dinner to get to know them a bit. They recorded a number of takes of 'Love Me Do' and, much against their wishes, 'How Do You Do It'. Photographer Dezo Hoffmann recorded the session for posterity.
September 5
– *The Cavern* (evening) with The Dennisons and Gus Travis & The Midnighters.
September 6
– *The Cavern* (lunchtime).
– *Rialto Ballroom, Liverpool,* with Rory Storm & The Hurricanes, The Big Three and The Mersey Beats.
September 7
– *Newton Dancing School, Village Hall, Irby, Heswall in the Wirral.*

September 8
– *YMCA Birkenhead.*
– *Majestic Ballroom, Birkenhead.*
September 9
– *The Cavern* (evening) with Cyril Preston's Jazz Band with Clinton Ford and Billy Kramer & The Coasters.
September 10
– *The Cavern* (lunchtime).
– *Queen's Hall, Widnes in Cheshire,* the second of three Monday evening gigs supported by Geoff Stacey & The Wanderers and Rory Storm & The Hurricanes.
September 11
– *Abbey Road* The group recorded 'Love Me Do', 'P.S. I Love You' and 'Please, Please Me' using session drummer Andy White. Ringo played tambourine and maracas. This was the recording of 'Love Me Do' used for their first single, though the initial pressings used the version with Ringo's drumming recorded on the 4th. The difference is minimal.
September 12
– *The Cavern* (evening) with Freddie & The Dreamers, 16-year-old Simone Jackson (for whom The Beatles played backing), The Spidermen and Group One.
September 13
– *The Cavern* (lunchtime).
– *Riverpark Ballroom, Chester.*
September 14
– *Tower Ballroom, New Brighton, Wallasey.* Sam Leach's "Operation

Big Beat V" with Rory Storm & The Hurricanes, Gerry & The Pacemakers and Billy Kramer & The Coasters.
September 15
– *The Victory Memorial Hall, Northwich in Cheshire.*
September 16
– *The Cavern* (evening) with The Red River Jazzmen and Gerry & The Pacemakers.
September 17
– *The Cavern* (lunchtime).
– *Queen's Hall, Widnes,* the last of three Monday evening gigs supported by Billy Kramer & The Coasters and The Vikings.
September 19
– *The Cavern* (evening) with The Dakotas and The Big Three.
September 20
The Cavern (lunchtime).
September 21
– *Tower Ballroom, New Brighton, Wallasey,* with Rory Storm & The Hurricanes.
September 22
– *Majestic Ballroom, Birkenhead.*
September 23
– *The Cavern* (evening) with The Saints Jazz Band and Kingsize Taylor & The Dominoes.
September 25
– *Heswall Jazz Club, The Barnston Women's Institute, Heswall,* with Gerry & The Pacemakers.
September 26
– *The Cavern* (lunchtime).

– *The Cavern* (evening) with The Spidermen and Kingsize Taylor & The Dominoes.
September 28
– *The Cavern* (lunchtime).
– "A Grand River Cruise" aboard the M.V. Royal Iris, with Lee Castle & The Barons and Freddy (The Teddy) Fowell.
September 29
– *Oasis Club, Manchester.*
September 30
– *The Cavern* (evening) with The Red River Jazzmen and Clay Ellis & The Raiders.
October 1
– The group signed a second management contract with Brian Epstein. It ran for five years and gave him 25 per cent of their gross earnings.
October 2
– *The Cavern* (lunchtime).
October 3
– *The Cavern* (evening) with The Echoes and Billy Kramer & The Dakotas.
October 4
– *The Cavern* (lunchtime).
October 5
– The single **'Love Me Do'/'P.S. I Love You'** was released in the UK as PARLOPHONE 45R 4949. Brian Epstein is reputed to have bought 10,000 copies for his NEMS chain of record stores because he knew that was how many they would have to sell to make it into the Top 20.
– Radio Luxembourg played the record.
October 6
– The Beatles arrived at Dawson's Music Shop, Widnes, at 4 pm to autograph copies of 'Love Me Do'.
– *Horticultural Society Dance, Hulme Hall, Port Sunlight, Birkenhead.*
October 7
– *The Cavern* (evening) with The Swinging Blue Genes, The Red River Jazzmen and Ian & The Zodiacs.
October 8
– The Beatles recorded an interview session for EMI's The Friday Spectacular show on Radio Luxembourg. This consisted of new EMI releases played before a live audience of about 100 people at EMI's London headquarters on Manchester Square. The audience danced and

That was the one
– it gave us somewhere to go."

applauded the records and the artists were interviewed. Both sides of their new single were played.

October 9
– The Beatles visited the offices of *Record Mirror* to try and drum up publicity for themselves.

October 10
– *The Cavern* (lunchtime).
– *The Cavern* (evening) with Ken Dallas & The Silhouettes and The Four Jays.

October 11
– *Rialto Ballroom, Liverpool.*

October 12
– *The Cavern* (lunchtime).
– *Tower Ballroom, New Brighton, Wallasey.* A five-and-a-half-hour NEMS presentation. Brian Epstein placed The Beatles second to Little Richard on a bill which also included The Big Three, Billy Kramer & The Coasters, Pete MacLaine & The Dakotas, The Four Jays, Lee Curtis & The All Stars (with Pete Best on drums), The Mersey Beats, Rory Storm & The Hurricanes, Guy Travis & The Midnighters and The Undertakers. The concert was a huge success.
– EMI's *The Friday Spectacular* with The Beatles' record and interview was broadcast by Radio Luxembourg.

October 13
– *The Cavern* (evening) with The Zenith Six Jazz Band, Group One and The Dennisons.

October 15
– *Majestic Ballroom, Birkenhead.*

October 16
– *La Scala Ballroom, Runcorn in Cheshire,* with The Chants.

October 17
– *The Cavern* (lunchtime) with Johnny Sandon & The Remo Four.
– *The Cavern* (evening) with Johnny Sandon & The Remo Four, Group One and The Swinging Blue Genes.
– Between shows at the Cavern the group appeared on Granada Television's *People and Places* singing 'Some Other Guy' and 'Love Me Do', transmitted live from Manchester. This was their first television appearance.

October 19
– *The Cavern* (lunchtime).

Little Richard:
"Man, those Beatles are
fabulous.
If I hadn't seen them
I'd never have
dreamed they were
white. They have
a real authentic
negro sound."

October 20
– *Majestic Ballroom, Hull.*

October 21
– *The Cavern* (evening) with The Fourmost and The Red River Jazzmen.

October 22
– *Queen's Hall, Widnes,* with Lee Curtis & The All Stars, The Mersey Beats and The Chants.

October 25
– The group recorded 'Love Me Do', 'A Taste of Honey' and 'P.S. I Love You' for the BBC Light Programme's *Here We Go* at the BBC studios in Manchester.

October 26
– *The Cavern* (lunchtime).
– *Public Hall, Preston,* with Mike Berry, The Outlaws and The Syd Munson Orchestra. Presented by the Preston Grasshoppers Rugby Football Club.
– The Beatles on *Here We Go* was broadcast by the BBC Light Programme.
– 'Love Me Do' entered the New Musical Express charts at number 49.

Paul: "If you want to know when we knew we'd arrived, it was getting in the charts with 'Love Me Do'.

October 27
– *Hulme Hall, Port Sunlight, Birkenhead.*
– Before playing this gig the group recorded an interview with a boys' club to be broadcast to the patients of Cleaver and Clatterbridge Hospitals, Wirral, on the hospital radio show *Sunday Spin.*

October 28
– *Liverpool Empire* as support for Little Richard. Also on this NEMS Enterprises Pop Package Show were Craig Douglas (backed by The Beatles), Jet Harris (formerly bassist with The Shadows) & The Jetblacks, Kenny Lynch, The Breakaways and Sounds Incorporated. Brian had tried to book Sam Cooke as a "surprise guest" but he was not available.
– The Beatles' appearance on the hospital radio show, *Sunday Spin* was transmitted.

October 29
– The Beatles made a second visit to Granada Television's Manchester studios to record for *People and Places.*

They performed 'Love Me Do' and 'A Taste Of Honey'.

October 30
– The Beatles flew to Hamburg for 14 nights at the Star-Club sharing the bill with Little Richard.

November 1 – 14
– *Star-Club, Grosse Freiheit, Hamburg,* with Little Richard.

November 2
– The Beatles' second appearance on Granada Television's *People and Places* was aired.

November 15
– The group flew to London from Hamburg.

November 16
– The Beatles recorded a second appearance for EMI's *The Friday Spectacular* show on Radio Luxembourg, appearing on stage at EMI's headquarters for a an interview between the playing of both sides of their record while the audience danced and applauded.
– The Beatles visited the Fleet Street offices of *Disc,* and garnered a few column inches in the next issue.

November 17
– *Matrix Hall, Coventry,* with The Mark Allen Group and Lee Teri. Regarded by the group as a disappointing performance.

November 18
– *The Cavern* (evening) with The Mersey Beats and The Pete Hartigan Jazz Band in a "Welcome Home" gig.

November 19
– *The Cavern* (lunchtime).
– *Smethwick Baths, Smethwick in Staffordshire.*
– *Adelphi Ballroom, West Bromwich.* Three gigs in one day.

November 20
– *Floral Hall, Southport.* Two sets.

November 21
– *The Cavern* (lunchtime).
– *The Cavern* (evening) with Johnny Templar & The Hi Cats and Ian & The Zodiacs.

November 22
– *The Cavern* (lunchtime).
– *Majestic Ballroom, Birkenhead.*

November 23
– *St James's Church Hall, Gloucester Terrace, London.* The Beatles auditioned for Ronnie Lane, the

Light Entertainment auditioner for BBC TV. They played a ten-minute set for him, and four days later Brian Epstein received a rejection letter.
– *Tower Ballroom, New Brighton, Wallasey.* "12th Annual Lancashire and Cheshire Art's (sic) Ball", held in aid of a children's charity, with the Llew Hird Jazz Band, Billy Kramer & The Coasters and The Pipes and Drums of 1st Battalion Liverpool Scottish Regiment (Queen's Own Cameron Highlanders).
– The Beatles' second appearance on Radio Luxembourg's *The Friday Spectacular* was aired.

November 24
– *Royal Lido Ballroom, Prestatyn, Wales.*

November 25
– *The Cavern* (evening) with The Zenith Six Jazz Band, The Fourmost and The Swinging Blue Genes.

November 26
– *Abbey Road.* The group recorded 'Tip Of My Tongue', 'Ask Me Why' and 'Please, Please Me'. George Martin was pleased with the results and told the group that 'Please, Please Me' would be a number one hit. The 'Tip Of My Tongue' recording didn't survive.

November 27
– The group recorded 'Love Me Do', 'Twist and Shout' and 'P.S. I Love You' for the BBC Light Programme's *Talent Spot* at the BBC Paris Studio on Lower Regent Street.

November 28
– *The Cavern* (evening) with Johnny Sandon & The Remo Four and Dee Young & The Pontiacs.
– *The 527 Club*, top floor of Lewis's Department Store, Liverpool. "The Young Idea Dance" for the shop staff.

November 29
– *Majestic Ballroom, Birkenhead.*

November 30
– *The Cavern* (lunchtime) with The Dakotas.
– *Town Hall, Earlstown, Newton-le-Willows in Lancashire.* "The Big Beat Show".

December 1
– *The Victory Memorial Hall, Northwich in Cheshire.*
– *Tower Ballroom, New Brighton, Wallasey.*

December 2
– *Embassy Cinema, Peterborough.* The Beatles went down badly in both sets of this Frank Ifield concert. Also on the bill were Susan Cope, The Tommy Wallis & Beryl Xylophone Team, The Lana Sisters and The Tod Taylor Four.

December 3
– The group appeared on *Discs-a-Go-Go*, live from Bristol's TWW (Television Wales and West) studio.

December 4
– The Beatles sang 'Love Me Do', 'P.S. I Love You' and 'Twist And Shout' live on *Tuesday Rendezvous*, a children's show presented by Gary Marshall, transmitted live from Associated-Rediffusion's Kingsway Studio, London.
– The Beatles' appearance on *Talent Spot* was broadcast on the BBC Light Programme.

December 5
– *The Cavern* (lunchtime).
– *The Cavern* (evening) with Gerry & The Pacemakers, Johnny Sandon & The Remo Four and The Statesmen.

December 6
– *Club Django, Queen's Hotel, Southport.*

December 7
– *The Cavern* (lunchtime).
– *Tower Ballroom, New Brighton, Wallasey.*

December 8
– *Oasis Club, Manchester.*

December 9
– *The Cavern* (evening) with The Fourmost, The Swinging Blue Genes and The Zenith Six Jazz Band. George Martin attended this performance to see if a live album could be recorded at The Cavern.

December 10
– *The Cavern* (lunchtime).

December 11
– *La Scala Ballroom, Runcorn in Cheshire,* with Johnny Sandon & The Remo Four and The Mersey Beats.

December 12
– *The Cavern* (lunchtime).
– *The Cavern* (evening) with The Fourmost, The Mersey Beats, Robin Hall and Jimmy MacGregor.

December 13
– *Corn Exchange, Bedford,* with Robin Hall and Jimmy MacGregor.

On the brink of success, aboard a Liverpool tugboat.

December 14
– *Music Hall, Shrewsbury.*

December 15
– *Majestic Ballroom, Birkenhead.* The regular evening show was followed at midnight by The *Mersey Beat* Poll Winners Award Show. The Beatles were voted most popular group for second year running and closed the show at 4 am.

December 16
– *The Cavern* (evening), with The Fourmost, The Swinging Blue Genes, Gerry & The Pacemakers and The Red River Jazzmen.

December 17
– The Beatles played live on Granada Television's *People And Places* show.

December 18 – 31
– *The Star-Club, Grosse Freiheit, Hamburg.* The Beatles' fifth and last residency in Germany, arranged before their chart success and growing concert revenues.

December 27
– 'Love Me Do' got to number 17 in the Record Retailer's Top 50 charts, it's highest position.

December 31
– *Star-Club.* Ted 'Kingsize' Taylor recorded The Beatles' final night at the Star Club. The 30 songs on his tape were later released on an unauthorised album.

19**63**

January 1
– The Beatles' engagement at the Star Club ended and they flew from Hamburg to London.

January 2
– The group flew from London to Scotland but the plane, due to land in Edinburgh (where Neil Aspinall was waiting for them with the van), was diverted to Aberdeen. Their first night's booking at the Longmore Hall in Keith had to be cancelled because snowdrifts had blocked the roads and so, with nothing to do until the following evening, John flew back to Liverpool.

January 3
– John flew from Liverpool to Scotland.
– *Two Red Shoes Ballroom, Elgin, Morayshire.*

January 4
– *Town Hall, Dingwall, Ross and Cromarty.*

January 5
– *Museum Hall, Bridge of Allan, Stirlingshire.*

January 6
– *Beach Ballroom, Aberdeen.*

January 8
– The group appeared live on Scottish TV's *Round-Up*, transmitted locally from The Theatre Royal, Glasgow, and presented by Paul Young and Morag Hood. The band mimed 'Please Please Me'.

January 10
– *Grafton Rooms, Liverpool,* where they headed a bill of five acts.

January 11
– *The Cavern* (lunchtime) with Kingsize Taylor & The Dominoes.
– *Plaza Ballroom, Old Hill, Staffordshire.*
– The single **'Please Please Me'/'Ask Me Why'** was released in the UK as PARLOPHONE 45-R 4983.
– The Beatles appeared on ABC TV's *Thank Your Lucky Stars*, performing 'Please Please Me'.

January 12
– *Invicta Ballroom, Chatham in Kent.*

January 13
– Alpha TV Studios, Birmingham, where the group recorded an appearance on ABC TV's *Thank Your Lucky Stars*. They closed the first half of the show miming to 'Please Please Me'.

January 14
– *Wolverham Welfare Association Dance, Civic Hall, Wirral.*

January 16
– Granada TV Centre, Manchester. Rehearsal for a live appearance on the *People And Places* programme to be broadcast later in the day.
– Playhouse Theatre, Manchester, to rehearse for a session on the BBC Radio programme *Here We Go*.
– Granada TV Centre, for the *People And Places* transmission, for which they mimed to 'Please Please Me' and 'Ask Me Why'.
– Playhouse Theatre, Manchester to record their spot on *Here We Go*, for which they sang 'Chains', 'Please Please Me', 'Three Cool Cats' and 'Ask Me Why'. 'Three Cool Cats' was edited out when the programme was broadcast .

January 17
– *The Cavern.*
– *Majestic Ballroom, Birkenhead.*
– 'Please Please Me' entered the charts.

January 18
– *Floral Ballroom, Morecombe, Lancashire.*
– Roadie Neil Aspinall went down with flu so Les Hurst, Gerry & the Pacemakers' roadie, stood in for him.

January 19
– *Town Hall Ballroom,* Whitchurch in Shropshire. Once again, Les Hurst stood in for Neil Aspinall.
– *Thank Your Lucky Stars* was broadcast.

January 20
– *The Cavern* with Pete Hartigan's Jazzmen, The Dennisons, The Merseybeats and The Swinging Blue Genes. Neil, sweating and feverish, hauled their gear. He explained to Brian Epstein that he just could not do the drive to London the next day. Fortunately, he bumped into Mal Evans on the stairs of the Cavern where he

Left: The Beatles' characteristic logo – with a dropped 't' – arrived in early 1963.

Mal Evans watches over The Beatles backstage.

worked and asked, **"Mal, can you run the boys to London and back for me?"**

Mal, a GPO telephone engineer who had taken to dropping in to The Cavern on his way back to the Post Office after lunch, agreed. After a while he extended his visits to include the evenings and got to know George Harrison. They left the club together one day and Mal invited him back to listen to some records. George suggested that Mal should work on the door of The Cavern; that way he would hear the music free and get

paid in his spare time. Mal, an imposing 6 feet 2 inches, was gentle and polite, but had the outward appearance of a tough bouncer.

January 21
– *EMI House, London,* to record EMI's plug show *Friday Spectacular* for Radio Luxembourg hosted by Shaw Taylor and Muriel Young with an audience of 100 teenagers. They were interviewed, and 'Please Please Me' and 'Ask Me Why' were played.
– The Beatles were signed in the US by Vee Jay Records.

January 22
– *BBC Paris Studio, London,* where they were interviewed live on the radio programme *Pop Inn* to promote their new single 'Please Please Me'.
– *Playhouse Theatre, London,* to rehearse and record their first appearance on the BBC pop radio programme *Saturday Club,* presented by Brian Matthew. They recorded 'Some Other Guy', 'Love Me Do', 'Please Please Me', 'Keep Your Hands Off My Baby' and 'Beautiful Dreamer'.
– *BBC Paris Studio, London,* to record a BBC Light Programme show *The Talent Spot,* presented by Gary Marshal. They sang 'Please Please Me', 'Ask Me Why' and 'Some Other Guy' before a studio audience.

January 23
– *The Cavern* (evening), with The Fourmost, Ken Dallas & The Silhouettes and Freddie Starr & The Midnighters.

January 24
– The Beatles signed copies of 'Please Please Me' at NEMS record shop in Liverpool and gave a short acoustic performance to the assembled fans.
– *Assembly Hall, Mold, Wales.*

January 25
– *Co-operative Hall, Darwen.* A local Baptist Church youth club event with supporting acts The Electones, The Mike Taylor Combo and The Mustangs with Ricky Day.
– The Beatles session on BBC Radio's *Here We Go* was broadcast, presented by Ray Peters.
– Radio Luxembourg's *Friday Spectacular* broadcast.

January 26
– *El Rio Club, Macclesfield in Cheshire,* with Wayne Fontana & The Jets.
– *King's Hall, Stoke-on-Trent in Staffordshire.* Paul and John began work on 'Misery', intended for Helen Shapiro, backstage at this gig.
– The Beatles' first appearance on the BBC's *Saturday Club* was broadcast.

January 27
– *Three Coins Club, Manchester.*

January 28
– *Majestic Ballroom, Newcastle upon Tyne.*

Mal Evans

On January 23 The Beatles drove back to Liverpool from London in freezing temperatures. The windscreen of the van shattered and their stand-in roadie Mal Evans drove with no glass. The group were so cold they lay huddled on top of each other in the back.

John Lennon told Neil Aspinall what had happened: "You should have seen Mal. He had this paper bag over his head with just a big split in it for eyes. We were all in the back of the van doing the same thing. It was freezing. The windscreen shattered. Mal had to knock out the rest of the broken glass and just drive on. It was perishing. Mal looked like a bank robber."

The Beatles had a gig the next lunchtime and an out of town gig that evening. Mal showed up at Neil's with the van in perfect condition, windscreen replaced. Neil: "We never knew how he'd managed to get it fixed again so quickly and, even if we didn't say so, it was something we remembered. Ten out of ten to Mal for not just bringing back the van and leaving it for someone else to get a new windscreen put in." Mal's efficiency was to lead him to a career with The Beatles which lasted out the decade.

January 29
– BBC's *Talent Spot* broadcast.
January 30
– *The Cavern* (evening) with Johnny Sandon & The Remo Four and The Dakotas.
January 31
– *The Cavern* (lunchtime).
– *Majestic Ballroom, Birkenhead.* Two sets.
February 1
– *Assembly Rooms, Tamworth in Staffordshire.*
– *Maney Hall, Sutton Coldfield in Warwickshire.*
February 2
– *Gaumont Cinema, Bradford.* The first gig on their nationwide tour with Helen Shapiro, where they were effectively bottom of the bill. The programme opened with The Red Price Band, followed by The Honeys, compere Dave Allen, The Beatles, Dave Allen and Danny Williams who closed the first half. The Red Price Band again opened the second set, followed by The Kestrels and Kenny Lynch, and then David Allen introduced 16-year-old Helen Shapiro. The Beatles wore burgundy suits with

velvet collars, designed by Paul, and their hair brushed forward "French style".
– Their set was 'Chains', 'Keep Your Hands Off My Baby', 'A Taste of Honey', and 'Please Please Me'.
– John and Paul finished 'Misery' on the coach but Helen's management didn't even bother to show it to her. Kenny Lynch, however, was interested and has the distinction of being the first outsider to record a Lennon and McCartney song. It was also on the coach that John and Paul came up with the idea of running up to the microphone together and shaking their heads and singing, 'Whooooooo!', even though 'She Loves You' was not yet out.
– 'Please Please Me' entered the Music Week charts at number 16.
February 3
– *The Cavern* (evening), an eight-hour "Blues Marathon" with The Fourmost, The Dominoes, The Hollies, Earl Preston & The TT's, The Merseybeats, The Swinging Blue Genes and The Roadrunners.
February 4
– *The Cavern* (last lunchtime session).

John: "We don't really bother about what we **do on the stage.** We practise what we call **'Grinning at nothings'.** One-two-three, and we **all grin at nothing!** When we go out with Helen Shapiro I don't know how we'll manage. I thought I might **lie on the floor** like **Al Jolson."**

*Opposite: Brian Epstein at The Cavern.
Below Right: John favoured Rickenbacker guitars in the studio as well as on tour.*

February 5
– *Gaumont Cinema, Doncaster* (Helen Shapiro tour).
February 6
– *Granada Cinema, Bedford* (Helen Shapiro tour)
February 7
– *Regal Cinema, Wakefield* (Helen Shapiro tour).
February 8
– *ABC Cinema, Carlisle* (now in Cumbria) (Helen Shapiro tour).
February 9
– *Empire Theatre, Sunderland* (Helen Shapiro tour).
February 11
– *Abbey Road.* All ten new tracks needed to make the Please Please Me album were recorded in one ten-hour session (the other four tracks were already out as sides A and B of their two singles). The tracks were chosen by George Martin from their The Cavern set in an attempt to re-create the atmosphere of the group's live performance.
February 12
– *Azena Ballroom, Sheffield.*
– *Astoria Ballroom, Oldham.*
February 13
– *Majestic Ballroom, Hull.*
February 14
– *Locarno Ballroom, Liverpool.* St Valentine's Day dance.
February 15
– *Ritz Ballroom, King's Heath, Birmingham.*
February 16
– *Carfax Assembly Rooms, Oxford.*
February 17
– Teddington Studio Centre, Middlesex, to record an appearance on ABC TV's *Thank Your Lucky Stars* where they sang 'Please Please Me'.
February 18
– *Queen's Hall, Widnes.* Two sets, promoted by Brian Epstein.
February 19
– *Cavern Club* (evening) with Lee Curtis & The All Stars, The Pathfinders and Freddie Starr & The Midnighters. The queue began to form two days before the doors opened. Bob Wooler announced from the stage that The Beatles' 'Please Please Me' now occupied the number one position in the *NME* charts. It was also, apparently,

Paul: "We'd been playing the songs for months **and months and months** before getting a record out. So we came into the studio at **ten in the morning,** started it, did one number, had a **cup of tea,** relaxed, did the next one, a couple of overdubs... we just worked through them, like the stage act. And by about **ten o'clock** that night, we'd done **ten songs** and we just reeled out of the studios, John **clutching** his throat tablets!"

the last time that any of The Beatles saw Pete Best. Afterwards they drove through the night to London.
February 20
– The group appeared live on the BBC Light Programme's *Parade of the Pops*, presented by Denny Piercy, singing 'Love Me Do' and 'Please Please Me'. This was their first live BBC transmission.
– *St James Street Swimming Baths, Doncaster.*
February 21
– *Majestic Ballroom, Birkenhead.* Two sets.
February 22
– *Oasis Club, Manchester.*
February 23
– *Granada Cinema, Mansfield in Nottinghamshire* (Helen Shapiro tour).
– 'Please Please Me' reached number one in the *Disc* singles charts .
– ABC Television transmitted The Beatles on *Thank Your Lucky Stars*.
February 24
– *Coventry Theatre, Coventry* (Helen Shapiro tour).

February 25
– *Casino Ballroom, Leigh in Lancashire,* for Brian Epstein's NEMS Enterprises "Showdance".
– The single **'Please, Please Me'/'Ask Me Why'** was released in US as VEE JAY VJ 498.
February 26
– *Gaumont Cinema, Taunton in Somerset,* with Danny Williams heading the bill in place of Helen Shapiro who had a cold and Billie Davis standing in to complete the line-up (Helen Shapiro tour).
February 27
– *Rialto Theatre, York* (Helen Shapiro tour, still without Helen Shapiro).
February 28
Granada Cinema, Shrewsbury (with Helen Shapiro back on stage).
– In the tour coach on the way to this gig, John and Paul wrote 'From Me To You', which was to be their next single.
March 1
– *Odeon Cinema, Southport* (Helen Shapiro tour).
March 2
– *City Hall, Sheffield* (Helen Shapiro tour).
– Didsbury Studio Centre: After their second set, The Beatles drove to Manchester to be interviewed live with Brian Epstein by David Hamilton for ABC TV's evening talk show, *ABC At Large.* A short clip of them playing 'Please Please Me' was shown.
March 3
– *Gaumont Cinema, Hanley in Staffordshire.* The last show on the Helen Shapiro tour. The Beatles now closed the first half of the show.
March 4
– *Plaza Ballroom, St Helens.*
March 5
– *Abbey Road.* The group recorded 'From Me To You'.
March 6
– *Playhouse Theatre, Manchester.*

Northern Songs

Northern Songs Limited was set up to control John and Paul's songwriting copyrights. John and Paul naively thought that they would own 100 per cent	of the company, but it turned out that Dick James and his accountant Charles Silver took 51 per cent, John and Paul had 20 per cent each and Brian Epstein owned	10 per cent. Dick James and Charles Silver always had the controlling vote. They both became multi-millionaires on the strength of a negligible investment.

The Beatles recorded another session for the BBC Light Programme's *Here We Go*, singing 'Misery', 'Do You Want To Know A Secret' and 'Please Please Me'.

March 7
– *Elizabethan Ballroom, Nottingham,* with Gerry & The Pacemakers, The Big Three and Billy J. Kramer with The Dakotas. Everyone on the bill was managed by Brian Epstein, who promoted the event. This was the first of six "Mersey Beat Showcase" events promoted by NEMS, where the artists accompanied by 80 paying fans were taken by coach to

Another dressing room before another show before another audience that can't hear a word they sing or a note they play.

venues across the country. Bob Wooler, DJ from The Cavern, was compere.
March 8
– *The Royal Hall, Harrogate.*
March 9
– *Granada Cinema, East Ham, London.* Their second package tour, this time supporting Tommy Roe and Chris Montez. The Beatles wiped the stage with them on the first night and took over top billing. Their set for this tour was 'Love Me Do', 'Misery', 'A Taste Of Honey', 'Do You Want To Know A Secret', 'Please Please Me' and 'I Saw Her Standing There'.
March 10
– *Hippodrome Theatre, Birmingham* (Roe/Montez tour).
March 11
– EMI House to record their last interview for *Friday Spectacular* to be broadcast on Radio Luxembourg.
March 12
– *Granada Cinema, Bedford* (Roe/Montez tour). John came down with a cold and was unable to play this concert. George and Paul took over the vocals.
– The Beatles appeared on BBC Light Programme's *Here We Go*, presented by Ray Peters.
March 13
– *Abbey Road.* An over-dub session to put harmonica on to 'Thank You Girl'.
– *Rialto Theatre, York* (Roe/Montez tour). John was still in bed with a heavy cold.
March 14
– *Gaumont Cinema, Wolverhampton* (Roe/Montez tour, without John).
March 15
– *Colston Hall, Bristol,* with John back on stage to play both sets (Roe/Montez tour).
March 16
– *Broadcasting House, London.* The Beatles performed live on the BBC Light Programme's *Saturday Club* presented by Brian Matthew. They Sang 'I Saw Her Standing There', 'Misery', 'Too Much Monkey Business', 'I'm Talking About You', 'Please Please Me' and 'The Hippy, Hippy Shake'.
– *City Hall, Sheffield* (Roe/ Montez tour).

March 17
– *Embassy Cinema, Peterborough* (Roe/Montez tour).
March 18
– *Regal Cinema, Gloucester* (Roe/Montez tour).
March 19
– *Regal Cinema, Cambridge* (Roe/Montez tour)
March 20
– *ABC Cinema, Romford* (Roe/Montez tour).
March 21
– BBC Piccadilly Studios, London, to record 'Misery', 'Do You Want To Know A Secret' and 'Please Please Me' for BBC Light Programme's *On The Scene.*
– *ABC Cinema, West Croydon* (Roe/Montez tour).
March 22
– *Gaumont Cinema, Doncaster* (Roe/Montez tour).
– The album PLEASE PLEASE ME was released in the UK as Parlophone PMC 1202 (mono) and PCS 3042 (stereo).

SIDE A: **'I Saw Her Standing There', 'Misery', 'Anna (Go To Him)', 'Chains',**

'Boys', 'Ask Me Why', Please
Please Me';
SIDE B: 'Love Me Do', 'P.S. I Love You',
'Baby It's You', 'Do You Want To
Know A Secret', 'A Taste Of Honey',
'There's A Place', 'Twist And Shout'.
March 23
– City Hall, Newcastle upon Tyne
(Roe/Montez tour).
March 24
– Empire Theatre, Liverpool
(Roe/Montez tour).
March 25
– The Beatles spent the day being

*The Beatles in action at the
launch party for their
Please Please Me album at
the offices of EMI, April 5.*

photographed and filmed by
Dezo Hoffmann.
March 26
– Granada Cinema, Mansfield
(Roe/Montez tour).
March 27
– ABC Cinema, Northampton
(Roe/Montez tour).
March 28
– ABC Cinema, Exeter (Roe/
Montez tour).
– The Beatles' recording for the BBC
Light Programme's *On The Scene*
was transmitted.

March 29
Odeon Cinema, Lewisham, London
(Roe/Montez tour).
March 30
– Guildhall, Portsmouth
(Roe/Montez tour).
March 31
– De Montfort Hall, Leicester.
The last night of the Roe/Montez tour.
April 1
– BBC Piccadilly Studios, London. The
group recorded two programmes for
the BBC Light Programme's *Side By
Side*, presented by John Dunn, in which

Julian Lennon

It was three days before John went to visit Cynthia and his new son. Cynthia: "Years later, John said something in an interview which was to hurt me very much. He told *Playboy* magazine: 'Julian was born out of a bottle of whisky on a Saturday night.' John was with Yoko Ono then but I was still offended and so was Julian. It was so untrue. I could tell that John said it to impress the interviewer but it still hurt. For a start we didn't even drink whisky in those days, but the worst part was the implied denial of our love. We were very much in love and very happy - Julian truly was a love child."

the resident act, The Karl Denver Trio, invited a guest group each week. For the first show, The Beatles sang 'Side By Side' with The Karl Denver Trio, followed by 'I Saw Her Standing There', 'Do You Want To Know A Secret', 'Baby It's You', 'Please Please Me', 'From Me To You' and 'Misery'. For the second show they once more sang 'Side By Side' with The Karl Denver Trio followed by 'From Me To You', 'Long Tall Sally', 'A Taste Of Honey', 'Chains', 'Thank You Girl' and 'Boys'.

April 3
– *Playhouse Theatre, London,* to record a session for BBC Radio's *Easy Beat,* presented by Brian Matthew, before a teenage studio audience. The Beatles performed 'Please Please Me', 'Misery' and 'From Me To You'.

April 4
– *BBC Paris Studio, London,* to record a third *Side By Side* broadcast. The Beatles performed 'Too Much Monkey Business', 'Love Me Do', 'Boys', 'I'll Be On My Way' and 'From Me To You'. The BBC already had two tapes of The Beatles playing the theme tune with The Karl Denver Trio.
– *Roxburgh Hall, Stowe School, Bucks.* After the recording session The Beatles went to play an afternoon session at the boys' public school in Stowe, where the all-male audience sat in neat rows and did not scream.

April 5
– EMI House, London. During an award ceremony in which they were presented with their first silver disc for the single 'Please Please Me', the group gave a private performance for executives of EMI.
– *Swimming Baths, Leyton, London.*

April 6
– *Pavilion Gardens Ballroom,* Buxton, Derbyshire.

April 7
– *Savoy Ballroom, Portsmouth.*
– The Beatles' appearance on *Easy Beat* was aired by the BBC.

April 8
– John and Cynthia's son, John Charles Julian Lennon, was born at 6 am.

April 9
– *BBC Paris Studio, London,* to do a live interview for the BBC Light Programme lunchtime show *Pop Inn,* during which their forthcoming single 'From Me To You' was played.
– Associated-Rediffusion's Wembley Studios for a live appearance on the children's programme *Tuesday Rendezvous.* They mimed 'From Me To You' and 'Please Please Me'.
– *The Ballroom, Gaumont State Cinema, Kilburn, London.*

April 10
– *Majestic Ballroom, Birkenhead.*

April 11
– *Co-operative Hall, Middleton in Lancashire.*
– The single **'From Me To You'/'Thank You Girl'** was released in the UK as Parlophone R 5015.

April 12
– *Cavern Club,* for a Good Friday, eight-hour "R&B Marathon", with The Fourmost, The Dennisons, The Nomads, The Panthers, Faron's Flamingoes, The Flintstones, The Roadrunners and Group One.

April 13
– *Studio E, Lime Grove Studios, London,* for extensive rehearsals and the recording of an appearance on BBC Television's *The 625 Show.* They performed: 'From Me To You', 'Thank You Girl' and were joined by the rest of the cast to close the show with 'Please Please Me'.
– At a party held that evening by Shadows' guitarist Bruce Welch

at his house in North Harrow, The Beatles met Cliff Richard for the first time.

April 14
– *ABC Television's Teddington Studio Centre, Teddington.* The Beatles mimed to 'From Me To You' for an edition of *Thank Your Lucky Stars.*
– That evening, The Beatles saw The Rolling Stones play at the Crawdaddy Club in the Station Hotel, Richmond. The Beatles appeared at the club identically dressed in long suede leather jackets with matching hats acquired in Hamburg. It was an intentionally intimidating image, later described by Jagger as a "four headed monster".

April 15
– *Riverside Dancing Club, Bridge Hotel, Tenbury Wells in Worcestershire.*

– The Beatles' interview on *Friday Spectacular* was broadcast on Radio Luxembourg.

April 16
– *Granada TV Centre, Manchester.* The Beatles mimed live to 'From Me To You' on *Scene At 6.30.*
– BBC screened *The 625 Show* at the same time.

April 17
– *Majestic Ballroom, Luton.*

April 18
– *Royal Albert Hall, London,* with Del Shannon, The Springfields, Lance Percival, Rolf Harris, The Vernon Girls, Kenny Lynch, Shane Fenton & The Fentones and George Melly. A two-part concert, the second half of which was broadcast live by BBC radio as *Swinging Sound '63.* In the first half The Beatles played 'Please Please Me' and 'Misery' and in the second 'Twist And Shout' and 'From Me To You'. The show closed

Jane Asher

During rehearsals at the Royal Albert Hall on April 18 The Beatles met 17-year-old Jane Asher in the Green Room. She was writing a celebrity piece about them for *Radio Times* magazine and was posed as a screaming fan by the BBC photographer. After the show, Jane returned with them to the Royal Court Hotel where they were staying and afterwards they all went to *NME* journalist Chris Hutchins' apartment on the King's Road. Jane and Paul started a relationship which would continue until 1968.

with a fade-out from the entire cast performing Kurt Weill's 'Mack The Knife'.
– The Rolling Stones had received front-row tickets from The Beatles and back-stage passes. After the gig, Brian Jones and The Stones' then-manager Giorgio Gomelsky helped Mal Evans and Neil Aspinall load the van with The Beatles' stage gear. Some fans mistook Brian for one of The Beatles and mobbed him for autographs. He was overwhelmed, and Gomelsky remembered Brian walking away afterwards in a daze, down the big steps at the rear of the building, saying:

April 19
– *King's Hall, Stoke-on-Trent.*
The second of Brian Epstein's "Mersey Beat Showcase" events.

April 20
– *Ballroom, Mersey View Pleasure Grounds, Frodsham in Cheshire.*

April 21
– *Empire Pool, Wembley,* for the *NME*'s '1962-63 Annual Poll-Winners' All Star Concert', starring Cliff Richard and The Shadows. As the poll had been conducted in 1962, The Beatles hadn't actually won anything but were included because of their two recent number one singles. They played 'Please Please Me', 'From Me To You', 'Twist And Shout' and 'Long Tall Sally' to an audience of 10,000 people.
– *Pigalle Club, Piccadilly, London.* with Dave Antony and the Druids.
– The BBC Light Programme broadcast the first of The Beatles' *Side By Side* programmes.

April 23
– *Floral Hall, Southport.*

April 24
– *Majestic Ballroom, Finsbury Park, London.* Another of Brian Epstein's "Mersey Beat Showcase" promotions, with Gerry & The Pacemakers, Billy J. Kramer and The Big Three, to an audience of 2,000 people.

April 25
– *Ballroom, Fairfield Hall, Croydon.* Another "Mersey Beat Showcase" evening, with Gerry & The Pacemakers, Billy J. Kramer and The Big Three.

"That's
what I want, Giorgio.
That's what I
want!"

April 26
– *Music Hall, Shrewsbury.*

April 27
– *The Victory Memorial Hall, Northwich in Cheshire.*

April 28
– George, Paul and Ringo flew to Santa Cruz, Tenerife for a 12 day holiday.
– At Brian's expense, John and Brian Epstein flew to Torremolinos, Spain for a vacation together, leaving Cynthia and her new born baby in Liverpool.

May 11
– *Imperial Ballroom, Nelson.*
A record 2,000 attendance.

May 12
– *Alpha TV Studios, Birmingham,* for another recorded *Thank Your Lucky Stars* appearance. They mimed 'From Me To You' and 'I Saw Her Standing There'.
– The BBC Light Programme broadcast the second of The Beatles' *Side By Side* programmes.

May 14
– *Rink Ballroom, Sunderland.*

May 15
– *Royal Theatre, Chester.*

May 16
– *Television Theatre, London,* for their second appearance on national BBC TV. They shared the bill with a glove puppet, Lenny the Lion, The Raindrops and Patsy Ann Noble on children's programme *Pops and Lenny* which went out live before an invited audience. With the show's namesake, the puppet, The Beatles performed 'From Me To You', a short version of 'Please Please Me' and joined Lenny The Lion and the rest of the cast for a version of 'After You've Gone'.

May 17
– *Grosvenor Rooms, Norwich.*

John's holiday with Brian

John: "I was on holiday with Brian Epstein in Spain, where the rumours went around that he and I were having a love affair. Well, it was almost a love affair, but not quite. It was never consummated. But it was a pretty intense relationship. It was my first experience with a homosexual that I was conscious was homosexual... We used to sit in a cafe in Torremolinos looking at all the boys and I'd say, 'Do you like that one? Do you like this one?' I was rather enjoying the experience, thinking like a writer all the time: I am experiencing this." While John was there, he wrote 'Bad To Me' for Billy J. Kramer, one of Brian's artists.

May 18
– *Adelphi Cinema, Slough,* on tour with Gerry & The Pacemakers, Tony Marsh, Erkey Grant, Ian Crawford, The Terry Young Six, Daiv Macbeth, Louise Cordet and, initially heading the bill but rapidly demoted to second spot, Roy Orbison. The Beatles' set for this tour was 'Some Other Guy', 'Do You Want To Know A Secret', 'Love Me Do', 'From Me To You', 'Please Please Me', 'I Saw Her Standing There' and 'Twist & Shout'.
– *Thank Your Lucky Stars* was broadcast by ABC TV.
May 19
– *Gaumont Cinema, Hanley in Staffordshire* (Roy Orbison tour).
May 20
– *Gaumont Cinema, Southampton* (Roy Orbison tour).
May 21
– *Playhouse Theatre, London,* to record the BBC Light Programme's *Saturday Club.* They were interviewed by presenter Brian Matthew and performed 'I Saw Her Standing There', 'Do You Want To Know A Secret', 'Boys', 'Long Tall Sally', 'From Me To You' and 'Money (That's What I Want)'.
– They also recorded a session for a new radio programme *Steppin' Out,* for which they did 'Please Please Me', 'I Saw Her Standing There', 'Roll Over Beethoven', 'Thank You Girl' and 'From Me To You' before a live audience.
May 22
– *Gaumont Cinema, Ipswich* (Roy Orbison tour).
May 23
– *Odeon Cinema, Nottingham* (Roy Orbison tour).
May 24
– *Studio Two, Aeolian Hall, London,* to record the first programme in their own BBC Light Programme series: *Pop Go The Beatles.* The programme began and closed with a rocked-up version of 'Pop Goes The Weasel' recorded by The Beatles with the aid of their guests for this programme, The Lorne Gibson Trio. The Beatles performed 'From Me To You', 'Everybody's Trying To Be My Baby', 'Do You Want To Know A Secret', 'You Really Got A Hold On Me', 'Misery'

*Above: On stage at the Majestic Ballroom, Birkenhead. Before long shows where the audience could reach and out and touch The Beatles would be a thing of the past.
Below: John and Ringo with Roy Orbison.*

and 'The Hippy Hippy Shake' as well as bantering with presenter Lee Peters.
– *Granada Cinema, Walthamstow, London* (Roy Orbison tour).
– *May 25 City Hall, Sheffield* (Roy Orbison tour).
– The Beatles appear on the BBC Light Programme's *Saturday Club.*
May 26
– *Empire Theatre, Liverpool* (Roy Orbison tour).
May 27
– *Capitol Cinema, Cardiff,* (Roy Orbison tour).
– The single **'From Me To You'/'Thank You Girl'** released in US as VEE JAY VJ 522.
May 28
– *Gaumont Cinema, Worcester* (Roy Orbison tour).
May 29
– *Rialto Theatre, York* (Roy Orbison tour).
May 30
– *Odeon Cinema, Manchester* (Roy Orbison tour).
May 31
– *Odeon Cinema, Southend-on-Sea* (Roy Orbison tour).
June 1
– *BBC Paris Studio, London.*

The Beatles recorded the second and third programmes in their *Pop Go The Beatles* series. On the second programme they sang 'Too Much Monkey Business', 'I Got To Find My Baby', 'Youngblood', 'Baby It's You', 'Till There Was You' and 'Love Me Do'. Their guests were The Countrymen. For the third programme they performed 'A Shot Of Rhythm And Blues', 'Memphis, Tennessee', 'A Taste Of Honey' and 'Sure To Fall (In Love With You)' with Carter-Lewis & The Southerners as their guests.
– *Granada Cinema, Tooting, London* (Roy Orbison tour).
June 2
– *Hippodrome Theatre, Brighton* (Roy Orbison tour).
June 3
– *Granada Cinema, Woolwich, London* (Roy Orbison tour).
– The Beatles on BBC Radio's *Steppin' Out* was broadcast.
June 4
– *Town Hall, Birmingham* (Roy Orbison tour).
– The first of the *Pop Go The Beatles* programmes was broadcast by the BBC Light programme.
June 5
– *Odeon Cinema, Leeds* (Roy

"Really **sorry** Bob. **Terribly** worried to realise **what** I had done. What **more** can I **say?**"

Orbison tour). Girls from local high schools were noticeably 'absent' during the few days preceding this event as they queued in shifts, day and night, in order to be sure of tickets.

June 7
– *Odeon Cinema, Glasgow* (Roy Orbison tour).

June 8
– *City Hall, Newcastle upon Tyne* (Roy Orbison tour).

June 9
– *King George's Hall, Blackburn.* The last concert of the Roy Orbison tour.

June 10
– *The Pavilion, Bath,* with The Colin Anthony Combo and Chet & The Triumphs.

June 11
– The BBC Light Programme broadcast the second programme in the series *Pop Go The Beatles.*

June 12
– *Grafton Rooms, Liverpool.* A charity event in aid of the NSPCC at which The Beatles played for free.

June 13
– *Palace Theatre Club, Stockport.*
– *Southern Sporting Club, Manchester.*

June 14
– *Tower Ballroom, Wallasey.* Another of Brian Epstein's "Mersey Beat Showcase" promotions.

June 15
– *City Hall, Salisbury.*

June 16
– *Odeon Cinema, Romford,* with Billy J. Kramer & The Dakotas, The Vikings with Michael London, Gerry & The Pacemakers, and compere Vic Sutcliffe. The last of the "Mersey Beat Showcase" concerts.

June 17
– *BBC Maida Vale Studios, London,* to record the fourth of the *Pop Go The Beatles* programmes, this time with The Bachelors as "guests". The Beatles recorded 'I Saw Her Standing There', 'Anna (Go To Him)', 'Boys', 'Chains', 'P.S. I Love You' and 'Twist And Shout'.

Dezo Hoffmann photographed the session and did a separate photo session afterwards in Delaware Road.

The group drove to Liverpool.

June 18
– Paul's 21st birthday party was held in a marquee in the back garden of his Aunt Jin's house at 147 Dinas Lane, Huyton.
– The BBC Light Programme broadcast the third edition of *Pop Go The Beatles.*

June 19
– *Playhouse Theatre, London,* to record their second appearance on BBC Radio's *Easy Beat* before a live, screaming audience. They performed 'Some Other Guy', 'A Taste Of Honey,' 'Thank You Girl' and 'From Me To You'.

June 20
– Acting on orders from Brian Epstein, John sent Bob Wooler a telegram reading:
– The Beatles Limited was formed.

June 21
– *Odeon Cinema, Guildford.*

June 22
– *Television Theatre, London:* John taped a BBC TV *Juke Box Jury,* hosted by David Jacobs, with fellow jurors Katie Boyle, Bruce Prochnik and Caroline Maudling. John voted every one of the records presented as a "miss".
– Afterwards he was driven to the Battersea Heliport where he flew by

Opposite: Humble despite the avalanche of accolades that came their way, The Beatles bowed low as a matter of course at the end of each song.
Above: On stage at Birkenhead.

specially chartered helicopter to join the others in Wales, landing at the Penypound Football Ground, in Abergavenny.
– *Ballroom, Town Hall, Abergavenny.* A civic reception in which the group met the Mayor and Mayoress, Councillor and Mrs J.F. Thurston, was held when Paul, George and Ringo arrived in Abergavenny with Neil Aspinell in the group's van.

After the show, the group signed autographs at three pence each, proceeds going to the local committee of the Freedom From Hunger Campaign.

June 23
– *Alpha TV Studios, Birmingham,* to tape a session for *Summer Spin* – the summer name for *Thank Your Lucky Stars.* The whole show was a celebration of the Mersey scene. The programme was presented by Pete Murray. The group mimed 'From Me To You' and 'I Saw Her Standing There'.
– The Beatles' appearance on *Easy Beat* was transmitted.

June 24
– *Playhouse Theatre, London,* for another recording session for BBC Radio's *Saturday Club* presented by Brian Matthew. The Beatles sang 'I Got To Find My Baby', 'Memphis, Tennessee', 'Money (That's What I Want)', 'Till There Was You', 'From Me To You' and 'Roll Over Beethoven'.

The Bob Wooler Incident

At Paul's 1st birthday party. The Beatles' old friend Bob Wooler teased John about his trip to Spain with Brian Epstein but John was drunk and in a belligerent mood. He leapt on Bob Wooler and beat him up. John said, "He called me a queer so I battered his bloody ribs in." Next John attacked a woman who was standing nearby. When Billy J. Kramer intervened, Lennon yelled, "You're nothing Kramer, and we're the top." Brian Epstein drove Bob Wooler to the hospital to get his eye treated and to check for broken ribs.

John: "The Beatles' first national coverage was me beating up Bob Wooler at Paul's 21st party because he intimated I was homosexual. I must have had a fear that maybe I was homosexual to attack him like that and it's very complicated reasoning. But I was very drunk and I hit him and I could have really killed somebody then. And that scared me... That was in the *Daily Mirror,* it was the back page..."

June 25
– *Astoria Ballroom, Middlesbrough.*
– The BBC Light Programme broadcast the fourth *Pop Go The Beatles* programme.

June 26
– *Majestic Ballroom, Newcastle upon Tyne.* Before this show Paul and John wrote their next single, 'She Loves You', in their hotel room.

June 27
– Paul attended Billy J. Kramer's recording session to watch him cut John's 'Bad To Me' and 'I Call Your Name'.

June 28
– *Queen's Hall, Leeds,* with Acker Bilk and his Paramount Jazz Band to an audience of 3,200.

June 29
– The Beatles appeared on the BBC Light Programme's *Saturday Club.*
– The Beatles appearance on ABC TV's *Summer Spin* Mersey Beat special was aired. John's appearance on BBC TV's *Juke Box Jury* was broadcast, clashing with ABC TV's *Summer Spin.*

June 30
– *ABC Cinema, Great Yarmouth.* The first of a ten-week series of seaside concerts. They played: 'Some Other Guy', 'Thank You Girl', 'Do You Want To Know A Secret', 'Misery', 'A Taste Of Honey', 'I Saw Her Standing There', 'Love Me Do', 'From Me To You', 'Baby It's You', 'Please Please Me' and 'Twist And Shout'.

July 1
– *Abbey Road.* The Beatles recorded their next single 'She Loves You'/'I'll Get You'.

July 2
– *Maida Vale Studios, London,* to record the first of 11 new *Pop Go The Beatles* programmes, this time presented by Rodney Burke. The Beatles performed 'That's All Right (Mama)', 'Carol', 'Soldier Of Love (Lay Down Your Arms)', 'Lend Me Your Comb , 'Clarabella' and 'There's A Place'. Their first guest act was Duffy Power with The Graham Bond Quartet.

July 3
– *Playhouse Theatre* to rehearse and record a session for BBC Light Programme's *The Beat Show* with the NDO (Northern Dance Orchestra) and The Trad Lads. The show's host was Gay Byrne and The Beatles performed

Above: George and his father Harry.

'From Me To You', 'A Taste Of Honey' and 'Twist And Shout'.

July 4
– The BBC Light Programme broadcast *The Beat Show.*
– The Beatles, accompanied by Jane Asher's brother Peter, saw The Rolling Stones play the Scene Club, Soho.

July 5
– *Plaza Ballroom, Old Hill, Dudley,* with Denny & The Diplomats.

July 6
– *Northwich Carnival, Verdin Park.* That afternoon The Beatles attended the carnival and Paul crowned the Carnival Queen.
– *The Victory Memorial Hall, Northwich.*

July 7
– *ABC Theatre, Blackpool.*

July 8
– *Winter Gardens, Margate.* The Beatles' set: 'Roll Over Beethoven', 'Thank You Girl', 'Chains', 'Please Please Me', 'A Taste Of Honey', 'I Saw Her Standing There', 'Baby It's You', 'From Me To You' and 'Twist And Shout'.

July 9
– *Winter Gardens, Margate.*

July 10
– *Aeolian Hall, London,* to record two more *Pop Go The Beatles* shows. For the sixth programme they did 'Sweet Little Sixteen', 'A Taste Of Honey', 'Nothin' Shakin' (But The Leaves On The Trees)', 'Love Me Do', 'Lonesome Tears', 'In My Eyes' and 'So How Come (Nobody Loves Me)' and had Carter-Lewis & The Southerners as their guests.

For the seventh programme they recorded 'Memphis, Tennessee', 'Do You Want To Know A Secret', 'Till There Was You', 'Matchbox', 'Please Mister Postman' and 'The Hippy Hippy Shake' with The Searchers as their guests. After the recording session they drove back to Margate in time for the first house.
– *Winter Gardens, Margate.*

July 11
– *Winter Gardens, Margate.*

July 12
– *Winter Gardens, Margate.*
– The EP **Twist And Shout** was released

in the UK as PARLOPHONE GEP 8882 (mono only):

SIDE A: 'Twist And Shout', 'A Taste Of Honey';

SIDE B: 'Do You Want To Know A Secret', 'There's A Place'.

July 13
– *Winter Gardens, Margate.*
July 14
– *ABC Theatre, Blackpool.*
July 15
– Paul was fined £17 at Birkenhead Magistrates Court for speeding. He did not attend.
July 16
– *BBC Paris Studio, London.*
Programmes eight, nine and ten of

Pop Go The Beatles were recorded and stockpiled in one long session. For programme eight they recorded 'I'm Gonna Sit Right Down And Cry (Over You)', 'Crying, Waiting, Hoping', 'Kansas City'/Hey-Hey-Hey!', 'To Know Her Is To Love Her', 'The Honeymoon Song' and 'Twist And Shout'. They had as their guests The Swinging Blue Jeans.

The ninth programme featured 'Long Tall Sally', 'Please Please Me', 'She Loves You', 'You Really Got A Hold On Me', 'I'll Get You' and 'I Got A Woman' and would have The Hollies as guests when it was broadcast.

Programme ten featured 'She Loves

On stage at the Regal Cinema, Cambridge.

You', 'Words Of Love', 'Glad All Over', 'I Just Don't Understand', '(There's A) Devil In Her Heart' and 'Slow Down' with guests Russ Sainty & The Nu-Notes.
July 17
– *Playhouse Theatre, London,* to record a BBC Light Programme *Easy Beat.* They performed four numbers before the usual live teenage audience: 'I Saw Her Standing There', 'A Shot Of Rhythm And Blues', 'There's A Place' and 'Twist And Shout'.
July 18
– *Abbey Road.* The Beatles worked on material for their second album: 'You Really Got A Hold On Me',

'Money (That's What I Want)', '(There's A) Devil In Her Heart' and 'Till There Was You'.

July 19
– *Ritz Ballroom, Rhyl.*

July 20
– *Ritz Ballroom, Rhyl.* Afterwards, The Beatles drove back to Liverpool.

July 21
– *Queen's Theatre, Blackpool.* Four thousand fans blocked the streets of Blackpool before the concert, an early intimation of Beatlemania to come.

The Beatles met with Don Haworth from BBC TV Manchester to discuss the possibility of a half-hour serious documentary on The Beatles and the Mersey scene. They were interested and plans went ahead.

– The recent *Easy Beat* recording was transmitted by the BBC Light programme.

July 22
– *Odeon Cinema, Weston-super-Mare,* The opening of a six night engagement. Dezo Hoffman spent the day with the group on the beach at Bream Down, where he got them to pose in Victorian swimming costumes, ride donkeys and also made an amateur film of them cavorting on the beach. Dezo Hoffmann: On the way back they stopped at a Go-Kart track.

"I had the idea of hiring bathing huts, old fashioned **swimming costumes** *etc.* **They loved dressing up in** **silly** *costumes,* **John kept his on back at the hotel long after the session was** **over."**

July 23
– *Odeon Cinema, Weston-super-Mare.*
– *Pop Go The Beatles* was broadcast by the BBC Light Programme.

July 24
– *Odeon Cinema, Weston-super-Mare.*

July 25
– *Odeon Cinema, Weston-super-Mare.*

July 26
– *Odeon Cinema, Weston-super-Mare.*
– The album INTRODUCING THE BEATLES was released in the US as VEE JAY VJLP 1062 (mono) and SR 1062 (stereo).
 SIDE A: 'I Saw Her Standing There', 'Misery', 'Anna (Go To Him)', 'Chains', 'Boys', 'Love Me Do';
 SIDE B: 'P.S. I Love You', 'Baby It's You', 'Do You Want To Know A Secret', 'A Taste Of Honey', 'There's A Place', 'Twist And Shout'.

July 27
– *Odeon Cinema, Weston-super-Mare.*

July 28
– *ABC Cinema, Great Yarmouth.*

July 30
– *Abbey Road.* The Beatles recorded 'Please Mister Postman' and 'It Won't

Be Long' in a morning session.
– *Playhouse Theatre, London,* for two BBC Light Programme recordings: an interview with Phil Tate for the "Pop Chat" spot on *Non Stop Pop*, and a session for Saturday Club where they played 'Long Tall Sally', 'She Loves You', 'Glad All Over', 'Twist And Shout', 'You Really Got A Hold On Me' and 'I'll Get You'.
– Back at *Abbey Road* for an evening session, The Beatles worked on 'Till There Was You', 'Roll Over Beethoven', 'It Won't Be Long' and 'All My Loving'.
– *Pop Go The Beatles* was broadcast by the BBC Light Programme.

July 31
– *Imperial Ballroom, Nelson.*

August 1
– *Playhouse Theatre, Manchester,* to record two more sessions for The BBC Light Programme's *Pop Go The Beatles.* For the 11th show in the series, they recorded 'Ooh! My Soul', 'Don't Ever Change', 'Twist And Shout', 'She Loves You', 'Anna (Go To Him)' and 'A Shot Of Rhythm & Blues' and their guests were Cyril Davies' Rhythm & Blues All-Stars with Long John Baldry. The 12th show featured Brian Poole & The Tremeloes as guests and The Beatles playing 'From Me To You', 'I'll Get You', 'Money (That's What I Want)', 'There's A Place', 'Honey Don't' and 'Roll Over Beethoven'.
– The first issue of *The Beatles Book* was published in collaboration with Brian Epstein.

August 2
– *Grafton Rooms, Liverpool.*

August 3
– *Cavern Club.* The Beatles' last performance at the club. Tickets sold out within half an hour of going on sale.

August 4
– *Queen's Theatre, Blackpool.* The Beatles had to enter the theatre through a trap door on the roof, reached through scaffolding in the next-door builder's yard, because the normal entrances were totally blocked by fans.

August 5
– *Urmston Show.* An annual bank holiday show held in a giant marquee. The Beatles topped a four-act bill, which included Brian Poole & The

Ringo is escorted from the Gaumont Cinema, Bournemouth, during the 1963 summer season.

Tremeloes. David Hamilton was the compere.

August 6
– *Springfield Ballroom, St Saviour, Jersey.*
– The Beatles relaxed by go-karting and swimming. It was while in the Channel Islands that John Lennon met up again with Royston Ellis and Ellis introduced him to Polythene Pam.

August 7
– *Springfield Ballroom, St Saviour, Jersey.*

August 8
– *Auditorium, Candie Gardens, Guernsey.* The Beatles flew to Guernsey in a 12-seater plane.

August 9
– *Springfield Ballroom, St Saviour, Jersey.*

August 10
– *Springfield Ballroom, St Saviour, Jersey.*

August 11
– *ABC Theatre, Blackpool.*
– Mal Evans met the group in the van when they arrived at Manchester Airport after their week in the Channel Islands. It was his first day as a full-time employee of the group. The pressure of work and the need for personal security had led Brian Epstein to ask Mal to work as a combined roadie/bodyguard for the group.

August 12
– *Odeon Cinema, Llandudno.* The first night of a six-night season at the seaside with two houses each night.

August 13
– *Odeon Cinema, Llandudno.* After the second show the group returned to Liverpool for the night.

August 14
– In the morning they drove to Granada TV Centre, Manchester, to record two songs; 'Twist And Shout' and 'She Loves You' for *Scene*. The first was transmitted that night.
– *Odeon Cinema, Llandudno.*

August 15
– *Odeon Cinema, Llandudno.*

August 16
– *Odeon Cinema, Llandudno.*

August 17
– *Odeon Cinema, Llandudno.*

August 18
– *Alpha TV Studios, Birmingham,* to record an appearance for ABC TV's *Lucky Stars* (Summer Spin) presented by Pete Murray. They mimed 'She Loves You' and 'I'll Get You', the 'A' and B-sides to their next single
– *Princess Theatre, Devon.*

August 19
– *Gaumont Cinema, Bournemouth,* with Billy J. Kramer & The Dakotas and Tommy Quickly. Another summer seaside residency.
– The Beatles held a 20th birthday party for Billy J. Kramer in their dressing room between the two houses
– Granada transmitted The Beatles singing 'She Loves You' on *Scene*.

August 20
– *Gaumont Cinema, Bournemouth.*

August 21
– *Gaumont Cinema, Bournemouth.*

August 22
– While in Bournemouth, The Beatles stayed at the Palace Court Hotel where, probably on this day, Robert Freeman shot the famous monochrome photograph for the With The Beatles album.
– After lunch, The Beatles and Robert Freeman, drove to the Southern ITV Centre, Southampton, where they recorded an appearance for the *Day By Day* programme, miming 'She Loves You', which was broadcast that evening.
– *Gaumont Cinema, Bournemouth.*

August 23
– *Gaumont Cinema, Bournemouth.*
– The single **'She Loves You'/'I'll Get**

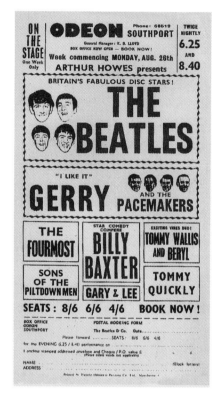

You' was released in the UK as PARLOPHONE R 5055. Demand for the new single was so great that EMI pressed over a quarter of a million copies in the four weeks before its official release.

August 24
– *Gaumont Cinema, Bournemouth.*
– The Beatles' July 30 recording for *Saturday Club* with presenter Brian Matthew was transmitted by the BBC Light Programme. The Beatles performing on *Lucky Stars* (Summer Spin) was broadcast by ABC TV.

August 25
– *ABC Theatre, Blackpool.*

August 26
– *Odeon Cinema, Southport,* with Gerry & the Pacemakers, the Foremost, Billy Baxter, Tommy Quickly, Tommy Wallis and Beryl, Gary & Lee and the Sons of the Piltdown Men. Another one-week seaside residency. The Beatles set consisted of 'Roll Over Beethoven', 'Thank You Girl', 'Chains', 'A Taste Of Honey', 'She Loves You', 'Baby It's You', 'From Me To You', 'Boys', 'I Saw Her Standing There' and 'Twist And Shout'.
– Paul received his third speeding conviction this year and was fined £31 and disqualified from driving for one year.

August 27
– *Odeon Cinema, Southport.*
– The Beatles were filmed playing 'Twist And Shout' and 'She Loves You' on stage, but with no audience, at The Little Theatre in Southport as part of the BBC TV Manchester documentary being made by Don Haworth. After a change of clothes to suggest a different occasion, they played 'Love Me Do'. Audience shots were then dubbed in from the previous night's concert. In the end their commercial recordings of these songs were used in the "documentary" which finished up about as close to reality as their movie *A Hard Day's Night*.
– The BBC Light Programme broadcast edition 11 of *Pop Go The Beatles*.

August 28
– *Odeon Cinema, Southport.*
– The Beatles were interviewed at the BBC's Manchester studios and also filmed as if backstage making up before

The With The Beatles Cover

Robert Freeman: "I suggested a black and white photograph... The boys liked the idea and the session was set up for noon the following day in the hotel dining room. The large windows let in a bright sidelight and the dark maroon velvet curtains were pulled round as a backdrop... We decided to use the black turtleneck sweaters which they wore at the time, to keep the picture simple." Ringo was placed in the bottom right corner as he was the last to join the group and had to kneel on a stool to be comfortable in the right position for the shot. Freeman received £75 for the cover, rather than the original £25 EMI originally proposed.

a concert, and waiting in the wings with their instruments, all for Haworth's *The Mersey Sound* documentary.

August 29
– *Odeon Cinema, Southport.*
– The Beatles acted an airport arrival for the "documentary" and also took a Mersey ferry between the Pier Head and Wallasey, signing autographs and meeting fans.

August 30
– *Odeon Cinema, Southport.*
– Ringo was filmed pushing his way through extras outside his childhood home at 10 Admiral Grove in the Dingle for Don Haworth's film.
– The BBC Light Programme broadcast the "Pop Chat" interview on *Non Stop Pop.*

August 31
– *Odeon Cinema, Southport.*
The final show in Southport.

September 1
– *ABC TV's Didsbury Studio Centre, Manchester.* The group recorded an appearance on the variety show *Big Night Out* presented by comedians Mike and Bernie Winters. They mimed 'From Me To You', 'She Loves You' and 'Twist And Shout' before a studio audience of 600 (broadcast September 7).

September 3
– *Aeolian Hall, London,* to record the last three programmes in the *Pop Go The Beatles* series, presented by Rodney Burke. For the 13th edition The Beatles recorded 'Too Much Monkey Business', 'Love Me Do', 'She Loves You', 'Till There Was You', 'I'll Get You' and 'The Hippy Hippy Shake'. Their guests were Johnny Kidd & The Pirates. For the 14th they played 'Chains', 'You Really Got A Hold On Me', ' Misery', 'A Taste Of Honey' (which was later edited into the preceding programme), 'Lucille' and 'From Me To You'. The Marauders were their guests. For the 15th and final session they played 'She Loves You', 'Ask Me Why' '(There's A) Devil In Her Heart', 'I Saw Her Standing There', 'Sure To Fall (In Love With You) and 'Twist And Shout.' Their guests were Tony Rivers & The Castaways.

– The BBC Light Programme broadcast edition 12 of *Pop Go The Beatles.*

September 4
– *Gaumont Cinema, Worcester.*

September 5
– *Gaumont Cinema, Taunton.*

September 6
– *Odeon Cinema, Luton.*
– The EP **The Beatles' Hits** was released in the UK as PARLOPHONE GEP 8880 (mono only).
>   SIDE A: **'From Me To You', 'Thank You Girl';**
>   SIDE B: **'Please, Please Me', 'Love Me Do'.**

September 7
– *Playhouse Theatre, London,* to rehearse and record a session for the BBC Light Programme's fifth birthday edition of *Saturday Club.* The Beatles performed 'I Saw Her Standing There', 'Memphis, Tennessee', 'Happy Birthday Saturday Club', which was written especially for the occasion by John, 'I'll Get You', 'She Loves You' and 'Lucille'.

After the recording, Paul did an interview with Rosemary Hart for the BBC Home Service series *A World Of Sound.*
– *Fairfield Hall, Croydon.*
– 'She Loves You' reached number one in the charts where it stayed for seven weeks.
– The Beatles' appearance on Mike and Bernie Winters' *Big Night Out* was broadcast by ABC TV.

September 8
– *ABC Theatre, Blackpool.*

September 10
– John and Paul attended a Variety Club of Great Britain luncheon at the Savoy Hotel where they received the award for 'Top Vocal Group of the Year'.

The Beatles and fellow Liverpudlian Billy J. Kramer hold up Susan Maughan outside London's Savoy Hotel, September 10.

– The BBC Light Programme broadcast edition 13 of *Pop Go The Beatles.*

September 11
– *Abbey Road,* to continue work on the With The Beatles album. They worked on 'I Wanna Be Your Man' (Paul has no memory of it being intended as anything other than a vehicle for Ringo), 'Little Child', 'All I've Got To Do' and 'Not A Second Time'. Finally, they made a number of takes of George's 'Don't Bother Me'.

September 12
– *Abbey Road.* In preparation for their Australian tour they recorded three message clips for Bob Rogers, an important DJ on Sydney station 2SM, and an open message to be used by any radio station. After this they continued work on 'Hold Me Tight', 'Don't Bother Me', 'Little Child' and 'I Wanna Be Your Man'.

The Rolling Stones

On the afternoon of September 10, The Rolling Stones' manager, ex-Beatles publicist Andrew Oldham, was walking down Jermyn Street when a taxi pulled up beside him, waiting for traffic lights. The window rolled down and a Liverpudlian voice said, "Get in, Andy." It had been only a few months since he had stopped working as The Beatles' press agent.

In the cab were John and Paul, returning to their hotel after lunch. Knowing that The Beatles liked The Rolling Stones, Andrew told them that he was looking for songs for them to record. John and Paul immediately suggested that he might like to hear one they had just written, called 'I Wanna Be Your Man', which they thought might be suitable.

Andrew was on his way to meet the Stones at Ken Colyer's Studio 51 in Great Newport Street, Soho, and John and Paul said they would join him. At the club they borrowed a couple of guitars from Brian and Keith and launched into the number. There was only one problem: the song didn't have a middle eight.

After a quick conference John and Paul told them that if they really liked the song, they would finish it off for them. They disappeared into a side room and reappeared a few minutes later. "Forget something?" asked Bill Wyman.

"No," said Paul. "We've just finished the middle eight. How does this sound?"

It became the Rolling Stones' first Top 20 hit.

September 13
– *Public Hall, Preston.*
– *Imperial Ballroom, Nelson, Lancashire.* After the Preston show Paul drove to Nelson to take his place on the panel of judges at the "Miss Imperial 1963" contest, part of an annual "Young Ones Ball" promotion by local newspaper *The Nelson Leader*.
September 14
– Press interviews at NEMS

Liverpool offices.
– *The Victory Memorial Hall, Northwich.*
September 15
– *Royal Albert Hall, London.* This was the annual "Great Pop Prom" promoted by *Valentine*, *Marilyn* and *Roxy* magazines in aid of the Printers' Pension Corporation. The Beatles appeared with 11 other acts. The compere was Alan Freeman.

– The Beatles did a photo session with The Rolling Stones, who were also on the bill, on the steps to the rear of the hall.
– The single **'She Loves You'/ 'I'll Get You'** was released in the US as Swan 4152.
September 16
– John and Cynthia flew to Paris on holiday where they were joined later by Brian Epstein. George and his

Paul: **"Standing up on those steps behind the Albert Hall in our new gear,** the smart trousers, the rolled collar. Up there with **The Rolling Stones** we were thinking, 'This is it - **London!, The Albert Hall! We felt like Gods!"**

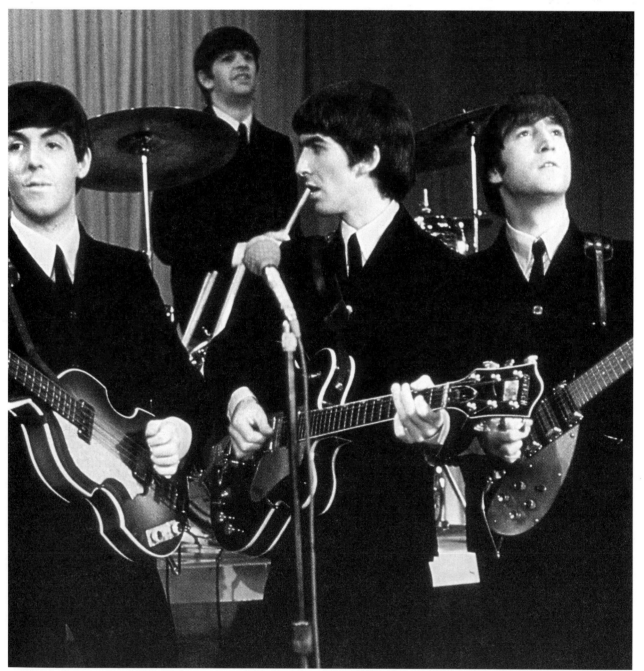

brother Peter visited their sister Louise in Benton, Illinois, USA.
– Paul, Jane, Ringo and Maureen, went to Greece.

Ringo: "I did a lot of swimming during the day while Paul had a bash at the water skiing. During the evenings we used to join in with the local Greek group called The Trio Athenia. 'Cause they didn't play pop stuff - not until we turned up at any rate. Now they'll have a go at half our Top Ten."

September 17
– The BBC Light Programme broadcast the 14th edition of *Pop Go The Beatles*.

September 24
– The BBC Light Programme broadcast the final edition of *Pop Go The Beatles*.

October 2
– Paul and Ringo arrived back in England via Zürich and Frankfurt. John, Cynthia and Brian flew direct from Paris.

October 3
– *Abbey Road.* Ringo overdubbed his vocal on 'I Wanna Be Your Man' and John and Paul put theirs on 'Little Child'.
– George flew in from the USA in time to join the others in an interview with Michael Colley for the BBC Light Programme's *The Public Ear*.
– Ringo drove to Southend, Essex, to see The Everly Brothers, Bo Diddley and The Rolling Stones play the Odeon Cinema.

October 4
– *Associated-Rediffusion's studios at Television House, London,* to record their first appearance on *Ready, Steady, Go!* They mimed 'Twist And shout', 'I'll Get You' and 'She Loves You' live and were interviewed by Keith Fordyce and Dusty Springfield.

October 5
– *Carnegie Hall, Glasgow.* The first of three Scottish gigs.
– The special fifth birthday edition of *Saturday Club* was broadcast by the BBC Light Programme.

October 6
– *Carlton Theatre, Kirkaldy.* A total

Paul: "We used to go to Greece because in Greece they never recognised us. Everywhere else, in Germany, in Italy, in the south of France, it was 'There's The Beatles!' and we had to run for our bloody lives. So we'd go to Greece, and then one year everyone recognised us in Greece too. So we figured, 'Whoa, this is the point of no return'. But then you learn either to get out now or realise that this is fame, this is what happens with fame. This is celebrity, We thought 'Well, we'd better get on with it, come to terms with it'."

of 3,000 fans crowded into the two performances.

October 7
– *Caird Hall, Dundee.*

October 9
– *BBC Paris Studio, London,* to record 'She Loves You' for the BBC Light Programme comedy show, *The Ken Dodd Show.*
– Don Haworth's BBC television "documentary", *The Mersey Sound,* was broadcast to great acclaim.

October 11
– *Ballroom, Trentham.*

October 12
– The Beatles rehearsed for their appearance the following night on *Sunday Night At The London Palladium.*

October 13
– *London Palladium.* The Beatles topped the bill at ATV's Val Parnell's *Sunday Night At The London Palladium,* transmitted live from the theatre to an audience of 15 million viewers. They played 'From Me To You', 'I'll Get You', 'She Loves You' and 'Twist And Shout', and joined the other acts, which included Brook Benton and Des O'Connor, as well as compere Bruce

Forsyth, to wave goodbye to the audience and viewers from the revolving stage which traditionally ended the show.

October 14
– The British press discovered Beatlemania with headline coverage of The Beatles' appearance on *Sunday Night At The London Palladium* and the mass hysteria that the group caused in its fans.

October 15
– *Floral Hall, Southport.*
– It was announced that The Beatles had been invited to appear on *The Royal Variety Show.*

October 16
– *Playhouse Theatre, London,* to record their final session for BBC Light Programme's *Easy Beat.* They played 'I Saw Her Standing There', 'Love Me Do', 'Please Please Me', 'From Me To You' and 'She Loves You'.
– The Beatles were interviewed about the *Royal Variety Show* announcement by Peter Woods for BBC Light Programme's *Radio Newsreel.*

October 17
– *Abbey Road.* The Beatles recorded

The Origins of Beatlemania

Outside the London Palladium on October 13, fans blocked Argyll Street and spilled over into Great Marlborough Street, stopping traffic. Fans in the audience screamed so much that John yelled for them to "Shut up!". It was this manifestation of Beatles fans' adulation that led the following day's newspapers to coin the term "Beatlemania". The event was also covered by the late news on ITV.

Above: A fan grabs George on stage in Stockholm, October 26.
Opposite: London Airport, October 23.

George: "But I sense **the atmosphere** here too. You know, you can **always** tell the **places** where **living** people."

both sides of their next single – 'I Want To Hold Your Hand' and 'This Boy' – using EMI's new four-track machine for the first time. (EMI was very backward technologically and it is entirely typical that they were just installing four-track equipment when American studios, such as Atlantic Records, had been using eight-track equipment since the Fifties.)
– The Beatles also worked on 'You Really Got A Hold On Me', and made 'The Beatles' Christmas Record' for their fan club members.
– Fans blocked Bond Street when Paul arrived to take a girl out to lunch who had won a "Why I Like The Beatles" magazine competition.

October 18
– *Granada Television Centre, Manchester,* to mime 'She Loves You' for that evening's edition of *Scene at 6.30.*

October 19
– *Pavilion Gardens Ballroom, Buxton.*

October 20
– *Alpha TV Studios, Birmingham,* to record a headline appearance for ABC TV's *Thank Your Lucky Stars.* They mimed 'All My Loving', 'Money (That's What I Want)' and 'She Loves You' while 3,000 fans blocked the streets and attempted to storm the studios.
– The BBC Light Programme broadcast the final appearance by The Beatles on *Easy Beat.*

October 23
– *Abbey Road.* The Beatles completed work on 'I Wanna Be Your Man', Ringo's track for the new album.
– That afternoon The Beatles flew BEA to Stockholm International Airport, Arlanda, arriving to a scene of screaming fans and uncharacteristic Swedish chaos. Bouquets of flowers were thrust at them from all directions as they posed for pictures in their overcoats on the tarmac. Hundreds of girls had taken the day off school to be there to welcome them, and the press later described the scene as "The Battle of Stockholm Airport". On the state radio station, Sveriges Radio, a DJ called Klas Burling (the Swedish Brian Matthew) played nothing but Beatles records.

The police managed to escort the group to the Hotel Continental where the girls took up their position outside. Quite a lot managed to get inside The Beatles' suite as well, and everyone partied late into the night.

October 24
– The Beatles held a chaotic press conference. Surrounded by heavy security because of the crowds of fans, they attempted to do a little sightseeing, and were taken, rather unnecessarily, to an English-style pub.
– *Karlaplansstudion, Stockholm,* to record (without rehearsal) an interview and a live set for Klas Burling's Sveriges Radio show, *Pop '63,* which for this edition was renamed *The Beatles pupgrupp från Liverpool på besök i Stockholm* (The Beatles pop group from Liverpool visiting Stockholm). The group played a lively seven numbers: 'I Saw Her Standing There', 'From Me To You', 'Money (That's What I Want)', 'Roll Over Beethoven', 'You Really Got A Hold On Me', 'She Loves You' and 'Twist And Shout'. The local group Hasse Rosen & The Norsemen also appeared on the show.

That night they visited the Nalen, the main teenage dance hall. It happened to be celebrating its 75th anniversary, so all the local celebrities were there.

Ringo: "A bit more elegant than the Cavern."

October 25
– *Nya Aulan, Karlstad,* with local group The Phantoms. This venue was a secondary school hall and the group played two performances of their standard set for the tour: "Long Tall Sally', 'Please Please Me', 'I Saw Her Standing There', 'From Me To You', 'A Taste Of Honey', 'Chains', 'Boys', 'She Loves You' and 'Twist And Shout'. As in England their performance was almost entirely drowned by screams.

October 26
– *Kungliga Tennishallen, Stockholm,* where The Beatles were billed second to Joey Dee & The Starlighters for the two shows. The audience clearly thought otherwise.
– ABC TV's *Thank Your Lucky Stars* premiered 'All My Loving' and 'Money (That's What I Want)'.

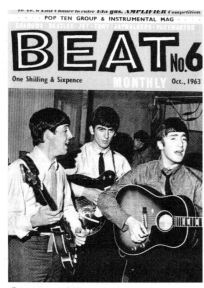

October 27
– *Cirkus, Gothenburg.* The Beatles played an afternoon show as well as two houses in the evening.

October 28
– *Waidele record shop, Borås,* where they spent half an hour signing records.
– *Boråshallen, Borås.*

October 29
– *Sporthallen, Eskilstuna,* with Jerry Williams, The Violents, Trio Me' Bumba, The Telstars and Mona Skarström.

October 30
– *Narren-teatern, Stockholm,* to record an appearance on the Sveriges Television show *Drop In* before a live audience in a small theatre in the Grona Lund amusement park. They were persuaded by presenter Klas Burling to extent their set from two to four numbers and performed 'She

Loves You', 'Twist And Shout', 'Long Tall Sally' and 'I Saw Her Standing There'. Also on the bill were Gals & Pals and the young singer Lill-Babs who appeared in many photographs with the group.

October 31
– The Beatles flew SAS back to London where hundreds of screaming teenage girls had gathered on the roof of the Queen's Building at Heathrow Airport to welcome them back to Britain. By coincidence, Ed Sullivan happened to be passing through the airport at that time and witnessed the scene. It impressed him very much and led him to book the group for his show when they were still virtually unknown in the USA.

November 1
– *Odeon Cinema, Cheltenham.* The first night of The Beatles' Autumn Tour, with The Rhythm & Blues

Quartet, The Vernons Girls, The Brook Brothers, Peter Jay & The Jaywalkers and The Kestrels. The compere was Frank Berry. The Beatles' standard set for the tour was: 'I Saw Her Standing There', 'From Me To You', 'All My Loving', 'You Really Got A Hold On Me', 'Roll Over Beethoven', 'Boys', 'Till There Was You', 'She Loves You', 'Money (That's What I Want)' and 'Twist And Shout'.
– The EP **The Beatles** (No.1) was released in the UK as PARLOPHONE GEP 8883 (mono only).
> SIDE A: **'I Saw Her Standing There', 'Misery';**
> SIDE B: **'Anna (Go To Him)', 'Chains'.**
– The single **'I Wanna Be Your Man'** by The Rolling Stones, written by Lennon & McCartney, was released in the UK as DECCA F 11764.

November 2
– *City Hall, Sheffield* (Autumn Tour).

November 3
– *Odeon Cinema, Leeds* (Autumn Tour).
– The Beatles appeared on *The Ken Dodd Show*, broadcast by The BBC Light Programme.
– The Beatles' interview on *The Public Ear* was aired by the BBC Light Programme.

November 4
– *Prince Of Wales Theatre, London,* for the Royal Command Performance, in the presence of Their Majesties the Queen Mother and Princess Margaret, accompanied by Lord Snowdon. Bernard Delfont risked offending the crustier members of the establishment and press by inviting The Beatles to appear at the Royal Variety Performance along with more traditional acts. The Beatles were seventh to perform but were clearly the headline act. On the bill were Marlene Dietrich, Max Bygraves, Harry Secombe, Buddy Greco, Wilfred Bramble & Harry H. Corbett, Charlie Drake, Michael Flanders & Donald Swann, Joe Loss & His Orchestra, Susan Maughan, Nadia Nerina, Luis Alberto Del Parana & Los Paraguayos, Tommy Steele, Eric Sykes & Hattie Jacques, The Clark Brothers, Francis Brunn, the Billy Petch Dancers, Pinky

& Perky and The Prince of Wales Theatre Orchestra.

November 5
– An Associated-Rediffusion television crew filmed The Beatles in the back of a car driving around London for a documentary called *The Beatles and Beatlemania*, to be included in their current affairs programme. *This Week.*
– *Adelphi Cinema, Slough* (Autumn Tour). Watched by 30 policemen waiting to cope with the expected crowds, Ringo led an on-stage jam session with George and several Jaywalkers before the concert.

November 6
– *ABC Cinema, Northampton* (Autumn Tour).

November 7
– The Beatles flew to Dublin. They were interviewed at the airport by Frank Hall for Radio Telefis Eireann's television programme *In Town*, shown that evening. They were accompanied by playwright Alun Owen, who remained with them for three days, making notes for their projected first film. At that time, it still had not been decided whether the film should be fact or fiction, nor did it have a name. The resulting film was fiction but based so completely on their lives that it had a strong documentary feel. Alun Owen: **"It's most important to get to know The Beatles, to find out exactly what makes them tick. And also to ascertain which things cause those fantastic crowd receptions."**
– *Adelphi Cinema, Dublin* (Autumn Tour)

November 8
– The Beatles filmed an interview with Jimmy Robinson of Ulster TV near the Irish border which was included in that evening's edition of *Ulster News.*
– Broadcasting House, Belfast to record an interview with Sally Ogle for that evening's *Six Ten* programme.

November 9
– *Granada Cinema, East Ham, London* (Autumn Tour). The crowds outside the venue were so great that when The Beatles sent out for food, it had to be given a police escort to reach them. They watched through the

---

"Rattle yer jewellery"

The Beatles wore fancy new black outfits for the Royal Variety Show on November 4: high V-necks, black ties and blindingly white shirts. The curtains opened and they went straight into 'From Me To You' with not one scream from the audience. This was followed by 'She Loves You', then Paul announced that they would sing something from *The Music Man*: "This one's been covered by our favourite American group - Sophie Tucker," he cracked and they played 'Till There Was You'. John introduced 'Twist And Shout' with his famous remark: "In the cheaper seats, you clap your hands. The rest of you, just rattle your jewellery," a comment which had worried Brian Epstein a great deal in rehearsal, when John had said, "rattle your fucking jewellery". No encores were allowed but the applause went on so long it delayed Dickie Henderson's announcement of the next act. Afterwards they met the Queen Mother who asked them where they would be playing next. When told their next concert was in Slough, she remarked, "Oh, that's near us" (meaning Windsor Castle, just two miles from Slough). Later the Queen Mother announced that she found them "most intriguing".

"Dublin was **fantastic.**
The fans there really do **go mad.**
Girls who fainted in the
crowds outside the theatre were carried
into their seats by attendants.
Outside there was the **biggest riot** yet.
It's a fact that **cars were overturned**
and the **police** had to make **several arrests.**

Inside it was **incredible** for **noise** and appreciation."

RECORD MIRROR, PETER JAY, NOVEMBER 7

John, Ringo and Paul with Harry Secombe, Tommy Steele and Marlene Dietrich at rehearsals for the Royal Variety Show, November 4.

windows as it was marched across the road through the crowd.

November 10
– *Hippodrome Theatre, Birmingham* (Autumn Tour).
– *The Royal Variety Show* was transmitted by ATV and on the radio by the BBC Light Programme.

November 11
– The Beatles *pupgrupp från Liverpool på besök i Stockholm* was broadcast on Sveriges Radio.

November 12
– Paul had gastric flu which caused their Portsmouth Guildhall concert to be postponed until December 3.
– They were interviewed at the Guildhall by Jeremy James for Southern TV's *Day By Day* programme that evening.
– BBC TV's *South Today* programme broadcast an interview with the band by John Johnston recorded at their hotel, The Royal Beach in Southsea.

November 13
– *Westward TV Studios, Plymouth.* The Beatles were interviewed by Stuart Hutchison for *Move Over, Dad* (a local teenagers' programme). So many fans blocked the streets outside that an ingenious route, using interconnecting tunnels, had to be devised to get them to the studio.

– *ABC Cinema, Plymouth* (Autumn Tour).

November 14
– *ABC Cinema, Exeter* (Autumn Tour).

November 15
– *Colston Hall, Bristol* (Autumn Tour).

November 16
– *Winter Gardens, Bournemouth* (Autumn Tour). The three rival American television networks - NBC, CBS and ABC - were permitted to film the hysterical audience and part of the show. Paul and John were interviewed by John Darsa for the CBS coverage. *Life* magazine photographer Terence Spencer with his assistant also arrived at their hotel, the Branksome Towers, outside Bournemouth and was quickly accepted into the inner circle. Brian Epstein was particularly keen on the publicity that a large spread in *Life* would produce. However, The Beatles did not turn up for the shoot that would have given them the January 31, 1964, cover, which went to Geraldine Chaplin instead.
– The Beatles interview on *Move Over, Dad* was transmitted by Southern TV.

November 17
– *Coventry Theatre, Coventry* (Autumn Tour).

November 18
– *EMI House, London,* to receive silver discs for Please Please Me and the not yet released With The Beatles from EMI Chairman Sir Joseph Lockwood. They also received silver EPs for Twist And Shout from George Martin and a silver EP and single for Twist And Shout and 'She Loves You' from Gerald Marks, the editor of *Disc*. After the presentation there was a cocktail party followed by a formal lunch in the boardroom with company executives and their guests.

November 19
– *Gaumont Cinema, Wolverhampton* (Autumn Tour).

November 20
– *ABC Cinema, Manchester* (Autumn Tour). Backstage at the ABC were news crews from Pathé News, Granada TV and BBC Radio. Pathé filmed part of the concert to be screened in British cinemas as The

Beatles Come To Town during Pathé News. The Granada TV crew filmed the group at the same time and interviewed them about their forthcoming tour of the US.
– Michael Barton did a two-minute interview broadcast that same evening on the BBC North Home Service programme *Voice Of The North*. Barton also interviewed George about the Liverpool and Hamburg rock scenes for a North Home Service programme called *Wacker, Mach Schau*.

November 21
– *ABC Cinema, Carlisle* (Autumn Tour).
– Paul's interview on *The World of Sound* was broadcast by the BBC Home Service.

Right: Ringo with Eric Morecambe, December 2; Below: The Beatles hoist fellow Liverpudlian Ken Dodd at Manchester, November 25.

November 22
– *Globe Cinema, Stockton-on-Tees* (Autumn Tour).
– The album WITH THE BEATLES was released in the UK as PARLOPHONE PMC 1206 (mono) and PCS 3045 (stereo).
  SIDE A: 'It Won't Be Long', 'All I've Got To Do', 'All My Loving', 'Don't Bother Me', 'Little Child', 'Till There Was You', 'Please Mister Postman';
  SIDE B: 'Roll Over Beethoven', 'You Really Got A Hold On Me', 'I Wanna Be Your Man', '(There's A) Devil In Her Heart', 'Not A Second Time', 'Money (That's What I Want)'.

November 23
– *City Hall, Newcastle upon Tyne* (Autumn Tour).

November 24
– *ABC Cinema, Hull* (Autumn Tour).

November 25
– *Granada TV Centre, Manchester*. The Beatles mimed 'I Want To Hold Your Hand' and 'This Boy' and were later interviewed with Ken Dodd by Gay Byrne for *Granada's Scene* and *Late Scene Extra* programmes.

November 26
– *Regal Cinema, Cambridge* (Autumn Tour).
– Jean Goodman interviewed The Beatles in their dressing room for the local BBC TV show *East At Six Ten*.

November 27
– *Rialto Theatre, York* (Autumn Tour). All the lights in the theatre fused and the curtains would not work and had to parted manually.
– The BBC North Home Service programme *Wacker, Mach Schau* was broadcast.
– Granada's *Late Scene Extra* with The Beatles miming to 'I Want To Hold Your Hand' was broadcast.

November 28
– *ABC Cinema, Lincoln* (Autumn Tour). Ringo had earache and had to cut short rehearsals to go to hospital and have his ear syringed but was back in time for the show.

November 29
– *ABC Cinema, Huddersfield* (Autumn Tour). Between sets The Beatles gave individual interviews to

Gorden Kaye for *Music Box*, a record request show for local hospitals.
– The single **'I Want To Hold Your Hand'/'This Boy'** was released in the UK as PARLOPHONE R 5084. Advance sales passed the million mark before it was released, the first time this had ever happened in Britain.

November 30
– Empire Theatre, Sunderland (Autumn Tour).

December 1
– *De Montfort Hall, Leicester* (Autumn Tour).

December 2
– *Elstree Studio Centre, Borehamwood*, to record an appearance on Associated-Rediffusion's *Morecambe And Wise Show*. The group sang 'This Boy', 'All My Loving' and 'I Want To Hold Your Hand' live before a small studio audience and did comedy sketches with Eric and Ernie. The Beatles, Eric and Ernie, all dressed in striped blazers, closed the show with 'Moonlight Bay'.
– *The Ballroom, Grosvenor House Hotel, Park Lane*, in aid of a charity for spastics. The group was part of a cabaret-style floor show and the audience wore evening dress.

December 3
– *Guildhall, Portsmouth* (Autumn Tour). The concert that had been postponed in November because of Paul's gastric 'flu.

"The Beatles must be the **only** people in **showbiz** ever to have turned down a *Life* cover." TERENCE SPENCER

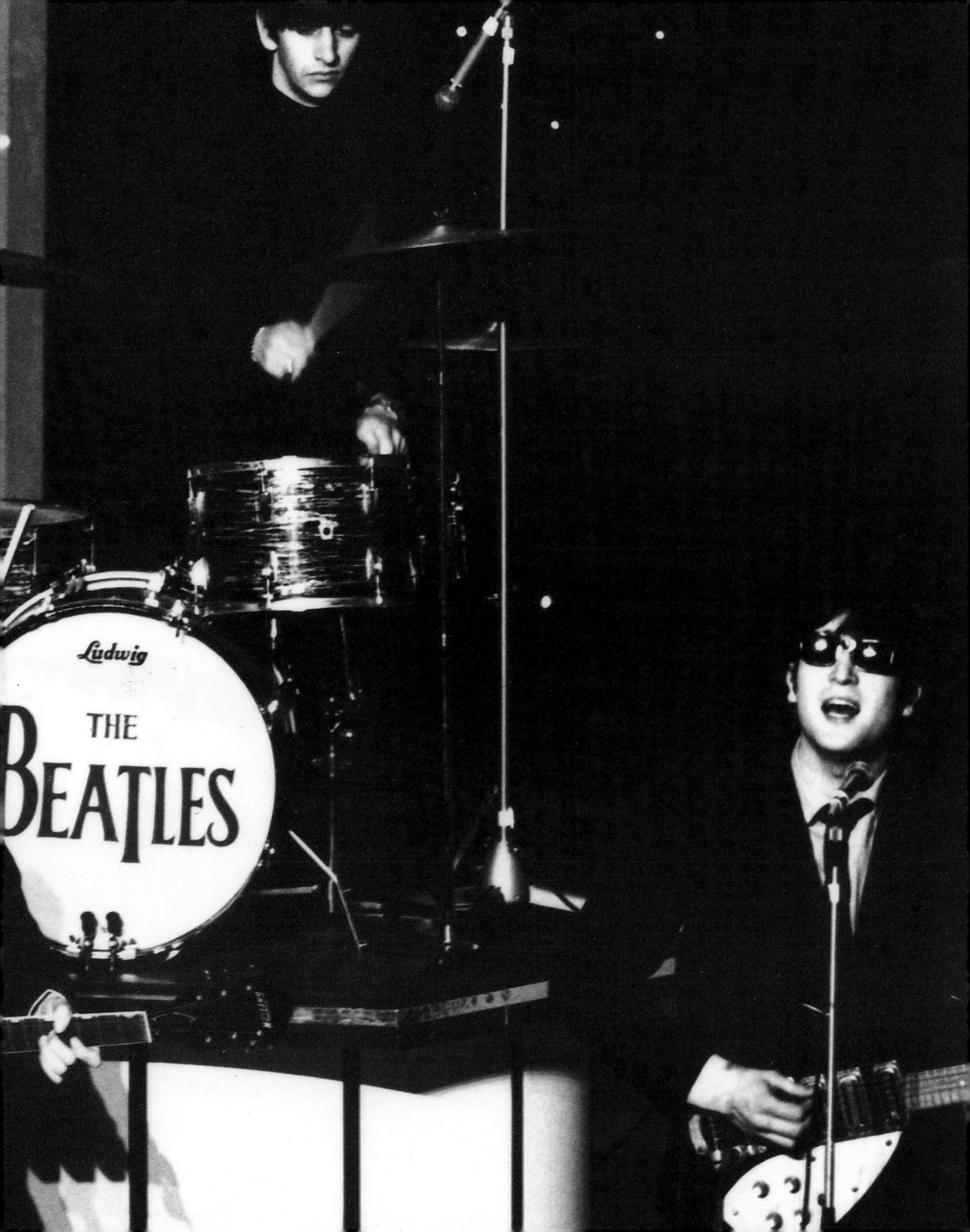
Ludwig
THE
BEATLES

HIT

"**Elvis** is great, his songs are **rubbish.**"

December 7
– Empire Theatre, Liverpool.
The Beatles comprised the entire panel for a special edition of BBC-TV's *Juke Box Jury* before an audience of 2,500 members of The Beatles' Northern Area Fan Club. As usual, the compere was David Jacobs:

The Chants: 'I Could Write A Book' [Liverpool group]

John: "It's gear. Fabulous. Fab. It's it."

Paul: "I talked to The Chants recently about the disc. They said it's powerful. It is."

Ringo: "I'll buy it."

George: "It's great. Enough plugs and they've got a hit."

David Jacobs: "Are they being too generous?"

Unanimous hit.

Elvis Presley: 'Kiss Me Quick'

Paul: "What I don't like about Elvis are his songs. I like his voice. This song reminds me of Blackpool on a sunny day."

Ringo: "Last two years Elvis has been going down the nick."

George: "If he's going back to old tracks, why not release 'My Baby Left Me'? It'd be a number one."

John: "It'll be a hit. I like those hats with 'Kiss Me Quick' on."

Unanimous hit.

Swinging Blue Jeans: 'Hippy Hippy Shake'

Ringo: "Good, but not as good as the original by Chan Romero."

George: "It's a popular song around Liverpool. We used to do it. Could be a hit."

John: "The boys nearly made it before. I like Bill Harry's version as well!"

Paul: "Doesn't matter about Chan Romero's disc. Nobody remembers. It's as good as a new song."

Unanimous hit.

Paul Anka: 'Did You Have A Happy Birthday?'

Ringo: "Not for me. I've never bought one of his records."

George: "Okay. But I wouldn't buy it. Guitar phrasing is like that on Cliff's latest."

John: "Tune's not bad, but I don't like gallop tunes."

Paul: "I quite liked it."

Unanimous miss.

Shirley Ellis: 'The Nitty Gritty Song'

John: "I like it."

Paul: "I like this kind of record, but it doesn't say anything."

Ringo: "We all like this sort of thing but it won't be a hit."

George: "Won't be a hit in England. We haven't got around to that sort of thing yet."

David Jacobs: "You mean British teenagers are behind the Americans?"

George: "We've liked this type of thing for years but it hasn't really caught on."

Unanimous miss.

Steve and Eydie: 'I Can't Stop Talking About You'

Ringo: "SHE carries him, actually!"

George: "It could easily make the twenty. So relaxed."

John: "They're relaxed because they're getting on a bit. I don't like it."

Three to one hit.

Billy Fury: 'Do You Really Love Me?'

Unanimous miss.

Bobby Vinton: 'There, I've Said It Again'

George: "Quite nice, but I don't think the public will buy it."

John: "Get an old song and everybody does it again at the same time."

Paul: "Secretly, teenagers don't want old songs brought back."

Ringo: "Nice and smooth, 'specially if you're sitting in one night - and not alone."

Unanimous miss.

The Orchids: 'Love Hit Me'

John: "Just a big con - a pinch from The Crystals and Ronettes."

Paul: "It's good for a British record."

Ringo: "It'll sell a few, but not many."

George: "I'd rather have British groups pinch from The Crystals than the other stuff."

A three to one miss. Then it was revealed that The Orchids were there in the audience.

John: "A lousy trick."

The Merseybeats: 'I Think Of You' [No time for discussion, only a vote. Unanimous hit.]

– Next, the Fan Club audience saw a special concert, shown later the same day as *It's The Beatles!* For this they played 'From Me To You', 'I Saw Her Standing There', 'All My Loving', 'Roll Over Beethoven', 'Boys', 'Till There Was You', 'She Loves You', 'This Boy', 'I Want To Hold Your Hand', 'Money (That's What I Want)', 'Twist And Shout' and 'From Me To You'.

– The BBC Light Programme then recorded a two-minute interview to use on their Christmas Day special *Top Pops of 1963*.

– Finally, protected by a police cordon, they made a dash to the nearby Odeon Cinema.

– Odeon Cinema, Liverpool (Autumn Tour).

December 8
– Odeon Cinema, Lewisham, London (Autumn Tour).

Paul: "People will **whistle** this **one."**

Opposite: With David Jacobs at the Juke Box Jury TV Special in Liverpool, December 7. Below: Photocall at Lewisham, December 8.

"If they **press** any **harder** they'll come through as **chips.**"

The scene that greeted The Beatles at Wimbledon Palais, December 14.

December 9
– *Odeon Cinema, Southend-on-Sea* (Autumn Tour). A BBC-TV news crew interviewed the group in their dressing room.
December 10
– *Gaumont Cinema, Doncaster* (Autumn Tour). Backstage, The Beatles gave an interview to the Australian radio journalist Dibbs Mather for the BBC Transcription Service.
December 11
– *Futurist Theatre, Scarborough* (Autumn Tour).
December 12
– *Odeon Cinema, Nottingham* (Autumn Tour).
December 13
– *Gaumont Cinema, Southampton,* the last concert on the Autumn Tour.
December 14
– *Wimbledon Palais.* The Beatles' Southern Area Fan Club concert. An afternoon performance, after which The Beatles sat behind the Palais bar and shook hands with all 3,000 of their SFC members. Most of them stood in an orderly line to shake hands with the group but a few girls fainted. They very soon had to stop giving autographs as the line grew too long. Some girls managed to tousle their hair or kiss their hands.

Their live performance was completely drowned out by screams. Worried that the fans might cause damage to their stage, the Palais management enclosed it in a steel cage, prompting John to quip,
December 15
– *Alpha TV Studios, Birmingham,* to record ABC TV's *Thank Your Lucky Stars.* An all Merseyside show. The Beatles mimed 'I Want To Hold Your Hand', 'All My Loving', 'Twist And Shout' and 'She Loves You' and were presented with two gold discs.
– The Beatles' Christmas flexi-disc was sent out to the 28,000 members of their fan club.
December 17
– *Playhouse Theatre, London,* to record a Christmas edition of *Saturday Club* for the BBC Light Programme. They played 'All My Loving', 'This Boy', 'I Want To Hold Your Hand', 'Till There Was You', 'Roll Over Beethoven'

The Beatles with Cilla Black, The Searchers and Billy J. Kramer and The Dakotas at the all-Merseybeat Thank Your Lucky Stars, December 15.

and 'She Loves You'. Then they parodied Dora Bryan's recent hit 'All I Want For Christmas Is A Beatle' with 'All I Want For Christmas Is A Bottle'. This was followed by a half minute medley entitled 'The Chrimble Mudley' which combined 'Love Me Do', 'Please, Please Me', 'From Me To You', 'I Want To Hold Your Hand' and 'Rudolph The Red-Nosed Reindeer'.

December 18
– *BBC Paris Studio, London,* to record *From Us To You,* a two-hour Beatles Boxing Day bank holiday special for the Light Programme. 'From Me To You' was recorded as 'From Us To You' as the signature tune to begin and end the programme, and the show was hosted by Rolf Harris. Guests were Susan Maughan, Jeanie Lambe, Kenny Lynch, Joe Brown & The Bruvvers, The Kenny Salmon Seven and Alan Elsdon's Jazzband with Mick Emery. The Beatles and Rolf Harris joined together for a version of 'Tie Me Kangaroo Down, Sport' and the group performed 'She Loves You', 'All My Loving', 'Roll Over Beethoven', 'Till There Was You', 'Boys', 'Money (That's What I Want)', 'I Saw Her Standing There' and 'I Want To Hold Your Hand'.

December 21
– *Gaumont Cinema, Bradford.*

The first of two special previews of *The Beatles' Christmas Show,* performed as a concert without costume or comedy sketches.

Chris Charlesworth, who would become a music writer, attended this show with his father:
– The Christmas Special edition of *Saturday Club* was broadcast by the BBC Light Programme.

December 22
– *Empire Theatre, Liverpool.* Second of the *The Beatles' Christmas Show* previews.

December 23
– *It's The Beatles,* a 15-part weekly series of 15-minute spots presented by Peter Carver, began transmission on Radio Luxembourg.

December 24
– *Astoria Cinema, Finsbury Park, London,* with The Barron Knights & Duke D'Mond, Tommy Quickly, The Fourmost, Billy J. Kramer & The Dakotas, Cilla Black and Rolf Harris. The show ran for 16 nights, with two houses per night, finishing on January 11, 1964, and was seen by almost 100,000 people.

December 25
– The Beatles flew home to Liverpool.

December 26
– The Beatles flew from Liverpool to London.
– *Astoria Cinema, Finsbury Park, London. The Beatles Christmas Show.*
– *From Us To You,* a two hour Beatles Boxing Day bank holiday special was broadcast by the BBC Light Programme.
– The single **'I Want to Hold Your Hand'/'I Saw Her Standing There'** was released in the US as CAPITOL 5112.

December 27
– *Astoria Cinema, Finsbury Park, London. The Beatles' Christmas Show.*

December 28
– *Astoria Cinema, Finsbury Park, London. The Beatles' Christmas Show.*

December 30
– *Astoria Cinema, Finsbury Park, London. The Beatles' Christmas Show.*

December 31
– *Astoria Cinema, Finsbury Park, London. The Beatles' Christmas Show.* (One house only, to allow time for New Year celebrations.)

"There were very few boys in the audience... it was almost all girls and they just screamed like crazy. Rolf Harris was the compere and he had to come on for ten minutes just before The Beatles closed the show because, unlike the other acts, they used their own equipment and it had to be set up behind the curtains. Harris was completely drowned out by the screams but he asked for it by drawing sketches of the four Beatles on his easel pad. The Beatles were only on for about 25 minutes and they were also drowned out. I couldn't hear a note they sang or played, even though I was quite near the front, on Paul's side, but **it was the most exciting** thing I'd ever seen in my life... an unbelievable experience. The next day all I could think about was getting a guitar."

The Beatles in costume for a sketch in their Christmas show.

The Beatles' Christmas Show

Peter Yolland designed the show for children. It opened with a speeded up film made from stock clips while the soundtrack announced: "By land, by sea, by air, come the stars of The Beatles Christmas Show..." The curtains parted to reveal a large cardboard helicopter landing on the stage. Compere Rolf Harris played the role of airline ticket collector and introduced each member of the cast individually as they stepped off.

Naturally, the final passengers to leap out were The Beatles, carrying BEA tote bags and wearing glasses.

In one sketch, a follow spot picked up four men in white coats on a blacked out stage. Three of them hurried away as the commentator, imitating a current toothpaste advertisement, said "Three out of four doctors...". The remaining "doctor" was John Lennon who completed the phrase, "... leaves

one doctor!" This was the level of script writing and The Beatles were very disappointed with it.

Tommy Quickly threw cotton wool stage snowballs at the audience and The Fourmost played a version of 'White Christmas', at one point doing a Beatles imitation by switching one of their guitars to the left hand.

One awful sketch was called 'What A Night', written by Peter and Ireland Cutter who wrote most of Laurel and

Hardy's material. John played Sir John Jasper, a moustache twirling, top hatted, whip carrying villain who threw Ermyntrude, the pathetic heroine, played by George in drag, into the path of an express train, named the "Beeching Express" after the current transport minister, infamous for cutting most of the branch line services in Britain. Ringo danced across the stage and sprinkled everyone with paper snow before

George was saved by the timely arrival of Fearless Paul the Signalman.

The Beatles were finally announced by a roll of drums from Ringo. They played 'Roll Over Beethoven', 'All My Loving', 'This Boy', 'I Wanna Be Your Man', 'She Loves You', 'Till There Was You', 'I Want To Hold Your Hand', 'Money (That's What I Want)' and ended, as usual, with 'Twist And Shout' sung by John. This show was repeated 30 times.

19**64**

January 1
– The Beatles continued their residency at the *Astoria Cinema, Finsbury Park, London*, with *The Beatles' Christmas Show.*
– A BBC clip of The Beatles singing 'She Loves You' was shown on TV's *The Jack Paar Show*, the first film of The Beatles shown to US audiences. Brian Epstein was angry with the BBC for selling the clip because it interfered with his own careful marketing strategy.

January 2
– *Astoria Cinema, Finsbury Park, London. The Beatles' Christmas Show.*

January 3
– *Astoria Cinema, Finsbury Park, London. The Beatles' Christmas Show.*

January 4
– *Astoria Cinema, Finsbury Park, London. The Beatles' Christmas Show.*

January 5
– George and Ringo recorded an interview for the BBC Light Programme magazine *The Public Ear* at their Green Street flat.
– *Astoria Cinema, Finsbury Park, London. The Beatles' Christmas Show.*

January 6
– *Astoria Cinema, Finsbury Park, London. The Beatles' Christmas Show.*

– Afterwards The Beatles went to the *Talk Of The Town*, on Charing Cross Road, to see Alma Cogan, but arrived too late and missed her performance.

January 7
– The Beatles recorded an appearance for Saturday Club at the *Playhouse Theatre, London.* They performed 'All My Loving', 'Money (That's What I Want)', 'The Hippy Hippy Shake', 'I Want To Hold Your Hand', 'Roll Over Beethoven', Johnny B. Goode' and 'I Wanna Be Your Man'.
– *Astoria Cinema, Finsbury Park, London. The Beatles' Christmas Show.*

January 8
– *Astoria Cinema, Finsbury Park, London. The Beatles' Christmas Show.*

January 9
– *Astoria Cinema, Finsbury Park, London. The Beatles' Christmas Show.*

January 10
– *Astoria Cinema, Finsbury Park, London. The Beatles' Christmas Show.*

January 11
– *Astoria Cinema, Finsbury Park, London.* The final night of *The Beatles' Christmas Show.*
– 'I Want To Hold Your Hand' entered the American Cashbox charts at number 80.

Above: Alma Cogan.
Right: With Bruce Forsyth at the London Palladium.

January 12
– *London Palladium*. The Beatles appeared on the ATV television variety show *Val Parnell's Sunday Night At The London Palladium* with Alma Cogan, Dave Allen and compere Bruce Forsyth. The Beatles played 'I Want To Hold Your Hand', 'This Boy', 'All My Loving', 'Money (That's What I Want)' and 'Twist And Shout'. As before, they appeared on the carousel at the end of the show where, by tradition, all the featured artists stood and waved goodbye as it slowly revolved.

This was their first meeting with Alma Cogan, who invited them back to her flat at Stafford Court in Kensington High Street which she shared with her mother and younger sister. They arrived at her flat long before she did as they made a quick getaway in their Austin Princess, leaving Alma to change in her dressing room, but her sister was there to greet them.

– George and Ringo's interview on *The Public Ear* was broadcast by the BBC Light Programme.

January 13
– The single **'I Want To Hold Your Hand'/'I Saw Her Standing There'** was released in the US as CAPITOL 5112. It went straight into the charts.

January 14
– At 5:15 pm The Beatles' Comet 4B left for Le Bouget airport, then the main Paris airport, to begin a three-week residency at the Paris Olympia. With them were Brian Epstein, Mal Evans and press representatives but not Ringo who was unable to meet the others in London that day because Liverpool airport was fogbound. London was also blanketed, but by late afternoon it had lifted enough for the rest of the group to get to France.

The Beatles' Austin Princess was at the airport to meet them, as were 60 fans and the press. More fans were waiting at the George V Hotel, filling the lobby. That evening, Bruno Coquatrix, the director of the Olympia, called in to see them, as did a representative from their French record label, Odeon.

Sunday Night at the London Palladium.

George: "We miss the **screams,**
but the audiences are great.
Now roll on **America."**

John and Paul shared a suite because they were committed to writing six new songs for their forthcoming film, a song for Billy J. Kramer and one for Tommy Quickly. They had a piano brought in and got to work while George had a night out on the town at the Club Eve.

January 15
– John and Paul got up around noon as usual and ate a regular English breakfast of orange juice, cornflakes, scrambled eggs and a pot of tea. A stroll down the Champs Elysées brought a crowd of photographers and sightseers but they were driven back to the hotel before it got out of hand. Ringo arrived on the five o'clock flight. That night they did a try-out concert at the Cyrano Theatre in Versailles with all the other artists who would be appearing on the Olympia bill: Trini Lopez, Sylvie Vartan and a full music hall variety act including a juggler. Lopez closed the first half. Sylvie Vartan preceded The Beatles, an unenviable position. The show began at nine and lasted until after midnight with French fans dancing in the aisles and chanting for "Les Beat-les!". In France they drew a male crowd rather than female, and because there was much less screaming they could actually hear the music. Next day the press reported their every move.
– In New York, DJ Scott Muni reported that he had received more than 12,000 applications for a Beatles fan club.

January 17
– *Olympia Theatre, Paris.* The afternoon matinée was sold out to fans whereas the evening audience was made up of more expensively dressed, older Parisians who wanted to see what all the fuss was about. The ancient music hall was not equipped for modern amplification and the fuses blew three times as the theatre could not supply enough power for their amps. Mal rushed on stage to make emergency repairs. There were no screams or shrieks, but the audience clapped in time and appreciated the music.
The audience was well behaved, but

backstage a riot was going on. Cameramen were everywhere and an argument erupted when a French photographer was not allowed in to take exclusive pictures. A fight broke out which spilled onto the stage. George had to move quickly to prevent his guitar from being damaged by the brawling mob and Paul stopped singing to call for order. Gendarmes arrived and added to the chaos. No-one was allowed backstage for the remaining dates.

The Olympia was in many ways a dry run for Carnegie Hall, Epstein's policy being to book his group into the most prestigious venues possible. The Olympia was the best music hall in France, where the first night guaranteed an audience in full evening dress, minks and diamonds. It was a beautiful, classic theatre with sumptuous furnishings. However, the dressing room was tiny and the Olympia was unused to Beatlemania: people with tickets had been prohibited from entering the theatre, whereas others found someone already in their seats. It was chaos. The theatre was ringed with armed police and beyond them a cordon of fans chanting "Beat-les, Beat-les, Beat-les!" As the group left the stage a few more punches were exchanged. Predictably, French chauvinism showed in the press reports the next day, though *France Soir* suggested that French pop idols must be jealous because never before had the French clapped along so loudly with the beat.

January 18
– *Olympia Theatre, Paris.*
January 19
– *Olympia Theatre, Paris.* Three sets. The matinée was broadcast live on the Paris station Europe-1's *Musicorama* show. The songs performed were 'From Me To You', 'This Boy', 'I Want To Hold Your Hand', 'She Loves You' and 'Twist And Shout'.
January 20
– *Olympia Theatre, Paris.*
– Europe-1 broadcast an interview with The Beatles.
– The album MEET THE BEATLES was released in the US as CAPITOL ST 2047.

Above: John and Ringo with Brian Epstein at the George V in Paris.

Number One in America

On the evening of January 17 a telephone call brought the news that 'I Want To Hold Your Hand' had reached number one in America. It had taken only three weeks to reach the top position. Road manager Mal Evans reported that the group went mad: "They always act this way when anything big happens – just a bunch of kids, jumping up and down with sheer delight. Paul climbed on my back demanding a piggyback. They felt that this was the biggest thing that could have happened. And who could blame them? Gradually they quietened down, ordered some more drinks and sat down to appreciate fully what happened. It was a wonderful, marvellous night for all of them. I was knocked out..." The Beatles celebrated until 5 am.

Up until now, only a handful of British acts had ever made the charts in the US; the UK was a wasteland for popular music as far as American record buyers were concerned. The Beatles changed all that and opened the door for a tidal wave of British acts which transformed the face of American popular music forever, destroying the old Brill-Building Tin-Pan-Alley tradition and heralding the idea that popular music could be something other than mere "entertainment".

Beatlemania was hotting up in the US in the classic showbusiness manner: a flurry of lawsuits. *Billboard* reported, "The Beatles, the nation's hottest recording property today, are becoming the object of the nation's hottest lawsuits. The rock'n'rolling English group has a series of singles and LPs out on three labels – Capitol, Vee Jay and Swan. And each is becoming involved in a series of suits and countersuits between the various companies." Dealers across the country were receiving telegrams from one or more of the companies threatening that legal action would be taken if they persisted in selling the other's product.

Meanwhile, WABC's Beatles fan club was receiving between 2,000 and 3,000 letters a day and *Cashbox* was predicting, "Won't be long before every group with long hair will be sought by American companies."

Sightseeing on the Champs Elysees on January 15, the day before the Paris Olympia opening.

SIDE A: 'I Want To Hold Your Hand', 'I Saw Her Standing There', 'This Boy', 'It Won't Be Long', 'All I've Got To Do', 'All My Loving';
SIDE B: 'Don't Bother Me', 'Little Child', 'Till There Was You', 'Hold Me Tight', 'I Wanna Be Your Man', 'Not A Second Time'.

January 22
– *Olympia Theatre, Paris.*

January 23
– *Olympia Theatre, Paris.*

January 24
– *Olympia Theatre, Paris.*
– The Beatles recorded an interview for American Forces Network (AFN) in their Paris studio.

January 25
– *Olympia Theatre, Paris.*
– AFN broadcast their interview with The Beatles in the show *Weekend World*. *Cashbox* magazine finally hits the stands showing 'I Want To Hold Your Hand' at number one, up from number 43. It was number three in Billboard, up from 45.

January 26
– *Olympia Theatre, Paris.*

January 27
– The single **'My Bonnie'/'The Saints'** by Tony Sheridan & The Beatles was released in the US as MGM K 13213.
– The album INTRODUCING THE BEATLES was released in the US as VEE JAY VJLP 1062.

SIDE A: 'I Saw Her Standing There', 'Misery', 'Anna (Go To Him)', 'Chains', 'Boys', 'Ask Me Why';
SIDE B: 'Please, Please Me', 'Baby It's You', 'Do You Want To Know A Secret', 'A Taste Of Honey', 'There's A Place', 'Twist And Shout'.

January 28
– John and George flew back to London on their second day off from the Olympia. George had dinner with Phil Spector and The Ronettes.

January 29
– John and George flew to Paris on the early morning flight.
– At the *Pathé Marconi Studio* in Paris The Beatles recorded 'Can't Buy Me Love' and German language versions of 'I Want To Hold Your Hand' and 'She Loves You'.
– *Olympia Theatre, Paris.*
– The single 'Do You Want To Know A Secret'/'Bad To Me' by Billy J. Kramer & The Dakotas, written by Lennon & McCartney, was released in the US as LIBERTY 55667.

January 30
– *Olympia Theatre, Paris.*
– The single **'Please, Please Me'/'From Me To You'** was released in the US as VEE JAY VJ 581.

January 31
– *Olympia Theatre, Paris.*
– The single **'Sweet Georgia Brown'** by Tony Sheridan & The Beatles was

British European Airways, now BA, incorporated their own logo with the name of the group on The Beatles' hand luggage.

released in the UK as POLYDOR NH 52-906. The track was recorded in May 1961 in Hamburg but Sheridan added a new vocal track in 1963 for this release.

February 1
– *Olympia Theatre, Paris.*

February 2
– *Olympia Theatre, Paris.*

February 3
– The Beatles visited the American Embassy in Paris to obtain visas and work permits.
– *Olympia Theatre, Paris.*

February 4
– *Olympia Theatre, Paris.*

February 5
– The Beatles returned to London from Paris and held the usual press conference at the airport.

February 7
– The EP **All My Loving** was released in the UK as PARLOPHONE GEP 8891.
SIDE A: **'All My Loving', 'Ask Me Why';**
SIDE B: **'Money (That's What I Want)', 'P.S. I Love You'.**
– The Beatles flew to New York City on Pan Am flight 101, where 3,000 fans were waiting at JFK airport. Their party consisted of Paul, Ringo, George, John and Cynthia plus Neil Aspinall, Mal Evans, publicist Brian Sommerville, Brian Epstein and record producer Phil Spector. The group were unusually subdued. Ringo told *Liverpool Post* reporter George Harrison (no relation):

The German singles

German EMI, Electrola Gesellschaft, insisted that The Beatles would not get large sales in that country unless the lyrics were sung in German. The Beatles thought this was nonsense, and so did George Martin, but he did not want to give them an excuse for not doing their best to sell Beatles records. He managed to persuade John and Paul to re-record 'She Loves You' and 'I Want To Hold Your Hand' in German. Someone from Electrola Gesellschaft translated the lyrics and was on hand at the recording to make sure the accents didn't sound like a comedy

record. George Martin turned up at the studio in Paris on January 27 but The Beatles did not. After an hour's wait – a not unusual delay for The Beatles – Martin called the George Cinq Hotel, but none of them would come to the telephone. They told Neil Aspinall to inform George Martin that they would not be coming. A furious George Martin told Neil, "You just tell them I'm coming right over to let them know exactly what I think of them." Not long afterwards he burst into the drawing room of The Beatles' suite where, as he described it, the scene was one straight out of Lewis Carroll:

"Around a long table sat John, Paul, George, Ringo, Neil Aspinall and Mal Evans, his assistant. In the centre, pouring tea, was Jane Asher, a beautiful Alice with long golden hair. At my appearance, the whole tableau exploded. Beatles ran in all directions, hiding behind sofas, cushions, the piano... 'You bastards,' I yelled. 'I don't care if you record or not, but I do care about your rudeness!'"

The Beatles slowly reappeared and muttered sheepish apologies. Two days later they cut the German language version of the songs.

"They've got **everything** over there, will they want **US** too?"

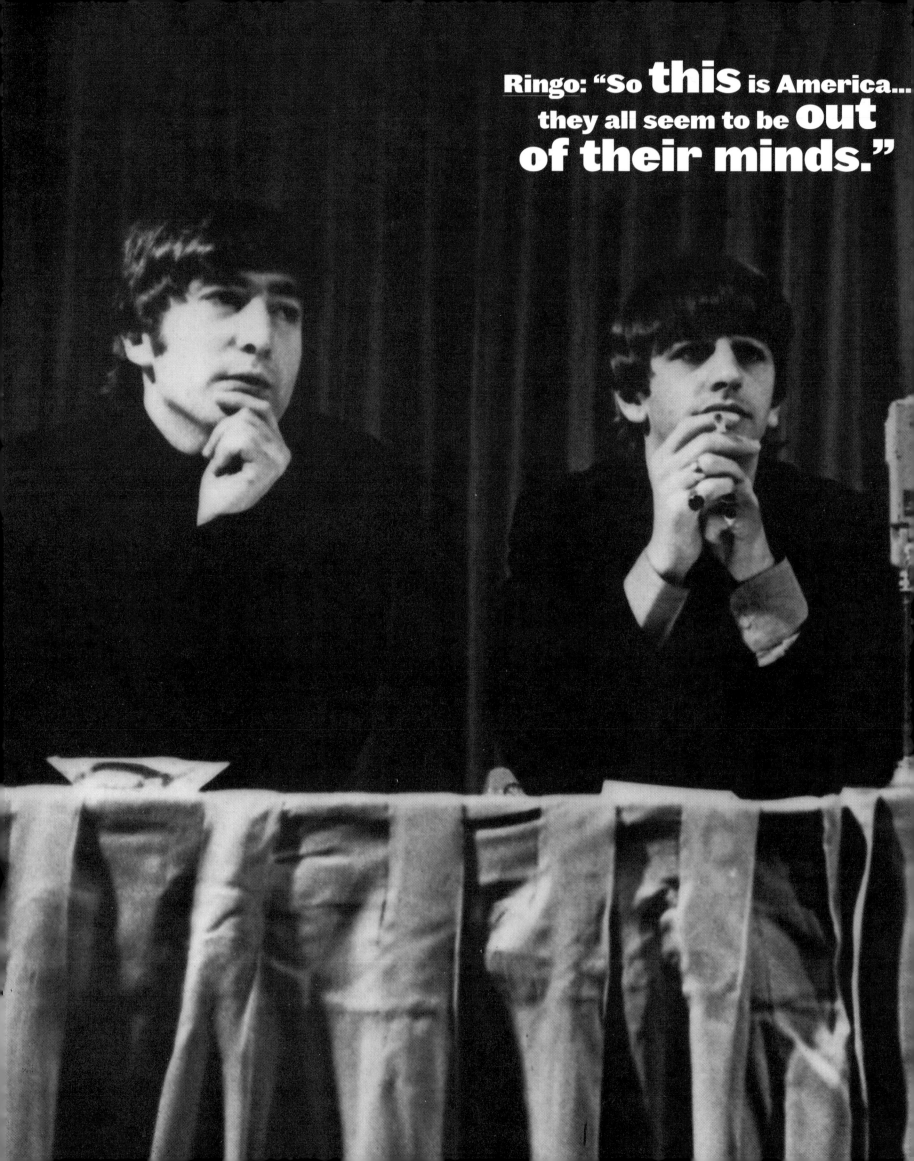

Ringo: "So **this** is America... they all seem to be **out** of their minds."

Paul: "What have **we** got to give a country like America? Yes, I know that we've got a record at the top of **the charts**, but that doesn't mean that they'll go for **us personally**, does it?"

"We love you Beat-les, oh yes we dooo! We love you Beat-les and we'll be true!"

During the rehearsal for The Beatles' appearance on the Ed Sullivan Show in New York Neil Aspinall substituted for George who was in bed with a sore throat.

They needn't have worried. Ed Sullivan had already received 50,000 applications for tickets to his show which only seated 728, and fans had been gathering at JFK since the previous afternoon.

The Beatles' Boeing 707 touched down at 1:20 pm to scenes never before witnessed at Kennedy. It was a cold clear day. Five thousand fans, mostly young girls taking a day off school, were crowded four deep on the upper arcade of the arrivals building, waving "We Love You Beatles" placards and home-made banners welcoming The Beatles to America.

In addition to the screaming teenagers, they were met by over 200 reporters and photographers from radio, television, magazines and newspapers.

The Beatles themselves thought at first that the President's plane was about to land, then it dawned on them: the reception was for them.

For days the radio stations had been whipping the fans into a frenzy, and it was Murray the K at 1010 WINS who first announced the supposedly secret details of their airline, time of arrival and flight number. The information was quickly repeated on WINS rival stations: WABC and WMCA.

Over 100 yelling journalists were waiting for the group as they emerged from immigration, and at first they couldn't see for the flash bulbs. "So this is America," said Ringo. "They all seem to be out of their minds." – The scene at the Plaza, New York's grandest hotel, was chaotic with hundreds of fans being held at bay by police barricades and 20 mounted police. They kept up a constant mantra-like chant, interspersed with shouts of "We want The Beatles!" That evening

"We've never seen **anything** like this before, **ever.** Never. Not even for **kings** and **queens.**"
AIRPORT OFFICIAL, JFK

a stream of guests visited the ten-room Presidential suite, including The Ronettes, DJ Murray the K and George's sister, Louise, who lived in Illinois but had flown in to see him. – The Beatles recorded an interview with Brian Matthew on the telephone from the BBC in London to be broadcast the next morning on *Saturday Club.* Then they looked at some of their fan mail: 100,000 letters were waiting for them when they arrived in New York.

February 8
– Another press conference was held in the Plaza's Baroque Room. Afterwards John, Paul and Ringo went for a photo-opportunity walkabout in Central Park followed by about 400 girls. George had strep throat and stayed inside, tended by his sister Louise Caldwell.

At 1:30 pm The Beatles travelled by limousines to CBS studios at 53rd Street for a sound check. On the way, fans charged at the cars en masse and it was up to mounted police to get them through. The studios themselves were guarded by 52 police officers and ten mounted police. At the studios The Beatles had to join AFRA (the US equivalent of the Musicians' Union) and sign forms. Neil Aspinall stood in for George at the camera position run-through for the next day's live show. The studio staff were surprised when The Beatles asked to hear a playback of their rehearsal; no other musical act had ever bothered. The Beatles were interviewed by The Ronettes.

That evening John, Paul and Ringo went to the 21 restaurant for dinner with Capitol Records executives.

The road to New York

Tom Wolfe, writing in the *New York Herald Tribune* reported on The Beatles' arrival in his customary style, noticing the small details which characterised the event: [Though in fact Paul, George and Ringo took one limo, John another and Brian was left to hail a cab to get to town].

"The Beatles left the airport in four Cadillac limousines, one Beatle to a limousine, heading for the Plaza Hotel in Manhattan. The first sortie came almost immediately. Five kids in a powder blue Ford overtook the caravan on the expressway, and as they passed each Beatle, one guy hung out the back window and waved a red blanket.

"A white convertible came up second, with the word BEETLES scratched on both sides in the dust. A police car was close behind that one with the siren going and the alarm light rolling, but the kids, a girl at the wheel and two guys in the back seat, waved at each Beatle before pulling over to exit with

the cops gesturing at them.

"In the second limousine, Brian Sommerville, The Beatles' press agent, said to one of The Beatles, George Harrison: 'Did you see that, George?' Harrison looked at the convertable with its emblem in the dust and said, 'They misspelled Beatles.'

"But the third sortie

succeeded all the way. A good – looking brunette, who said her name was Caroline Reynolds of New Canaan, Conn., and Wellesley College, had paid a cab driver $10 to follow the caravan all the way into town. She cruised by each Beatle, smiling vainly, and finally caught up with George Harrison's limousine at a light at Third

Avenue and 63rd Street.

"'How does one go about meeting a Beatle?' she said out the window.

"'One says hello,' Harrison said out the window.

"'Hellow!' she said. 'Eight more will be down from Wellesley.' Then the light changed and the caravan was off again."

George Martin joined them. The Beatles ate chops whereas executives ate pheasant. Paul ate crepe suzettes. Back at the hotel they listened to the radio till late at night.

– That morning The Beatles' recorded telephone interview with Brian Matthew was broadcast on BBC Light Programme's *Saturday Club*.

February 9

– *Studio 50, West 53rd Street.* Rehearsals for the *Ed Sullivan Show* took up the morning. In the afternoon The Beatles recorded numbers for another *Ed Sullivan Show* to be broadcast after they had left the country. This would be their third show – their first was to be done live that evening and the second was to be a live show from Florida on February 16. For the "third" show, they recorded 'Twist And Shout', 'Please, Please Me' and 'I Want To Hold Your Hand'. There was a different audience for the third show recording than that which attended the live transmission that evening. Other guests included Gordon and Sheila MacRae and The Cab Calloway Orchestra.

That evening, for the 8 pm live show, The Beatles performed 'All My Loving', 'Till There Was You' and 'She Loves You' followed by an Anadin advert. Then came Ed's other guests – Georgia Brown & Oliver Kidds, Frank Gorshin, Tessie O'Shea – and the show closed after a Kent cigarette advert with 'I Saw Her Standing There' and 'I Want To Hold Your Hand'. Thirteen-and-a-half minutes of television had changed the face of American popular music. The Nielsen ratings showed that 73,700,000 people had watched The Beatles on Ed Sullivan, not just the largest audience that Sullivan had ever had, but the largest audience in the history of television.

Half an hour before they appeared on stage, Brian Sommerville handed them a telegram: "Congratulations on your appearance on the Ed Sullivan Show and your visit to America. We hope your engagement will be a successful one and your visit pleasant. Give our best to Mr. Sullivan. Sincerely, Elvis & The Colonel." George read the telegram and asked, deadpan, "Elvis who?"

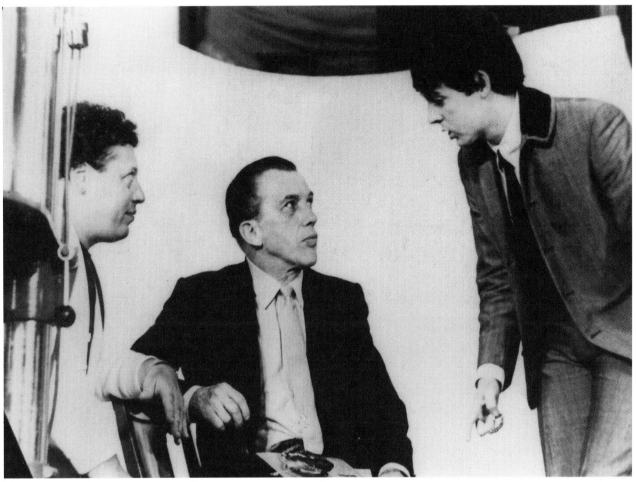

Above: Paul with Ed Sullivan. Below: Ringo at the Peppermint Lounge.

After the show Murray the K took The Beatles, minus George who still had a sore throat, to the Playboy Club. **Paul: "The bunnies are even more adorable than we are."** Protected by a police escort, they risked walking the few blocks to 59th Street where they were quickly ushered up to the Penthouse lounge for dinner. Afterwards they went on to the Peppermint Lounge, home of the Twist, where Ringo excelled at twisting to Beatles tunes with a young dancer called Geri Miller. They left at 4 am.

February 10

– The day was taken up with press interviews and presentations. At one ceremony, Capitol Records president Alan Livingstone presented The Beatles with golden discs to mark the sale of a million copies of 'I Want To Hold Your Hand' and a million dollars worth of sales of the album Meet The Beatles. The evening was spent at

clubs. Once again, they returned to the Plaza at 4 am.

February 11

– A snow storm blanketed the East Coast and all flights were cancelled so a special carriage was attached to the Pennsylvania Railroad express, the Congressman, to take them to Washington, DC. The carriage, an old Richmond, Fredericksburg and Potomac Railroad sleeper car called The King George, was already filled with press when they arrived, and at each stop, more cameramen poked their lenses through the windows. Two thousand fans braved eight inches of snow to welcome them at Washington's Union Station. There was a press conference then they visited WWDC, the first American radio station to play a Beatles record, where they were interviewed by DJ Carroll James. He asked about their influences:

John: "Small Blind Johnny."
Carroll James: "Small Blind Johnny?"
John: "Oh yes, he played with Big Deaf Arthur."
Carroll James: "John, they call you the chief Beatle…"
John: "Carroll. I don't call you names!"
Carroll James: "Excluding America and England, what are your favourite countries you've visited?"
John: "Excluding America and England, what's left?"

The party checked into The Shoreham Hotel, taking the whole of the seventh floor which was sealed off from the fans. One family refused the leave their rooms on the seventh floor so the hotel cut off the central heating, hot water and electricity, telling them that there had been a power failure. The disgruntled family moved.

A total of 8,092 fans, mostly girls, saw the show at the *Washington Coliseum*, protected by 362 police officers, one of whom found the volume so loud he stuck a bullet in each ear as ear plugs. The Beatles' set consisted of: 'Roll Over Beethoven', 'From Me To You', 'I Saw Her Standing There', 'This Boy', 'All My Loving', 'I Wanna Be Your Man', 'Please, Please Me', 'Till There Was You', 'She Loves You', 'I Want To Hold Your Hand', 'Twist And Shout' and 'Long Tall Sally'. Also on the bill were The Chiffons and Tommy Roe.

Above: John plays up to the camera and Paul fools around with a Beatle wig at the Peppermint lounge.

Paul: "Most exciting yet."

The Embassy incident

After the February 11 show there was a reception at the British Embassy, given by Lady Ormsby-Gore. There had been a formal dance to benefit The National Association for the Prevention of Cruelty to Children, and The Beatles were required to hand out the raffle prizes at the end of the affair. The British community, arrogant debutantes and aristocrats, disgraced themselves, and one woman even snipped off a lock of Ringo's hair just behind his left ear. John pushed all the autograph seekers away saying, "These people have no bloody manners," and grabbing Ringo, said, "I'm getting out of here." Ringo calmed him down, they did their stuff and left. Brian was told firmly never to expose them to that kind of gathering again.

February 12

– The Beatles took the two-hour train ride back to New York but their limousine could not get through the waiting crowds of fans. It was Lincoln's birthday, a public holiday, so school was out and 10,000 fans were waiting at Penn Station. They had to be spirited back to the hotel by normal New York City yellow cabs. After a quick shave, shower and change of clothes, they were smuggled out of the Plaza down the back elevator and out through the kitchens in order to get to nearby *Carnegie Hall* for a double header at the most prestigious venue in the country. The audience was warmed up by a folk'n'roll group called The Briarwoods. Backstage they received a gold disc from Swan Records for selling a million copies of 'She Loves You'. Shirley Bassey was among their visitors.

– Promoter Sid Bernstein took Brian Epstein outside into the snow laden air after the show and offered him $25,000 plus a $5,000 donation to the British Cancer Fund for a *Madison Square Garden* concert in a few days time. Tickets could be printed and would sell out at once, he assured Brian. **"Let's leave this for next time,"** said Brian.

That night, their last in New York City, they left the Plaza at 1:30 am to visit the Headliner Club and then the Improvisation coffee house in Greenwich Village. They returned at dawn and a reporter who was still waiting outside asked if it had been a quiet night.

– Granada Television screened *Yeah, Yeah, Yeah! – The Beatles In New York*, an instant documentary by the Maysles Brothers.

Paul: "No. We met **Stella Stevens, Tuesday Weld** and **Jill Haworth –** and they're not exactly **quiet** girls."

February 13

– National Airlines Flight 11 left New York at 1.30 pm, and arrived at Miami at 4 pm. At Miami there were 7,000 fans waiting, whipped into a frenzy by rival radio stations WFUN and WQAM who announced their arrival time, but The Beatles leapt straight from the plane into a waiting limousine and were off to the Deauville Hotel in Miami Beach. Their convoy of three black limousines had motorcycle outriders front and back and made the eight miles of expressway into the city in record time, going through red lights, driving on the wrong side of the road, as fans lining the streets cheered and waved.

– Murray the K accompanied them, and even shared a room with George in their three-bedroom suite, guarded by Pinkerton detectives. (Disgruntled George never figured out how the pushy New York DJ had pulled that one off.) That evening they visited the Mau Mau Lounge where they saw The Coasters and danced the "Mashed Potato". Murray the K took them to see Hank Ballard and The Midnighters at the Miami Peppermint Lounge. There they were besieged by autograph hunters so they didn't stay long.

– After being inundated with requests, Granada Television repeated *Yeah, Yeah, Yeah! – The Beatles In New York* by the Maysles Brothers.

February 14

– A short rehearsal for the *Ed Sullivan Show*. A photo session for *Life* magazine in the swimming pool at the home of a Capitol Records executive, followed by a tour round Miami Harbour in a luxury houseboat provided by a Bernard Castro. Two reporters were found to have stowed away and the boat returned to shore to put them off. Their private bodyguard, Sgt Buddy Bresner, took them home to meet his wife and kids – Dottie, Barry, Andy and Jeri – and fed them a typical American meal: roast beef, green beans, baked potatoes, peas, salad and a huge strawberry ice cake. That evening they stayed in the hotel, taking in the floor shows in the hotel's night clubs: first comedian Don Rickells, then Myron Cohen and singer Carol Lawrence. They had no dinner because Bresner's massive lunch had filled them up.

February 15

– The group, wearing swimming trunks, rehearsed in the hotel's Napoleon Room. At 2 pm The Beatles did a dress rehearsal for *the Ed Sullivan Show* before an audience of 2,500, many of whom had queued outside since early morning. The rest of the day was spent fishing.

(THE *Morning* KANSAS CITY STAR)

The Kansas City Times

★ ★ ★   KANSAS CITY, FRIDAY, SEPTEMBER 18, 1964—

Police Hold Tide of Beatlemania

[ADDITIONAL STORIES AND PICTURES ON PAGES 3, 8 AND 20.]

By Robert K. Sanford
(A Member of The Star's Staff)

WHEN the announcer said, "The Beatles!" and the four British singers bounced onto the stage a concerted scream rose in Municipal Stadium and hundreds of flashbulbs lit the park like harsh fireflies.

The scream tore on and on. The performers, jolly and jaunty, sounded some practice guitar chords, said "Ha" and "Hi" into the microphones and abruptly ripped into a tune called "Twist and Shout."

The scream, from an audience of 20,280, reached frightening intensity. A man smoking a cigar in the front row put his hands over his ears and puffed.

The Beatles played for 31 minutes, 12 songs perhaps, and only as they left did the screaming die, sinking into a mournful moan.

"They are gone, gone," a girl said. "I'll never see them again."

And so the night of the Beatles, the biggest entertainment promotion in the area in the memory of many of the teen-agers who attended, came and passed.

Physically, it was accomplished rather efficiently, with a line of 100 policemen separating the crowd from the bandstand. No one was hurt. There were no crushing stampedes, no ugly incidents.

Many Seats Empty

The crowd did not fill the 41,000 seats arranged for the event, but it was a sizable crowd in any estimate, one of the four or five biggest crowds to see the Beatles on their American tour.

The spectators were from several states, and their cars were directed and their property and limbs protected by about 350 police in the stadium area.

The spectators were admonished several times previous to the Beatles' appearance to stay in their seats or the show would be stopped. By and large they did. Only at the end, when the Beatles were rushed from the field in a black limousine, did a section of several hundred teen-age girls rush to the line of policemen. They yelled goodbye and waved.

One of the quartet raised a hand in farewell in the back window of the car as it sped away. Then the girls began to cry.

Finley Loses Money

Charles O. Finley, owner of the Kansas City Athletics and the man who brought the Beatles here for $150,000, lost money. He did not make a public appearance at the show. His manager, Pat Friday, gave a check for $25,000 to Children's Mercy hospital although no profit was made on the venture.

An Athletics official said ticket sales of about 28,000 were needed to break even. The gate was estimated at something more than $100,000, but considerably short of the $150,000.

Finley said he was delighted with the performance and that he considered the behavior of Kansas City teen-agers indeed commendable. He praised the work of the police and of U. M. K. C. and Rockhurst college students who acted as ushers.

So, concerning the physical aspects—the security, the traffic, the crowds—all went well. Reason prevailed.

Some Worn Out

But the event left some of the Beatle followers emotionally torn. As the crowds left the park, fully 10 minutes after all the shouting, there were groups of exhausted girls still seated in the playing field area and the stands. They were crying.

Why?

"Because they (the B's) just left and didn't say anything," a girl explained, rubbing her eyes. "Now they are gone forever."

"Ah, they'll be back again," a policeman said.

"What do you care?" the girl wept. "You were down in front there and you didn't care and I was way back here and I couldn't even get close to them. . ."

"Now wait a minute, honey," he said. "It's not my fault."

Then he walked away.

Ear Stoppers Needed

Many of the policemen who manned the barricade in front of the blaring loudspeakers put cotton in their ears. For others not so well prepared, the sound of the mass scream —a fearful sound because it seems out of control—will linger, not gently, in their memory.

The Beatle music, the incessant beat and the hard blare of electric guitars pushed to volume limits, can be heard on jukeboxes in a hundred thousand joints and drugstores. The scream had no volume control.

Scarlett Peterson, 14, Topeka, sat on the front row with no shoes and wore a button that said, "I Love Paul." (That's Paul McCartney. The others are Ringo Starr, George Harrison and John Lennon).

Why the button?

"Because Paul is left-handed like me and plays bass guitar and has brown eyes and black hair."

With blue-tipped fingernails she pushed back a lock of her blond hair.

"You'll have to get out of our seats, girls," a woman said. "These are our seats."

Scarlett and her friends walked out, unoffended.

A girl with a legitimate front-row seat was Tina Mitchell, 15, of 7205 Flora avenue, president of the Leabets (Beatles spelled inside-out), the Kansas City fan club. She thought the show was grand and she had grand news.

A friend with her, Vicki Mucie, 14, of 3545 Warwick boulevard, had come into ownership of a cigarette butt that Paul reportedly had smoked at the afternoon press conference downtown.

What was she going to do with it?

"I'm going to frame it along with a jelly bean that John stepped on in Denver when I saw them there."

It was a yellow jelly bean and the cigarette butt was filter-tipped.

Yes, jelly beans were thrown at the Beatles in their Kansas City performance, too. Why? Because the Beatles love jelly beans, silly.

There were stories of great sacrifice and effort among the followers. Mary Jo Berger, 15, Edwardsville, Ill., carried a sign which she tried to show to the Beatles and was told to go back to her seat.

The sign said:
"You're the greatest
"Charlie O.
"For you got us
"Dear Ringo.
"I wish I may
"I wish I might
"Get to talk to
"Him tonight."

One of Mary Jo's friends from Edwardsville chose to walk out of the stadium with one shoe on and one shoe off. Why?

"Because sometime when they were singing I suddenly found my shoe in my hand."

The Beatles left the stadium at 9:15 o'clock. At 11:13 o'clock their airplane left the ground at Municipal Air Terminal on the way to Dallas.

Most of the time before they left they spent in the plane, passengers in the world of aviation, where, experts tell us, as in all of life, the noise level is increasing every year.

BEATLEMANIA IN KANSAS CITY—Appeared thus last night as 20,208 screaming spectators—most of them teen-age girls—cheered their idols during a 31-minute performance at the Municipal Stadium. Many of the girls were weeping when the performance was over. Four other acts took up the rest of the 2-hour show.

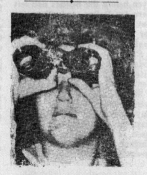

BEATLEMANIA ANALYZED

Frightening, Says Child Expert

By DR. BERNARD SAIBEL

The experience of being with 14,000 teen-agers to see the Beatles is unbelievable and frightening.

And, believe me, it is not at all funny, as I first thought when I accepted this assignment.

THE HYSTERIA and loss of control go far beyond the impact of the music. Many of those present became frantic, hostile, uncontrolled, screaming, unrecognizable beings.

If this is possible — and it is — **parents and adults have a lot to account for to allow this to go on.**

This is not simply a release, as I at first thought it would be, but a very destructive process in which adults allow the children to be involved — allowing the children a mad, erotic world of their own without the reassuring safeguards of protection from themselves.

THE EXTERNALS are terrifying. Normally recognizable girls behaved as if possessed by some demonic urge, defying in emotional ecstacy the restraints which authorities try to place on them.

The hysteria is from the girls and when you ask them what it is all about, all they can say is: "I love them."

Some, restrained from getting up on the stage after the Beatles left, asked me to touch the drums for them.

THERE ARE A LOT of things you can say about why the Beatles attract the teen-age crowd.

The music is loud, primitive, insistent, strongly rhythmic and releases in a disguised way (can it be called sublimation?) the all too tenuously controlled, newly acquired physical impulses of the teen-ager.

Mix this up with the phenomena of mass hypnosis, contagious hysteria and the blissful feeling of being mixed up in an all-embracing, orgiastic experience and every kid can become "Lord of the Flies" or the Beatles.

What is it all about?

Why do the kids scream, faint, gyrate and in general look like a primeval, protoplasmic upheaval and go into ecstatic convulsions when **certain** identifiable and expected trade-marks come forth such as "Oh, yeah!" a twist of the hips or the thrusting out of an electric guitar?

WELL, THIS MUSIC (and the bizarre, gnome - like, fairy - tale characters who play it) belongs to the kids and is their own—different, they think, from anything that belongs to the adult world.

Besides, kids, like the other separate and distinct parts of humanity, are competitive. If there is a youngster who can scream loudly, there is one who can scream louder.

If there is one who belongs to the cognoscenti (those in the know), there is one who is more sensitive and more appreciative of this art than any of the others. And to prove it, she faints and all can see how much more affected she is, because she has to be carried out on a stretcher — a martyr, a victim of her capacity for deep understanding and overwhelming emotion.

REGARDLESS OF the causes or reasons for the behavior of these youngsters last night, it had the impact of an unholy bedlam, the like of which I have never seen. It caused me to feel that such should not be allowed again, if only for the good of the youngsters.

It was an orgy for teenagers.

DR. BERNARD SAIBEL, lower center, SURROUNDED BY SCENES OF FRENZY
Child-guidance expert wore look of concern.

Limousine Besieged

MOB SCENE: Teen-agers swarmed on and around the Beatles' limousine yesterday afternoon as the automobile entered the Edgewater Inn a few minutes after their arrival in Seattle. Several girls flung themselves onto the car and pounded on the windows.

– ABC TV's Dick Clark's *American Bandstand* broadcast a telephone interview with the group.

February 16

– *The Ed Sullivan Show* was done in the Deauville Hotel itself. CBS gave out 3,500 tickets when the hall only held 2,600. The police had to deal with riots when fans holding perfectly valid tickets were turned away. The group played, 'She Loves You', 'This Boy', 'All My Loving', 'I Saw Her Standing There', 'From Me To You' and 'I Want To Hold Your Hand'. Joe Louis and Sonny Liston were both in the audience. Mitzi Gaynor topped the bill but the 70,000,000 viewers were mostly tuned in to watch The Beatles.

The owner of the hotel, Maurice Lansberg, gave a small party for the performers and technicians on the show. Self-service: lobster, beef, chicken, and fish.

February 17

– The Beatles tried their hand at water-skiing.

Above: With boxer Cassius Clay, soon to become known as Muhammad Ali, at his training camp in Miami. Below: Ringo in Miami.

– The single 'I Wanna be Your Man' by The Rolling Stones, written by Lennon & McCartney, was released in the US as London 9641.

February 18

– On their day off, The Beatles, probably at Paul's instigation, requested a visit to Cassius Clay's training camp where he was preparing for his rematch with the champion, Sonny Liston. The photographers went crazy as ex-heavyweight champ Clay picked up Ringo as if he weighed only a few ounces.

– They had a barbecue in the grounds of a millionaire's home, eating the biggest steaks they had ever seen, and tried their hand with speedboats. That evening they went to a drive-in movie, where they saw Elvis Presley's *Fun In Acapulco*.

February 21

– The Beatles returned to London from Miami, via New York.

February 22

– The Beatles arrived back in London at 8:10 am to a tumultuous welcome. They gave a press conference in the Kingsford-Smith suite at the airport which was shown by BBC TV later as part of the sports programme *Grandstand*. News of their return was also featured on radio news and other programmes.

Paul spent the evening in Canterbury, seeing Jane Asher act in *The Jew Of Malta*.

February 23

– *ABC TV's Teddington Studio Centre.* Without even a day off to get over jet-lag, The Beatles taped an appearance for Mike & Bernie Winters' variety show *Big Night Out* before a live audience. They appeared in various skits, including a river cruise which was also filmed by ITN and used in its news bulletin that evening. They mimed to 'All My Loving', 'I Wanna Be Your Man', 'Till There Was You', 'Please Mister Postman', 'Money (That's What I Want)', and 'I Want To Hold Your Hand'.

Afterwards they went to an all-night party at Alma Cogan's apartment in Kensington.
– The Beatles' third appearance on the *Ed Sullivan Show* was screened.

February 24
– Ringo went to Liverpool to see his family.

February 25
– Ringo took the first flight from Liverpool to London to attend a recording session.
– *Abbey Road.* They finished 'Can't Buy Me Love', recorded 'You Can't Do That' and began work on Paul's 'And I Love Her' and John's 'I Should Have Known Better'.
– George's 21st birthday. He received 52 mail-sacks holding about 30,000 cards. Two fans sent him a door so that he could use one of the thousands of 21st keys he was sent.

February 26
– *Abbey Road.* Further work on 'And I Love Her' and 'I Should Have Known Better'.

February 27
– *Abbey Road.* 'And I Love Her' was finished, plus complete recordings made of John's 'Tell Me Why' and 'If I Fell'.

February 28
– *BBC Studios at 201 Piccadilly.* The Beatles recorded a second *From Us To You* bank holiday special for the Light Programme. The group was interviewed by Alan ("Fluff") Freeman and taped 'You Can't Do That', 'Roll Over Beethoven', 'Till There Was You', 'I Wanna Be Your Man', 'Please Mister Postman', 'All My Loving', 'This Boy' and 'Can't Buy Me Love'. As before they taped their own version of the show's theme tune *From Us To You* to open and close the programme.
– The single 'A World Without Love' by Peter & Gordon was released in the UK as COLUMBIA DB 7225. It had been written by John and Paul and given to Jane Asher's brother who had just received a record contract from EMI.
– The single **'Why'/'Cry For A Shadow'** by Tony Sheridan & The Beatles (A-side) and The Beatles (B-side) was released in the UK as POLYDOR NH 52-275.

Jane Asher: "The song came up one night when Paul and John were round at our home. They hadn't really finished it, but Peter and Gordon were mad keen about it right away. So the boys worked on it."

Above: Peter and Gordon. Right: On March 2 The Beatles' Hard Day's Night train passes through Taunton where Paul acknowledges an older fan.

February 29
– ABC TV's *Mike and Bernie Winters' Big Night Out* featuring The jet-lagged Beatles was broadcast.

March 1
– *Abbey Road.* 'I'm Happy Just To Dance With You' was written for George who was not yet writing songs. This was followed by 'Long Tall Sally' with Paul in fine Little Richard form, and 'I Call Your Name'.

March 2
– The Beatles began filming *A Hard Day's Night*, directed by Richard Lester, with a screenplay written by Alun Owen. Filming began at 8:30 am on Paddington Station, with The Beatles hurriedly joining Equity minutes before boarding the train.

The first week was spent filming on a specially hired train going from Paddington to Minehead and back, covering 2,500 miles in six days. After the crowds on the first day, they boarded the train at Acton station to avoid Paddington. There was a special dining car laid on for The Beatles and crew but when there was a 40-minute break they used the time set aside for eating to sit still instead of rolling from side to side.

Filming started at 8.30, very early for them, and each day they were given a shooting schedule. Since they all had

equal parts, there was never a great deal of dialogue to be learned. On the train, the dialogue was recorded using microphones inside their shirts, but even then there were many retakes because the levels were not high enough. One of the actresses on the train the first day was Patti Boyd, with whom George struck up an immediate friendship.
– The single **'Twist And Shout'/'There's A Place'** was released in the US as TOLLIE 9001.

March 3
– Filming on location, between London and Minehead.

March 4
– Filming on location, between London and Minehead.

March 5
– Filming on location, between London and Minehead.
– The group have drinks with Jeffrey Asher at Vincent's, the Oxford Sportsmen's club, before attending a dinner at Brasenose College, Oxford, that Archer had organised to celebrate their fundraising work for Oxfam.
– The single **'Komm, Gib Mir Deine Hand'/'Sie Liebt Dich'** was released in Germany as ODEON 22671.

March 6
– Filming on location, between London and Minehead.

March 9
– Filming on location, between London and Newton Abbott, Devon. This was the last day of railway location filming.

Recording at Studio
Two, Abbey Road,
February 1964.

NEMS Enterprises

On March 9 NEMS Enterprises Limited moved from Liverpool to new headquarters on the fifth floor of Sutherland House, 5 & 6 Argyll Street, London. The press office, previously at 13 Monmouth Street, London, was also moved to the new office suite. A press release, dated March 2, listed the management staff as: J. Alistair Taylor, General Manager; J.B. Montgomery, Accounts; Tony Barrow, NEMS Press Officer; Brian Sommerville, Beatles' Personal Press Representative; Wendy Hanson, Personal Assistant to Brian Epstein.

NEMS then managed The Beatles, Gerry & The Pacemakers, Billy J. Kramer, The Dakotas, Cilla Black, The Fourmost, Tommy Quickly, Sounds Incorporated and The Remo Four. In Brian's accompanying letter to his staff he said: "First of all as our organisation is very much in the public eye, it is most important that we present the best possible 'front'. By this I mean that all visitors must be treated with utmost courtesy. That work must be carried out smoothly and efficiently without fuss. And most important, that the offices themselves must be kept tidy and clean at all times."

March 10
– Filming at The Turk's Head, Twickenham.
– That evening they visited Tony Sheridan at Brian Epstein's apartment.

March 11
– Filming at Twickenham Film Studios, miming to 'I Should Have Known Better' in a mock-up of the train's guard's van. Studio technicians rocked the set during filming. At one point Richard Lester stopped the shoot because the technicians were rocking the set in time with The Beatles' music.

March 12
– Filming at Twickenham: hotel room sequences.

March 13
– The movie's closing sequence was filmed with a helicopter at Gatwick Airport.

March 16
– Ringo filmed his canteen sequence at *Twickenham Studios*.
– Ringo was made Vice-President of Leeds University Law Society.

– George and Brian Epstein attended a Cilla Black recording session for BBC's *Saturday Club*.
– The single **'Can't Buy Me Love'/ 'You Can't Do That'** was released in the US as CAPITOL 5150.

March 17
– Filming at *Les Ambassadeurs Club*.
– John recorded an interview with Jack de Manio for the BBC Home Service programme *Today* to promote his forthcoming book *In His Own Write*.

March 18
– Filming at Twickenham.
– While on the set they recorded an interview for the BBC Light Programme show *The Public Ear* in which they interviewed each other.
– John's interview was broadcast on the *Today* programme.

March 19
– The Variety Club of Great Britain 12th Annual Show Business Awards were presented at a luncheon at the Dorchester Hotel. Harold Wilson, Leader of the Opposition, presented The Beatles with the award for "Show

Below left: On the set for A Hard Days Night.

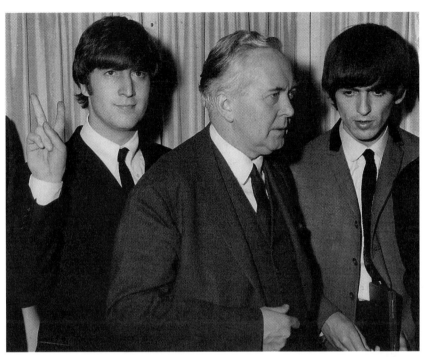

March 19, The Dorchester: Prime Minister Harold Wilson, whose Huyton constituency was in Liverpool, was quick to recognise the immense publicity value of being photographed with The Beatles.

Business Personalities of 1963" and, somewhat shrewdly, had his picture taken with them. John referred to his award, a heart shaped shield, as his "purple heart".

– The Beatles were filming that morning at Twickenham and returned to the set directly after the luncheon. Later that evening they recorded their first *Top Of The Pops* programme for the BBC. They mimed to 'Can't Buy Me Love' and 'You Can't Do That'.

– There had been a lot of discussion about a name for the film. Beatlemania was rejected, as was Moving On, Travelling On, Let's Go and Paul's suggestion, Who Was That Little Old Man? It was Ringo who came up with *A Hard Day's Night*. After a particularly heavy day he remarked, **"Boy, this has been a hard day's night!"** Everyone jumped on the idea immediately.

March 20

– Filming at Twickenham.

– Ringo was interviewed on the set by Peter Nobel for the BBC radio programme *Movie-Go-Round*.

– In the late afternoon they drove to the London headquarters of Associated Rediffusion and appeared live on *Ready, Steady, Go!* miming to 'It Won't Be Long', 'You Can't Do That' and

'Can't Buy Me Love'. They were interviewed by Cathy McGowan and took part in sketches.

– George took Hayley Mills to the midnight charity showing of *Charade* at the *Regal Cinema in Henley-on-Thames*.

– The single **'Can't Buy Me Love'/'You Can't Do That'** was released in the UK as PARLOPHONE R 5114.

March 22

– The Beatles interviewing themselves was broadcast on *The Public Ear* by the BBC Light Programme.

March 23

– Filming at the Scala Theatre, Charlotte Street, London, where they were to remain all week.

– The Duke of Edinburgh presented The Beatles with the Carl-Alan Award for Musical Achievement in 1963 at a ceremony at the *Empire Ballroom in Leicester Square* as part of the annual Carl-Alan Ballroom Dancing Awards. The presentation was broadcast live by BBC television.

– The single **'Do You Want To Know A Secret'/'Thank You Girl'** was released in the US as VEE JAY VJ 587.

– The EP **The Beatles** was released in the US as VEE JAY VJEP 1-903.

> SIDE A: **'Misery', 'A Taste Of Honey'**; SIDE B: **'Ask Me Why', 'Anna (Go To Him)'.**

– The EP format was unusual in the US, but Vee Jay only had a few tracks to play with and they released them in every possible format.

March 24

– Filming at the Scala Theatre, Charlotte Street, London.

– John did an interview to promote his new book for *Dateline London*, a BBC Overseas Service magazine programme.

March 25

– Filming at the Scala Theatre, Charlotte Street, London.

– The Beatles' appearance on *Top Of The Pops* was transmitted.

March 26

– Filming at the Scala Theatre, Charlotte Street, London.

March 27

– John and Cynthia, George and Patti left to spend the Easter weekend in Dromolan Castle, County Clare, Ireland. Ringo went to spend the weekend at Woburn Abbey as the guest of Lord Rudolph Russell, son of the Duke of Bedford. Paul remained in London.

– The press reported that they held the first six positions in the Australian singles charts.

March 30

– The single 'Bad To Me' by Billy J. Kramer & The Dakotas, written by Lennon & McCartney, was released in the US as IMPERIAL 66027.

– The BBC Light Programme broadcast their specially recorded Beatles bank holiday special, *From Us To You*.

March 31

– The group filmed a live concert at the *Scala Theatre, Charlotte Street, London*, for *A Hard Day's Night*. They mimed to 'Tell Me Why', 'And I Love Her', 'I Should Have Known Better' and 'She Loves You'. Thirteen-year old Phil Collins was in the audience as one of the 350 paid child extras.

That evening, The Beatles recorded a session for BBC Light Programme's *Saturday Club*. They did 'Everybody's Trying To Be My Baby', 'I Call Your Name', 'I Got A Woman', 'You Can't Do That', 'Can't Buy Me Love', 'Sure To Fall (In Love With You)' and 'Long Tall Sally'.

– John was interviewed about his book by Brian Matthew for the BBC Home Service programme *A Slice of Life*.

April 1

– Filming at the Scala Theatre, Charlotte Street, London.

In His Own Write

In His Own Write by John Lennon was published by Jonathan Cape. John: "Some journalist who was hanging round The Beatles came to me and I ended up showing him the stuff. They said, 'Write a book' and that's how the first one came about, and the second was your follow-up. Then I forgot about it."

To promote the book, John appeared live on the BBC television *Tonight* programme broadcast from Lime Grove. He was interviewed by Kenneth Allsop and read selections from the book, many of which first saw print as John's 'Beatcomber' column in *Mersey Beat*.

Paul: "When George Martin was scoring A Hard Day's Night [for the orchestral film soundtrack], he said, 'What is that note, John? It's been a hard day's night and I've been work-? Is it the seventh? Work-innnnggg?

"John said, 'Oh no, it's not that.'

"'Well is it workinnnggg?' He sings the sixth.

"John said, 'No.'

"George said, 'Well, it must be somewhere in between then!'

"John said, 'Yeah, man, write *that* down.' **And that's what I love! That's what I find interesting about music!"**

– A meeting was arranged at the London offices of NEMS between John and his father, Freddie. It lasted 20 minutes and George and Ringo were also present. They had not seen each other for 17 years.
– Paul visited a sick relative at Walton Hospital in Liverpool.

April 2
– Filming at the Scala Theatre, Charlotte Street, London.

April 3
– Filming at Twickenham Film Studios.
– The Beatles filmed answers to viewers questions for the Tyne Tees Television programme *Star Parade*.

April 4
– In the Billboard "Hot 100" chart for the week of April 4, The Beatles occupied no fewer than 12 places, including the top five, an unprecedented achievement. 'Can't Buy Me Love' was at number 1, followed by 'Twist And Shout' (2), 'She Loves You' (3), 'I Want To Hold Your Hand' (4), 'Please, Please Me' (5), 'I Saw Her Standing There' (31), 'From Me To You' (41), 'Do You Want to Know A Secret' (46), 'All My Loving' (58), 'You Can't Do That' (65), 'Roll Over Beethoven' (68) and 'Thank You Girl' (79). A week later two more singles entered the chart – 'There's A Place' (74)

and 'Love Me Do' (81).
– The Beatles' most recent *Saturday Club* session was broadcast on the BBC Light Programme.

April 5
– Filming the chase sequence at Marylebone Railway Station.

April 6
– Filming at Twickenham.

April 7
– Filming at Twickenham.

April 9
– Ringo filmed his solo spot for the film on the towpath of the Thames at Kew.
– The Beatles' Q & A session was broadcast on Tyne Tees Television.

April 10
– Filming at Twickenham.
– The album THE BEATLES' SECOND ALBUM was released in the US as Capitol ST 2080.
   SIDE A: 'Roll Over Beethoven', 'Thank You Girl', 'You Really Got A Hold On Me', 'Devil In Her Heart', 'Money (That's What I Want)', 'You Can't Do That';
   SIDE B: 'Long Tall Sally', 'I Call Your Name', 'Please Mister Postman', 'I'll Get You', 'She Loves You'.

April 12
– Filming at Marylebone Station which was closed on Sundays.

April 13
– Filming at Twickenham.

April 14
– Filming at Twickenham.

April 15
– Filming outside shots at the *Scala Theatre, Charlotte Street, London.*
– Paul was interviewed by David Frost for a BBC1 television show, *A Degree Of Frost.*

April 16
– Filming chase scenes in Notting Hill Gate.
– *Abbey Road.* Recording 'A Hard Day's Night'.

April 17
– Filming at Les Ambassadeurs.
– The group were interviewed by Ed Sullivan in the club's walled garden during a break in filming.
– The title *A Hard Day's Night* was announced as the name of The Beatles' first film.

April 18
– The morning was spent at Twickenham Film Studios.
– The afternoon was spent in rehearsal at The Hall Of Remembrance, Flood Street, Chelsea, for a TV Special for Rediffusion called *Around The Beatles.*
– The Beatles appeared on ATV's *The Morecambe and Wise Show* (recorded December 2, 1963).

April 19
– *IBC Studios, Portland Place,* to record their contribution to *Around The Beatles.* They played 'Twist And Shout', 'Roll Over Beethoven', 'I Wanna Be Your Man', 'Long Tall Sally', 'Can't Buy Me Love' and a greatest hits medley: 'Love Me Do'/'Please, Please Me'/'From Me To You'/'She Loves You'/'I Want To Hold Your Hand' and 'Shout!' They would mime to this tape on the actual show.
– Burglars broke into George and Ringo's flat in *Green Street, Knightsbridge.*

April 20
– Paul filmed at the Jack Billings TV School of Dance, Notting Hill, in a solo spot that was ultimately cut from the final film.

April 21
– Paul's second day of filming at the Jack Billings TV School of Dance.

April 22
– Outdoor locations shots filmed

On stage at the Scala
Cinema, filming concert
footage for Hard
Day's Night.

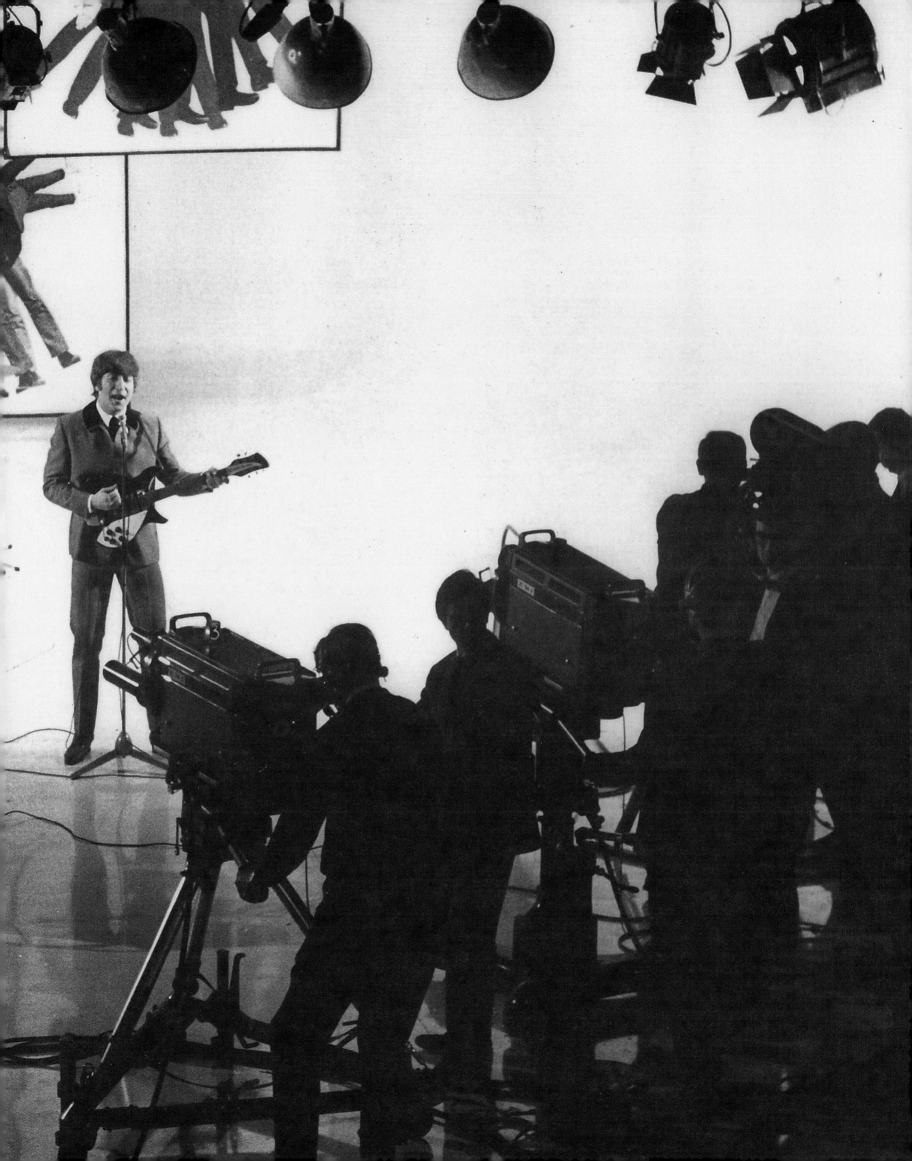

at the Hammersmith Odeon and in Notting Hill and Shepherd's Bush.
– The Beatles attended a press reception, hosted by the Rt. Hon. Sir Eric Harrison, Australian High Commissioner, at *Australia House*. Fans milled around outside in the pouring rain and the 700 guests all scrambled to get autographs.
Paul: "Will it be like this in Australia then? Blimey!"
The group was finally pushed into a private office containing a huge map of Australia made entirely of apples. Ringo grabbed one and ate it, telling the Ambassador, **"It's bonza, mate!"** Each member of the group was presented with a hamper of two magnums of Australian champagne, and tins of fruit. John asked, **"Where's the Aussie beer we've heard so much about then?"** Sir Eric grew more and more irritated at the proceedings.

April 23
– Filming at Thornbury Playing Fields, Isleworth, Middlesex.
– John cut short his day's filming in order to attend a Foyle's Literary Luncheon, given in his honour, at the Dorchester Hotel. The chairman was Osbert Lancaster and guests included Arthur Askey, Harry Secombe, Millicent Martin, Joan Littlewood, Helen Shapiro, Marty Wilde, Yehudi Menuhin, Victor Silvester, Mary Quant and cartoonist Giles. Brian Epstein was in attendance but, strangely, no other Beatles. Christina Foyle was put out when John restricted his speech to the words, **"Thank you very much and God bless you"**.

April 24
– Ringo's Sir Walter Raleigh puddle sequence was filmed in West Ealing. As it was the final day of shooting, The Beatles, the entire crew, and Murray the K, who was visiting, trooped across the road from the studios to the Turk's Head pub nearby where food and drinks had been laid on in a private room in the back.

April 25
– Rehearsals for *Around The Beatles* held at The Hall of Remembrance, Flood Street, Chelsea.

"There has never been a reception quite like this in Australia House and I hope there will never be another one. I guess I am what you would call a square but those photographers were just too much. They climbed all over the chairs and then when we went inside a closed office they were thrusting their cameras through the windows and rapping on the glass..."
SIR ERIC HARRISON

Above: April 22, With Sir Eric Harrison, the Australian High Commisioner.
Right: April 28, filming the Shakespearean scene for Around The Beatles.
Above Right: April 29, at Madame Tussauds, checking out their wax models.

April 26
– The Beatles topped the bill at the *New Musical Express* 1963-4 Annual Poll Winners' All-Star Concert held at Empire Pool, Wembley, in the afternoon. Ten thousand fans saw them receive their awards from Roger Moore and perform 'She Loves You', 'You Can't Do That', 'Twist And Shout', Long Tall Sally' and 'Can't Buy Me Love'.

April 27
– The Beatles attended a full dress rehearsal before a live audience for the *Around The Beatles* TV Special held at Rediffusion's studios in Wembley.
– The single **'Love Me Do'/'P.S. I Love You'** was released in the US as TOLLIE 9008.
– The single 'A World Without Love' by Peter & Gordon, written by Lennon & McCartney, was released in the US as CAPITOL 5175.
– The single **'Why'/'Cry For A Shadow'** by Tony Sheridan & The Beatles (A- side) and The Beatles (B-side) was released in the US as MGM K 13227.
– John's *122* was published in the US.
– NEMS Enterprises increased its share capital to 10,000 £1 shares. Brian gave The Beatles 250 shares each.

April 28
– The *Around The Beatles* TV Special was taped at Rediffusion's Wembley Studio. As well as the numbers they had already recorded, The Beatles

played Act V Scene 1 of Shakespeare's *A Midsummer Night's Dream* with John taking the female role of Thisbe, Paul as Pyramus, George as Moonshine and Ringo as Lion. Paul later named his cat Thisbe.

April 29
– *ABC Cinema, Edinburgh.* Stayed overnight at the Roman Camp Hotel, Callander, Perthshire.
– An interview with BBC Radio Scotland was broadcast on Scottish News.

April 30
– The group was interviewed in the afternoon by BBC Scotland for the news programme *Six Ten*, then they recorded an interview at the Theatre Royal, Glasgow for STV's *Roundabout* programme.
– That evening they played two sets

"Why didn't you leave us alone? How would you like a microphone always stuck in your face when you are on holiday?"

at the *Odeon Cinema, Glasgow*.

May 1
– The Beatles were driven to the BBC's Paris Studio in the West End of London to record their third *From Us To You* bank holiday special for the BBC Light Programme, introduced by Alan Freeman. They played: 'I Saw Her Standing There', 'Kansas City'/'Hey-Hey-Hey-Hey', 'I Forgot To Remember To Forget', 'You Can't Do That', 'Sure To Fall (In Love With You)', 'Can't Buy Me Love', 'Matchbox' and 'Honey Don't'.

May 2
– John and Cynthia, George and Patti flew to Honolulu on holiday but the pressure from the press was relentless and they were forced to leave. They flew on to Papeeti, in Tahiti. A reporter asked John, **"Why are you leaving Hawaii so soon?"** John snapped back at him, George was asked, **"How long will you stay in Tahiti?"** to which he replied, **"An hour."**
– Paul and Jane, Ringo and Maureen, took a holiday in St Thomas, Virgin Islands. They travelled under aliases: Paul was Mr Manning, Jane was Miss Ashcroft, Ringo was Mr Stone and Maureen Miss Cockroft. They left from Luton Airport and flew to Paris. From they flew to Lisbon, where they spent the night at the Ritz Hotel.
– An exhibition of Stuart Sutcliffe's paintings opened at the Walker Art Gallery in Liverpool.

May 3
– From Lisbon, Paul and Jane, Ringo and Maureen, flew to Puerto Rico and from there to the Virgin Islands – a convoluted route designed to avoid the press.

In St Thomas, they hired a yacht, complete with crew: Captain Bolyard and his wife Peggy.
Paul: "Fantastic scenery in those islands – we really felt we were in another world. I remember taking the dinghy out to do some spear fishing. I had this clumsy old spear with me – honestly, it was big enough to catch whales. So I dove – or is it dived? – off the boat and

started hunting around for fish. There were lots of little fish kicking around down below, but suddenly I saw some barracudas. Miniature sharks. Nasty fellows those! You can annoy other fish but barracudas are NOT for stirring. They're for avoiding. I tried to get them to go away but it didn't work. So I ran for my life – well, swam for it, anyway! You couldn't see me for bubbles. Of course I didn't catch anything that trip."

Paul walked barefoot on the beach and got spines in his feet. He was over-confident out in the sun and got burned. They swam and collected conch shells (with the conch still inside). They went ashore at Little Dix Bay in Virgin Gorda, in the British Virgin Islands and spent the evening listening to a calypso band and having a dance. At the hotel they saw James Garner in *Boy's Night Out*.

May 5
– STV broadcast the interview they made with The Beatles during their visit to Glasgow.

May 6
– Rediffusion's TV Special *Around The Beatles* was screened.

May 8
– The single 'One And One Is Two' by The Strangers With Mike Shannon, written by Lennon & McCartney, was released in the UK as PHILLIPS BF 1335.

May 10
– The Beatles' appearance at the *NME* Poll Winners' concert at Empire Pool, Wembley, was screened by ABC Television as a special called *Big Beat '64*.

May 11
– The EP **Four By The Beatles** was released in the US as CAPITOL EAP 2121.
SIDE A: 'Roll Over Beethoven', 'All My Loving';
SIDE B: 'This Boy', 'Please Mister Postman'.

May 18
– Paul's appearance on *A Degree Of Frost* was broadcast by BBC1.
– The *From Us To You* Beatles Bank

Paul and Jane Asher aboard the yacht Happy Days near the Virgin Islands.

Paul: "There was something about the atmosphere there that made me get quite keen on writing new songs in the evenings. I did a couple while I was there which we recorded when we got back, 'The Things We Said Today' and 'Always And Only' ('It's For You')... When you went out at night, the moon lit up everything. You could look into the water and actually see the bottom of the bay. Everything clear and cool and clean.

Fab! I found myself just wanting to get some ideas down on paper for songs. All that palm beach stuff!
"After a while I decided to buy myself a cheap guitar, just to keep in practice. But I didn't take it away with me – I gave it to Peggy as a little keepsake. It would have been a bit much to take it all the way back to good ol' England."

Holiday Special was broadcast by the BBC Light Programme.

May 21
– The single **'Sie Liebt Dich'/'Komm, Gib Mir Deine Hand'** was released in the US as SWAN 4182.

May 24
– The Beatles' interview with Ed Sullivan was screened along with a clip filmed for *A Hard Day's Night*, but not used in the film, of them miming to 'You Can't Do That'.

May 26
– John and George returned to London from their holiday.

May 27
– John and George attended Cilla Black's 21st birthday party, given by Brian Epstein at his London flat. Afterwards they went to the *London Palladium* to see Cilla's show.
– Paul and Jane, Ringo and Maureen returned from their holiday in St Thomas, Virgin Islands.

May 29
– Paul attended a Billy J. Kramer recording session to see him work on 'From A Window'.
– The single **'Ain't She Sweet'/'If You Love Me Baby'**, the A-side by The Beatles and B-side by Tony Sheridan & The Beatles, was released in the UK as POLYDOR NH 52-317.
– The single 'Nobody I Know' by Peter & Gordon, written by Paul McCartney, was released in the UK as COLUMBIA DB 7292

"Didn't think we could miss you **so much.** Get well soon."

May 30
– The Beatles gave a press conference to discuss their world tour at NEMS London offices presided over by Derek Taylor, their new press representative.

May 31
– *Prince of Wales Theatre, London,* with Kenny Lynch, Cliff Bennett & The Rebel Rousers, The Vernons Girls, The Lorne Gibson Trio, The Chants and The Harlems. Brian Epstein's "Pop's Alive" show. They did two sets, playing 'Can't Buy Me Love', 'All My Loving', 'This Boy', 'Roll Over Beethoven', 'Till There Was You', 'Twist And Shout' and 'Long Tall Sally'.

Before the show Ringo took delivery of a £350 Ludwig drum kit, supplied by Drum City.

June
– Paul bought a steel blue Aston Martin DB5 just before leaving for their world tour.

June 1
– *Abbey Road.* The Beatles worked on songs intended to be used on the A Hard Day's Night album: 'Matchbox', 'I'll Cry Instead' and 'Slow Down'. Carl Perkins, the composer of 'Matchbox', was in the studio to watch them. George had been so influenced early on by Perkins that on the Johnny Gentle tour he had called himself Carl Harrison.
– The single **'Sweet Georgia Brown'/'Take Out Some Insurance On Me Baby'** by Tony Sheridan & The Beatles was released in the US as ATCO 6302.

June 2
– *Abbey Road.* John's 'Any Time At All' and Paul's 'Things We Said Today' were recorded.
– At the studio The Beatles recorded an interview with Bob Rogers for Australian television ATN 7.
– Paul and Jane saw Cilla Black play the London Palladium.

June 3
– Ringo collapsed during a morning photo session for *Saturday Evening Post* in Barnes and was taken to University College Hospital suffering from acute tonsillitis and pharyngitis, requiring complete rest and quiet.
– That evening, with Ringo not there, the remaining Beatles recorded demo versions of their own compositions: George did 'You'll Know What To Do' (unreleased), Paul did a demo of 'It's For You' to give to Cilla Black and John recorded 'No Reply' which he gave to Tommy Quickly for a single before The Beatles used it.

June 4
– The Beatles' Austin Princess, driven by their chauffeur "Big" Bill Corbett, took John, Paul, George and Jimmy Nicol to Heathrow Airport for their flight to Denmark. They were swiftly taken aboard their plane ahead of the other passengers, and signed autographs for the captain and crew. Over 6,000 fans were waiting in Copenhagen airport, with most of the yelling coming from boys rather than girls. Fans attempted to storm the doors of the Royal Hotel, opposite the Tivoli Gardens, when they checked in and the crowd of 10,000 fans brought the centre of Copenhagen to a standstill. The crowds were controlled by Danish police assisted by visiting members of the British Royal Fusiliers.

They had to rehearse their repertoire for Jimmy Nicol, Ringo's stand-in, and Mal Evans introduced a new way of getting them to remember the playlist - he taped it onto their guitars.

Before the first of their two shows at the KB Hallen, they were visited by the British Ambassador. They played two packed out-houses, with 4,400 fans in each. The first set consisted of: 'I Want To Hold Your Hand', 'I Saw Her Standing There', 'You Can't Do That', 'All My Loving', 'She Loves You', 'Till There Was You', 'Roll Over Beethoven', Can't Buy Me Love', This Boy' and 'Long Tall Sally'. For the second set, and the rest of the tour, the order of the first two numbers was switched round. Ringo's 'I Wanna Be Your Man' was left out of the set. There were riotous scenes at the end of the second performance when the MC announced that The Beatles would not be coming back onstage and a potted delphinium was thrown at him.
– Back at the Royal The Beatles ate smorrebrodsseddel, a sort of jam sandwich, and Paul sent Ringo a get-well cable:

June 5
– They arrived at Amsterdam's Schiphol Airport at 1 pm and were presented with bunches of flowers and traditional Dutch hats. After the usual press conference they went straight to Hillegom, 26 miles outside Amsterdam, to rehearse and record a television show for VARA TV at the Treslong café-restaurant. They mimed to 'Twist And Shout', 'All My Loving', 'Roll Over Beethoven', 'Long Tall Sally', 'She Loves You' and 'Can't Buy Me Love', but before they could complete the last number, they were engulfed by fans, mostly boys. Mal Evans, Derek Taylor and Neil Aspinall did their best to clear the stage but eventually Neil signalled the group to leave. John, Paul and George ran for cover, leaving Jimmy Nicol playing along to the music.

After the concert that evening they toured Amsterdam's red-light district, the Walletjes.

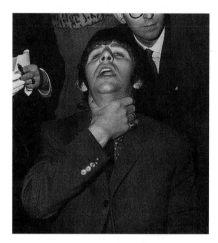

Bottom left: Copenhagen-bound with Jimmy Nicol as Ringo's temporary replacement.
Left: Ringo draws attention to the condition that prevented him joining the group on tour.

Jimmy Nicol

With The Beatles due to leave on a world tour, a substitute drummer was urgently required. George Martin suggested Jimmy Nicol who suddenly found himself a temporary member of the most famous group on Earth. The Beatles cancelled a recording session and spent the time at Abbey Road rehearsing with Jimmy Nicol instead.

Jimmy: "I was having a bit of a lie down after lunch when the phone rang. It was EMI asking if I could come down to the studio to rehearse with The Beatles. Two hours after I got there I was told to pack my bags for Denmark."

John: "**When we hit town**, **we hit it,** we were not **pissing** about. You know, there's photographs of me **grovelling** about, **crawling** about in Amsterdam **on my knees,** coming out of **whore houses** and things like that, and people saying, 'Good morning, John...' The police escorted me to the places because they never wanted a **big scandal.**"

– The single 'Like Dreamers Do' by The Applejacks, written by <u>Lennon</u> & <u>McCartney</u>, was released in the UK as Decca F 11916.

June 6

– The Beatles made a highly publicised tour of the Amsterdam canals in one of the glass-topped tourist boats. Some fans dived into the canal and the police used very rough tactics in getting them out. All police leave was cancelled and 15,000 police were on duty for The Beatles'

canal trip, watched by 50,000 fans.

– The concerts were held at the Exhibition Hall in Blokker, about 36 miles from Amsterdam. They travelled there in two white Cadillacs with motorcycle outriders which, curiously, had sidecars. In between sets they managed to get a bit of rest in their dressing room but inadvertently insulted the good people of Blokker. They were expected at a civic reception at a local restaurant and a visit to a traditional Dutch village had also

Below: George, Paul and John, at Sydney Airport.

been laid on. No-one told them and they slept peacefully while everyone waited for them to appear.

The fans were particularly boisterous, since many were boys.

Paul: "Sometimes we thought they were going to get out of hand but nobody ever started any real trouble."

June 7

– The 10:15 am BEA flight to Hong Kong from London, Heathrow, was held up for an hour to enable The Beatles to make the connection from their flight from Amsterdam, which caused some grumbles in the British press later. The plane stopped to refuel at Zürich, Beirut, Karachi, Calcutta and Bangkok. In Beirut, police turned fire fighting foam on the hundreds of fans who invaded the runway. In Karachi Paul attempted to buy a few souvenirs at the airport but even at 2 am shrieking fans appeared from nowhere and he was forced back on to the plane. They managed a 6 am cup of tea in the terminal building at Calcutta with no trouble but at Bangkok about 1,000 fans, mostly in school uniforms, rampaged through the airport chanting, "Beatles come out!". They did go down the ramp to sign autographs and be kissed. <u>John</u> and <u>Paul</u> had a pillow fight on board, filmed by Australian TV cameraman Mayo Hunter and transmitted on *The Seven Network* shortly after the plane landed in Australia.

June 8

– The Beatles arrived at Kai Tak Airport in Hong Kong and were quickly transferred to the 15th floor of the President Hotel in Kowloon, by-passing customs and immigration formalities. <u>Paul</u> and Neil ordered a couple of the famous 24-hour suits. That evening, tired and jet-lagged, The Beatles were expected to attend the Miss Hong Kong Pageant, held in the hotel. When they refused there were so many tears that <u>John</u> went down to the Convention Hall to make an appearance. He shook the contestants' hands and made a few choice remarks about the beauty of oriental girls.

The Beatles' arrival in Sydney

The Beatles flew to Sydney on June 11, stopping for fuel in Darwin where, at 2:35 in the morning, 400 fans stood waiting at the airport for a glimpse of the group. The Beatles went through customs and immigration and met the press. John: "You men must be from the nose-papers. Well don't blow the story up too big!" It was raining heavily and very cold when they arrived at Sydney's Mascot International Airport, despite

which 2,000 fans managed to give them a damp welcome. The Beatles were paraded around the airport in an open-topped milk truck so by the time they reached the Sheridan Hotel they were soaked to the skin. A woman, soaking wet, threw her six-year-old mentally handicapped child up into the back of the truck yelling, "Catch him Paul!" Paul, drenched and unsteady as the truck bumped around the airport, managed to

catch the terrified child. "May God bless you!" the woman shouted.

"He's lovely! Great!" shouted Paul. "You take him now." The woman ran after the truck until the driver saw her and slowed. She took her child and kissed it. "He's better! Oh, he's better!" she wept.

They checked into their hotel in Potts Point, Sydney. Their luggage had not yet arrived from the airport but Paul and John had enough dry clothes with them

to change. George went out on the balcony to wave to fans dressed only in a bath towel wrapped around his waist.

Once they had dried off and warmed up, they launched straight into a round of interviews, press conferences, photo sessions and meetings with promoters and civic dignitaries.

Adelaide Television screened interview with The Beatles by Ernie Sigley done in Sydney.

George: "The best flight I remember was the one to Hong Kong. It took several hours and I remember them saying, 'Return to your seats because we're approaching Hong Kong' and I thought, 'We can't be there already.' We'd been sitting on the floor drinking and taking Preludins for about 30 hours and so it seemed like a ten-minute flight.

"On all those flights we were still on uppers and that's what helped us get through because we'd drink a whisky and coke with anyone, even if he was the Devil, and charm the pants off him."

June 9
– *Princess Theatre, Kowloon, Hong Kong* with The Maori Hi-Five. The Beatles played two shows, but since the Chinese promoter had charged outrageous ticket prices, not all the seats were full, and many of the thousands of fans who greeted them at the airport could not afford to see the shows. A ticket cost the equivalent of one week's pay. They did no sightseeing, thinking it might be too dangerous.

June 11
– Ringo was discharged from University College Hospital, London.

June 12
– Ringo, accompanied by Brian Epstein, flew to Australia via San Francisco, Honolulu and Fiji. He forgot his passport and the plane was delayed. Eventually he left without it. He climbed the steps alongside actress Vivien Leigh. Brian introduced her but Ringo didn't know who she was. His passport finally arrived at the airport and was put on another plane to be given to him during his stopover in San Francisco.

– *Centennial Hall, Adelaide*, two sets with Sounds Incorporated, Johnny Devlin, Johnny Chester and The Phantoms. The compere was Alan Field. More than 50,000 applications had been made for the four concerts at this 3,000 seater hall. Their set was the same as in Denmark and Holland: 'I Saw Her Standing There', 'I Want To Hold Your Hand', 'You Can't Do That', 'All My Loving', 'She Loves You', 'Till There Was You', 'Roll Over Beethoven', Can't Buy Me Love', This Boy' and 'Long Tall Sally'.

That night, The Beatles had a private party in their hotel suite, ignoring

a society extravaganza held in their honour in the Adelaide Hills.

June 13
– In the afternoon Ringo arrived in San Francisco and gave a press conference at the airport while changing planes. The conference turned into chaos as reporters scrambled to get autographs, and Ringo was hurried away to board the Quantas flight to Sydney.

Four thousand fans were still camped outside the South Australia Hotel, Adelaide, when The Beatles woke up just after noon. The group held a small reception for their Fan

Club organisers before the show.
– *Centennial Hall, Adelaide.* Two sets.
– The Beatles held a private party in their suite.

June 14
– Ringo arrived in Sydney to the usual shrieking fans and clamouring pressmen. At the inevitable press conference, Ringo told reporters about his rings, his taste in alcohol ("I've switched from Scotch to Bourbon") and said, **"I've heard you've got a bridge or something here. No one ever tells me anything, they just knock on my door and drag me out of bed to look at rivers and things. At the moment I love it all. I mean, wouldn't you, if you got off a plane to all this?"** He was asked if he ever had his hair cut, to which he replied curtly: **"Of course, it'd be down by my ankles if I didn't."**

After 90 minutes in Sydney, Ringo and Brian Epstein flew on to

Above right: Ringo and Brian Epstein leave London for Australia.

The Adelaide reception

The Beatles flew from Sydney to Adelaide in a chartered Ansett ANA jet, arriving at 11:57 am. Police estimated that 200,000 people lined the ten miles route of their motorcade from the airport to the city centre. At least 30,000 blocked the area around the City Hall where they met Mayor Irwin, the City Council and their families who presented them with toy koala bears. John told them, "Wherever we go, anywhere in the world, this reception which Adelaide has given us will stick in our memories." Everywhere they went, they were interviewed by Adelaide DJ Bob Francis from 5DN, even on the balcony of the Town Hall. He had booked the suite next to them in the Southern Australia Hotel and had a landline installed to give his listeners hourly reports.

Melbourne where the crowd at the airport was already large, waiting to greet the other members of the group due to arrive five hours later. When Brian and Ringo arrived at the Southern Cross Hotel, a crowd of 3,000 fans were already gathered outside. Police Inspector Mike Patterson decided to make a run for it and hoisted Ringo onto his immense shoulders and charged into the crowd. Unfortunately, he tripped over The Beatles own PR woman and pitched Ringo into the waiting arms of the crowd. Patterson quickly pulled him free and got him into the hotel but he was as white as a sheet. His first words were: **"Give us a drink. That was the roughest ride I've ever had."** He went straight to his room to lie down.

The other Beatles left their hotel at 12:15 pm and flew from Adelaide to Melbourne in their chartered Ansett ANA Fokker Friendship. They arrived at Essendon Airport to a frenzied welcome from a crowd of 5,000. The crowd outside the hotel was so large that army and navy units had been called in as reinforcements when steel barriers were knocked down and the casualties began to mount up. Their route into the city was lined by 20,000 fans, most of whom moved on to the hotel which was under a state of siege. Protected by 12 motorcycle outriders, the group neared their hotel at 4 pm and were driven into a garage entrance while a dummy police car with siren blaring pulled up at the hotel's front door as a diversion. In front of the hotel, 300 police and 100 military battled with the crowd, cars were crushed, people broke bones, fell from trees and more than 150 girls fainted. Fifty people, many of them adults, were taken to hospital with injuries sustained in the crush. Scores of girls had their sweaters torn off and many lost their shoes.
– To relieve the crush, The Beatles were asked to show themselves, and all five appeared on the first floor balcony. The roar of the crowd was like that at a Nuremburg rally, prompting John to give them a Nazi salute and shout 'Sieg Heil', holding his finger to his

upper lip as a moustache.
– Once The Beatles had been properly reunited there was a press conference with all five of them, after which Jimmy Nicol's services were no longer needed.
Jimmy: **"The boys were very kind but I felt like an intruder. They accepted me, but you can't just get into a group like that – they have their own atmosphere, their own sense of humour. It's a little clique and outsiders just can't break in."** The Beatles celebrated their reunion with a party with local girls until 4 am. Jimmy Nicol was not present.
June 15
– Jimmy Nicol slipped out of The Beatles' Melbourne hotel on Bourke Street at 8 am in the morning accompanied by Brian Epstein to drive to the airport, **"after 12 fabulous days with the world at my feet"**. Jimmy didn't say goodbye to The Beatles, who were

sleeping off their all-night party.
Jimmy: **"I don't think I should disturb them."** At the airport Brian paid him his agreed fee of £500 and gave him a gold watch, engraved, "To Jimmy, with appreciation and gratitude - Brian Epstein and The Beatles."

EMI held a reception for the group at the Epsilon Room of the hotel, where the wrath of a furious John Lennon was directed on EMI executives when John saw that EMI had designed a different sleeve for With The Beatles for Australia. (Australian union rules meant that all album sleeve artwork had to be re-photographed and made up. The With The Beatles sleeve would have lost too much detail if subjected to this absurd treatment so they made a different one. John was not in the mood to listen to the convoluted explanation.)
– *Festival Hall, Melbourne,* two sets, after which they attended a private party given by Melbourne socialites in the rich suburb of Toorak.

Melbourne, in the top left hand corner, three Beatles can be seen waving down to the immense crowds.

George: "We can't hear **ourselves** singing, so how can **they** hear us? There's **never** a **pause** in their **screaming.** They're great!"

– The single 'Nobody I Know' by Peter & Gordon, written by Paul McCartney, was released in the US as CAPITOL 5211.
– A recording of one of their shows on the 12th was broadcast by 5DN as *Beatles Show.*

June 16
– The Beatles attended a civic reception at Melbourne Town Hall. Police closed several streets as 15,000 fans took the day off school to catch a glimpse of the group on the Town Hall balcony. They arrived half an hour late because the ticker tape reception slowed their car down. Mayor Leo Curtis had foolishly given tickets for the reception to any fan who wrote in and the reception, planned for 150 people, had swelled to 350. Ringo was asked to speak and gave them a classic Ringo line: (It was 1:15 pm.) The Mayor then asked for autographs, prompting a melée as fans and dignitaries scrambled to touch the group. Ringo demanded that they leave immediately and the Mayor took them to his wife's chambers on the second floor.

Away from the crowds, The Beatles relaxed and sat around listening to a university student play the didgeridoo and joining the Curtis family in a sing-song around the piano which Paul played. They stayed half and hour longer than planned and the event was described by Brian Epstein afterwards as **"the most happy, informal moment since the tour began."** The press, however, thought The Beatles had stormed out of the reception and ran headlines like: "Beatles Walk Out! Anger At Rude Guests."
– *Festival Hall, Melbourne,* two sets.

June 17
– George managed to get out for an afternoon's motoring in an MG in the Dandenong Mountains with tour organiser Lloyd Ravenscroft. Meanwhile, John, Paul and Ringo had a hairdresser come in to cut their hair.
– *Festival Hall, Melbourne,* two sets. Channel Nine filmed the final concert for a TV show: *The Beatles Sing For Shell* (the oil company).

June 18
– The Beatles flew into Sydney at 11.40 am, where a relatively small

"I wish you'd had this reception a little **earlier** instead of **dragging** me out of **bed** at this early hour."

crowd of 1,200 fans were waiting for them, guarded by 300 police. They were rapidly transferred to their old suite in the Chevron Hotel before the usual press conference where Ringo got in a few good lines.

Reporter: "I'm from Perth, Western Australia.
Ringo: "Are you bragging or complaining?"
Same Reporter: "I have flown 2,000 miles to record this interview."
Ringo: "Gee, your arms must be tired."
– *Sydney Stadium, Sydney, NSW.* The jelly baby throwing habit, the result of an ill-considered publicity statement, really got out of hand in Australia.

George: "Wherever we've been since then – America, Europe and now Australia, that stupid story has gone ahead with the result that we get jelly babies chucked at us till we're really fed up."

Paul stopped the show twice to ask the audience. Each time his request was met by screams and another hail of jelly babies. Paul shrugged his shoulders, **"Well, I asked you, anyway."** Afterwards they spoke about it to the press.

Paul: "I keep asking them not to chuck those damned things, but they don't seem to have the sense to realise we hate being the target for sweets coming like bullets from all directions. How can we concentrate on our jobs on the stage when we are having all the time to keep ducking to avoid sweets, streamers and the other stuff they keep throwing at us?"
John: "It's ridiculous. They even throw miniature koala bears and gift-wrapped packages while we are going round on the revolving stage. We haven't a chance to get out of the way."
Ringo: "It's all right for you lot. You can jump aside and dodge them, but I'm stuck at

"Please don't throw those **sweets** at us. They get in our **eyes."**

the drums and can't move, so they all seem to hit me."

Despite that, The Beatles liked the audience.

It was Paul's 22nd birthday and his principal guests were 17 beautiful girls, winners of the *Daily Mirror* "Why I Would Like to be a Guest at a Beatle's Birthday Party" competition. At 3 am Ringo passed out drunk, but the party was carefully monitored and nothing untoward occurred.

June 19
– *Sydney Stadium, Sydney, NSW.*
– The EP **Long Tall Sally** was released in the UK as Parlophone GEP 8913.
   SIDE A: 'Long Tall Sally', 'I Call Your Name';
   SIDE B: 'Slow Down', 'Matchbox'.

June 20
– *Sydney Stadium, Sydney, NSW.* Someone in the audience threw an egg, hitting John on the foot. He looked in the direction it came from and yelled, **"What d'you think I am, a salad?"** No more eggs were thrown.
– The Beatles did a telephone interview with Colin Hamilton for the BBC Light Programme show *Roundabout.*

June 21
– As they were packing to leave, a tapping on the windows of suite 801 revealed 20-year-old Peter Roberts, an "exile" from Netherton, Liverpool, who had scaled the drainpipes of the hotel in total darkness to say hello.

John: "I knew before he opened his mouth where he was from because I knew nobody else would be climbing up eight floors... I gave him a drink because he deserved one and then I took him around to see the others."
– Ten thousand fans saw them off at the airport, the biggest turn-out yet. They flew the 1,500 miles to Auckland, New Zealand, where 7,000 screaming fans were waiting at the airport and they received a "traditional" welcome of nose-rubbing kisses from laughing Maori women in native costume.

John: "My wife'll kill me when she hears about this!"
Three thousand more fans watched them drive to Hotel St George where

129

they were smuggled in through a bottle shop because of the crush of fans.

June 22

– *Town Hall, Wellington, North Island, NZ.* The sound system was so primitive that as they came off stage, John screamed **"What the fucking hell is going on here?"** It turned out that the PA operator had never turned his speakers up before and was scared to do so. The second house was considerably louder but the sound quality was still bad. **Paul: "We have sung through worse mics, but not very often; usually during the early days; we expected better here."**

Ringo was now recovered sufficiently for his vocal spot, 'Boys', to be put back on the set list.

After the concert, Mal Evans had to get out of the car and use his muscle to clear a way through to the hotel because the local police thought that two men would be enough to control a crowd of 5,000 fans. Auckland Chief Constable, Superintendent Quinn, refused a police escort for The Beatles between their hotel and the Town Hall because: **"We provide such escorts only for royalty and other important visitors"**. This smug attitude by the authorities caused problems throughout New Zealand.

June 23

– *Town Hall, Wellington, North Island, NZ.*

John: "You know, The Beatles' tours were like Fellini's *Satyricon*. I mean, we had that image, but man, our tours were like something else. If you could get on our tours, you were in... Australia, what, just everywhere. **Just think of *Satyricon* with four musicians going through it. Wherever we went there was always a whole scene going on. We had our four bedrooms separate from... tried to keep them out of our room. And Derek's and Neil's rooms were always full of fuck knows what, and policemen and everything... they didn't call them groupies then, they called it something else. If we couldn't get groupies, we would have whores and everything, whatever was going."**

June 24

– *Town Hall, Auckland, North Island, NZ.* The Beatles tour encountered more hostility from the smug local establishment in Aukland. The Inspector of Police, ignoring the wishes of the public he was paid to serve, greeted the tour management with, **"We didn't want 'em here and I don't know why you brought 'em."** Because so few police were on duty, The Beatles' Cadillac was stuck 30 feet from the Royal Continental Hotel where they were staying. Mal, Neil and Lloyd Ravenscroft had to lock The Beatles in the car and push it to the garage door, fighting off fans all the way. It took 20 minutes and about 200 fans managed to get into the garage with them. They then had to throw the fans out one by one before The Beatles could go to their rooms.

John later told an American interviewer: **"It was a bit rough. I thought definitely a big clump of my hair had gone. I don't mean just a bit. They'd put about three policemen on for three or four thousand kids and they refused to put more on. 'We've had all sorts over 'ere, we've seen them all,' they said, and they had seen them all as we went crashing to the ground."**

– After this incident John lost his temper and refused to play any more unless more police were provided.

June 25

– *Town Hall, Auckland, North Island, NZ.* Mayor Robinson hosted a civic welcome for the group, against vocal opposition from other members of the council. A crowd of 7,000 fans gathered outside the Town Hall to see The Beatles rub noses with three Maori girls in native costumes and pretend to attack Mayor Robinson with Maori pois.

June 26

– *Town Hall, Dunedin, South Island, NZ.* The local police ignored the advice from the tour managers and only allocated three policemen to control the thousands of fans who gathered outside the New City Hotel.

When they arrived the police had only left a three foot hole in their barrier outside the hotel through which The Beatles literally had to fight their way as fans easily overwhelmed the three Dunedin constables. Paul's face was scratched and John lost some of his hair as Mal and Neil fought back the crowd to get the group through. John Lennon's expressed opinion of the Dunedin local authorities was rich and colourful.

– That night John, Ringo and DJ Bob Rogers played a joke on Paul involving a nude girl which Paul did not find at all amusing.

– The album A HARD DAY'S NIGHT (Original Soundtrack Album) was released in the US as UNITED ARTISTS UAS 6366.

SIDE A: 'A Hard Day's Night', 'Tell Me Why', 'I'll Cry Instead', 'I Should Have Known Better' (by George Martin & Orchestra), 'I'm Happy Just To Dance With You', 'And I Love Her' (by George Martin & Orchestra); SIDE B: 'I Should Have Known Better', 'If I Fell', 'And I Love Her', 'Ringo's Theme (This Boy)' (by George Martin & Orchestra), 'Can't Buy Me Love', 'A Hard Day's Night' (by George Martin & Orchestra).

June 27

– *Majestic Theatre, Christchurch, South Island, NZ.* A crowd of 5,000 fans turned out to watch the group land and drive to the Clarendon Hotel in the city centre. En route a 13-year-old girl threw herself at their limousine, bouncing off the bonnet onto the road. She got what she wanted because the group took her into the hotel and gave her a cup of coffee.

– The BBC Light Programme show *Roundabout* broadcast the telephone interview done with The Beatles in Sydney.

June 28

– The group flew to Brisbane, via Auckland and Sydney. They arrived in Sydney on a TEAL flight at 9:35 pm. A crowd of 4,000 fans watched them walk a short distance to their chartered Ansett ANA Fokker Friendship aircraft and half an hour later they were gone.

June 29

– The Beatles arrived in Brisbane

just after midnight where 8,000 fans were waiting. The group were driven past the crowd in an open-topped truck but hiding in the crowd was a vocal core of Beatles haters who pelted the group with eggs, tomatoes and bits of wood. The group were taken quickly to Lennon's Hotel where they declared, **"No more unscheduled appearances. For as long as we're in Brisbane, it's the hotel and hall for us."**
– *Festival Hall, Brisbane.* The two houses of 5,500 were sold out but once again a gang of egg throwers had managed to get in and marred the concert for others. The Beatles made a few well-known gestures to the crowd but played on. That night The Beatles and 20 Brisbane girls partied till the early hours, dancing to Motown records.

June 30
– The Beatles secretly left the hotel in two hire cars and spent the day on the Gold Coast, mostly on the huge sweep of white sand between Broadbeach and Surfers' Paradise.
– *Festival Hall, Brisbane.*

July
– Paul bought his father a five-bedroom house called "Rembrandt" on the Wirral, 15 miles from Liverpool. Paul's brother Michael moved in with his father.

July 1
– Early in the morning a Rolls Royce delivered the group to Brisbane airport to catch a plane for Sydney. Then began the long Quantas-V flight home, refuelling in Singapore – where Paul and Ringo disembarked to wave to the 600 waiting fans – and Frankfurt.
– Australian Channel Nine broadcast The Beatles *Sing For Shell.*

July 2
– The Beatles arrived at Heathrow Airport, London, at 11.10 am.
– Paul played piano and John watched when Cilla Black recorded 'It's For You' at Abbey Road. Cilla: **"Paul was at the recording session when I made 'Anyone Who Had A Heart'. He said that he liked the composition and he and John would try to produce something similar. Well they came up with this new number, but for my money it's nothing like the 'Anyone' composition. That was some session we had when I made the new recording. John and Paul joined me, and George Martin. We made one track and then everyone had a go at suggesting how they thought it should be recorded. And everyone had different ideas. George said it should**

Above: Ringo submits to the traditional bumping at Lime Grove Studios on his 24th birthday, July 7. Below: John and Cynthia leave Heathrow after The Beatles' return from Australia.

John: **"A Hard Day's Night** was sort of interesting, since it was the first time. **We loathed the script** because it was somebody trying to write like we were in real life. In retrospect Alun Owen didn't do a bad job, but at the time we were **self-conscious about the dialogue. It felt unreal."**

be one way, Paul and John another and I just added my suggestions while they were thinking of what else they could do with the composition."

July 6
– The premiere of *A Hard Day's Night.* Piccadilly Circus was closed for traffic as Princess Margaret, Lord Snowdon, The Beatles, their wives and girlfriends attended the world premiere of the film at the London Pavillion.
– The single 'Like Dreamers Do' by The Applejacks, written by Lennon & McCartney, was released in the US as LONDON 9681.
– The single **'Ain't She Sweet' / 'Nobody's Child'** by The Beatles on the A-side and Tony Sheridan & The Beatles on the B-side was released in the US as ATCO 6308.

July 7
– *Lime Grove Studios, London.* The Beatles mimed 'A Hard Day's Night', 'Things We Said Today' and 'Long Tall Sally' for BBC TV's *Top Of The Pops.*
– After this, they went to Rediffusion's studios at Television House to record an interview about the film, which was broadcast that evening on Granada Television's *Scene At 6:30.*
– John was interviewed by journalist Chris Hutchins about *A Hard Day's Night* for the BBC Light Programme's *The Teen Scene.*
– Brian Epstein bought Ringo a pair of diamond cufflinks for his birthday. Ringo spent the evening celebrating with his parents.
– Paul presented his father with a £1,200 racehorse, Drake's Drum, for Jim's 62nd birthday. His father unwrapped a parcel containing a picture of the horse, and said, **"That's very nice, son, but what do I need a picture of a horse for?" "That's not the present! I bought you the bloody horse!"** It placed second in its first race. Paul remarked, **"There you are, I told you my dad was the best jockey in the business."**

July 8
– BBC TV's *Top Of The Pops* aired

The Beatles' performances of the A- and B- sides of their new single taped the previous day.

July 10

— 3,000 screaming fans were waiting in the bright sunshine at Speke Airport when The Beatles landed to attend the Northern premiere of *A Hard Day's Night* and appear as guests of honour at a civic reception. They were driven to the Town Hall in a police cavalcade led by motorcycle police. The route was lined shoulder to shoulder with police but on a dozen occasions the screaming girls managed to break through the police cordons and bring their motorcade to a screeching halt.

They arrived at the Town Hall at 6.55 pm, 25 minutes behind schedule, to be welcomed by Elizabeth "Bessie" Braddock, MP for Liverpool's Exchange Division, wearing her Cavern Club membership badge. They all hugged her and she said **"It's great to see you love."** After a meal

they made an appearance on the balcony overlooking Castle Street to be greeted by screaming crowds and the Liverpool City Police Band playing 'Can't Buy Me Love'.

The Lord Mayor, Alderman Louis Caplan, addressed the 714 guests from the Minstrel Gallery of the Town Hall's large ballroom with The Beatles and a large group of their relatives at his side: 14 members of the Lennon family and 16 from Ringo's. He said how proud Liverpool was of the group and what great ambassadors they were for the city. Each Beatle then said "Hello" from the gallery.

They had not expected such a warm reception. John was quoted in the Liverpool Echo as saying, "It beats our reception at Adelaide — our previous best — by miles. The boys are flabbergasted. This is the proudest moment of our lives. We never expected so many people would turn out. We thought there would only be a few people standing on the odd street corner.

"What really delighted us more than anything is that everybody here, from the top nobs down to the humblest Scouser, has been so nice and sung praise after praise, which I'm sure we really don't deserve."

Everyone was there, from Lord and Lady Derby and the Bishop of Liverpool to members of the local rock bands and friends from the Cavern days. Everyone needed a pass as the Liverpool police put on the biggest security operation in their history.

Shortly before 9 pm they left for the Odeon Cinema for the charity premiere of *A Hard Day's Night*. *The Echo* reported a battle by police to clear the milling crowds sufficiently for them to get away and, "even when they did get through, thousands flocked behind them like the tail of a comet".

At the Odeon the Liverpool City Police Band struck up the 'Z-Cars Theme', a popular television police show set in Liverpool, following it

Above: John with his Aunt Mimi.
Below: With the Municipal Police Band at Liverpool Town Hall, July 10.
Opposite: The convoy through the streets of Liverpool.

with a rather more restrained medley of Beatles hits. Compere David Jacobs introduced The Beatles and everyone went wild. *The Echo* said, "The Odeon Cinema last night had more of the atmosphere of a big family show than a glittering premier. It was an occasion when the distinguished relatives in the dress circle joined their younger brethren in the stalls for a night out with the city's favourite sons."
– BBC1's *Look North* news programme broadcast part of their press conference and an interview with the group conducted by Gerald Harrison.
– Granada Television's *Scene At 6:30* broadcast their own interview,

done at the airport, as well as film of the balcony ceremony.
– The single **'A Hard Day's Night'/'Things We Said Today'** was released in the UK as Parlophone R 5160.
– The album A HARD DAY'S NIGHT was released in the UK as Parlophone PCS 3058.
SIDE A: **'A Hard Day's Night', 'I Should Have Known Better', 'If I Fell', 'I'm Happy Just To Dance With You', 'And I Love Her', 'Tell Me Why', 'Can't Buy Me Love';**
SIDE B: **'Anytime At All', 'I'll Cry Instead', 'Things We Said Today', 'When I Get Home', 'You Can't Do**

That', 'I'll Be Back'.
– The single 'I'll Keep You Satisfied' by Billy J. Kramer & The Dakotas, written by Lennon & McCartney, was released in the US as Imperial 66048.
– The Beatles' first appearance on *the Ed Sullivan Show* was repeated by CBS-TV.

July 11
– The Beatles flew from Liverpool to London in the early hours of the morning to appear live on ABC TV's *Lucky Stars* (Summer Spin). They mimed to 'A Hard Day's Night', 'Long Tall Sally', 'Things We Said Today' and 'You Can't Do That'.

July 12
– *Hippodrome Theatre, Brighton,* with The Shubdubs, featuring Jimmy Nichol.
On his way there, George's new E-Type Jaguar was involved in a minor road accident in the New Kings Road, Fulham. Pedestrians collected bits of the broken glass as souvenirs.

July 13
– The single **'A Hard Day's Night'/ 'I Should Have Known Better'** was released in the US as Capitol 5222.

July 14
– *Broadcasting House, Portland Place, London,* to appear on the first edition of *Top Gear*, the BBC's new rock programme. They played 'Long Tall Sally', 'Things We Said Today', 'A Hard Day's Night', 'And I Love Her', 'I Should Have Known Better', 'If I Fell' and 'You Can't Do That'. The presenter was Brian Matthew.
– Paul was interviewed by Michael Smee for the BBC Overseas Service programme *Highlight*.

July 15
– John and Cynthia bought "Kenwood" in Saint George's Hill, Surrey. The mock-Tudor mansion in a private estate next to the golf course cost him £20,000.

July 16
– The first edition of *Top Gear* was broadcast by the BBC Light Programme.

July 17
– The Beatles recorded their fourth Bank Holiday Special *From Us To You* for the BBC Light Programme. They played 'Long Tall Sally', 'If I Fell', 'I'm Happy Just To Dance With You', 'Things We Said Today', 'I Should Have Known Better', 'Boys', 'Kansas City'/'Hey-Hey-Hey-Hey'. John read the closing credits.
– The single 'From A Window' by Billy J. Kramer & The Dakotas, written by Lennon & McCartney, was released in the UK as Parlophone R 5156.

July 18
– The Beatles flew to Blackpool to spend the day rehearsing for the next day's live broadcast of *Mike and Bernie Winters' Big Night Out* from the ABC Theatre, Blackpool.

July 19
– *ABC Theatre, Blackpool.* The Beatles appeared in a live transmission of *Mike and Bernie Winters' Big Night Out*. They played 'A Hard Day's Night', 'And I Love Her', 'If I Fell', 'Things We Said Today' and 'Long Tall Sally' as well as participating in various sketches with Mike and Bernie.

July 20
– The single **'I'll Cry Instead'/'I'm Happy Just To Dance With You'** was released in the US as Capitol 5234.

July 10: An unpleasant incident

The only sour note to the day came from the uncle of Anita Cochrane, who plastered Liverpool with 30,000 leaflets recounting his niece's affair with Paul and its outcome. Anita Cochrane, an 18-year-old Beatles fan, discovered that she was pregnant after partying with Paul at Stuart Sutcliffe's flat in Gambier Terrace. Unable to contact him by registered letters and telegrams, she eventually retained a lawyer who threatened legal action. Allegedly, it was only then that NEMS responded, offering her £5 a week maintenance. Brian Epstein is said to have intervened personally and offered £5,000 in exchange for renouncing all claims on Paul (published figures vary depending on source). The agreement said that Anita must never bring Paul to court or say or imply that he was the father of her child, Philip Paul Cochrane, nor must she ever reveal the terms of the agreement. All seemed to be well until today's civic reception for The Beatles when her outraged uncle intervened.

– The single 'And I Love Her'/'If I Fell' was released in the US as CAPITOL 5235.
– The album SOMETHING NEW was released in the US as CAPITOL ST 2108.
SIDE A: 'I'll Cry Instead', 'Things We Said Today', 'Anytime At All', 'When I Get Home', Slow Down', 'Matchbox';
SIDE B: 'Tell Me Why', 'And I Love Her', 'I'm Happy Just To Dance With You', 'If I Fell', 'Komm, Gib Mir Deine Hand'.

July 23
– The Night Of A Hundred Stars, *London Palladium,* with Judy Garland, Sir Laurence Olivier, et al. The Beatles took part in a sketch and played a brief set for this benefit concert in aid of the Combined Theatrical Charities Appeals Council.

July 25
– *BBC Television Centre, Shepherd's Bush.* George and Ringo each made appearances as members of the *Juke Box Jury* panel. George's edition was transmitted live that evening, while Ringo's was taped and screened the following week.

July 26
– *Opera House, Blackpool.*

July 28
– The Beatles flew to Stockholm, Sweden, on the 11:10 am flight from Heathrow Airport, London. Johanneshovs Isstadion, Stockholm,

Zsa Zsa Gabor rehearses with The Beatles at the London Palladium, July 23.

with The Kays, The Moonlighters, The Streaplers, Jimmy Justice, The Mascots and The Shanes. The group did two houses each night in the ice hockey stadium.

July 29
– *Johanneshovs Isstadion, Stockholm.*

July 30
– The Beatles flew from Stockholm to London, arriving mid-afternoon.

July 31
– The single 'It's For You' by Cilla Black, written by Lennon & McCartney, was released in the UK as PARLOPHONE R 5162.

August 1
– Ringo's appearance on *Juke Box Jury* was broadcast by BBC TV.

August 2
– *Gaumont Cinema, Bournemouth,* with The Kinks, Mike Berry and Adrienne Poster (later known as Posta).

August 3
– The BBC Light Programme broadcast The Beatles' fourth Bank Holiday Special *From Us To You.*
– A documentary, *Follow The Beatles,* filmed while they were making *A Hard Day's Night,* was screened by BBC1.

August 9
– *Futurist Theatre, Scarborough.*

August 10
– The single 'Do You Want To Know A Secret'/'Thank You Girl' was released in the US as OLDIES 45 OL 149.
– The single 'Please, Please Me'/'From Me To You' was released in the US as OLDIES 45 OL 150.

– The single 'Love Me Do'/'P.S. I Love You' was released in the US as OLDIES 45 OL 151.
– The single 'Twist And Shout'/'There's A Place' was released in the US as OLDIES 45 OL 152.

August 11
– *Abbey Road.* The Beatles began work on what was to be The Beatles For Sale album. They recorded John's 'Baby's In Black'.

August 12
– The film *A Hard Day's Night* opened simultaneously in 500 American cinemas.
– *The New York Times:* "This is going to surprise you – it may knock you right out of your chair – but the film with those incredible chaps, The Beatles, is a whale of a comedy."

The New York World-Telegram & Sun: "A Hard Day's Night turns out to be funnier than you would expect and every bit as loud as the wildest Beatle optimist could hope."

The New York Herald Tribune: "It is really an egghead picture, lightly scrambled, a triumph of The Beatles and the bald."

The New York Daily News: "The picture adds up to a lot of fun, not only for the teenagers but for grown-ups as well. It's clean, wholesome entertainment."

The New York Journal-American: "The picture turned out to be a completely wacky, off-beat entertainment that's frequently remindful of the Marx Brothers' comedies of the '30's."

The New York Post: "A Hard Day's Night suggests a Beatle career in the movies as big as they've already been in stage and dancehall. They have the songs, the patter, and the histrionic flair. No more is needed."

The Washington Post: "The main thing about it is that you can't hear it because the audience sort of over-participates."

The Washington Evening Star: "The film appears to be a genuinely funny British comedy; though nobody may ever really know. Its stars seem agreeable personalities with a zest for spoofing themselves and their idolaters and it looks as if it might be fun if you could hear it as well as see it."

– The single 'From A Window'/'I'll Be On My Way' by Billy J. Kramer & The

Dakotas, written by Lennon & McCartney, was released in the US as IMPERIAL 66051.
– Ringo was interviewed by Chris Hutchins for the BBC Light Programme's *The Teen Scene*, during one of Brian Epstein's "At Home" parties at his flat in Whaddon House, William Mews.

August 14
– *Abbey Road.* The Beatles worked on 'I'm A Loser', 'Mr Moonlight' and 'Leave My Kitten Alone' which was not released until the 1995 Anthology 1 CD.

August 16
– *Opera House, Blackpool*, with The Who, then known as The High Numbers.

August 18
– The Beatles set off on their 25-date American Tour. Their Clipper took them first to Winnipeg, Canada, where 500 fans stood screaming on the airport roof as the group did a couple of Hello America radio interviews from the plane. The plane stopped again in Los Angeles, where there were 2,000 fans and even more interviews. Finally, at 6:24 pm The Beatles touched down at San Francisco International Airport to mass hysteria from 9,000 screaming West Coast fans. The plan was for them to make a brief appearance at "Beatlesville" before being taken by limousine to the Hilton Hotel. Beatlesville was a small platform, about a mile northwest of the main airport buildings, surrounded by a cyclone fence and guarded by 180 San Mateo County Sherriffs. However, the chaos and screaming was so intense when they arrived that The Beatles remained in their limousine and held a quick strategy conference.

Eventually they decided it was worth the risk and, after a considerable delay, they entered the compound to wave to the crowd. Ringo was the first in but his presence caused mass hysteria: thousands of girls pushed forward, some trying to scale the fence as other fans charged a barrier of parked cars but were driven back by counter-attacking deputies. No sooner had Paul, George and John mounted the stage than the deputies herded them all back to their limousine and rushed

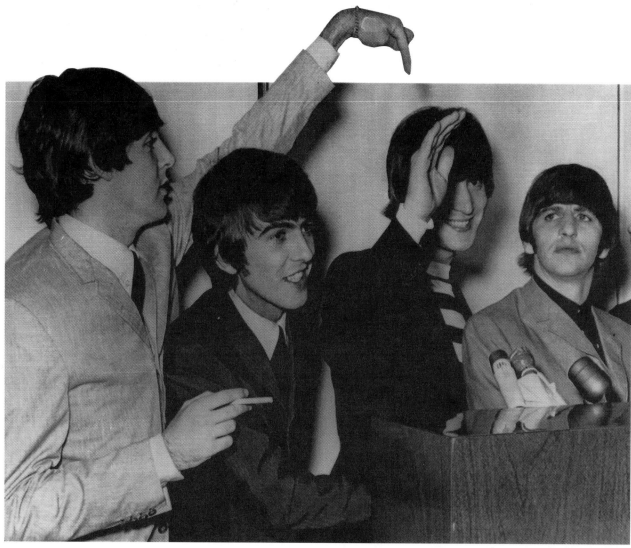

Press conference at the San Francisco Hilton, August 19.

them away from the hysterical scene. The link fences were being pushed over by the sheer weight of fans, those in front crushed against the links, with only the burly police straining with all their weight to keep the fences upright.

That night, John, Ringo, Derek Taylor, Billy Preston (Little Richard's organist and later an Apple artist) and Diana Vero, Brian Epstein's secretary, spent a few hours in a small club in Chinatown called The Rickshaw where they met Dale Robertson, the cowboy actor.

August 19
– *Cow Palace, San Francisco, California*, with The Bill Black Combo, The Exciters, The Righteous Brothers and Jackie DeShannon. The group's standard set for the tour was: 'Twist And Shout', 'You Can't Do That', 'All My Loving', She Loves You', Things We Said Today', Roll Over Beethoven', 'Can't Buy Me Love', If I Fell', 'I Want To Hold Your Hand',

'Boys', 'A Hard Day's Night' and 'Long Tall Sally'. Sometimes they would open with 'I Saw Her Standing There' and close with 'Twist And Shout'.

The Beatles played a total of 29 minutes. The gross was $91,670, the net take $49,80. They left behind an astonished populace, 17,130 delirious fans, 19 schoolgirls so overcome with emotion that first aid was necessary and one boy with a dislocated shoulder. *The San Francisco Examiner* reported "Although it was publicised as music, all that was heard and seen of the Mersey Sound was something like a jet engine shrieking through a summer lightning storm because of the yelling fans. It had no mercy, and afterwards everyone still capable of speech took note of a ringing in the ears which lasted for as long as The Beatles had played.

"The eerie scene of four young men with shaggy hairdos wiggling on the stage and moving their lips inaudibly

"You can figure it this way, that's **16,000** kids who aren't out **stealing hubcaps."**

DEPUTY SHERIFF

was exaggerated by the flashes from a hundred cameras like sheet lightning in the Midwest."

Thousands of cameras would have been a more accurate assessment.

The Cow Palace was nearly filled by 7 pm, an hour before showtime. When The Beatles appeared the girls screamed for a solid four minutes forty-five seconds. *The San Francisco Examiner* reported: "As soon as they left, the screaming stopped abruptly." Fifty fans were hurt and two arrested, fifty more were forcibly prevented from climbing on stage. At the end of the set, The Beatles dropped their instruments on stage, ran for the waiting car and were gone before the audience knew they had finished playing.

On the 15th floor of the hotel, 35 girls were rounded up all together trying to sneak past the guards. Some of the girls were dressed as maids. The Beatles did not stay to party, but flew straight to their next venue instead.

August 20

– Convention Center, Las Vegas, Nevada. At 1 am The Beatles' chartered plane touched down at Old McCarran Field in Las Vegas, and they were promptly driven to the Sahara Hotel where, despite a curfew, 2,000 fans were waiting to scream a welcome. The fans were dispersed by police using dogs. They spent the morning in their

Above: Paul in Las Vegas. Below: The Beatles cast fishing lines from their suite at the Edgewater Hotel in Seatlle.

penthouse suite on the 18th floor of the hotel while fans attempted to scale the walls, climb the garbage shoot and use the freight elevator. The group left for the 8,000-seater Convention Center at 2:30 for a sound check. The afternoon show opened at 4 pm but it was not until 5:30 that The Beatles took the stage to the usual screams, shrieks and showers of jelly babies.

After the concert the police used brutal tactics to force the fans away from backstage when The Beatles made their exit. One reporter had her foot run over by a police motorcycle, another girl was bruised in the ribs by a cop's night-stick. The Beatles made $30,000 for their trouble. The police were concerned that underage fans would enter gambling casinos if The Beatles visited them so they were requested to stay away. The Beatles had two slot machines in their rooms, but otherwise did no gambling.

August 21

– Seattle Center Coliseum, Seattle, Washington. The group stayed at the Edgewater Inn, later to become legendary as a rock star/groupie hangout, immortalised by Frank Zappa. All four of them dropped fishing lines out of their windows but no-one caught anything. At the press conference before their show, Paul criticised some of the American magazines, "that have printed some pretty terrible stories about us".

The *Seattle Post-Intelligencer* reported on the concert: "The original plan was for 16 Seattle police officers to escort the British quartet down a corridor, across 18 feet of open space and onto the stage. As The Beatles and their cortege whipped from the corridor, a phalanx of youngsters swept down a ramp from the balcony. The officers nearest the ramp pivoted like grid-iron tackles. Youngsters bounced off blue clad soldiers. Ringo, John, Paul and George were gone like gazelles, down a short tunnel toward the stage. Out of the chute like Brahma bulls, they bounced to their places as the Coliseum rose in one vast adolescent moan. Then the screams split the vaulted ceiling."

The band hit the stage at 9:25 and all 14,720 girls in the audience seemed to have brought their cameras. The

auditorium was illuminated with sheet lightning from the flash bulbs. While the band was onstage, the police recruited Navy volunteers from the audience and formed them in a double chain from the stage exit to the dressing room corridor. The Beatles played their final note, dropped their instruments, leaped to the back of the stage and out through the door. Hundreds of teenagers swept down the ramps straight into the cordon of United States Navy officers, standing with locked arms. The Beatles put their heads down and ducked their way through the narrow passage between the straining bodies and made it to the corridor mouth which the police promptly plugged after them. The car that was to have taken The Beatles back to the hotel was so badly damaged by fans that it had to be abandoned and it was another hour before the crowds had thinned enough for the group to be spirited out of the building in an ambulance. The next day, a hotel maid discovered two 16-year-old girls hiding under the bed in a fourth floor room and another in the closet.

August 22

– Empire Stadium, Vancouver, British Columbia, Canada. The show began at 8:14 and The Beatles came on at 9:23. Despite the long show, many reporters still thought that The Beatles' 29-minute set was too short. William Littler, in a grumpy piece in the *Vancouver Sun*, said, "Seldom in Vancouver's entertainment history have so many (20,261) paid so much ($5.25 top price) for so little (27 minutes) as did the audience which screamed at The Beatles in Empire Stadium Saturday night."

Three attempts were made to smash the ten-foot high stadium gates, and it finally buckled under the strain seconds after The Beatles began their performance, but only a dozen or so fans managed to get in before police and ushers got it closed again and held it shut with their bodies. Their exit was timed to perfection. They completed 'Long Tall Sally', bowed low while unstrapping their guitars, bolted from the stage into waiting limousines and with motorcycle outriders, they

"We slipped them in pretty easily. They're just **four** **little bits of fellas.** If they hadn't been dressed **so crazily,** we would **never** had known them."

DEPUTY POLICE INSPECTOR THOMAS RENAGHAN

<u>John:</u> **"I don't mind not being as popular as Ringo, or George or Paul** because if the group is popular **that's what matters."**

America: as the stadiums became larger The Beatles' sound shrank until it was barely audible above the screams.

were out of the stadium fewer than 30 seconds from their last note. The Beatles drove straight to the airport where they caught a plane to Los Angeles.

Thousands of teenagers left their seats and rushed the stage, crushing hundreds of young girls against the restraining fence. Dozens of girls suffered broken ribs and hundreds were treated for hysteria and shock.

August 23
– *The Hollywood Bowl, Hollywood, California.* For the concert, 18,700 people filled the Bowl, sold out four months earlier, for their concert. Outside 600 teenagers who were unable to get tickets shrieked, shouted and pushed to get in. Police made several arrests for disturbing the peace, trespassing and destroying property. A compact car was parked alongside the stage in which the group made their getaway as the concert ended at 10 pm. About 60 teenagers ran to the closest gate to see them drive off and used a photographer's car as a vantage point; the roof and bonnet of which were caved in. There was a huge traffic jam in the neighbourhood afterwards as thousands of parents converged on the Bowl to take their children home after the show. Police and firemen had set up roadblocks and closed off the whole Bowl area; local residents were given passes in order to get to their homes

After the concert there was a private party for the movie colony in the Bel-Air home of Mr & Mrs Alan Livingstone, president of Capitol Records. More than 500 attended the $25 a ticket affair which raised about $10,000 for the Haemophilia Foundation of Southern California. In the *San Fernando Valley Citizen-News*, <u>Paul</u> was photographed holding Rebel Lee Robinson, granddaughter of Edward G. Robinson.

Before the show, there was a press conference in which the group received five golds records and the key to California. When asked what they thought of Goldwater they gave a thumbs down sign. Dozens of teenage girls had managed to sneak into the conference and one of them asked <u>Paul</u> if he would like to learn to fly. It turned out her father had his own plane and she would be happy to teach him.
– The Beatles stayed in a rented house at 356 St. Pierre Road, in Brown Canyon, Bel-Air. That night, West Los Angeles police took more than 50 adolescents into technical custody for violating a 10 pm curfew as over 400 fans milled around at the junction of Sunset Boulevard and Bel-Air Road hoping to see The Beatles. St. Pierre Road itself was blocked by police. Over $5,000 worth of damage was done to shrubs and flowers by the fans and many residents turned on their sprinkler systems to try and ward off the teenagers, but to no avail.

August 24
– <u>John</u> managed to sneak out with Derek Taylor and Neil Aspinall for a few hours' shopping, but the outing was cut short when he was recognised.
– The single **'Slow Down'/'Matchbox'** was released in the US as Capitol 5255.

August 25
– <u>Paul</u> and <u>George</u> visited Burt Lancaster's house to watch a private screening of Peter Sellers' *A Shot In The Dark*. <u>Ringo</u> was watching a Jack Good TV show when Jayne Mansfield turned up at the doorstep. (<u>Paul</u> had said he would like to meet her.) <u>John</u> greeted her and she tugged at his hair and asked **"Is this real?"**

That evening <u>John</u> and Jayne went to the Whiskey A-Go-Go where they were

joined by <u>George</u>. <u>George</u> asked photographers to leave them alone and when one of them refused, <u>George</u> threw water at him.

<u>George</u>: "I finally decided to baptise him by chucking the ice-water at the bottom of my glass over him." When no-one could see, Jayne put her hand on <u>John</u>'s thigh and scared him.

August 26
– *Red Rocks Amphitheater, Denver, Colorado.* Though 2,000 seats remained empty, the 7,000 fans who bought tickets created a box-office record for this open-air stadium.

August 27
– *Cincinnati Gardens, Cincinnati, Ohio.* The press conference before the show was more animated than usual. *The Cincinnati Enquirer* reported: "A newspaperman from Dayton, who said the four ought to be able to handle a crowd of 30,000 without police protection, was told by Lennon, 'Well, maybe you could. You're fatter than we are.'... Teenagers stand up and scream piercingly – and painfully – when The Beatles appear. Why? They were asked. McCartney said none of them knew, but he had heard teenagers pay to go to their shows just to scream. 'A lot of them don't even want to listen,' he said, 'because they have got the records.'

"A reporter asked what they thought of the psychiatrist who drew an analogy between the hysteria generated by their beat and the speeches of the Nazi dictator Adolf Hitler. Lennon said abruptly, 'Tell him to shut up. He's off his head.'

"A questioner asked McCartney what he thought of columnist Walter Winchell. McCartney answered bluntly, 'He said I'm married and I'm not.' 'Maybe he wants to marry you,' Harrison suggested...

"The four answered a question admitting that the show that comes after the show is sometimes the one to see. They said they whooped it up until 4 or 5 in the morning, depending on how much sleep they need."

There were 17,000 in the audience, girls fainted and one went into convulsions. As usual, the show itself was drowned out by screaming. *The Cincinnati Enquirer* ran a headline: "Teenagers Revel In Madness: Young Fans

"Some Long Island **fans** in the crowd outside say they are **switching** to The Rolling Stones because you didn't **wave** to them from the hotel windows."

Drop Veneer Of Civilisation For Beatles." The newspaper reported: "The estimated 115 degree temperature melted bouffant hairdos as well as inhibitions. Well groomed girls who had hoped, without really hoping, that they would attract the eye of a Beatle, began to look like Brillo pads. A priest turned around in the crowd, looked at a reporter with tears in his eyes and said, 'I don't believe it. Just look at them. Look at their faces!' A technician from a television station was trying to measure the sound with an instrument. He gave up when the instrument recorded its maximum reading and broke."

The Beatles ran from the stage, straight to their Cadillac limousines and headed to Lunken Airport where their chartered plane was waiting to take them to New York. They took off shortly after midnight.

August 28
– Forest Hills Tennis Stadium, Forest Hills, New York. When The Beatles' plane touched down at 3:02 am at Kennedy Airport, 3,000 fans were waiting for them, and another few hundred were stationed outside the Delmonico Hotel, at Park Avenue and 59th Street, where they were staying, even though their hotel was supposed to be a secret. By the next morning there were thousands of fans there. The girls overturned a concrete plant tub outside the hotel and tried all manner of ingenious ways to get in: pretending they lived there and delivering fake packages. Two girls arrived dressed as nurses to tend The Beatles. Deputy Police Inspector Thomas Renaghan, chief of Manhattan North detectives said the damage wasn't too bad. "We slipped them in pretty easily. They're just four little bits of fellas. If they hadn't been dressed so crazily, we would never had known them."

As The Beatles pushed through the police barricades to reach the hotel, one fan managed to snatch Ringo's St Christopher medal from his neck. Fans stayed outside until 4 am, screaming every time anyone came near any of the windows in the hotel. Many of them carried portable radios tuned in to the various Beatles stations. Police used bullhorns to ask hotel guests to stay away from the windows.

The girls were restrained by police barricades erected on the other side of Park Avenue, but anyone appearing at a window caused screams and chaos as the girls spilled out into the street, disrupting the traffic. They were encouraged by radio reporters who thrust microphones in front of their faces and yelled, **"Okay, let's hear it for The Beatles!"**

At the press conference, heavily infiltrated with fans, a reporter said, Someone in The Beatles party mumbled, **"If they want to go away for that reason, let them,"** but Paul responded, **"The police said no. They told us to stay away from the windows, boys. After all, we can't get into trouble with the police chief."**

The Beatles were asked what they thought of the "oversized roughnecks" who appeared at the airport scene the previous night. **"That was us,"** replied Paul.

John said at the press conference: The girl who stole Ringo's medal, Angie McGowan, returned it and posed for photographs while first Ringo, then Paul, kissed her on the cheek.

The stadium's 15,983 seats were sold out and extra field seats were added at $6.50 each, a steep price in those days. The fans were kept from The Beatles by an eight-feet-high fence topped with barbed wire. The group flew to the stadium by helicopter from the Wall Street heliport.

Bob Dylan, accompanied by his road manager and journalist Al Aronowitz, came to visit the group at their hotel after the show, and turned The Beatles and Brian Epstein on to marijuana for the first time.

August 30
– Convention Hall, Atlantic City, New Jersey. The Beatles stayed at the Lafayette Motel in Atlantic City. At 2:15 pm, in order to get through the crowds of fans, the group had to sneak out of the motel in the back of a fish truck. Six miles west of Atlantic City they transferred to the tour bus which took them straight to the Philadelphia Convention Hall.

There were 19,000 fans in the audience. Five ambulances were

New York: Ringo with Angie McGowan, who snatched his St Christopher medal.

on hand to treat casualties among the 500 teenagers outside the auditorium, and a police sergeant collapsed from exhaustion.

August 31
– The group spent their rest days holed up at the Lafayette Motel. Paul used the time to get through to Elvis on the phone.

Ringo: "Paul had a nice talk with him... Though we haven't met him, we consider ourselves good friends and appreciate what each of us is doing. El and his manager were very generous to us, showering us with presents and keepsakes. These include some very expensive silver guns and holsters which the four of us and our manager Brian received."

September 2
– *Convention Hall, Philadelphia, Pennsylvania*, before an audience of 13,000 fans.

Before the show there was the usual press conference where 50 police, 25 VIPs and 25 reporters crowded into a meeting room near the hall.

September 3
– *State Fair Coliseum, Indianapolis, Indiana.* At the obligatory press conference, this one held at the State Fair Radio Building, a reporter asked The Beatles if teenagers screamed at them because they were revolting against their parents. **Paul: "They've been revolting for years."**
John: "I've never noticed them revolting." Paul was asked if he was anti-religious. **"I'm not religious, but I'm not anti-religious. I'm not an atheist; I'm agnostic. I just don't know."** They were asked if they would like to be able to walk down the street without being recognised.
John: "We used to do this with no money in our pockets. There's no point in it."

The Beatles spent two nights in Indianapolis in all, staying at the Speedway Motel on West 16th Street. The group all agreed that the shows at the Coliseum were "quite quiet"

Above: Ringo, John and Brian Epstein.
Opposite: "Often Was Heard Disparaging Words" reads the curious caption in George's US newspaper.

"These Beatles make about fifty million bucks a year and they don't even have to buy a haircut in this country."

compared to other venues. They set foot on the Coliseum stage at 6:21 before an audience of 12,413 screaming fans, mostly girls. After the press conference they did an evening show, this time to 16,924 fans. Thirty girls were treated for hysteria, one fan cut his arm when he was shoved against a glass door and a girl cut her hand while climbing a fence. When The Beatles boarded their chartered plane at Weir Cook Municipal Airport, they were $85,231.93 the richer. ($1,719.02 had already been deducted for state gross income tax. There was some debate in the press as to whether The Beatles (NEMS Ltd) counted as a foreign corporation - if not, then they owed the federal government a further $42,000.)
– Mrs Jeane Dixon, the psychic who forecast the assassination of President Kennedy, predicted that The Beatles' plane would crash on take-off from Indiana en route to Denver, Colorado, and that three Beatles would die and the fourth be seriously maimed. She was wrong.

September 4
– *Milwaukee Auditorium, Milwaukee, Wisconsin.*

September 5
– *International Amphitheater, Chicago, Illinois.* There had been plans for a civic welcome and 100,000 people were expected but Special Events Director Colonel Jack Reilly cancelled the arrangements saying

he did not have sufficient police to spare **"for a bunch of singers"**. Paul commented on TV and radio, **"So we shall have to go in by the back door again and the fans won't get a chance to see us or we to see them. It's a great big drag."**

Nonetheless Chicago was ready for The Beatles. The Andy Frain Organisation sent ten of its ushers to The Beatles' concert the previous night in Milwaukee to scout the tactics of The Beatles' fans, and the 170 ushers and 35 usherettes were specially selected as being non-Beatles fans so that they would not succumb to the hysteria. Stationed around the auditorium were 320 Chicago cops. One of them, patrolman Anthony Dizonne, remembered the Frank Sinatra days. **"This is kind of like Sinatra multiplied by 50 or 100,"** he observed.

The Beatles' plane flew into the rarely used Midway Airport an hour late. They were due at 3:40 pm but by the time they arrived over 5,000 fans were waiting for them. The girls were kept behind a chain-link fence as the group were bundled into a long black limousine and roared off to the Stock Yard Inn attached to the amphitheater at 42nd Street and Halsted. The crowds outside were so thick that the group had to enter through the kitchens. *The Chicago Sun-Times* reported only one casualty at the airport, a 14-year-old girl who was treated for a cut finger.

At the concert, fans were frisked and all large signs confiscated because they would block the view for others. Jelly beans, candy kisses and anything else that the fans were likely to throw at the group were also confiscated. Despite this, Paul was hit in the face by a spent flashbulb.

After the show half a dozen fans were taken to Evangelical Hospital in various states of emotional and physical exhaustion. One girl was poked in the eye but left the ambulance to rejoin the audience.

After the show, they hurried into waiting cars and drove straight back to the airport where they flew on to Detroit. A police guard was mounted

"You're behaving like a bunch of children. This plane is in danger of crashing unless you sit quietly. It is vital that you fasten your seat belts..."

on their hotel room to prevent fans from tearing it apart for souvenirs.

September 6
– *Olympic Stadium, Detroit, Michigan.* Two shows in the home of Tamla Motown.

September 7
– *Maple Leaf Gardens, Toronto, Canada.* The Beatles flew into town in their charter Electra and parked at the old airport terminal. The first people on board were two immigration nurses who were only interested in getting the group's autographs. They were followed by an immigration officer who had the same thought in mind. George told a reporter from the *Toronto Daily Star*, "We don't like being asked for autographs by the officials. Everywhere we go it's always the police guarding us, or the journalists or the relatives of the promoters who ask us to sign."

They barely made it into the King Edward Hotel. Paul's shirt was ripped and torn: **"I thought I was for it, but an immense copper lifted me up and shoved me into the elevator."**

Ringo: "We got separated from John and George coming in but the police were very good."

In order to get them from the hotel to the gig, the police used a paddy wagon and fooled the fans by leaving from the back of the hotel. Paul told the *Daily Star* reporter that they had amused themselves by making sign language at a group of office girls in the National Trust building across from their hotel, **"Normally we don't look out the windows because fans go a little potty but we were amazed at seeing the girls there on Labor Day and gave them a cheery wave or two."**

– The paper ran another news item headed "Beatles' Blonde Snubs Mayor": "Mayor Philip Givens couldn't get to see The Beatles. The mayor and his wife called at the singers' hotel suite at 1.30 pm today to pay their respects. According to the Mayor, they got 'a very rude reception'. When they knocked, the mayor said, a blonde answered and took his card. 'Then she said, "Two of them are asleep and two of them are with relatives. Nobody gets in," and slammed the door in my face'."

There were 35,522 paying customers at the two shows, which resulted in a cheque for $93,000 for the group. Some 4,000 men and women police and Mounties were on duty at the Maple Leaf Gardens and a five block area around the Gardens was roped off and patrolled for 12 hours before the group was due to arrive.

Showtime for the first set was 4 pm but The Beatles did not appear before 5:30, introduced by Jungle Jay Nelson of station CHUM. A thoughtful review in the *Toronto Telegram* said, "They don't rely on obvious sexuality, either in movement or song, but obviously there is a large element of sexuality in their appeal. Any sexuality is once removed: it occurs in the eye of the beholder rather than from any overt action by The Beatles."

Between sets there was the usual press conference. First The Beatles posed with local disc jockeys, fan club presidents and Miss Canada, then the questions began: **"What time do you get up in the morning?"**
John: "Two o'clock in the afternoon."

They were asked if they thought they were setting a good example by smoking.
George: "We don't set examples."
Paul: "Why should we?"
Ringo: "We even drink."

It has been said that you appeal to the maternal instinct in these girls...
John: "That's a dirty lie."

They were asked why they didn't record all the songs that they write.
Paul: "It's just not good policy to flood the market with records like they did in America. Naughty them."

How long do you think you'll last?
John: "Longer than you."

September 8
– *The Forum, Montreal, Quebec, Canada.* The two houses were seen by 21,000 fans.

On the plane from Montreal to Jacksonville, Florida, after the concert, Ringo, who was normally ill-at-ease

John: "The best view of the country is over the blue shoulder of a policeman."

"The Beatles are 100 feet away, they came thousands of miles to be here. The only thing preventing their appearance is cine-cameramen."

on planes, relaxed and threw a cushion at someone. Immediately a pillow fight ensued with all the first-class pillows winging through the air. Suddenly a voice came over the intercom, Everyone froze, then returned to their seats and quietly fastened themselves in. Then Paul appeared, returning to his seat, a huge grin on his face at pulling one over on his mates.

September 9
– The Beatles' plane was re-routed by Hurricane Dora, and landed instead at Key West at 3:30 am. Even in the middle of the night hundreds of teenagers were waiting to scream a welcome.

September 11
– *Gator Bowl, Jacksonville, Florida.* After a rest day in Key West, mostly spent drinking, The Beatles finally got to Jacksonville. Once there, they had a hard time reaching the Gator Bowl. After a press conference at their hotel, The George Washington, two dozen police battled about 500 Beatles fans for 15 minutes in the hotel's parking garage at the intersection of Julia and Monroe Streets trying to get The Beatles out of the elevator and into their limousine. It took the group 15 minutes to move 25 feet. Eventually the police drove a flying wedge through the crowd with motorcycle outriders and managed to transfer the group to their trailer at the Gator Bowl by 7:15.
– Despite the screaming girls, The Beatles had to refuse to go on until newsreel and television cameramen had left the arena. Newsreel footage, and particularly footage of the group playing, was a valuable commodity and the cameramen refused to leave. Eventually Derek Taylor stepped up to the microphone, shirt-sleeved, and issued an ultimatum. He said that the film made as newsreels was ultimately sold and shown in cinemas with no royalties paid to The Beatles.

After the announcement Captain C. L. Raines and Captain I. L. Griffin gave the order to end the movie-making. Police officers physically restrained eight cameramen, covered their camera lenses with their hands

Hurricane Dora

The September 11th concert ran smoothly, though a strong wind, the aftermath of Hurricane Dora, whipped their hair and threatened their instruments as they played. Fans charged the stage after the last number but were restrained by a police blockade and a six-foot fence. Although 30,000 tickets had been sold, only 23,000 showed up. Around 7,000 out-of-town fans who bought tickets were unable to see the concerts because Hurricane Dora had destroyed roads and bridges. President Johnson was in Jacksonville inspecting the damage as The Beatles played. That evening, a few minutes after midnight, their aircraft took off for Boston from Imeson Airport. No fans had discovered their travel plans, so for once there was no hysteria at the airport.

and led them by the arm from the performance area.

– Derek Taylor spoke to a *Florida Times-Union* reporter on the plane who reported, "Taylor was somewhat apologetic for the showdown he had brought about over the cameramen, but he said a great deal of money was involved. He said this was the first time in the tour history he'd had to make such a speech."

In Detroit, earlier, The Beatles had announced that they would refuse to appear on stage in Jacksonville if the audience was segregated. They had heard that blacks in Florida were only allowed to sit in the balconies at concerts. Their statement read,

It turned out that there never were plans for the concert to be segregated.
– The single 'I Don't Want To See You Again' by Peter & Gordon, written by <u>Paul McCartney</u>, was released in the UK as Columbia DB 7356.

September 12
– *Boston Garden, Boston, Massachusetts.*

September 13
– *Civic Center, Baltimore, Maryland.*
– The Beatles stayed at the Holiday Inn, where mounted police were required to restrain the fans. At the Civic Arena, two girls had themselves delivered in a large cardboard box labelled "Beatles Fan Mail" but were discovered by a guard checking all deliveries.

September 14
– *Civic Arena, Pittsburgh, Pennsylvania.* The Beatles' Lockheed Electra arrived at Greater Pittsburgh Airport half an hour late at 4:36 pm to the screams of 4,000 fans, mostly girls, some of whom had been waiting since 9:00 am. The plane parked at

Gate 16 and the girls began to scream. The organisers were taking no chances and private detectives boarded the plane, then followed the group out and into the waiting limousine which sped quickly away, surrounded by motorcycle police. There were 120 police at the airport including 15 on horseback, a security force even more elaborate than that used by presidents. Teenagers lined Parkway West to see The Beatles' motorcade drive into town. Five thousand fans surrounded the Civic Arena where The Beatles gave a press conference, then ate a catered meal before showtime.

The paid attendance was 12,603, the City Amusement tax was $6,251 and the Federal Levy $5,001.

September 15
– *Public Hall, Cleveland, Ohio.* In Cleveland The Beatles stayed at the Sheraton-Cleveland which, as usual, was inundated with fans: a girl of 11 showed up with a stolen key to a $35-a-night room, a boy hid in a packing case being trucked in, an underage fan tried to get into the Kon Tiki Bar, saying he had reservations for cocktails and one girl fainted on the sidewalk outside but recovered enough to say that she thought the nearest first aid station was in the hotel.

The police requested that they stay on the floor on which the press conference was to be held, rather than the presidential suite because too many fans knew they were registered to stay in those rooms. On Public Square outside the only time the police cordons broke was when The Beatles appeared at a window and waved. Traffic was restricted to one mile an hour in case fans surged forward, but the rush hour proceeded smoothly without too much delay.

"We will **not appear** unless **negroes** are allowed to sit **anywhere.**"

"We have **never** had a show stopped. These policemen are a bunch of **amateurs.**"

Shortly after The Beatles took the stage a great wave of teenagers began pushing to the front, slowly taking the police line with them. More than 100 police leaned into the crowd but they were steadily forced back towards the stage, threatening the safety of the group. Inspector Michael Blackwell and Deputy Inspector Carl C. Bare panicked and decided to stop the show.

Bare charged out of the wings onto the stage, shouldered The Beatles aside, grabbed a microphone and bellowed, The Beatles, however, were in the middle of 'All My Loving' and carried on playing. Bare turned and walked towards John, who instead of stopping, did a little dance and made a face at

him. Then Inspector Blackwell came storming out, gesturing to the group to get off the stage. He grabbed George by the elbow and steered him to the wings. George turned on him, **"What the hell do you think you are doing? Get your hands off me!"** The crowd shouted in protest but the music stopped and The Beatles slowly left the stage. The steel safety curtain came down and Blackwell and Bare stared down the booing fans.

In their dressing room The Beatles complained to the news director of local radio station KYW, Art Schreiber. **"This had never happened to us before,"** said John. In the wings Brian diplomatically sided with the police. **"The police were**

"Sit down! The show is over!"

Inspector Carl Bare of the Cleveland Juvenile Bureau stops the show.

absolutely right. This has never happened before, but it was clear to me from the start that there was something very wrong. The enthusiasm of the crowd was building much too early."

After lecturing the audience, Blackwell allowed the show to continue after a ten-minute delay, but only on condition that the audience remained in their seats and that the house lights stayed up. Derek Taylor asked them to remain in their seats and the fans began to chant, **"DON'T STAND UP, DON'T STAND UP, DON'T STAND UP"**. The curtain rose again and the group picked up where they left off and the rest of the show went well.

Later, Blackwell said, **"I don't blame the children. They're young and they can't be expected to behave like adults. And I don't blame The Beatles – there is nothing wrong with their act. But if we hadn't stopped it there would have been serious injury. One little girl was knocked down in the charge and there were 300 other youngsters about to trample her."** One girl was trampled but not seriously hurt. Another fainted.

Afterwards 500 fans attacked the stage door, but to no avail. The Beatles were already speeding away, using back roads, to their waiting aircraft at Cleveland Hopkins Airport. The police had cleverly run a riot bus, a converted paddy wagon, at high speed out of the hall while The Beatles escaped through the back door. The riot bus had been on duty all through the day, running between the Sheraton-Cleveland Hotel and Public Hall. At first the fans were fooled into thinking The Beatles were in it, but soon realised it was a decoy. In the end they ignored it. Just before showtime it made the trip again, this time with The Beatles as passengers, and the fans dismissed it.

The Sheraton-Cleveland Hotel refused to sell the bed linen that The Beatles had used, **"because the idea seems to be against good taste"** said the manager.

September 16
– *City Park Stadium, New Orleans, Louisiana.* The Beatles were scheduled to arrive at New Orleans Lakefront Airport where they were to be flown by helicopter to the Congress Inn. However, that was not what happened. First of all the helicopter blew a tyre, so limousines were ordered instead, but they went to Moisant Field, New Orleans International Airport by mistake. It turned out that this was to the good because that was where The Beatles' charter plane landed. They piled into the limousines and were off, complete with flashing blue lights and screaming sirens, at 3 am. Unfortunately The Beatles' car got separated from the rest of the motorcade and followed a different route. There were a few hundred fans near the hotel, standing along the road designated their official route, and when they saw The Beatles in an unguarded car they quickly surrounded it, screaming hysterically.

Police soon arrived and forced the fans aside, but as The Beatles' car was backing up, it hit a Kenner police patrol car, causing slight damage. Finally The Beatles made it to the motel, ran through the lobby, the laundry room then outside and to their motel rooms: a three room suite – Room 100. By 4 am most of the crowd had faded away. Two of The Beatles were sleeping, the other two were preparing to eat.

At the concert some 700 teenagers broke away from the stand and attempted to crash through the barriers keeping them from the stage. It took 225 New Orleans police more than 20 minutes to restore order. Mounted police patrolled the area around the stage while the fans who broke through onto the football field were roped off to one side. More than 200 fans collapsed and had to be revived with smelling salts and one girl had her arm broken but refused to go to hospital until after the show.

September 17
– *Municipal Stadium, Kansas City, Missouri.*

The Kansas Concert

September 17 was originally supposed to be a rest day but after seeing the amazing reception the group received elsewhere in the country, a wealthy promoter, Charles O. Finley, approached Brian Epstein with an offer of $100,000 to add Kansas City to their tour. Brian asked The Beatles if they would mind and without even looking up they said, "Whatever you think, Brian." Brian turned the offer down, despite the fact it was an enormous figure for the time. But Finley saw it as a matter of civic pride and was determined that Kansas City should see The Beatles. He offered $150,000,

a higher figure than an American artist had ever received and almost guaranteed to show a loss. The 41,000 seater stadium was half full, with 20,280 paying spectators. Finley, the owner of Kansas City Athletics, lost between $50,000 and $100,000 for sponsoring the show. Despite this he donated a further $25,000 to Mercy Hospital. He said, "I don't consider it any loss at all. The Beatles were brought here for the enjoyment of the children in this area and watching them last night they had complete enjoyment. I'm happy about that. Mercy Hospital benefited by $25,000.

The hospital gained, and I had a great gain by seeing the children and the hospital gain." An Athletics official said that ticket sales of 28,000 were needed to break even.

The Beatles flew in at 2 am in pouring rain. About 100 fans waited, staring at them from behind a wall of wet policemen. George slipped on the wet runway apron on his way to the limousine which transferred them to the Muehlebach Towers where they had the $100-a-day, 18th-floor terrace penthouse. It took seven bellmen to carry in the 200 items of luggage The Beatles party had

with them. A Kansas City actress had sent up a Missouri country ham, apple cider, a mincemeat pie and a watermelon.

To commemorate this extraordinary concert, The Beatles added 'Kansas City'/'Hey-Hey-Hey-Hey' to their repertoire, which the local fans loved. Excitement ran so high that the concert had to be stopped, with a threat of cancellation, if the audience did not calm down. They did and The Beatles played on.

The Muehlebach Towers sold the group's bed linen – 16 sheets and eight pillow cases – to a Chicago man for $750.

September 18
– *Memorial Coliseum, Dallas, Texas.* In Dallas the stage was three times higher than was normally used, which put Ringo some 15 feet above the ground. Before the show there was a press conference, as usual, mostly attended by 13-year-old girls from radio stations no-one had ever heard of before. Ringo was asked about the girls who had fallen to their knees and eaten the grass The Beatles walked upon. **Ringo: "I hope they don't get indigestion."**

Someone arranged for Paul to telephone Methodist Hospital and encourage Cheryl Howard, the 10-year-old victim of a hit-and-run driver who was fighting for her life. **"A pity you can't be with us tonight at the programme,"** he told her.

There were the usual scenes outside their hotel, the Cabana, where fans jumped into the fountain after finding all doors to the hotel blocked. When the group returned to the hotel they jumped from their car but were cut off from the back entrance by several hundred fans. George was knocked to his knees and Ringo almost went under but they made it through. During the struggle a girl was pushed through a glass door and was severely cut about the face. Several others were injured. After the show they drove straight to Dallas Love Field where their plane took off at 11:08, taking The Beatles to a ranch in Missouri for a rest.

September 19
– Oxfam printed half a million Christmas cards drawn by John Lennon.

September 20
– *Paramount Theater, Broadway, New York City,* "An Evening With The Beatles" with Steve Lawrence and Edie Gorme. One of the few charity concerts The Beatles gave, this on behalf of the United Cerebral Palsy Fund of New York, this performance was attended by 3,682 members of society, who paid up to $100 a ticket. Ed Sullivan visited the dressing room, Gloria Steinham was there, doing a story for *Cosmopolitan*, and Bob Dylan and his manager Albert Grossman went back to their motel with the band after the show. They stayed at the Riviera Motel, near Kennedy Airport, ready for the next morning's departure. That evening Brian Epstein accused press officer Derek Taylor of taking his limousine from outside the Paramount and called him a swine. Derek replied in kind and resigned, both as The Beatles' press officer and as Brian's personal assistant. He worked for a further three months showing his successor the ropes and was later to return to run the Apple press office.

September 21
– The Beatles' Flight BA 510 landed at Heathrow Airport, London, at 9:30 pm by which time thousands of fans had gathered on the roof of the Queen's Building to greet them. Continuous

Beatles music had been playing throughout the building and regular flight reports were announced, as their Boeing 707 crossed the Atlantic.
– The single 'I Don't Want To See You Again' by Peter & Gordon, written by Paul McCartney, was released in the US as Capitol 5272.

September 24
– Brickey Building Company Limited was formed by Ringo, to give himself and his fellow Beatles a reliable building and decorating service.

September 27
– *Prince Of Wales Theatre, London.* Ringo acted as one of a panel of celebrity judges in the final of The National Beat Group Competition, a charity event in aid of Oxfam. The second half of the show was broadcast live by BBC2 as *It's Beat Time*. Paul and Jane attended a party given to celebrate the first anniversary of The Pretty Things.

September 29
– *Abbey Road.* The Beatles worked on 'Every Little Thing', 'I Don't Want To Spoil The Party' and 'What You're Doing'.

September 30
– *Abbey Road.* The Beatles finished 'Every Little Thing' and worked on 'What You're Doing' and 'No Reply'.

October 1
– Paul went to see *Goldfinger*, the new James Bond movie.
– Alf Bicknell, The Beatles' new chauffeur, started work. He was to be their driver until August 1966

when they stopped touring.

October 2
– Rehearsals at the *Granville Theatre, Fulham,* for Jack Good's American TV show *Shindig.*
– That evening Paul attended an Alma Cogan recording session and played tambourine on the track 'I Knew Right Away' (the B-side of her single 'It's You').

October 3
– Shindig recorded live before a lively audience of Beatles Fan Club members at the Granville Theatre, Fulham. The Beatles performed 'Kansas City'/'Hey-Hey-Hey-Hey', 'I'm A Loser' and 'Boys'. They also took part in the finale with the Karl Denver Trio.

October 6
– *Abbey Road.* The Beatles arrived just after 2:30 pm. The entire session was spent recording 'Eight Days A Week' until 7:00 pm. John played his new composition, 'I Feel Fine', to the group.
After the session John, Paul and Ringo went to the Ad Lib where they spent the evening with Cilla Black, Mick Jagger and The Ronettes.

October 7
– Shindig shown by ABC-TV in the USA.

October 8
– That morning Ringo took his driving test in Enfield in order to avoid unwanted publicity. He passed first time. (He had previously been driving a Ford Zephyr around Liverpool, presumably without a licence.)
– *Abbey Road.* The Beatles were in studio two recording Paul's 'She's A Woman'.

October 9
– *Gaumont Cinema, Bradford.* Opening of The Beatles' four-week tour of Britain. They were delayed by heavy traffic and by police on the A1 who flagged them down in order to get autographs, and arrived in Bradford two hours late. Also on the bill were The Rustiks, Sounds Incorporated, Michael Haslam, The Remo Four, Tommy Quickly and Mary Wells. The MC was Bob Bain.
The Beatles' set for this tour consisted of 'Twist And Shout', 'Money (That's What I Want)', 'Can't Buy Me Love', 'Things We Said Today', 'I'm Happy Just To Dance With You', 'I Should Have Known Better', 'If I Fell', 'I Wanna Be Your Man', 'A Hard Day's Night' and 'Long Tall Sally'. Sixty police guarded the stage area, there were 40 firemen and 60 St John Ambulance men and nurses on hand to deal with fainting fans. Outside, the crowds were controlled by mounted police brought in from Wakefield. There were a few arrests and a firework was thrown.
The group spent the night at the Raggles Inn in Queensbury, celebrating John's 24th birthday, before leaving for Leicester the following morning.

October 10
– Ringo spent most of the day looking for cars. He eventually bought a Facel-Vega, which he tried out by driving at 140 mph up the M1.
– In the evening The Beatles played

the De Montfort Hall, Leicester
(British Tour).
– The music press reported that the next Beatles album was to be a gate-fold with a picture of The Beatles standing beneath the Arc de Triomphe at night with lighted matches held under their chins. It didn't happen.

October 11
– T*he Odeon Cinema, Birmingham*
(British Tour).

October 12
– The album SONGS, PICTURES AND STORIES OF THE FABULOUS BEATLES was released in the US as VEE JAY VJLP 1092.

> SIDE A: **'I Saw Her Standing There', 'Misery', 'Anna (Go To Him)', 'Chains', 'Boys', 'Ask Me Why';**
> SIDE B: **'Please, Please Me', 'Baby, It's You', 'Do You Want To Know A Secret', 'A Taste Of Honey', 'There's A Place', 'Twist And Shout'.**

October 13
– *The ABC Cinema, Wigan*
(British Tour).

October 14
– The group spent the day at Granada Television studios in Manchester miming 'I Should Have Known Better' and conducting an interview for the show *Scene At 6:30*.
– *The ABC Cinema, Ardwick, Manchester* (British Tour). Backstage The Beatles were interviewed by David Tindall for BBC1 news magazine *Look North*.

October 15
– *The Globe Theatre, Stockton-on-Tees* (British Tour).
– The group were interviewed by Tyne Tees Television for *North-East Newsview*.

October 16
– *The ABC Cinema, Hull*
(British Tour).
– The single **'If I Fell'/'Tell Me Why'** was released in Europe as PARLOPHONE DP 562 (a few hundred copies were accidentally released in the UK on January 29 1965).
– The Beatles on *Scene At 6:30* was broadcast by Granada Television.
– Tyne Tees Television broadcast their interview with The Beatles on *North-East Newsview*.

October 17

– The group drove back to London from Hull.

October 18
– *Abbey Road.* The Beatles finished 'Eight Days A Week'. They then worked on 'Kansas City'/'Hey-Hey-Hey-Hey', followed by 'Mr Moonlight', 'I Feel Fine' and Paul's 'I'll Follow The Sun'. George sang Carl Perkins' 'Everybody's Trying To Be My Baby' which they followed with 'Rock And Roll Music' and 'Words Of Love'.

October 19
– The group drove from London to Edinburgh to play *the ABC Cinema* (British Tour).

October 20
– *Caird Hall, Dundee* (British Tour). June Shields from Grampian Television interviewed The Beatles in their dressing room for the programme *Grampian Week*.

October 21
– *Odeon Cinema, Glasgow*
(British Tour).

October 22
– *Odeon Cinema, Leeds* (British Tour).

October 23
– The group drove back to London, then played the *Gaumont State Cinema, Kilburn* (British Tour).
– Grampian Television broadcast the Caird Hall interview on *Grampian Week*.

October 24
– Press conference to announce that The Beatles' new single was to be 'I Feel Fine'/'She's A Woman'.
– *Granada Cinema, Walthamstow, London* (British Tour).

October 25
– *Hippodrome Theatre, Brighton*
(British Tour).

October 26
– *Abbey Road.* The morning was spent listening to previous recordings. In the afternoon Ringo recorded his vocal for 'Honey Don't'. During the evening session the group recorded some material for a Christmas flexi-disc.
  Afterwards Paul and Ringo, accompanied by Jane and Maureen, went to the Ad Lib Club.

October 28
– *ABC Cinema, Exeter* (British Tour). Afterwards the group took their chauffeur, Alf Bicknall, for a night

out on the town to celebrate his 36th birthday.

October 29
– *ABC Theatre, Plymouth*
(British Tour).

October 30
– *Gaumont Cinema, Bournemouth*
(British Tour).
– The single 'It's You'/ 'I Knew Right Away' by Alma Cogan, with Paul on tambourine on the B-side, was released in the UK as COLUMBIA DB 7390.

October 31
– *Gaumont Theatre, Ipswich*
(British Tour).

November 1
– *Astoria Theatre, Finsbury Park, London* (British Tour).

November 2
– An extra date was added to the British Tour and The Beatles flew to Aldergrove Airport in Northern Ireland to play *King's Hall, Belfast.*

November 3
– The Beatles flew back to London from Belfast.

November 4
– *Ritz Cinema, Luton* (British Tour). BBC producer Joe McGrath visited John backstage to invite him to contribute to a new Dudley Moore television show, then unnamed, but

Actors Richard Chaimberlain (left), Raymond Massey and Anne Baxter imitate The Beatles on the set of Dr. Kildare, the long running American hospital series.

eventually called *Not Only... But Also*. John had previously run into Dudley Moore in a studio and told him,

"I like what you're doing and I'd like to be in on it."

– The EP Extracts From The Film *A Hard Day's Night* was released in the UK as PARLOPHONE GEP 8920.

> SIDE A: **'I Should Have Known Better', 'If I Fell'**;
> SIDE B: **'Tell Me Why', 'And I Love Her'**.

November 5

– *Odeon Cinema, Nottingham* (British Tour).

November 6

– *Gaumont Cinema, Southampton* (British Tour).

– They were interviewed in their dressing room by Tony Bilbow for the Southern Television programme *Day By Day*, broadcast that evening.

– The EP Extracts From The Film *A Hard Day's Night* (volume two) was released in the UK as PARLOPHONE GEP 8924.

> SIDE A: **'Anytime At All', 'I'll Cry Instead'**;
> SIDE B: **'Things We Said Today', 'When I Get Home'**.

November 7

– *The Capitol Cinema, Cardiff* (British Tour).

November 8

– *Empire Theatre, Liverpool* (British Tour).

November 9

– *City Hall, Sheffield* (British Tour).

November 10

– *Colston Hall, Bristol*. The last date of the British Tour.

November 13

– CBS-TV broadcast *The Beatles In America* – a full-length version of the Maysles Brothers documentary *Yeah, Yeah, Yeah! The Beatles On Tour* which covered their whole tour.

November 14

– *Television studios, Teddington,* where they recorded a *Thank Your Lucky Stars* show, renamed *Lucky Stars Special* in their honour. They mimed to 'I Feel Fine', 'She's A Woman', 'I'm A Loser' and 'Rock And Roll Music'.

Afterwards George and Paul went home while John and Ringo went with friends to the Flamingo Club in Soho to see Georgie Fame and The Blue Flames.

November 16

– The Beatles recorded 'I Feel Fine' and 'I'm A Loser' at *Riverside Studios, London,* for an edition of BBC TV's *Top Of The Pops* presented by Brian Matthew. They mimed to both sides of their new single: 'I Feel Fine' and 'She's A Woman'.

November 17

– The Beatles recorded a *Top Gear* show for the BBC Light Programme at the *Playhouse Theatre, London*. Brian Matthew interviewed them and they recorded 'I'm A Loser', 'Honey Don't', 'She's A Woman', 'Everybody's Trying To Be My Baby', 'I'll Follow The Sun' and 'I Feel Fine'.

November 20

– John filmed a surreal film sequence with Dudley Moore and Norman Rossington on Wimbledon Common, to accompany his reading from *In His Own Write* on Moore's new BBC2 programme *Not Only... But Also*.

November 21

– ABC Television broadcast *Lucky Stars Special*.

November 23

– *Wembley studios.* An appearance on *Ready Steady Go!* to promote their new record. They mimed to 'I Feel Fine', 'She's A Woman', 'Baby's In Black' and 'Kansas City'/'Hey-Hey-Hey-Hey'. They also chatted on camera with presenter Keith Fordyce.

– The single 'I Feel Fine'/'She's A Woman' was released in the US as CAPITOL; 5327.

– The album THE BEATLES' STORY was released in the US as CAPITOL STBO 2222 (a double album containing one live cut from The Beatles, recorded August 23, 1964, at the Hollywood Bowl).

> SIDE A: **'On Stage With The Beatles', 'How Beatlemania Began', 'Beatlemania In Action', 'The Man Behind The Beatles – Brian Epstein', 'John Lennon', 'Who's A Millionaire?'**
> SIDE B: **'Beatles Will Be Beatles', 'Man Behind The Music – George Martin', 'George Harrison'**
> SIDE C: **'A Hard Day's Night – Their First Movie', 'Paul McCartney', 'Sneaky Haircuts And More About Paul'**

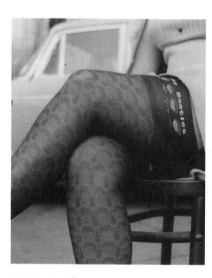

Beatles stockings....

> SIDE D: **'Twist And Shout' (live), 'The Beatles Look At Life', 'Victims of Beatlemania', 'Beatle Medley', 'Ringo Starr', 'Liverpool And All The World!'**.

November 24

– Paul attended the marriage of his father, James, aged 62, to Angela Williams, aged 35.

November 25

– The Beatles recorded a Boxing Day special edition of BBC Light Programme's *Saturday Club* show. The broadcast consisted of six songs: 'Rock And Roll Music', 'I'm A Loser', 'Everybody's Trying To Be My Baby', 'I Feel Fine', 'Kansas City'/'Hey-Hey-Hey-Hey' and 'She's A Woman', but four of these, all except the first and 'Kansas City' were previously recorded versions. It is possible that only two songs were taped this day, or that the new versions were not up to scratch. The programme also included banter with presenter Brian Matthew.

November 27

– The single **'I Feel Fine'/'She's A Woman'** was released in the UK as PARLOPHONE R 5200.

– The Beatles final appearance on *Ready Steady Go!* was shown by Rediffusion.

November 28

– Chris Hutchins visited John at Kenwood and interviewed him for the BBC Light Programme's *Teen Scene*.

– Afterwards John and Cynthia went Christmas shopping in London.

November 29

– John read from his book, *In His Own Write* on Dudley Moore's BBC2 programme *Not Only... But Also*. He was apparently shy and self-conscious about reading aloud, but this was quickly dispelled by Moore and Rossington's antics.

– John and George had a few drinks afterwards then went to the Crazy Elephant where they spent the evening with two members of The Miracles.

– Chris Hutchins' interview with John was broadcast by the BBC Light Programme's *Teen Scene*.

November 30

– Ringo gave an interview to *Melody Maker* about his forthcoming operation to have his tonsils removed. While in their office, he saw the weekly charts compiled and 'I Feel Fine' enter at number one.

December 1

– <u>Ringo</u> booked into University College Hospital to have his tonsils removed. He gave a brief press conference at the hospital before going to the ward.

December 2

– <u>Ringo</u>'s tonsils were removed. A record player and records were delivered to his bedside.

December 3

– <u>Ringo</u> still in hospital, but doing well and making a fast recovery.

– BBC's *Top Of The Pops* broadcast The Beatles miming both sides of their new single.

December 4

– The album BEATLES FOR SALE was released in the UK as PARLOPHONE PCS 3062.

SIDE A: 'No Reply', 'I'm A Loser', 'Baby's In Black', 'Rock And Roll Music', 'I'll Follow The Sun', 'Mr Moonlight', 'Kansas City'/'Hey-Hey-Hey-Hey';

SIDE B: 'Eight Days A Week', 'Words Of Love', 'Honey Don't', 'Every Little Thing', 'I Don't Want To Spoil The Party', 'What You're Doing', 'Everybody's Trying To Be My Baby'.

– Many of the tracks were oldies, played by The Beatles at the Cavern and in Hamburg.

December 8

– <u>George</u> visited <u>Ringo</u> in hospital, adding to the security problem caused by fans trying to sneak in.

– *The Daily Express* reported that <u>Paul</u> told them he would marry Jane Asher.

December 9

– <u>George</u> and Patti flew to the Bahamas for a break before *The Beatles' Christmas Show*.

– <u>Paul</u> visited <u>Ringo</u> in hospital, attracting even more press and fans.

December 10

– <u>Ringo</u> was finally released from University College Hospital.

December 15

– The album BEATLES '65 was released in the US as CAPITOL ST 2228.

SIDE A: 'No Reply', 'I'm A Loser', 'Baby's In Black', 'Rock And Roll Music', 'I'll Follow The Sun', 'Mr. Moonlight';

SIDE B: 'Honey Don't',

Right: John's fringe receives attention from George just before the group take the stage.

John: "The numbers on this LP are **different** from **anything** we've done before and you **could** call our new one a '**Beatles Country and Western** LP'."

'I'll Be Back', 'She's A Woman', 'I Feel Fine', 'Everybody's Trying To Be My Baby'.

December 18

– The flexi-disc, Another Beatles' Christmas Record, was sent out free to members of The Beatles Fan Club.

December 19

– <u>George</u> and Patti flew back to London from Nassau.

December 20

– Brian Epstein bought number 24 Chapel Street, Belgravia, London.

December 21

– The first day of rehearsals for *Another Beatles' Christmas Show* at the *Hammersmith Odeon*.

December 22

– The complete cast of *Another Beatles' Christmas Show* assembled on stage at the *Hammersmith Odeon* for

a rehearsal.

– During a break in rehearsals, Jimmy Savile (who was appearing in the show) recorded a brief interview with the group for BBC's *Top Of The Pops '64* Christmas show.

December 23

– Rehearsals for the Christmas Show.

December 24

– The Beatles opened their twice-nightly *Another Beatles' Christmas Show* at the *Hammersmith Odeon, London*.

– The Beatles performing 'A Hard Day's Night', recorded in July, was broadcast on BBC TV's *Top Of The Pops '64*.

December 26

– *Hammersmith Odeon, London: Another Beatles' Christmas Show.*

December 28

– *Hammersmith Odeon, London: Another Beatles' Christmas Show.*

December 29

– *Hammersmith Odeon, London: Another Beatles' Christmas Show.* (One performance instead of the usual two.)

December 30

– *Hammersmith Odeon, London: Another Beatles' Christmas Show.*

December 31

– *Hammersmith Odeon, London: Another Beatles' Christmas Show.*

– Afterwards <u>Paul</u>, Jane, <u>George</u> and Patti attended EMI producer Norman Newell's New Year's Eve party at his London flat.

Another Beatles' Christmas Show

The show was compered by Jimmy Savile, who brought fans to The Beatles' dressing room before the shows. The Mike Cotton Sound playing Georgie Fame's 'Yeh, Yeh!' opened. They were joined by Michael Haslem, a Brian Epstein protégé – one of those who didn't make it – who came on stage to sing 'Scarlet Ribbons'. The Yardbirds were on next followed by a pantomime sketch involving The Beatles dressed as Antarctic explorers looking for the Abominable Snowman, compered by Liverpudlian Ray Fell. The first half ended with Freddie and The Dreamers, beginning with 'Rip It Up', 'Bachelor Boy' and including 'Cut Across Shorty'.

The second half opened with Elkie Brooks followed by Sounds Incorporated, then finally Jimmy Saville introduced The Beatles dressed in blue Mohair suits and singing 'She's A Woman' with Paul taking vocals. John sang 'I'm A Loser', George did 'Everybody's Trying To Be My Baby' then John and Paul duetted on 'Baby's In Black.' Ringo sang 'Honey Don't' followed by John on 'A Hard Day's Night' and their current hit, 'I Feel Fine'. 'Long Tall Sally' was the finale. The drawings on the front and back covers of the programme were by John.

19**65**

January 1
– Hammersmith Odeon, London:
Another Beatles' Christmas Show.
January 2
– Hammersmith Odeon, London:
Another Beatles' Christmas Show.
January 4
– Hammersmith Odeon, London:
Another Beatles' Christmas Show.
January 5
– Hammersmith Odeon, London:
Another Beatles' Christmas Show.
January 6
– Hammersmith Odeon, London:
Another Beatles' Christmas Show.
January 7
– Hammersmith Odeon, London:
Another Beatles' Christmas Show.

Opposite: Paul with Richard Lester, director of A Hard Days Night *and* Help.

January 8
– Hammersmith Odeon, London:
Another Beatles' Christmas Show.
 After this evening's performance, The Beatles were given a private view of the Boat Show at the nearby Earl's Court Exhibition Hall. By midnight they were paddling around an artificial lake in a rubber dinghy and trying out the radio-controlled mini-powerboats.
January 9
– Hammersmith Odeon, London:
Another Beatles' Christmas Show.
– The album Beatles '65 reached number one in the US charts.
– John read from *In His Own Write* on Dudley Moore's BBC 2 programme *Not Only... But Also.*
January 11
– Hammersmith Odeon, London:
Another Beatles' Christmas Show.
January 12
– Hammersmith Odeon, London:
Another Beatles' Christmas Show.
January 13
– Hammersmith Odeon, London:
Another Beatles' Christmas Show.
January 14
– Hammersmith Odeon, London:
Another Beatles' Christmas Show.
January 15
– Hammersmith Odeon, London:
Another Beatles' Christmas Show.
– After that evening's performance, Ringo and George spent the evening at a party given by *Melody Maker* journalist Bob Dawbarn.
January 16
– Hammersmith Odeon, London:
Another Beatles' Christmas Show.
Christmas Show.
January 25
– John and Cynthia flew to the Alps to join George Martin and his

future wife Judy Lockhart-Smith on a skiing holiday.
January 27
– Maclen Limited was formed with John, Paul and Brian Epstein as directors.
January 28
– George and Patti flew to Europe on holiday.
January 29
– The European-only pressing of the single **'If I Fell'/'Tell Me Why'** was released in the UK as Parlophone DP 562 to a few record stores by accident. The single was pressed by EMI for foreign export only but these copies were sold by sales reps in error.
February 1
– The EP **4 By The Beatles** was released in the US as Capitol R 5365.
**Side A: 'Honey Don't', 'I'm A Loser';
Side B: 'Mr. Moonlight', 'Everybody's Trying To be My Baby'.**
February 3
– Ringo and Maureen had lunch with Paul Getty Jr.
February 4
– Paul and Jane flew to Hammamet, Tunisia, for a holiday, staying at a free villa provided by the British Embassy.
February 7
– John and Cynthia, George Martin and Judy returned to England from their holiday. George Martin was hobbling because he broke a toe on the ski slopes on his first day.
February 11
– Ringo married Maureen Cox at Caxton Hall Register Office, London; registrar Mr D.A. Boreham. John, George and Brian Epstein attended but Paul was still in North Africa.

Ringo and Maureen
Ringo had known Maureen since Cavern days and they had been going out together virtually ever since. "This means two married and two unmarried Beatles - two down and two to go," commented George. They drove to Hove, Sussex, for a brief honeymoon at the home of their solicitor David Jacobs on Princes Crescent.

February 12
– Ringo and Maureen gave a press conference in David Jacobs' back garden.

February 14
– Ringo and Maureen returned to London from their honeymoon.
– Paul and Jane returned to London from Tunisia.

February 15
– That morning John passed his driving test in Weybridge.
– *Abbey Road.* The group arrived at 2:30 and spent the afternoon recording John's 'Ticket To Ride'. The evening session from 7 until 10.30 was spent recording Paul's 'Another Girl' and George's 'I Need You'.
– The single **'Eight Days a Week' /'I Don't Want To Spoil The Party'** was released in the US as Capitol 5371.

February 16
– *Abbey Road.* An afternoon session completing 'I Need You' and 'Another Girl'. From 5 until 10 pm they recorded John's 'Yes It Is' but the session did not go well. John was unhappy with the results and swore a lot.
– During a break in recording, The Beatles collected various awards from EMI, presented by Sir Joseph Lockwood.

February 17
– *Abbey Road.* An afternoon session from 2 until 7.00 was spent recording Paul's 'The Night Before', after which they worked until 11 pm on George's 'You Like Me Too Much'.

February 18
– *Abbey Road.* The Beatles arrived at 10 am and spent the morning mixing. John's 'You've Got To Hide Your Love Away' was recorded during the afternoon session.
    Ringo recorded 'If You've Got Trouble' during the evening session but John and Paul, who wrote the song specifically for Ringo, were not happy with the results and the track was not used. The remainder of the evening session was spent recording Paul's 'Tell Me What You See'.
    The rest of the evening was spent in the clubs.
– Northern Songs was launched on the stock exchange.

John: "This was written in my **Dylan days** for the film *Help!*. When I was **a teenager** I used to write poetry, but was always trying to hide my **real feelings.**"

February 19
– *Abbey Road.* The group made a late start. John's 'You're Going To Lose That Girl' was recorded in a three-hour afternoon session beginning at 3.30.
– That evening The Beatles attended a private party given in their honour at The Connaught Hotel, Carlos Place, by the chairman of EMI, Sir Joseph Lockwood.

February 20
– *Abbey Road.* The group arrived around midday and recorded the unreleased 'That Means A Lot'. Work finished at 6 pm to allow them to pack for the flight to the Bahamas.

February 21
– The Beatles' baggage was collected, ready for the flight.

February 22
– The Beatles flew to the Bahamas from Heathrow in a chartered Boeing 707 to begin filming *Help!*; 1,400 fans waved goodbye. There was a refuelling stopover in New York en route but The Beatles did not leave the aircraft, despite US Customs and Immigration insisting that they should pass through US Customs. They lit up immediately after take-off and didn't stop giggling until the plane landed. In the Bahamas they stayed in a house in the grounds of the Balmoral Club near Cable Beach.

February 23
– Filming on New Providence island, Bahamas.

February 24
– Filming on New Providence island, Bahamas. The Beatles usually began work at 8:30 to get in a full day's shooting.

February 25
– Filming on New Providence island, Bahamas.

February 26
– Filming on New Providence island, Bahamas.

February 27
– Filming on New Providence island, Bahamas.

February 28
– Filming on New Providence island, Bahamas.

March 1 - 9
– Filming on New Providence island, Bahamas. The Beatles worked solidly during their stay in the Bahamas with no days off.

March 10
– The Beatles began the journey back to London.

March 11
– The Beatles arrived at Heathrow Airport at 7.05 am from the Bahamas.

March 13
– The Beatles took the 11 am flight to Salzburg, Austria to continue filming *Help!*. At Salzburg Airport, 4,000 fans were waiting to greet them, as well as the press. They gave a press conference in a nearby hotel before checking into the Hotel Edelweiss in Obertauern where all the filming took place.
– Paul turned out to be very good on skis and was said by their instructor to have the makings of a professional. John had spent a couple of weeks trying to learn before they went to Austria but never really got the hang of it. Many of the people on the set had legs in plaster which The Beatles naturally had to sign.
– 'Eight Days A Week' reached number one in the US charts.

March 14 - 17
– Filming at Obertauern.
– *Eight Arms To Hold You* was announced as the working title for The Beatles' new film.

March 18
– Filming at Obertauern.
– Hayling Supermarkets Limited was incorporated to control a supermarket on Hayling Island, Hampshire, run by John's old school friend Pete Shotton. The directors were Shotton, John and George Harrison.

March 19
– Filming at Obertauern.
– The Beatles gave a party for the cast after the day's filming.
– Brian Matthew interviewed the group for the BBC Light Programme's *Saturday Club* by telephone from their hotel at 8 pm.

March 20
– Final day's shooting at Obertauern.

John: "The most humiliating experiences were like sitting with the Mayor of the Bahamas, when we were making *Help!* and being insulted by these **fuckin' junked up middle-class bitches and bastards** who would be commenting on our **work** and our **manners.** I was always drunk, insulting them. **I couldn't take it.** It would hurt me. I would go **insane, swearing** at them."

– BBC Light Programme's *Saturday Club* broadcast Brian Matthew's interview recorded the previous evening.
– John and Ringo were interviewed on the telephone by Chris Denning for his weekly Radio Luxembourg show, *The Beatles*.

March 22
– The Beatles flew back to London from Austria.
– The album THE EARLY BEATLES was released in the US as CAPITOL T-2309 (mono) and ST-2309 (stereo).
  SIDE A: 'Love Me Do', 'Twist And Shout', 'Anna (Go To Him)', 'Chains', 'Boys', 'Ask Me Why';
  SIDE B: 'Please, Please Me', 'P.S. I Love You', 'Baby, It's You', 'A Taste Of Honey', 'Do You Want To Know A Secret'.

March 24
– With the location shooting completed, The Beatles continued to film *Help!* at Twickenham film studios.

March 25
– Filming at Twickenham.

March 26
– Filming at Twickenham.

March 28
– The Beatles were driven to the *Alpha Studios at Aston in Birmingham,* where they recorded an appearance on the ABC TV show *Thank Your Lucky Stars*. They were interviewed by Brian Matthew and mimed to 'Eight Days A Week', 'Yes It Is' and 'Ticket To Ride'.

March 29
– Filming at Twickenham.

March 30
– Filming at Twickenham during the day.
– *Abbey Road* in the evening where they did five more takes of Paul's 'That Means A Lot' but Paul was not happy with the results and at 10 pm they called it a day.

March 31
– Filming at Twickenham.

April 1
– Brian Epstein took a lease on *The Saville Theatre on Shaftesbury Avenue* to use as a showcase for his many showbusiness interests, even opening it as a rock venue on Sunday evenings when the theatre was normally dark.
– The Beatles filmed at Twickenham.

Above: John in the Bahamas. Right: Paul at Heathrow, March 11.

"I don't like the recording that much; **we did it too fast trying** to be commercial."

April 2
– Filming at Twickenham.

April 3
– ABC TV transmitted the edition of *Thank Your Lucky Stars* recorded on May 28.

April 5
– The Beatles filmed the "Rajahama" Indian restaurant sequence at Twickenham.

April 6
– At a break in filming at the Twickenham studios, TV talk show host Simon Dee presented the group with the Radio Caroline Bell Award for "Most Consistent and Best Recording Artistes of the Past Year". The Beatles managed to disrupt the inevitable speeches by ringing the bell at appropriate moments throughout the proceedings.
– The EP **Beatles For Sale** was released in the UK as Parlophone GEP 8931 (mono only):
SIDE A: **'No Reply', 'I'm A Loser';**
SIDE B: **'Rock And Roll Music', 'Eight Days A Week'**

April 7
– Filming at Twickenham.

April 8
– Filming at Twickenham.
– The Beatles all attended the opening night of Downstairs At The Pickwick, a new London nightclub. Michael Crawford was among the other guests.

April 9
– The single **'Ticket To Ride'/'Yes It Is'** was released in the UK as Parlophone R 5265.
– Filming at Twickenham.

April 10
– A promotional film of the group performing 'Ticket To Ride' and 'Yes It Is' was filmed at Riverside Studios for use on Top Of The Pops.

April 11
– The Beatles topped the bill at *the Empire Pool, Wembley*, at the *New Musical Express* Poll Winners show. They played 'I Feel Fine', 'She's A Woman', 'Baby's In Black', 'Ticket To Ride' and 'Long Tall Sally' to an audience of 10,000 people, and received their award from Tony Bennett.
  Afterwards they drove to the ABC Television studios at Teddington where

George: "We were waiting to shoot the scene in the restaurant when the guy gets thrown in the soup and there were a few Indian musicians playing in the background. I remember picking up the sitar and trying to hold it and thinking, 'This is a funny sound.' It was an incidental thing, but somewhere down the line I began to hear Ravi Shankar's name. The third time I heard it, I thought, 'This is an odd coincidence.' And then I talked with David Crosby of The Byrds and he mentioned the name. I went and bought a Ravi record; I put it on and it hit a certain spot in me that I can't explain, but it seemed very familiar to me. The only way I could describe it was: my intellect didn't know what was going on and yet this other part of me identified with it. It just called on me... a few months elapsed and then I met this guy from the Asian Music Circle organisation who said, 'Oh, Ravi Shankar's gonna come to my house for dinner. Do you want to come too?'"**

they appeared on *The Eamonn Andrews Show* to promote their new single.

April 12
– Filming at Twickenham.

April 13
– At Twickenham where they were filming The Beatles did a live interview for BBC Light Programme's *Pop Inn* to promote 'Ticket To Ride'. This was followed by a late-night session at *Abbey Road* to record the title song to *Help!*. John's original acoustic version was slow, but George Martin thought the fans would prefer a faster number. John went along with the idea but later said;
– Paul bought a house at 7 Cavendish Avenue in St Johns Wood, London, for £40,000.

April 14
– Location filming for *Help!* in Ailsa Avenue, not far from the Old Deer Park in Twickenham.
– *Help!* was announced as the title of the new film, replacing Eight Arms To Hold You.

April 15
– The *Top Of The Pops* session recorded on the 10th was broadcast by BBC TV.

April 16
– George and John were interviewed live by Cathy McGowan on *Ready, Steady, Go!* at the Rediffusion Television Studios in Wembley.

April 17
– Paul spent the day in disguise - cloth peaked cap, glasses, moustache and a big overcoat - in order to go furniture shopping in the Harrow Road and Portobello Road for his new house. A bartender in Ladbroke Grove was not fooled and recognised Paul when he asked for **"A drop o' the hard stuff,"** in an Irish accent.

April 18
– A part of their recorded appearance at the *New Musical Express* Poll Winners Show was broadcast on the *Big Beat '65* television special.

April 19
– The single **'Ticket to Ride'/'Yes It Is'** was released in the US as Capitol 5407.

April 20
– Filming at Twickenham.

April 21
– Brian Epstein sent a telegram to Elvis Presley in The Beatles' names to congratulate him on his first decade in the music business.
– Filming at Twickenham.

April 22
– Filming at Twickenham.

April 23
– Filming at Twickenham.

April 24
– Filming in Chiswick.

Right: Wembley, April 11: the NME Poll Winners show.

April 27
– Filming at Twickenham.
April 28
– Filming at Twickenham.
– Peter Sellers arrived on set to present the group with a Grammy Award, issued by the US National Academy of Recording Arts and Sciences. A Hard Day's Night had won the award in the "Best Vocal Performance by a Group" category.
April 29
– Filming at Twickenham.
– Chris Denning interviewed all four Beatles for his weekly Radio Luxembourg show, *The Beatles*.
– Jimmy Nicol, the drummer who stood in briefly for Ringo during the Australian tour of 1964, appeared in the London Bankruptcy Court with debts of £4,066 and assets of a nominal £50.
April 30
– Filming at Twickenham.
May 3
– The Beatles spent the day filming on Salisbury Plain with the assistance of the British Army's Third Tank Division. The Beatles, Eleanor Bron, Victor Spinetti, Roy Kinear, Leo McKern and the other actors and film

Above Right: Filming a scene from Help! on the Thames Embankment at Chiswick, April 24. Right: Bob Dylan. Opposite: John at the wheel of a Triumph Herald.

Bob Dylan

On May 9 The Beatles went to see Bob Dylan play the Royal Festival Hall. Afterwards they visited Dylan in his suite at the Savoy Hotel. The four Beatles filed into his reception room but the atmosphere remained tense until Allen Ginsberg broke the ice by falling off the arm of a settee into John Lennon's lap and asking him if he knew William Blake. "Never heard of him," snapped John but Cynthia spoke up, "Oh John, you liar, of course you have!" and everyone laughed. The rest of the evening was spent nightclubbing.

crew all stayed at the Antrobus Arms in Amesbury.
May 4
– Filming on Salisbury Plain. Spent the night at the Antrobus Arms.
May 5
– Filming on Salisbury Plain. Spent the night at the Antrobus Arms.
May 6
– Filming at Twickenham.
May 7
– Filming at Twickenham.
May 9
– Filming in New Bond Street. John and Ringo filming at Twickenham.
May 10
– Filming at Cliveden House, near Maidenhead in Berkshire.
– *Abbey Road*. The Beatles recorded two old rock'n'roll numbers 'Dizzy Miss Lizzy' and 'Bad Boy' aimed at the American market.
May 11
– Filming at Cliveden House.
May 16
– John attended a party given

for Johnny Mathis by Norman Newell.
May 18
– Twickenham for post-synchronisation work on the soundtrack to *Help!*.
– NBC-TV in the USA showed a pre-recorded interview with The Beatles by Peter Sellers in their Grammy Awards show *The Best On Record*. The programme also showed a clip of The Beatles playing 'I'm Happy Just To Dance With You' from *A Hard Day's Night*.
– Paul and Jane saw Gene Barry play *the Talk Of The Town* and visited him after the show. Afterwards they went on to Downstairs at the Pickwick Club.
May 21
– George and Patti spent the day shopping.
May 22
– 'Ticket To Ride' reached number one in the US charts.
– A brief clip of The Beatles singing 'Ticket To Ride' appeared in an episode of *Doctor Who* on BBC TV.

John: "I thought you had to drive tanks and win wars to win the MBE."

– John made a guest appearance in D.A. Pennebaker's film documentary of Bob Dylan's UK tour *Eat The Document*. John and Dylan were filmed talking in the back of a limousine.

May 25

– John and Cynthia returned to London from Cannes, where they had attended the Film Festival. That afternoon, before leaving, John recorded an interview with Martin Ogronsky for the CBS-TV *Merv Griffin Show*.

May 26

– The Beatles drove to the *BBC's Piccadilly Studios* where they recorded their last show for the BBC, a bank holiday special. They insisted that the name be changed from the usual *From Us To You*, to *The Beatles (Invite You To Take A Ticket To Ride)* which they thought was more suitable for their maturing image. They recorded live versions of 'Ticket To Ride', 'Everybody's Trying To Be My Baby', 'I'm A Loser', 'The Night Before', 'Honey Don't', 'Dizzy Miss Lizzy' and 'She's A Woman'.

May 27

– All The Beatles flew off on their holidays. Paul and Jane went to Portugal where they stayed in Bruce Welch's villa in Albufera. Paul wrote the lyrics to 'Yesterday' in the car on the way from the airport and completed them over the next two weeks.

June 1

– The interview with John recorded at the Cannes Film Festival was shown on the CBS-TV *Merv Griffin Show*.

Paul and Jane Asher arrive at Heathrow from Portugal, June 11.

Paul: "I fell out of bed. I had a piano by my bedside and I must have dreamed it because I tumbled out of bed and put my hands on the piano keys and I had a tune in my head. It was just all there, a complete thing. I couldn't believe it, it came too easy. In fact I didn't believe I'd written it. I thought maybe I'd heard it before, it was some other tune, and I went round for weeks playing the chords of the song for people, asking them, 'Is this like something? I think I've written it.' And people would say, 'No, it's not like anything else. But it's good...'"

John: "That was a good 'un."

June 3

– John and George, accompanied by Cynthia and Patti, attended Allen Ginsberg's 39th birthday party held in a basement flat in Chester Square, London. When they arrived, Ginsberg was wearing nothing but his birthday suit. The two Beatles looked around anxiously in case any photographers were present then quickly departed. **"You don't do that in front of the birds!"** hissed John to one of the organisers.

Ginsberg and John later became quite good friends and John himself was to appear naked on his Two Virgins album sleeve.

June 4

– The EP **Beatles For Sale 2** was released in the UK as PARLOPHONE GEP 8938 (mono only).

SIDE A: 'I'll Follow The Sun', 'Baby's In Black';
SIDE B: 'Words Of Love', 'I Don't Want To Spoil The Party'

June 7

– *The Beatles (Invite You To Take a Ticket To Ride)* was broadcast by BBC Light Programme as a Whit Monday special.

June 11

– Paul and Jane flew back from their holiday a day early at Brian Epstein's request in order to be in Britain when it was announced that The Beatles had been awarded the Member of the Order of the British Empire (MBE).

– The embargo on the news was lifted that evening and Paul was interviewed by telephone by Ronald Burns for the BBC Radio *Late Night News Extra* which also included an interview with Brian Epstein.

Ringo: "There's a proper medal as well as the letters, isn't there? I will keep it to wear when I'm old. It's the sort of thing you want to keep."

George: "I didn't think you got this sort of thing for playing rock'n'roll."

Paul: "I think it's marvellous. What does this make my dad?"

The MBE furore

Prime Minister Harold Wilson's decision to include The Beatles on his list of MBEs for the Queen to approve caused many outraged previous recipients to return their medals in protest. One of them was Hector Dupuis, a member of the Canadian House of Commons who claimed that he had been placed on "the same level as vulgar nincompoops". Dupuis received his medal for running the Canadian Selective Service, calling up young men for the armed services.

George: "If Dupuis doesn't want the medal, he had better give it to us. Then we can give it to our manager, Brian Epstein. MBE really stands for 'Mister Brian Epstein'."

The Beatles gave a press conference at Twickenham Film Studios on June 12, which was used in news bulletins around the world. John was 70 minutes late, to the annoyance of Brian Epstein, who had to fetch him personally by car to make him attend. John: "I set the alarm for eight o'clock and then just lay there. I thought, well, if anyone wants me they'll phone me. The phone went lots of times, but that's the one I never answer. My own phone didn't go at all. So I just lay there."

John was always uneasy about accepting the award. John: "We had to do a lot of selling out then. Taking the MBE was a sell-out for me. You know, before you get an MBE the Palace writes to you to ask if you're going to accept it, because you're supposed to reject it publicly and they sound you out first. I chucked the letter in with all the fan-mail, until Brian asked me if I had it. He and a few other people persuaded me that it was in our interests to take it, and it was hypocritical of me to accept it. But I'm glad, really, that I did accept it - because it meant that four years later I could use it to make a gesture. When my envelope arrived marked OHMS I thought I was being called up... I shall stick it on the wall or make it into a bell." In fact, he gave it to his Aunt Mimi who kept it on top of her television until he asked for it back in order to return it as a protest against Britain's involvement in the Biafra War.

June 14
– *Abbey Road*. <u>Paul</u> recorded 'Yesterday' with a string quartet, followed the gentle ballad with the up-tempo rocker, 'I'm Down' and finished the session with 'I've Just Seen A Face'.
– Afterwards <u>Paul</u> and Jane went to the Cromwellian Club.
– The album BEATLES VI was released in the US as Capitol T-2358 (mono) and ST-2358 (stereo).
   SIDE A: 'Kansas City'/'Hey-Hey-Hey-Hey', 'Eight Days A Week', 'You Like Me Too Much', 'Bad Boy', 'I Don't Want To Spoil The Party', 'Words Of Love';
   SIDE B: 'What You're Doing', 'Yes It Is', 'Dizzy Miss Lizzy', 'Tell Me What You See', 'Every Little Thing'.

June 15
– *Abbey Road*. <u>John</u>'s 'It's Only Love' was recorded during an afternoon session. Afterwards they spent a night in the clubs.

June 16
– <u>John</u> and <u>Ringo</u> spent the day at <u>John</u>'s house, sorting out songs for <u>Ringo</u> to sing. They were unhappy with the way that 'Troubles' had turned out and were thinking of changing it. They decided that <u>Ringo</u> should record 'Act Naturally'.
– The band did more post-synchronisation work at Twickenham for the film and later, at the Argyll Street office of NEMS, <u>John</u> did an interview and read "The Fat Budgie" section from *A Spaniard In The Works* to promote his new book on the BBC Radio show *The World Of Books*. He was also interviewed by Tim Matthews for the BBC Home Service news magazine *Today*, during which he also read the section of the book called "The National Health Cow".

June 17
– *Abbey Road*. <u>Ringo</u> recorded 'Act Naturally'. This was followed by the group recording 'Wait'. That night they were driven round the nightclubs.

June 18
– The Beatles were interviewed at the NEMS offices by the Italian-language section of the BBC World Service to coincide with their upcoming Italian dates.

Ringo and Paul at Heathrow en route to Paris, June 20.

John dodges a frenzied fan in Rome, June 29.

– Later, at the BBC's Lime Grove Studios, John appeared on BBC1's *Tonight* programme where he was interviewed by Kenneth Allsop and read from his book.

June 20

– The Beatles' European Tour opened in Paris. They arrived at Paris-Orly at 10 am and checked in to the George Cinq. Their reception was quiet by Beatles standards with only about 50 fans waiting outside their hotel. They played two concerts to 6,000 people each at *the Palais des Sports,* topping a bill which also featured The Yardbirds. The second show was broadcast on both French radio and television.

– Afterwards François Hardy visited them at the George Cinq.

The night was spent at Castell's nightclub, where they stayed until dawn.

– The Beatles' set during the European tour consisted of: 'Twist And Shout', 'She's A Woman', 'I'm A Loser', 'Can't Buy Me Love', 'Baby's In Black', 'I Wanna Be Your Man', 'A Hard Day's Night', 'Everybody's Trying To Be My Baby', 'Rock And Roll Music', 'I Feel Fine', 'Ticket To Ride' and 'Long Tall Sally'.

June 21

– Another night spent in Castell's.

– John's interview and reading from

"The National Health Cow" was broadcast on the BBC Home Service *Today* programme.

June 22

– The Beatles and their entourage flew to Lyons in the afternoon and played two shows at *the Palais d'Hiver.*

June 23

– The Beatles took the train to Milan.

June 24

– The Beatles played their first Italian show in Milan at *the Velodromo Vigorelli,* a 22,000-seater open-air arena. Brian Epstein was not pleased at all the empty seats, particularly during the afternoon show when many of the fans were at school or work and only 7,000 people attended. The press suggested that a combination of high prices and a heat wave had kept the fans away.

– John's book *A Spaniard in the Works* was published in UK by Jonathan Cape at 10s 6d.

June 25

– The Alfa Romero Racing Team drove the group to Genoa in four cars. There they played *the Palazzo dello Sport*, a 25,000 seater arena where, once again, there were many empty seats. The afternoon show attracted only 5,000 fans.

June 26

– The group travelled to Rome by special train from Genoa.

June 27

– Two shows in Rome at the *Teatro Adriano*. While The Beatles were playing 'I Wanna Be Your Man,' which Ringo always sang, Paul for some reason or other was laughing so hard he had to leave the stage. George was not amused and his displeasure was obvious. When Paul returned to the stage the microphone fell over and he continued laughing. This made John start laughing as well but George remained irritated by it all. At the end of the shows, Paul thanked the audience in Italian.

June 29

– Two more shows at *the Teatro Adriano, Rome*, though none of the shows there was more than half full.

June 30

– The group arrived in Nice where they stayed at the Gresta Hotel and played at *the Palais des Expositions*.

– After the show they spent the evening at La Fiesta nightclub. At 2 am The Beatles were still racing each other and members of their crew on the club's own go-kart track.

July 1

– The Beatles flew to Madrid where they visited the Jerez de la Frontera vineyard, while Brian Epstein saw a bullfight in the same arena in Madrid that the group were to play the next night.

– John's *A Spaniard in the Works* was published in the USA.

July 2

– *Plaza de Toros de Las Ventas, Madrid*. The Beatles were growing increasingly worried by the level of violence shown to the fans by the police and security in Italy and particularly in Spain.

July 3

– The group flew to Barcelona in the afternoon to play *the Plaza de Toros Monumental* at 10.30 that evening. This was followed by nightclubbing.

Above: Posing on their hotel terrace in Milan, June 24.
Below: Returning to London after their European tour, July 4.

– John's interview for *The World of Books* was transmitted on the BBC Home Service.

July 4

– When the group arrived home at London Heathrow at midday, 1,000 fans were waiting to greet them.

July 5

– A pre-recorded interview with John was broadcast on BBC Light Programme's *Teen Scene*.

– The single 'That Means A Lot' by P.J. Proby, written by Lennon & McCartney, was released in the US as LIBERTY 55806.

July 7

– Paul and Jane, George and Patti went to a party given by The Moody Blues in Roehampton.

July 11

– The album Beatles VI reached number one in the US album charts.

July 13

– Paul accepted five Ivor Novello Awards, presented by David Frost, on behalf of John and himself at a luncheon at the Savoy. John refused to attend. He had been upset by the press comments about their receiving the MBE and did not want to put himself on show again. Paul was 40 minutes late because he had forgotten about the engagement. On receiving the award he quipped, **"Thanks. I hope nobody sends theirs back now."**

July 14

– John, Cynthia, George, Patti, Ringo and Maureen spent the evening at the Bastille Night party at the Scotch St. James.

– Paul watched Jane in a repertory performance at *the Palace Theatre, Watford*.

July 15

– A film of Paul receiving the Ivor Novello Awards on the 13th was shown on Rediffusion Television's *Pick Of The Songs*, illustrated by clips of the various winners playing *Ready Steady Go!*.

July 17

– ABC TV's *Lucky Stars* Anniversary Show showed a film clip of The Beatles playing 'Help!'.

July 19

– Ringo and Maureen bought "Sunny Heights" in Weybridge for £37,000.

They moved in just before Christmas.
– The single **'Help!'/'I'm Down'** was released in the US as Capitol 5476.

July 23
– The single **'Help!'/'I'm Down'** was released in the UK as Parlophone R 5305.

John: "When 'Help!' came out in '65, I was actually crying out for help. Most people think it's just a fast rock'n'roll song. I didn't realise it at the time; I just wrote the song because I was commissioned to write it for the movie. But later, I knew I really was crying out for help. It was my fat Elvis period. You see the movie: He - I - is very fat, very insecure, and he's completely lost himself. And I am singing about when I was so much younger and all the rest, looking back at how easy it was. Now I may be very positive - yes, yes - but I also go through deep depressions where I would like to jump out the window... Anyway I was fat and depressed and I was crying out for help."

July 26
– Television Wales and West screened a clip from the film *Help!* on *Discs A Gogo*.

July 29
– Ten thousand fans gathered in Piccadilly Circus outside the *London Pavilion* on a humid summer evening for the royal premiere of *Help!*. The Beatles arrived in a black Rolls Royce and were presented to Princess Margaret and Lord Snowdon. Jane Asher wore a pure white Edwardian-style evening dress. There was a party afterwards at the Orchid Room of the Dorchester Hotel.

John: "The best stuff is on the cutting room floor, with us breaking up and falling about all over the place."

   Paul: "Filming *Help!* stretched us a bit, giving us more than one line at a time to say."

John: "*Help!* was too Disneyland. Later there was a rash of films similar to *Help!* and I could see what Richard Lester, the director, was doing. But he didn't really utilise us in that film. **He forgot about who and what we were, and that's** why the film didn't work. It was like having **clowns in a movie about frogs."**

Above: Paul meets Princess Margaret at the Help! premiere.
Right: George, Cynthia, John, Ringo and Maureen arrive at the Help! premiere.

– BBC's *Top Of The Pops* showed a film clip from *Help!*.

July 30
– The Beatles spent the day rehearsing on stage at Brian Epstein's *Saville Theatre*. They did two BBC interviews: one with Dibbs Mather for the British Information Service and the other with Lance Percival for his *Lance A Gogo* show on the BBC Light Programme.
– Later John, Paul and George drove to Blackpool in John's black-glass Rolls Royce. Ringo and Brian Epstein took the plane. The car was parked in the police station car park to keep it safe from fans but in the morning the windows were all cracked. John was angry, but it turned out that the windows had been fitted too tightly and had cracked with the movement of the car, not because they had been tampered with.

July 31
– Rehearsals for ABC TV's *Blackpool Night Out* and the upcoming American tour were held in Blackpool.

August 1
– The Beatles appeared on ABC TV's *Blackpool Night Out* along with Pearl Carr and Teddy Johnson, Mike and Bernie Winters, and Lionel Blair and his dancers. They performed 'I Feel Fine', 'I'm Down', 'Act Naturally', 'Ticket To Ride'. Paul

sang 'Yesterday' and they closed with 'Help!'.
– That evening Ringo and Brian flew back to London while the others followed in the Rolls Royce.

August 2
– Brian Epstein announced that The Beatles would not be doing a British tour this year. (They did play a nine-date tour in November/December)
– Paul and Jane, Marianne Faithfull and several other friends spent an evening on the town in London using The Beatles' Austin Princess to get around. They first met up with The Byrds at their hotel then continued to the Scotch St James's club in Mason's Yard.

August 3
– John took his Aunt Mimi down to Poole, in Dorset, to choose a bungalow.

August 6
– The album HELP! was released in the UK as Parlophone PMC 1255 (mono) and PCS 3071 (stereo).
   SIDE A: 'Help!', 'The Night Before', 'You've Got To Hide Your Love Away', 'I Need You', 'Another Girl', 'You're Going To Lose That Girl', 'Ticket To Ride';
   SIDE B: 'Act Naturally', 'It's Only Love', 'You Like Me Too Much', 'Tell Me What You See', 'I've Just Seen A Face', 'Yesterday', 'Dizzy Miss Lizzy'.

Heathrow, August 13: The Beatles leave for New York.

August 8
– John, Cynthia, George and Patti made a secretive trip to the Richmond Jazz Festival to see Eric Burdon and The Animals. They were unable to stay for long because they were recognised by fans and almost mobbed.
– The album Help! reached number one in the UK charts

August 9
– Brian Epstein's new signing, The Silkie, recorded John's 'You've Got To Hide Your Love Away' under John's supervision. Paul played guitar and George the tambourine during the six-hour session.

August 11
– The film Help! opened in New York.

August 13
– The Beatles arrived at JFK Airport to begin their third US tour. Their TWA flight touched down at 2:30 pm and was met by a huge battery of press, radio and TV reporters, but the police had the plane parked two miles from the main terminal so the thousands of waiting fans were unable to see them. They went straight to the Warwick Hotel at 6th Ave and 54th Street where they gave the obligatory press conference to about 250 reporters, fielded by their press officer Tony Barrow. The Beatles had the whole 33rd floor to themselves, with guards at all entrances to keep out unwanted visitors.
– The album HELP! was released in

the US as Capitol MAS-2386 (mono) and SMAS-2386 (stereo). It contained fewer songs and included music from Ken Thorne's film score.

SIDE A: 'The James Bond Theme' (The George Martin Orchestra), 'Help!', 'The Night Before', 'From Me To You Fantasy' (The George Martin Orchestra), 'You've Got To Hide Your Love Away', 'I Need You', 'In The Tyrol' (The George Martin Orchestra); **SIDE B: 'Another Girl', 'Another Hard Day's Night' (The George Martin Orchestra), 'Ticket To Ride', 'The Bitter End'/'You Can't Do That' (The George Martin Orchestra), 'You're Going To Lose That Girl', 'The Chase' (The George Martin Orchestra).**

August 14
– The police cleared the streets for a convoy of limousines to take The Beatles to rehearsals for the Ed Sullivan Show at CBS Studio 50 where they began work at 11 am. The group did not like the sound balance and continued rehearsals through the afternoon, watching playbacks until they were satisfied it was right. The final tape was made at 8:30 that evening. They performed 'I Feel Fine', Paul did 'I'm Down', then Ringo introduced himself and sang 'Act Naturally'. 'Ticket To Ride' was followed by Paul singing 'Yesterday' to a string quartet from the Ed Sullivan orchestra, and they ended with 'Help!', during which John forgot some of the words.

Paul: "I had to sing 'Yesterday' live in front of all those people. It was pretty nerve-wracking but it was very exciting. I know I was nervous. We'd recorded 'Yesterday' but I'd never really had to perform it anywhere."

August 15
– The Beatles played Shea Stadium.
– That evening Bob Dylan visited their hotel.

August 16
– This day had been left open as a rain check for Shea Stadium. They stayed in their hotel where visitors included The Supremes, The Exciters, The Ronettes, Del Shannon and Bob Dylan. They also taped a few interviews with DJs.

August 17
– The Beatles flew to Toronto, Canada, in the Lockheed Electra hired by Brian Epstein from American Flyers for the tour. Years later, George was on a flight from New York to Los Angeles and met the pilot. He said, **"George, you don't remember me, I'm the pilot from the American Flyers Electra plane that you did the tours on. You'd never believe that plane! It was just full of bullet holes, the tail, the wings, everything - just full of bullet holes. Jealous fellows who would be waiting around, knowing that The Beatles were arriving at such-and-such a time. They'd all be there trying to shoot the plane!"**

Shea Stadium

The police feared that fans would jam the tunnels in and out of Manhattan so the group was first escorted by limousine to the Manhattan East River Heliport and from there they flew to the World Fair site in Queens. There they transferred from the helicopter to a Wells Fargo armoured van where they were each given a Wells Fargo agent badge. As usual for those days, there was

a full bill, and 55,600 fans sat through the King Curtis Band, Cannibal and the Headhunters, Brenda Holloway, The Young Rascals and Sounds Incorporated before Ed Sullivan finally walked on stage to announce The Beatles. They did their standard 30-minute set of a dozen numbers then jumped straight back into the Wells Fargo van.

The usual set for this tour was: 'Twist And Shout',

'She's A Woman', 'I Feel Fine', 'Dizzy Miss Lizzy', 'Ticket To Ride', 'Everybody's Trying To Be My Baby', 'Can't Buy Me Love', 'Baby's In Black', 'I Wanna Be Your Man', 'A Hard Day's Night', 'Help!' and 'I'm Down'. Mick Jagger, Keith Richards and Andrew Loog Oldham were in the audience.

The concert was filmed and released as a documentary film called The Beatles At Shea Stadium.

"A single whistling sound of ten thousand children's larynxes a singing pierce the ears..."
ALLEN GINSBERG

– *Maple Leaf Gardens,* two shows to an audience of 35,000 fans each. News had leaked that the group were staying at the King Edward Sheraton and dozens of fans had booked themselves in, causing a difficult security problem.

August 18
– The Beatles flew in to Atlanta that morning and did just one concert, to 35,000 people at *the Atlanta Stadium.* The new baseball stadium had a very fine sound system which the group talked about for days after, since at most venues they could rarely hear themselves play. Their plane arrived at Houston airport at 2 am, having left Atlanta immediately after the gig. Local police had made no arrangements and fans swarmed out onto the runway as the plane taxied in to the terminal. Fans began climbing over the plane before it had even stopped moving, some of them smoking cigarettes next to the plane's fuel tanks. The group and Brian Epstein were unable to leave the plane until a forklift truck arrived for them.

August 19
– The Beatles played two sets to a total of 25,000 fans at *the Sam Houston Coliseum.* They were restrained performances in very hot weather with complete chaos backstage and no dressing room facilities. The group travelled to and from the show by armoured van.
– BBC's *Top Of The Pops* showed a film clip from *Help!.*

August 20
– The Beatles and entourage flew through the night from Texas, arriving in Chicago at three in the morning at Midway Airport. The police had heard of the trouble in Houston and had forbidden them to land at O'Hare because of the disruption it would cause. They put up at the O'Hare Sahara which had foolishly announced that The Beatles were to stay there, so the place was swarming with fans who made so much noise that no-one was able to get any sleep that night. Nonetheless their two sets at the huge *White Sox Park Stadium* before a total of 50,000 fans went very well.

Ringo's late for breakfast, an America hotel room, 1965.

August 21
– In the afternoon The Beatles flew from Chicago to Minneapolis, Minnesota, for one show before 22,000 people at the *Twin Cities Metropolitan Stadium.* Parts of the show were almost drowned out by a press helicopter circling above the crowd which particularly annoyed John. They stayed at the Leamington Motor Inn, which, like the hotel in Chicago, had announced that The Beatles were staying there. George had the best time in Minneapolis because someone gave him a new guitar. Brian Matthew arrived at the BBC straight from the airport to give the Saturday Club radio audience a first-hand report on the opening dates of The Beatles' American tour.

August 22
– Flying to Portland from Minneapolis, the group's Lockheed Electra flew through a deep gorge and, shortly before landing, one of the plane's four engines caught fire and they arrived belching black smoke and flames. The local press had a field day with this story, blowing it up out of all proportion, though it could have been dangerous had it occurred earlier.
– The Beatles played two shows at the *Portland Memorial Coliseum.* Carl Wilson and Mike Love of The Beach Boys visited them backstage. Allen Ginsberg was in the audience and was

greeted by John Lennon from the stage. He wrote a poem about the concert called "Portland Coliseum".

August 23
– The Beatles left Portland after their concert. With the Electra out of commission, they flew in a Constellation which lengthened the flight so they did not arrive in Los Angeles until a few hours before dawn. They rented a house at 2850 Benedict Canyon, Beverly Hills, but in fewer than ten hours the press and radio stations were giving out the supposedly secret address over the air. While The Beatles relaxed by the pool, the Beverly Hills police force had their work cut out keeping fans from invading their privacy. A dozen police were on duty plus a group of Burns Agency security men.

August 24
– Eleanor Bron, who had starred with the group in *Help!,* and The Byrds both visited The Beatles. Peter Fonda also came by when John was on an acid trip.
– That evening, the head of Capitol Records, Alan Livingstone, threw a party for the group during which they were presented with various awards. The guests included Edward G. Robinson, Jack Benny, Vince Edwards, Gene Barry, Richard Chamberlain, Jane Fonda, Rock Hudson, Groucho Marx,

John: "'She Said She Said' was written after an acid trip in LA during a break in The Beatles' tour, where we were having fun with The Byrds and lots of girls... Peter Fonda came in when we were on acid and he kept coming up to me and sitting next to me and whispering, 'I know what it's like to be dead'. He was describing an acid trip he'd been on."

Dean Martin, Hayley and Juliet Mills and James Stewart. The party ended with a screening of *What's New Pussycat* but Paul and George left before the end to attend a Byrds recording session in the early hours. The Byrds were recording 'The Times They Are A Changin'.
– The routine at Benedict Canyon consisted of breakfast at around 2 pm, sunbathing and swimming during the afternoon, then dinner followed by a private screening of the latest films. The house had a magnificent view across the canyon and was the perfect place for them to unwind.

August 25
– Two girl fans hired a helicopter to fly over the Benedict Canyon mansion

and jumped from it into the swimming pool. Brian complained to the police and no further helicopters came to bother them.

August 27
– The group remained trapped in their house but Paul put on his disguise and accompanied by Alf Bicknall, managed to do a bit of sightseeing.

August 28
– The Beatles travelled from Beverly Hills to San Diego in a luxury touring coach with ten seats, a fridge, bathroom, shower and plenty of food and drink. They took the coast highway for the two-hour journey. *The Balboa Stadium* was filled with 20,000 fans. The bus broke down on the way back to LA and

they had to stop at a mortuary to transfer to limousines for the remainder of the journey. Fans caught up with them and jumped all over the cars, ruining them.

August 29
– In the afternoon there was a large press conference at the Capitol Tower at Hollywood and Vine, during which Alan Livingstone presented The Beatles with gold discs for Help!.

An armoured truck took them from there to the *Hollywood Bowl* for the first of their concerts. The show was watched by 18,000 fans and one of them gave birth to a boy in the car park outside.

August 30
– The last night of their nine days

in Beverly Hills. Their second concert at the Bowl was a success and was taped by Capitol Records for a possible future live record. The group gave a pool-side party for the dozen or so press men and women who had accompanied them on the tour.
– BBC Radio broadcast *The Beatles Abroad*, a 45-minute programme of interviews recorded by Brian Matthew during the early days of the US tour.

August 31
– A total of 30,000 people saw the two shows at the *San Francisco Cow Palace*. The Beatles did their standard 12 number set and the show made news around the world because scores of fans fainted when loose seating allowed fans to push forward and rush the stage. The crowd got so out of hand at one point that the group had to leave the stage and wait in their backstage caravan until the situation had calmed down before returning to play. Johnny Cash and Joan Baez visited backstage. George played 'Greensleeves' and they both joined in the vocals.

September 1
– The Beatles flew back to London from the US.

September 2
– The Beatles arrived at London Airport.

September 4
– The single 'Help!' reached number one in the US charts.

September 6
– Paul and Jane went to see the play *The Killing of Sister George* starring Beryl Reid at the *Duke of York's Theatre*. They were driven by Alf Bicknell whom they invited in to watch with them. Paul enjoyed it, Jane was critical. Afterwards they cruised a few nightclubs.

September 10
– The single 'You've Got To Hide Your Love Away' by The Silkie, written by Lennon & McCartney, was released in the UK as Fontana TF 603.

September 11
– John, Paul and George returned to Liverpool to visit relatives for a few days.

September 12
– The album Help! reached number one in the US charts.
– The Beatles' August 14 recording for the *Ed Sullivan Show* was transmitted.

Meeting Elvis

On August 27 the Beatles met Elvis Presley at his home on Perugia Way in Bel Air next to the Country Club. They arrived at 11 pm to find Elvis waiting on the doorstep. He took them through a huge circular lobby lit with his favourite red and blue lights into an enormous living room dominated by a giant colour television set with the sound turned off. Brian Epstein and Colonel Tom Parker stood together at the side and watched the meeting.

The atmosphere was stilted at first, with no-one saying anything until Elvis blurted out, "If you damn guys are gonna sit here and stare at me

all night I'm gonna go to bed."

This broke the ice. Elvis produced guitars and he and The Beatles played along to rock records from Elvis's collection. Paul played piano and guitar while Elvis played bass. They found they had things in common, discussing incidents with fans and problems of being on the road. George told Elvis how their plane caught fire while landing in Portland and Elvis remembered a similar episode when his aircraft engine failed in Atlanta.

He said that it normally took him about 28 days to shoot one of his films which amazed The Beatles who thought their six

week shooting schedule had been rushed. John made a terrible gaffe by asking Elvis "Why don't you go back to making rock'n'roll records?" To Elvis this implied that his career had been all downhill but rather than argue the case, he blamed his film career:

"It's my movie schedule. It's so tight! I might just do one soon, though."

"Then we'll buy that!" John told him. It seemed to The Beatles later that Elvis had been stoned on something throughout the meeting. The visit lasted three hours and they left shortly after two in the morning. As Elvis waved them goodbye he called out, "Don't

forget to come and see us again in Memphis if you're ever in Tennessee." As The Beatles' limo pulled away, John turned to the others and asked, "Where's Elvis?" He later said: "It was like meeting Englebert Humperdinck."

Mal, Neil and Alf, their road managers, were also present during the visit and were amazed to find that Elvis had ten road managers, complete with their wives, living with him in the house, whereas The Beatles made do with three roadies for the four of them.

The Beatles were each given a complete set of Elvis albums, gun holsters with gold leather belts and a table lamp shaped like a wagon.

September 13
– Maureen gave birth to Zak Starkey at Queen Charlotte's Hospital, London.
– John, Paul and George returned from Liverpool.
– The single **'Yesterday'/'Act Naturally'** was released in US as CAPITOL 5498. This was not released in the UK until long after The Beatles split up.

September 17
– The single 'That Means A Lot' by P.J. Proby, written by Lennon & McCartney, was released in the UK as LIBERTY 10215.

September 20
– The single 'You've Got To Hide Your Love Away' by The Silkie, produced and written by Lennon & McCartney, was released in the US as FONTANA 1525.

September 25
– The Beatles cartoon series, *The Beatles*, made by King Features began broadcasting in the US. The series featured genuine Beatles songs and cartoon characters with voices by Paul Frees (John and George) and Lance Percival (Paul and Ringo). The series was produced by Al Brodax who later produced the cartoon film *Yellow Submarine*. The series was never shown in the UK.

October 1
– The single 'Yesterday' reached number one in the US. It remained unreleased in the UK because the group did not want their image as a rock'n'roll band damaged by the release of a solo ballad.

October 4
– Paul and John visited the recording studio to watch Alma Cogan record 'Eight Days A Week'.

Right: George and John at Heathrow.
Below: September 22: Ringo, Maureen and new-born son Zak leave Hammersmith Hospital.

John: "I was trying to **write** about an **affair** without letting my **wife know** I was **writing** about **an affair.**"

October 9
– All four Beatles attended a party given to celebrate the London opening of Lionel Bart's new musical *Twang*.
– Afterwards they celebrated John's birthday.

October 11
– Paul visited Decca Records Studios to watch Marianne Faithfull record 'Yesterday'. Marianne's version charted in the UK but came second to that by Matt Monro.
– The single **'Twist And Shout'/'There's A Place'** was released in the US as CAPITOL STARLINE 6061.
– The single **'Love Me Do'/'P.S. I Love You'** was released in the US as CAPITOL STARLINE 6062.
– The single **'Please, Please Me'/'From Me To You'** was released in the US as CAPITOL STARLINE 6063.
– The single **'Do You Want To Know A Secret'/'Thank You Girl'** was released in the US as CAPITOL STARLINE 6064.
– The single **'Roll Over Beethoven'/ 'Misery'** was released in the US as CAPITOL STARLINE 6065.
– The single **'Boys'/'Kansas City'/'Hey-Hey-Hey-Hey'** was released in the US as CAPITOL STARLINE 6066.

October 12
– *Abbey Road.* John's 'Run For Your Life' was recorded in an afternoon session, leading straight into 'Norwegian Wood', then still known as 'This Bird Has Flown'. George played sitar for the first time on a Beatles' recording; a cheap model bought at Indiacraft.

A 'Yesterday' tale

In Eric Burdon's autobiography, he says that Paul originally offered Chris Farlowe 'Yesterday':

"One day he phoned me at my Duke Street pad. 'Hey Eric, how ya doin', it's Chris Farlowe here,' he said in his hoarse voice. I asked how he was getting on. 'Oh, I'm OK. 'Ere listen, you'll never guess what happened. Paul McCartney - you know Paul out of The Beatles?' Yes, I had heard of him. 'Well he came round to our house in the middle of the night. I was out doing a show, but me mum was in and he left her a demo disc for me to listen to.' This was wonderful news. When was Chris going into the studio to cut this gift from the gods? 'Ah,' he growled. 'I don't like it. It's not for me. It's too soft. I need a good rocker, you know, a shuffle or something.'

'Yeah, but Chris,' I said. 'Anything to give you a start, man, I mean even if it's a ballad, you should go ahead and record it.'

'No, I don't like it,' he insisted. 'Too soft.'

'So what are you gonna do with the song?'

'Well, I sent it back, didn't I?'

'What was the title of the song?'

'"Yesterday",' he retorted."

Below left: Even John smiles as the group display their MBEs outside Buckingham Palace while, below, mounted police hold back the crowds in The Mall.

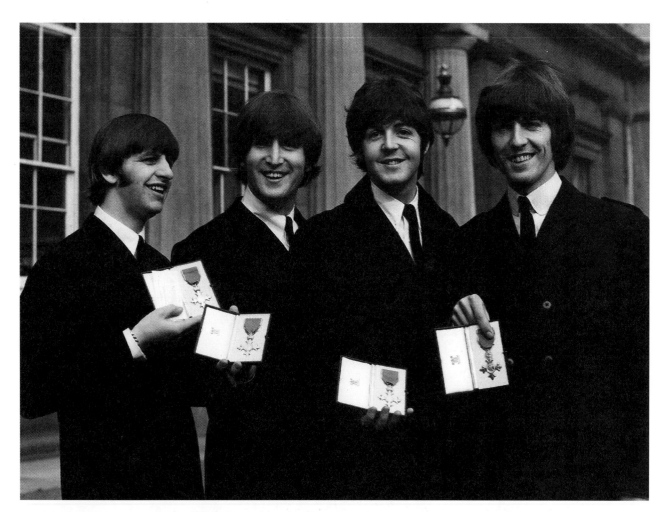

MBE day: October 26

The Beatles arrived at Buckingham Palace in John's black glass Rolls Royce in time for the 11 am honours ceremony in the Great Throne Room. Wearing dark suits and ties, they stood in a row while the Queen pinned the medals to the narrow lapels of their jackets. "How long have you been together now?" she asked.

"Oh, for many years," said Paul.

"Forty years," said Ringo, and everyone laughed.

"Are you the one that started it all?" the Queen asked Ringo.

He told her that the others started it. "I'm the little one," he said.

The Queen wore a pale gold gown. The room in Buckingham Palace was decorated in cream and gold, with six chandeliers overhead and an organ at one end. The band of the Coldstream Guards quietly played tunes from 'Humoresque' and 'Bitter Sweet'. Paul later described it as "a keen pad".

The Lord Chamberlain, Lord Cobbold, read out The Beatles' names. They stepped forward and bowed. The Queen shook hands, spoke to each, and pinned on the medals. They then stepped back into place and bowed again.

Paul described the Queen as "Lovely. Great! She was very friendly. She was just like a mum to us."

At the investiture 189 people received awards, including six who were knighted. The Beatles were awarded the MBE, the lowest of the five divisions of the order, for service to their country. It ranks 120th of the 126 titles of precedence and is the most widely given honour.

Outside, 4,000 Beatles fans chanted "Yeah, yeah, yeah" and jostled with police who managed to hold them back, but could not prevent them climbing the gates and lamp-posts outside the palace.

Immediately afterwards there was a press conference arranged in the downstairs bar of the Saville Theatre for The Beatles to discuss their MBEs and give their reaction to the protests.

October 13
– *Abbey Road.* The recording of 'Drive My Car' was the first time that The Beatles had recorded past midnight - something which would soon become the norm.

October 14
– John and Paul had a songwriting session at Kenwood.

October 15
– Paul and Jane saw Ben E. King play at the Scotch St James's. George, Patti, John and Cynthia arrived at the Scotch too late and missed the show.

October 16
– *Abbey Road.* 'Day Tripper' was recorded during an afternoon and evening session, followed by work on George's 'If I Needed Someone'.

October 18
– Abbey Road for the afternoon only, during which they completed 'If I Needed Someone' and worked on John's 'In My Life'.

October 20
– *Abbey Road.* Two extended sessions produced 'We Can Work It Out'.

October 21
– *Abbey Road.* The Beatles were in the studio from 2:30 until after midnight working on 'Norwegian Wood' and 'Nowhere Man'.

October 22
– *Abbey Road.* The Beatles were driven to Abbey Road at 10 am where they stayed until midnight working on 'Nowhere Man'.

October 24
– *Abbey Road.* The Beatles began work at 2.30 pm, working on Paul's 'I'm Looking Through You' and stayed until midnight. Afterwards all of them except John continued to the Scotch St. James's where Brian was holding a party.

October 26
– The Beatles were invested with their MBEs.

October 28
– *Abbey Road.* Mixing session for 'We Can Work It Out'.

– John Lennon arrived at the Ad Lib with a crowd of friends, driven in his Rolls Royce by The Beatles' chauffeur Alf Bicknall. When he learned that it was Alf's birthday he insisted on giving him a night out on the town. One of the entourage, John's friend Terry Doran, took charge of the car and after the Ad Lib, John took the whole party to dinner at the Savoy where François Hardy was in cabaret.

October 29
– *Abbey Road.* A new vocal track was added to 'We Can Work It Out'.

November 1

– The Beatles drove to Manchester to record *The Music Of Lennon And McCartney*, a special for Granada Television. Paul began 'Yesterday' and after 22 seconds the cameras cut away to a pregnant Marianne Faithfull performing her version. The group mimed to 'We Can Work It Out' and 'Day Tripper'. Other artists performed their own versions of Beatles songs.

– John became a director of Drutsown Limited, a company set up to control his literary income.

November 2

– The Beatles finished recording at Granada and returned to London.

November 3

– *Abbey Road*. An afternoon and an evening session ending at midnight recording Paul's 'Michelle'.

November 4

– *Abbey Road*. A 7 pm until 3 am session recording Ringo's 'What Goes On'.

November 6

– *Abbey Road*. A 7 pm until 3 am session working on Paul's 'I'm Looking Through You', but no-one was satisfied with the results.

November 8

– *Abbey Road*. The group rehearsed George's 'Think for Yourself' and at about 3 am recorded The Beatles Third Christmas Record, a flexi-disc issued free to fan club members only.

November 10

– *Abbey Road*. a 9 pm to 3 am session for John's 'The Word' and more work on 'I'm Looking Through You'.

November 11

– *Abbey Road*. A late night session beginning at 6 pm ending at 7 am working on 'Wait', recording Paul's 'You Won't See Me' and John's 'Girl'. They put the finishing touches to 'I'm Looking Through You' and their new album, Rubber Soul was finished.

November 15

– The afternoon was spent sequencing songs for the new album with George Martin.

November 16

– Paul saw Gene Pitney play in Slough and acted as MC, making the announcements from behind the stage

curtains so that no-one in the audience knew it was him: **"And to start the show in swinging style: The Mike Cotton Sound!"** He was there because Peter Asher's group, Peter and Gordon, were on the bill. Between houses, when the curtain was down, Paul played drums on stage.

November 17

– George and Patti spent the day shopping.

November 18

– John and Cynthia spent the day shopping.

November 23

– The Beatles filmed their own promotional film clips to promote the new album. This way they would be able to appear on television in the US, Japan and the rest of the world instead of being restricted to just a few British TV shows. They filmed all day at Twickenham Film Studios. Film versions were made of 'We Can Work It Out', 'Day Tripper', 'Help!', 'Ticket

To Ride' and 'I Feel Fine' which were shown all over the world during the Christmas period.

November 25

– Harrods opened for three hours in the evening to enable The Beatles to do late-night Christmas shopping in private.

November 27

– Paul saw his brother Michael in his group The Scaffold perform at the *Granada, East Ham* where they were on the bill of a Manfred Mann/Yardbirds concert, and attended the party after the show.

November 29

– The Beatles taped an interview with Brian Matthew at the *BBC Aeolian Hall* for use on the Christmas Day edition of BBC Light Programme's *Saturday Club*.

November 30

– Brian Matthew interviewed George and John separately at NEMS Argyll Street office for the BBC Overseas Service.

Paul with Beatles press attaché Derek Taylor.

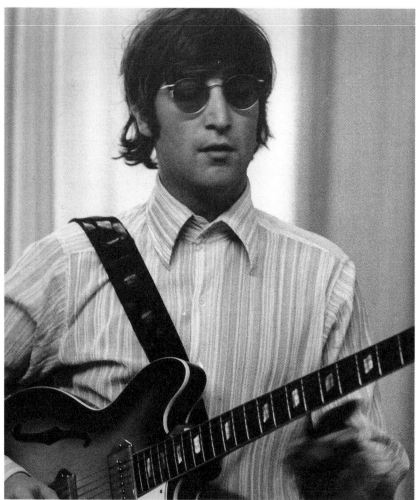

John: "We were just **getting better** technically and musically, that's all. Finally we took over the studio. In the early days, we had to take what we were given, we didn't know how you can get more bass. We were learning the technique on 'Rubber Soul'. **We were more precise about making the album,** that's all, and we took over the cover and everything. That was Paul's title, it was like 'Yer Blues', I suppose, meaning **'English Soul'** Just a pun. There's no great mysterious meaning behind it, it was just four boys working out what to call a new album."

December 1
– The Beatles spent the day practising at Mal and Neil's apartment in order to be on form for their upcoming British tour.
– An art exhibition at *the Nell Gwynne Club*, London included some of John's drawings.

December 2
– The Beatles drove to Berwick-on-Tweed. One of George's guitars fell off the back of the car en route and was smashed to pieces by following traffic.
– BBC TV's *Top Of The Pops* premiered the new promo films for 'Day Tripper' and 'We Can Work It Out'.
– John's company, Drutsown Limited, changed its name to Lennon Books Limited.

December 3
– The single **'Day Tripper'/'We Can Work It Out'** was released in the UK as Parlophone R 5389.

– The album RUBBER SOUL was released in the UK as Parlophone PMC 1267 (mono) and PCS 3075 (stereo).
   SIDE A: **'Drive My Car', 'Norwegian Wood (This Bird Has Flown)', 'You Won't See Me', 'Nowhere Man', 'Think For Yourself', 'The Word', 'Michelle';**
   SIDE B: **'What Goes On', 'Girl', 'I'm Looking Through You', 'In My Life', 'Wait', 'If I Needed Someone', 'Run For Your Life'.**
– EMI made an initial pressing of 750,000 copies to cope with the expected demand.
– The Beatles began their last UK tour in Glasgow, playing two sets at the *Odeon Cinema*. Also on the bill were their friends The Moody Blues. The Beatles' set consisted of: 'Dizzy Miss Lizzy', 'I Feel Fine', 'She's A Woman', 'If I Needed Someone', 'Ticket To Ride', 'Act

Naturally', 'Nowhere Man', 'Baby's In Black', 'Help!', 'We Can Work It Out', 'Day Tripper' and 'I'm Down'.
– Bad weather made Brian Epstein change their hotel from a small one just out of town to a grand hotel in the centre of Glasgow which posed a security problem.

December 4
– The group had a bad journey through snow to Newcastle for a concert at *The City Hall* (British Tour).

December 5
– *Liverpool Empire* (British Tour). All their friends and relatives attended the concert which turned out to be the last time The Beatles played their home town. During the second show, Paul joined support act The Koobas onstage to play drums on 'Dizzy Miss Lizzy'.
– The double-A side single, 'We Can Work It Out'/'Day Tripper', reached number one in the UK charts.
– The album Rubber Soul reached number one in the UK album charts.

December 6
– The album RUBBER SOUL was released in the US as Capitol T-2442 (mono) and ST-2442 (stereo). As usual it contained fewer tracks than the UK original:
   SIDE A: **'I've Just Seen A Face', 'Norwegian Wood (This Bird Has Flown)', 'You Won't See Me', 'Think For Yourself', 'The Word', 'Michelle';**
   SIDE B: **'It's Only Love', 'Girl', 'I'm Looking Through You', 'In My Life', 'Wait', 'Run For Your Life'.**
– The single **'Day Tripper'/'We Can Work It Out'** was released in the US as Capitol 5555.
– The EP **The Beatles Million Sellers** was released in the UK as Parlophone GEP 8946. (mono only)
   SIDE A: **'She Loves You', 'I Want To Hold Your Hand';**
   SIDE B: **'Can't Buy Me Love', 'I Feel Fine'.**

December 7
– The group drove to Manchester with no trouble but the city was covered in thick fog and it took them four hours to find the venue, arriving at the *ABC Cinema, Ardwick,* after they should have been on stage. Walter Shenson visited them backstage to discuss their third film.

December 8
– *Gaumont Cinema, Sheffield* (British Tour). After the show, The Moody Blues joined them for dinner at their hotel.

December 9
– The band drove to *Birmingham* through torrential rain and played the *Odeon Cinema* (British Tour).

December 10
– The Beatles returned to London and played the *Hammersmith Odeon* (British Tour).

December 11
– The band played the *Finsbury Park Astoria* (British Tour) to a tremendous London audience.

December 12
– The UK tour ended with a concert at *the Cardiff Capitol Cinema.* Ringo drove back to London after the show in order to go to the Scotch St James's Christmas party.

December 13
– John, Paul and George returned to London. They met with Brian to discuss their projected third film. The meeting ended in disagreement with the group turning down the script for Richard Condon's A Talent For Loving for which Brian had already bought the rights.

December 14
– John and Cynthia did Christmas shopping.

December 16
– Granada Television screened *The Music Of Lennon And McCartney* special.

December 17
– The Beatles Third Christmas Record flex-disc was sent to members of The Beatles fan club.

December 18
– John spent the night in the clubs.

December 19
– Paul and Jane saw a performance of Lionel Bart's musical *Twang* at *the Shaftesbury Theatre.*

December 23
– Paul did last-minute Christmas shopping. Among his Christmas gifts to the other Beatles were acetates of a special record called Paul's Christmas Album made in an edition of four copies only. On it Paul acted as a DJ playing his favourite tracks.

December 25
– BBC Light Programme's *Saturday Club* broadcast clips from a specially recorded interview.
– The pirate ship Radio Caroline broadcast a specially recorded Christmas message by the group who had always given their support to pirate stations.
– BBC TV's *Top Of The Pops* showed film clips of the group performing 'I Feel Fine', 'Help!', 'Ticket to Ride' and 'Day Tripper'.

December 26
– George was driven to Liverpool to pay a surprise visit to his mother and family in their new bungalow on Boxing Day. George and chauffeur Alf Bicknell had to sleep on camp beds in the attic.
– Radio Caroline broadcast a pre-recorded interview with Paul on its *Pop's Happening* programme.
– Paul was also in Liverpool to see his family, bringing his friend, Guinness heir, Tara Browne, with him. While they were out for a ride in country lanes in the Wirral, Paul fell off his moped and cut his lip badly enough to require several stitches.

December 31
– Paul, Jane, George and Patti attended a big New Year's party with EMI executives. John and Cynthia spent the evening at a party given by Norman Newell.
– John's father, Freddie Lennon, released a single, 'That's My Life (My Love And My Home)' on Pye Records.

Above: Manchester, December 7 – The Beatles wear face masks as a precaution against the fog. Below: Ringo and George at Hammersmith Odeon, December 10.

John: "I never saw him until I made a lot of money and he came back. I opened the *Daily Express* and there he was, washing dishes in a small hotel or something very near where I was living in the stockbroker belt outside London. He had been writing to me to try and get into contact. I didn't want to see him. I was too upset about what he'd done to me and to my mother and that he would turn up when I was rich and famous and not bother turning up before. So I wasn't going to see him at all, but he sort of blackmailed me in the press by saying all this about being a poor man washing dishes while I was living in luxury. I fell for it and saw him and we had some kind of relationship. He died a few years later of cancer. But at 65 he married a secretary who had been working for The Beatles, age 22, and they had a child, which I thought was hopeful for a man who had lived his life as a drunk and almost a Bowery bum."

John: "Oh Sure. I dug **the fame, the power, the money,** and playing to big crowds. **Conquering America** was the best thing.

You see we wanted to be bigger than Elvis – that was the main thing. At first we wanted to be Goffin and King, then we wanted to be Eddie Cochran, and then we wanted to be Buddy Holly, and **finally** we arrived at wanting to be bigger than the biggest – and that was **Elvis.** We reckoned we could make it because there were four of us. None of us would've made it alone, because Paul wasn't quite **strong enough,** I didn't have enough **girl-appeal,** George was **too quiet,** and Ringo was **the drummer.** But we thought that everyone would be able to dig at least one of us, and that's how it turned out."

DAILY
TRIUMPH
FOR BEATLES
SHOW BIZ
WELCOME
EXTRA
THE
BEATLES
BEATAX

Paul: "'Love Me Do' was our greatest philosophical song. For it to be simple and true means that it's incredibly simple."

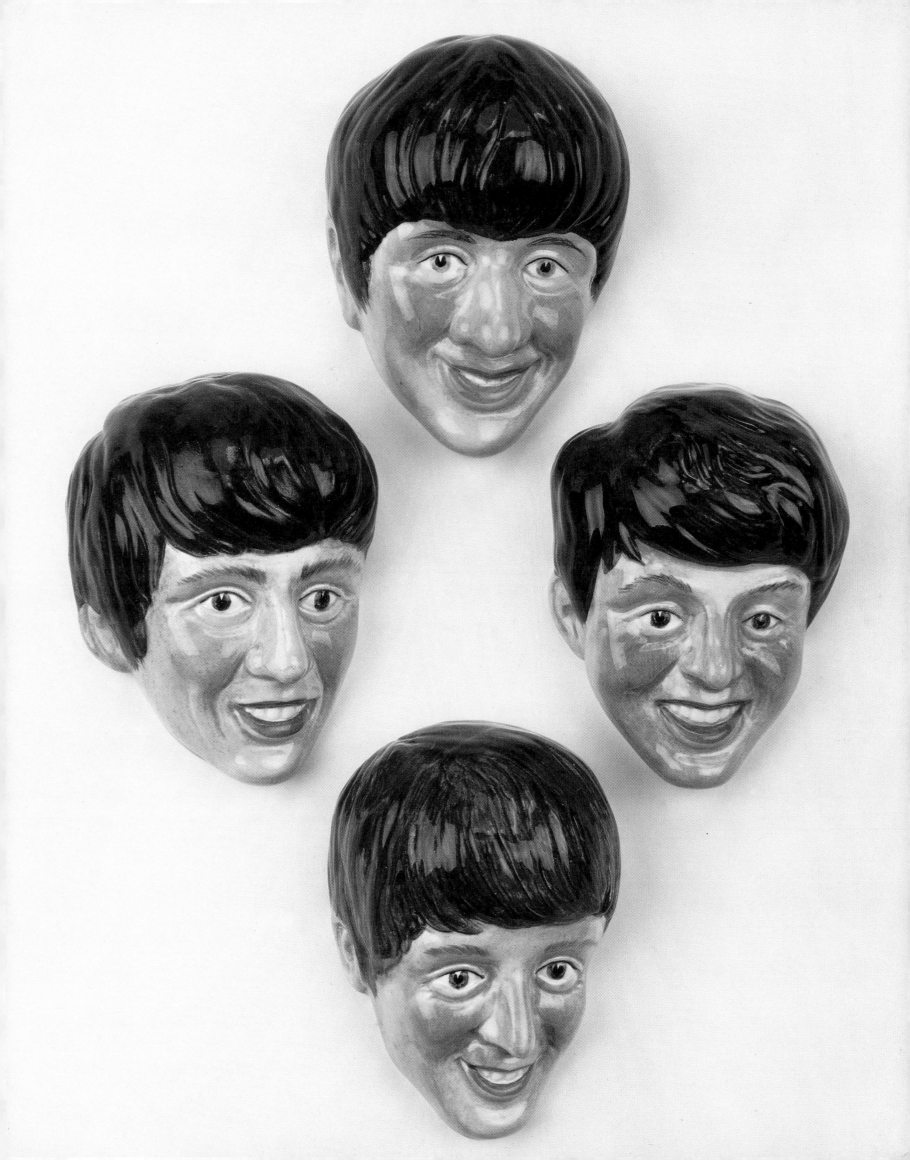

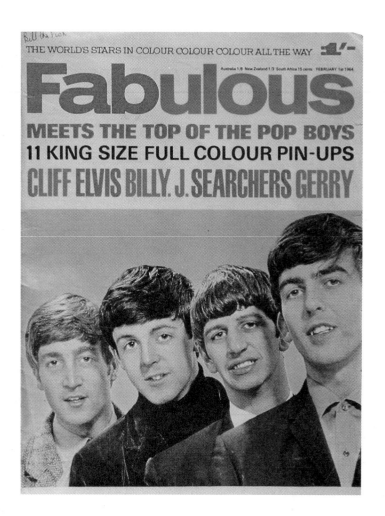

THE WORLD'S STARS IN COLOUR COLOUR COLOUR ALL THE WAY   1/-

Fabulous
MEETS THE TOP OF THE POP BOYS
11 KING SIZE FULL COLOUR PIN-UPS
CLIFF ELVIS BILLY. J. SEARCHERS GERRY

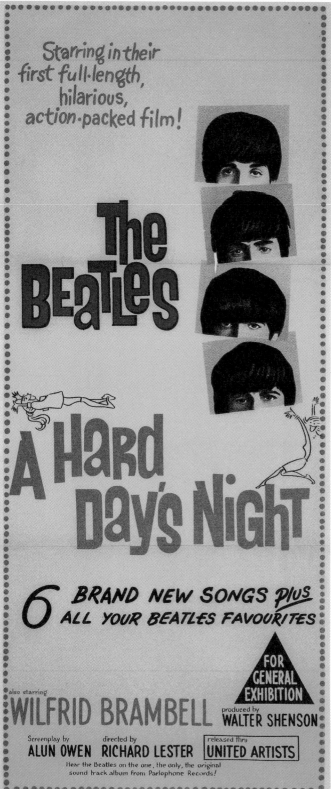

Starring in their first full-length, hilarious, action-packed film!

The BEATLES
A Hard Day's Night

6 BRAND NEW SONGS *plus* ALL YOUR BEATLES FAVOURITES

FOR GENERAL EXHIBITION

also starring **WILFRID BRAMBELL**   *produced by* **WALTER SHENSON**

Screenplay by **ALUN OWEN**   *directed by* **RICHARD LESTER**   *released thru* **UNITED ARTISTS**

Hear the Beatles on the one, the only, the original sound track album from Parlophone Records!

The BEATLES
COLOURING SET
pencil by number

PAUL
GEORGE
JOHN
RINGO

5 NUMBERED READY TO COLOUR PORTRAITS OF JOHN, PAUL, GEORGE, RINGO AND THE GROUP
6 BRILLIANT COLOURED PENCILS

Kitfix

NO PAINTS · NO WATER · NO MESS   ITS SO EASY!

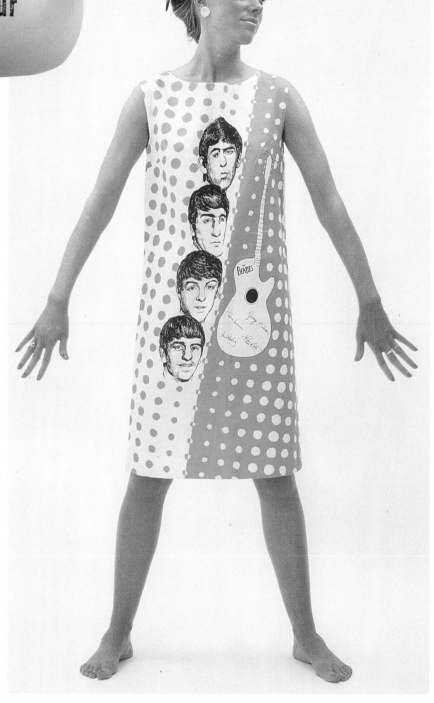

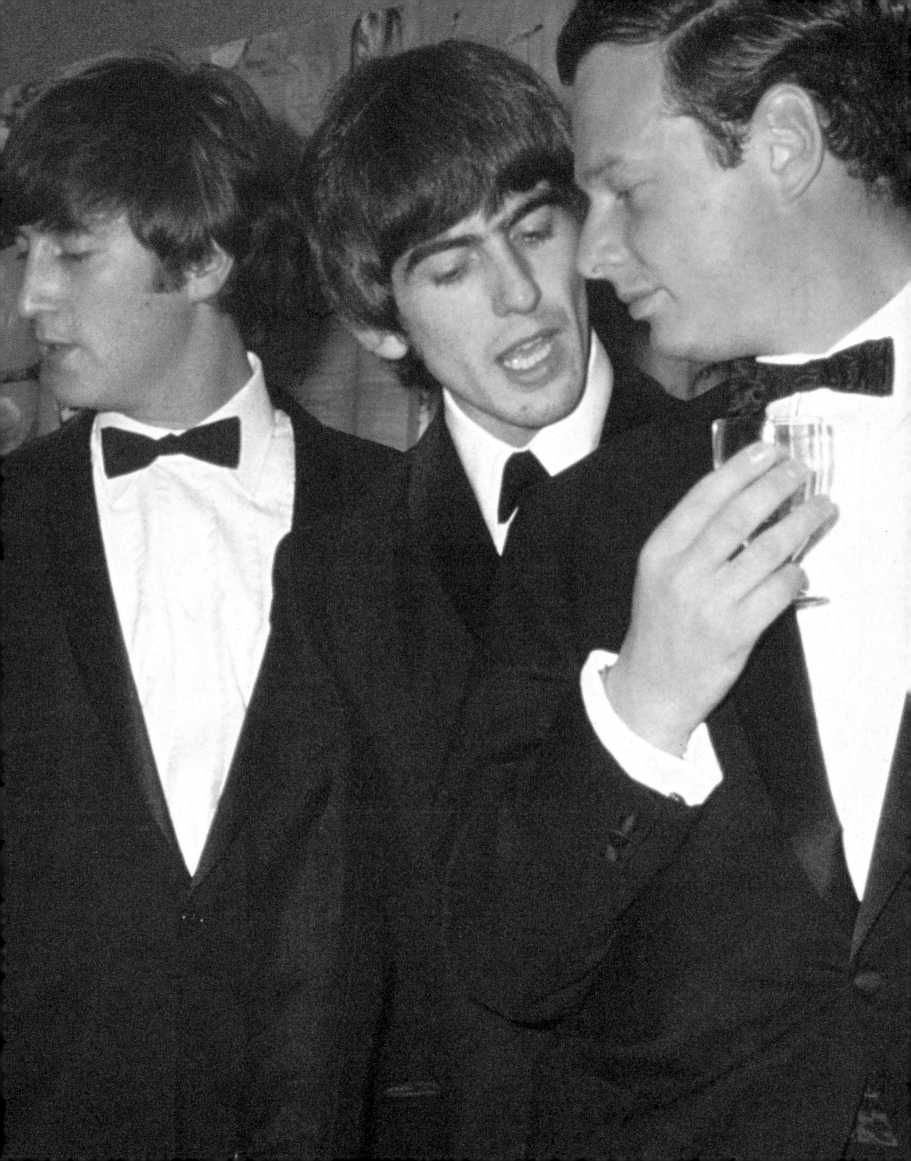

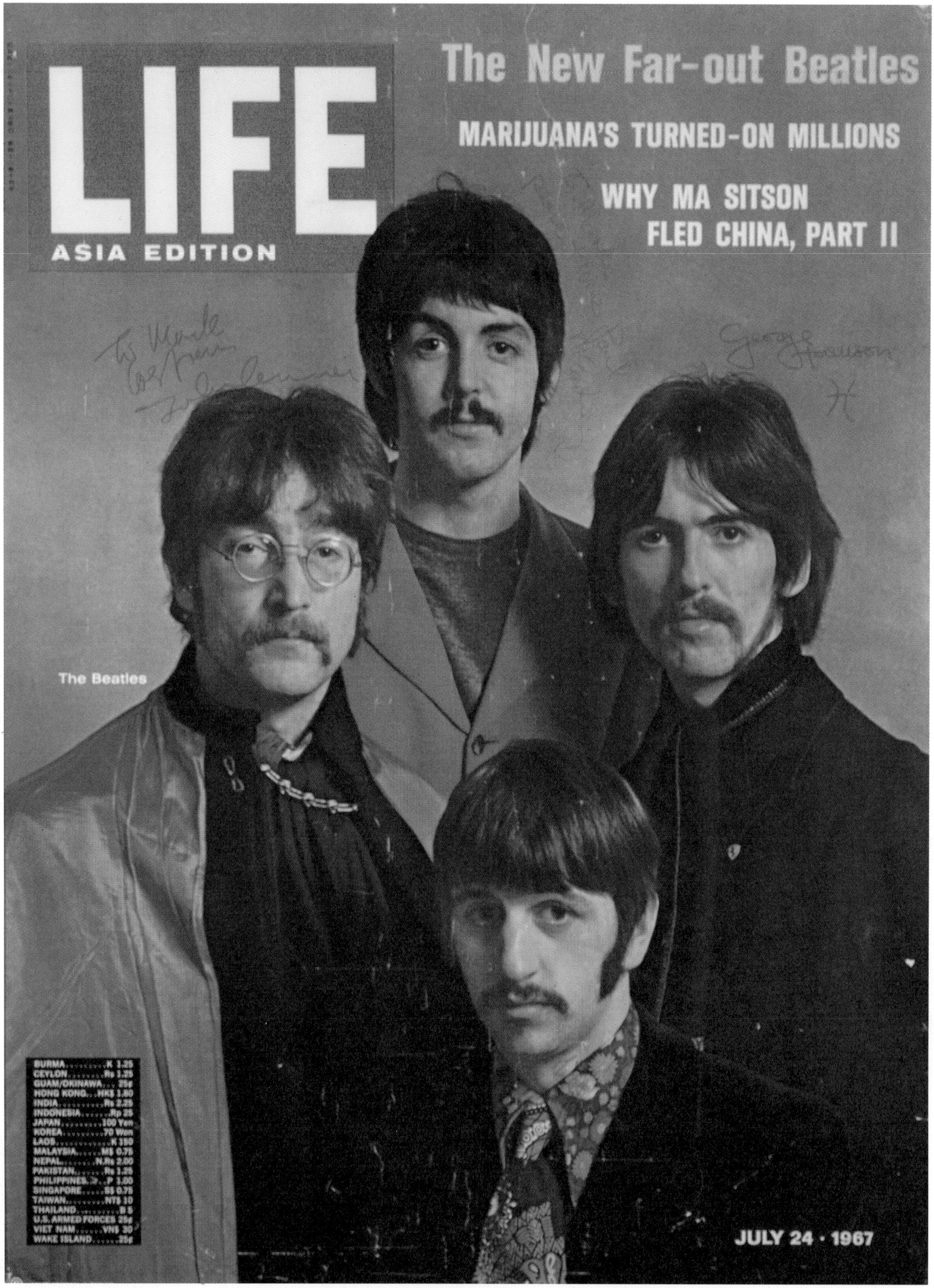

LIFE

ASIA EDITION

The Beatles

The New Far-out Beatles

MARIJUANA'S TURNED-ON MILLIONS

WHY MA SITSON FLED CHINA, PART II

BURMA	K 1.25
CEYLON	Rs 1.25
GUAM/OKINAWA	25¢
HONG KONG	HK$ 1.80
INDIA	Rs 2.25
INDONESIA	Rp 25
JAPAN	100 Yen
KOREA	70 Won
LAOS	K 350
MALAYSIA	M$ 0.75
NEPAL	N.Rs 2.00
PAKISTAN	Rs 1.25
PHILIPPINES	P 1.00
SINGAPORE	S$ 0.75
TAIWAN	NT$ 10
THAILAND	B 5
U.S. ARMED FORCES	25¢
VIET NAM	VN$ 30
WAKE ISLAND	25¢

JULY 24 · 1967

Page 177 Stuart Sutcliffe, in Hamburg, with the bass guitar he bought at John Lennon's suggestion so that he could become a Beatle. Stuart inspired much of The Beatles' image but he died without ever knowing the legacy of his influence.

Pages 178/179 The Fab Four in 1963, when being a Beatle was as good as it got.

Page 182/183 Like Royalty, The Beatles were welcomed wherever they went as no other pop performers before or since.

Page 184 Lennon & McCartney, whose songs became the soundtrack for the second half of the twentieth century.

Page 185 More than any other facet of their image, The Beatles' hairstyles cemented their unity.

Page 186/187 & 188/189 The Beatles on the set of their first movie A Hard Day's Night, rock'n'roll's greatest buddy movie.

Page 193 George and Patti.

Page 194/195 Brian Epstein with his principal clients. "We had complete faith in him when he was runnin' us," said John. "We'd never have made it without him and vice versa. Brian contributed as much as us in the early days, although we were the talent and he was the hustler."

Page 196/197 John: "We sometimes wrote together but all our best work we wrote apart."

Page 199 On June 25, 1967, The Beatles performed 'All You Need Is Love' on the BBC Our World Live worldwide TV link-up live from EMI's studio one. The viewing audience was estimated at over 300 million.

Page 200/201 Retaining the common touch, The Beatles visit a fish and chip shop in Taunton, Somerset, during the filming of Magical Mystery Tour, in September 1967.

Page 202 John during the filming of his promo for 'Strawberry Fields'.

Page 204/205 The Beatles in 1968, during a break from the 'White Album' sessions.

Page 208 John: "I'd never known love like this before, and it hit me so hard that I had to halt my marriage to Cyn. And don't think that was a reckless decision, because I felt very deeply about it and all the implications that would be involved."

1966

January 1

– The album Rubber Soul entered the Billboard Hot 100 charts.

January 5

– *CTS Studios,* The Beatles re-recorded and overdubbed sections of *The Beatles At Shea Stadium* soundtrack because the audience screaming and technical problems meant that the live sound was not up to exhibition standard. 'I Feel Fine' and 'Help!' were re-recorded from scratch.

– John and Cynthia entertained P.J. Proby at their home then drove back to London in John's black Rolls Royce to Proby's house off the King's Road, Chelsea, where he was giving a party. John returned home at dawn.

January 7

– John and Ringo met at John's to discuss The Beatles' next film.

January 8

– Paul went to Liverpool to visit his family.

– John, George and Ringo went to a party given by Mick Jagger at his home.

– The album Rubber Soul reached number one on the Billboard Hot 100 charts.

– The single 'We Can Work It Out' reached number one in the Billboard singles charts.

January 12

– John, Cynthia, Ringo and Maureen flew to Port of Spain, Trinidad, for a winter holiday.

January 13

– George and Patti met up with Mick Jagger and Chrissie Shrimpton for a night of dancing at Dolly's nightclub on Jermyn Street, in the West End.

January 21

– George married Patricia Anne Boyd

George marries Patti, January 21.

at the Leatherhead and Esher Register Office, Surrey. Paul and Brian Epstein were the Best Men. Afterwards there was a party at "Kinfauns", George's American-style villa in Esher.

January 22

– George and Patti gave a press conference before being driven to Heathrow to fly to Barbados for their honeymoon.

January 23

– John and Cynthia, Ringo and Maureen returned from Trinidad.

January 31

– Peter Sellers' send-up of 'A Hard Day's Night'/'Help!' was released in the US.

February 3

– Paul saw Stevie Wonder perform at the Scotch St. James's and visited with him backstage afterwards. Paul was very pleased to see him because he had always been one of his favourite Motown acts.

February 10

– 'Woman' by Peter & Gordon, written by Paul as Bernard Webb, entered the Billboard charts at number 83.

February 12

– John and Ringo spent a night at the Scotch St. James's.

February 21

– The single **'Nowhere Man'/'What Goes On'** was released in the US as CAPITOL 5587.

February 23

– Paul attended a lecture and taped performance by Luciano Berio at the Italian Institute. He and Berio spoke afterwards but there were too many press and Italian embassy people present for them to relax.

February 26

– The single 'Woman' by Peter &

Gordon, written by Paul as Bernard Webb, entered the UK charts at number 47.

February 28

– The Cavern was closed by the Official Receiver with debts of £10,000. The Police had to break down barricades to evict fans who had holed up inside to resist the closure.

March 1

– *The Beatles At Shea Stadium* was given its world premiere on BBC1 in black and white. It was originally filmed in colour, designed for the American market where it was shown in cinemas.

March 4

– *The London Evening Standard* published an interview with John Lennon by his friend Maureen Cleave.

His words upset no-one in Great Britain but when they were reprinted in the US, Christian fundamentalists reacted with hate and outrage.

– The EP **Yesterday** was released in the UK as PARLOPHONE GEP 8952 (mono). **SIDE A: 'Yesterday', 'Act Naturally'; SIDE B: 'You Like Me Too Much', 'It's Only Love'.**

March 6

– Paul and Jane went skiing in Klosters, Switzerland.

March 18

– NEMS had to confirm that Peter and Gordon's hit song, 'Woman' was written by Paul McCartney, though it was credited to Bernard Webb. Paul said he put a false name on it to see if it would still make the charts.

March 20

– Paul and Jane returned from their holiday in Klosters.

March 23

– Photo session to provide new pictures

John: "Christianity will go. It will vanish and shrink. I needn't argue about that. I'm right and I will be proved right. We're more popular than Jesus now. I don't know which will go first - rock 'n' roll or Christianity. Jesus was alright but his disciples were thick and ordinary. It's them twisting it that ruins it for me."

John: "I think that was one of his best songs, too, because the lyrics are good and I didn't write them."

of the group to publicise their next American album.

March 24
– All of The Beatles and their wives and girlfriends attended the premiere of Lewis Gilbert's film *Alfie*, starring Jane Asher.

March 25
– The Beatles did a photo session for Bob Whitaker at his studio at *1 The Vale, off the Kings Road, Chelsea*.
– While at Whitaker's studio, The Beatles recorded an interview with Radio Caroline DJ Tom Lodge which was released as a flexi-disc called *Sound Of The Stars* given away free in a promotion by *Disc And Music Echo*, part-owned by Brian Epstein.

March 26
– Drake's Drum, the racehorse that Paul bought for his father, won the Hylton Plate at the Aintree Racecourse in Liverpool, coming in at 20-1. Paul,

his father and his brother Michael watched the race.

March 28
– Ringo and George saw Roy Orbison at the *Granada Cinema, Walthamstow*.

April 1
– Paul and John visited Indica Books and Gallery in Mason's Yard. John bought a copy of Timothy Leary's *The Psychedelic Experience* and a reworking of the *Tibetan Book Of The Dead*, in the introduction of which he found the first line of 'Tomorrow Never Knows'.

April 6
– *Abbey Road*. An 8 pm until 1:15 am session recording the backing tracks for John's 'Tomorrow Never Knows'.

John: "That's me in my Tibetan Book of the Dead period. I took one of Ringo's malapropisms as the title, to sort of take the edge off the heavy philosophical lyrics."

"Often the backing I think of early on never comes off. With 'Tomorrow Never Knows' I'd imagined in my head that in the background you would hear thousands of monks chanting. That was impractical, of course, and we did something different. It was a bit of a drag, and I didn't really like it. I should have tried to get near my original idea, the monks singing; I realise now that was what it wanted."

Paul: "That was an LSD song. Probably the only one."

April 7
– *Abbey Road*. Paul's looped tapes were added to provide the unique solo on 'Tomorrow Never Knows'. They began work on Paul's 'Got To Get You Into My Life'.

Left: Paul with his father Jim in St John's Wood, London.

April 8
– *Abbey Road*. An afternoon and evening session resulted in the completion of a backing track for 'Got To Get You Into My Life.'
Afterwards they spent an evening in the clubs to unwind.

April 11
– *Abbey Road*. First they did more work on 'Got To Get You Into My Life' and then spent most of the afternoon and evening sessions on George's 'Love You To'.

George: "'Love You To' was one of the first tunes I wrote for sitar... this was the first song where I consciously tried to use sitar and tabla on the basic track. I overdubbed the guitars and vocal later."

April 13
– *Abbey Road*. During the first session of the day they completed 'Love You To', then after a break for dinner, they recorded the backing tracks for 'Paperback Writer', finishing up at 2:30 am.

April 14
– *Abbey Road*. The afternoon was spent completing 'Paperback Writer' and the evening, until 1:30 am, working on the future B-side 'Rain'.

The 'Butcher' Sleeve

At Bob Whitaker's studio on March 25, The Beatles posed in white coats, using sides of meat and broken dolls as props. John: "Bob was into Dali and making surreal pictures... it was inspired by our boredom and resentment at having to do another photo session and another Beatles thing. We were sick to death of it... That combination produced that cover."

The image was used as the sleeve for their next American album, Yesterday... and Today but provoked a very negative reaction and was withdrawn. It was used in the UK in ads for the single 'Paperback Writer'.

The Beatles receive awards from actor Clint Walker at the NME Poll Winners concert, May 1.

April 16
– *Abbey Road.* An afternoon and evening session during which they completed 'Rain'.
Ringo: "My favourite piece of me is what I did on 'Rain'. I think I just played amazing. I was into the snare and hi-hat. I think it was the first time I used this trick of starting a break by hitting the hi-hat first instead of going directly to a drum off the hi-hat... I think it's the best out of all the records I've ever made. 'Rain' blows me away. It's out of left field. I know me and I know my playing, and then there's 'Rain'."

April 17
– *Abbey Road.* The Beatles laid down the backing tracks for John's 'Dr. Robert'.

April 18
– John and George saw The Lovin' Spoonful play *The Marquee*.
– *The Cavern Club* was sold by a court receiver after going bankrupt.

April 19
– *Abbey Road.* 'Dr Robert' was completed.

April 20
– *Abbey Road.* A 12-hour session from 2:30 pm until 2:30 am working on John's 'And Your Bird Can Sing', and rehearsals for George's 'Taxman'.

April 21
– *Abbey Road.* 'Taxman' was finished, with Paul adding his distinctive guitar solo.
George: "I was pleased to have him play that bit on 'Taxman'. If you notice, he did like a little Indian bit on it for me."

April 22
– *Abbey Road.* The Beatles worked on 'Taxman' and 'Tomorrow Never Knows'.

April 23
– Paul spent the day at John's, songwriting and discussing the album.

April 26
– *Abbey Road.* The Beatles spent a 12-hour session, ending at 2:24 am, working on 'And Your Bird Can Sing'.

John: "I got home from the studio and I was **stoned** out of my mind on **marijuana** and, as I usually do, **I listened** to what I'd recorded that day. **Somehow** I got it on backwards and I sat there **transfixed** with the ear-phones on, with a big hash joint. **I ran in** the next day and said, **'I know what to do with it. I know... Listen to this!'** So I made them all play it **backwards.** The fade is me actually singing backwards – **'Sharethsm nowthsmea ness'.**"

April 27
– *Abbey Road.* John's 'I'm Only Sleeping' was virtually finished when they called it a day at 3 am.

April 28
– *Abbey Road.* The session was spent recording the eight-piece string section for Paul's 'Eleanor Rigby'.
Paul: "That started off with sitting down at the piano and getting the first line of the melody, and playing around with words. I think it was 'Miss Daisy Hawkins' originally, then it was her picking up the rice in a church after a wedding. That's how nearly all our songs start, with the first line just suggesting itself from books or newspapers.

"At first I thought it was a young Miss Daisy Hawkins, a bit like 'Annabel Lee', but not so sexy, but then I saw I'd said she was picking up the rice in church, so she had to be a cleaner; she had missed the wedding, and she was suddenly lonely. In fact she had missed it all - she was the spinster type.

"Jane Asher was in a play in Bristol then, and I was walking round the streets waiting for her to finish. I didn't really like 'Daisy Hawkins' - I wanted a name that was more real, and I got the name from a shop called 'Rigby'."

April 29
– *Abbey Road.* The day was spent adding vocals to 'Eleanor Rigby' and to 'I'm Only Sleeping'.

May 1
– NME Poll Winners concert at Empire Pool, Wembley, with The Spencer Davis Group, Dave, Dee, Dozy, Beaky, Mick & Titch, The Fortunes, Herman's Hermits, Roy Orbison, The Overlanders, The Alan Price Set, Cliff Richard, The Rolling Stones, The Seekers, The Shadows, The Small Faces, Sounds Incorporated, Dusty Springfield, Crispian St Peters, The Walker Brothers, The Who and The Yardbirds. The Beatles played a 15-minute set, but Brian Epstein would not allow ABC TV to film it because they had not reached an agreement over the terms. They were permitted to film them receiving their Poll Winners Awards. This was The Beatles last live appearance in the UK.

May 2
– BBC Playhouse Theatre, London. The Beatles were interviewed by Brian Matthew for the 400th edition of *Saturday Club*.
– Afterwards Paul and Ringo were interviewed separately for the BBC Overseas Service programme *Pop Profile*.

Paul: "I wrote that in bed one night. As a kids' story. And then we thought it would be good for Ringo to do."

May 5
– *Abbey Road.* George spent from 9:30 pm until 3 am recording the backwards guitar solo on 'I'm Only Sleeping'.

May 6
– *Abbey Road.* The session was spent adding vocals to 'I'm Only Sleeping'.

May 9
– *Abbey Road.* Paul and Ringo worked on Paul's 'For No One'.

May 13
– The Beatles had a night out at the Scotch St James's.

May 14
– *Melody Maker* reported that The Beatles had sold over 1,000,000 records in Denmark.

May 15
– ABC TV showed their film of The Beatles receiving their *NME* Poll Winners' awards.

May 16
– *Abbey Road.* Paul added his vocal to 'For No One'.

May 18
– *Abbey Road.* 'Got To Get You Into My Life' was recorded, using Eddie Thornton, Ian Hamer and Les Condon on trumpets and Peter Coe and Alan Branscombe on tenor saxes.

May 19
– *Abbey Road.* Beginning at 10 am The Beatles taped promotional clips of 'Paperback Writer' and 'Rain' in both colour and black and white for television stations around the world. Director Michael Lindsay-Hogg had worked with them before at *Ready Steady Go!* and they were to use him again in the future.

They had lunch at the Genevieve restaurant on Thayer Street, near EMI, and taped more film in the afternoon. That evening Alan Civil recorded his celebrated French horn solo on 'For No One'.

May 20
– The day was also spent shooting promotional films for 'Paperback Writer' and 'Rain', this time on location at Chiswick House, London.
– That evening John and Cynthia went to an all-night party with Mick Jagger and Chrissie Shrimpton.

May 21
– Early the next morning John, Cynthia, Mick and Chrissie went to Portobello Road market, getting there before the tourists.

May 26
– *Abbey Road.* The backing track for 'Yellow Submarine' was recorded.

May 27
– Accompanied by Keith Richards and Brian Jones, Paul and Neil Aspinall went to Dolly's Club on Jermyn Street to meet Bob Dylan the day his European tour reached London. Afterwards they all went back to Dylan's room at the Mayfair Hotel to listen to a set of test pressings he had with him from his most recent sessions.

Later that evening John and George attended Dylan's concert at the Albert Hall and watched as a faction of the audience jeered and booed when Dylan switched to electric instruments for the second half and, backed by The Band, gave them some rock'n'roll.

May 28
– The Beatles spent the day in Bob Dylan's hotel room, watching rushes of D.A. Pennebaker's film.

Top of The Pops, London, June 16.

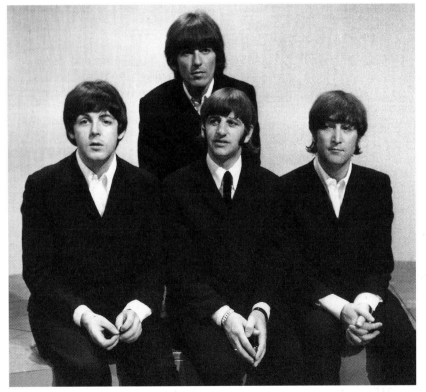

May 29
– The Beatles spent another evening with Bob Dylan at the Mayfair.

May 30
– The single **'Paperback Writer'/'Rain'** was released in the US as Capitol 5651.

May 31
– Ringo allowed photographer Leslie Bryce to shoot an "At Home" session at his house in Weybridge for *Beatles Monthly*.

June 1
– *Abbey Road.* The sound effects were added to 'Yellow Submarine', assisted by Brian Jones, Marianne Faithfull, Beatles' roadies Mal and Neil and various other friends.
– That evening George saw Ravi Shankar play a recital at the Albert Hall.

June 2
– *Abbey Road.* Most of the session was spent recording George's as-yet-untitled 'I Want To Tell You'.
– BBC television's *Top Of The Pops* premiered The Beatles' promotional films of 'Paperback Writer' and 'Rain'.

June 3
– *Abbey Road.* 'I Want To Tell You' was finished and 'Yellow Submarine' mixed in a session ending at 2:30 am.
– The tabloid newspapers reacted with suitable outrage at the photographs of The Beatles covered with meat and dolls used in the advertisements for the new single.

June 4
– The Beatles pre-recorded interview for the 400th edition of BBC Light Programme's *Saturday Club* was broadcast.

June 5
– The promotional films for 'Paperback Writer' and 'Rain' were aired on NBC TV's *Ed Sullivan Show*.

June 6
– *Abbey Road.* Most of the session was spent mixing. Paul added a vocal overdub to 'Eleanor Rigby'.

June 7
– A day spent at George's house rehearsing.

June 8
– *Abbey Road.* Paul's 'Good Day Sunshine' recorded.

June 9
– *Abbey Road.* 'Good Day Sunshine' completed.

June 10

– **'Paperback Writer'/'Rain'** was released in the UK as Parlophone R 5452.

June 14

– *Abbey Road.* The Beatles began work on <u>Paul</u>'s 'Here There And Everywhere'.

<u>John</u>: "This was a great one of his."

June 15

– The day was spent rehearsing for their appearance on *Top Of The Pops* to promote 'Paperback Writer'

– The album YESTERDAY... AND TODAY was released in the US as Capitol T-2553 (mono) and ST-2553 (stereo).

> SIDE A: **'Drive My Car', 'I'm Only Sleeping', 'Nowhere Man', 'Dr Robert', 'Yesterday', 'Act Naturally'.**
> SIDE B: **'And Your Bird Can Sing', 'If I Needed Someone', 'We Can Work It Out', 'What Goes On', 'Day Tripper'.**

June 16

– The Beatles went to the BOAC Air Terminal in Victoria to receive vaccinations against cholera in preparation for their forthcoming Far Eastern tour.

– After this they travelled in <u>John</u>'s black Rolls Royce to BBC Television Centre where they recorded their first live appearance on *Top Of The Pops*, which was also their last live television appearance playing music.

– *Abbey Road.* The band worked until 3 am on 'Here There And Everywhere'.

– The 'Butcher' sleeve on the Yesterday ... and Today album was withdrawn in the US. A new bland sleeve was pasted on top of the withdrawn copies and all new pressings just had the new sleeve. Collectors carefully peeled the replacement sleeves off and mint copies of the "Butcher" sleeve are now sold at rare record auctions for huge sums of money.

– The Beatles appeared on *Top Of The Pops* performing both sides of their new single live.

June 17

– *Abbey Road.* 'Here There And Everywhere' was completed and more work was done on 'Got To Get You Into My Life'.

Opposite: Top Of The Pops, London, June 16.
Below: Paul arrives back in Hamburg, June 26.

– <u>Paul</u> bought a 183-acre dairy farm in Machrihanish, Kintyre, Scotland.

June 20

– *Abbey Road.* A short visit to the studio after tea for the mixing of 'Got To Get You Into My Life'.

– The album Yesterday... and Today was re-released in the US with a new innocuous sleeve.

June 21

– *Abbey Road.* <u>John</u>'s 'She Said She Said' was recorded between 7 pm and 3:45 am.

June 22

– The Beatles attended a pre-opening party at Sibylla's nightclub on Swallow Street in which <u>George</u> had a financial stake.

June 23

– The Beatles took the 11 am flight to Munich where they were met by the press before a fleet of white Mercedes whisked them off to the Bayerischer Hof Hotel. They arrived late for a press conference at the hotel because they were trapped in the lift for ten minutes on the way down from their floor. Later, when no-one was about, they took a late-night dip in the pool.

June 24

– *Circus-Krone-Bau,* with Cliff Bennett & The Rebel Rousers, The Rattles and Peter & Gordon. Two sets, at 5:15 and 9:00 pm, the second of which was filmed by ZDF, German television. Their set for the tour

consisted of: 'Rock And Roll Music', 'She's A Woman', 'If I Needed Someone', 'Day Tripper', 'Baby's In Black', 'I Feel Fine', 'Yesterday', 'I Wanna Be Your Man', 'Nowhere Man', 'Paperback Writer' and 'I'm Down'. Among their guests at the hotel was Bettina Derlien, the barmaid from the Star Club.

June 25

– Early in the morning, The Beatles arrived at Munich railway station in a fleet of Mercedes with motorcycle police guarding them. They boarded the Royal train, previously used by the Queen of England, to take them to Essen. They each had their own suite of rooms, and were on board in time for breakfast.

– *Grugahalle, Essen.* They gave a press conference between their two shows and had a meal in their dressing room. They got back to their train, which travelled through the night to Hamburg, at about 2 am.

– The promotional film for 'Paperback Writer' was shown in the UK on the final edition of ABC TV's *Thank Your Lucky Stars.*

June 26

– Their train arrived in Hamburg at 6 am and they moved into the Schloss Hotel in Tremsbüttel, 30 miles away from Hamburg and the fans. They slept until 1:30 pm then made a balcony appearance for the several hundred fans gathered outside. <u>John</u> visited

Below Left: Newly attired in their Japanese Airlines happi coats, The Beatles arrive in Tokyo, June 30. Right: John faces the press at Heathrow, July 8.

shrine to Japan's war dead, and it was therefore seen as sacreligious for a rock'n'roll group to play there. Because of these threats, the Japanese lined the route from the airport and the perimeter of the hotel with 30,000 uniformed men. It went on to become one of the main rock venues in Tokyo.

July 1
– *Nippon Budokan Hall.* Japanese television filmed the first of today's two concerts.

July 2
– *Nippon Budokan Hall.* The final day of concerts. Fan hysteria was so great and the army security so tight that The Beatles were unable to leave their hotel. In order to buy some souvenirs, local tradesmen were brought to their suite and The Beatles bought a variety of kimonos, bowls and other goods at suitably inflated prices.

July 3
– The Beatles flew to Hong Kong, where they rested in the VIP lounge while their plane refuelled, before continuing to Manila in the Philippines (then under the dictatorship of Ferdinand Marcos) where a crowd of 50,000 fans was waiting to greet them. The Filipinos, having noted the behaviour of the Japanese authorities, were not to be outdone. With typical heavy-handedness, military police burst into the plane and seized The Beatles, dragging them down the stairs and into protective custody.

George: "These gorillas, **huge guys,** no shirts, **short sleeves,** took us right off the plane. They confiscated our 'diplomatic **bags'.** They took all four of us, **John, Paul, Ringo and me,** without Brian or Neil or Mal. Then they removed us in a boat to Manila Bay **surrounded** by a ring of **cops, guns** everywhere... straight away we thought we were all **busted** because we thought they would **find all the dope in our bags.**"

Astrid Kirchherr who gave him several letters written by Stuart Sutcliffe. Dr Bernstein, their Reeperbahn days doctor, and Bert Kaempfert were among their many visitors. The Beatles played two sets at *Ernst Merck Halle* with the usual press conference in between. Afterwards John and Paul went for a walk around the Reeperbahn after midnight, revisiting their old haunts.

June 27
– The Beatles returned to Heathrow airport, then left for Tokyo on the inaugural flight by Japanese Airlines over the North Pole. Unfortunately, a typhoon warning caused the plane to be grounded at Anchorage, Alaska, where they spent the night at the Westwood Hotel. That evening The Beatles visited

the hotel's club, 'The Top Of The World' on the top floor, and a local DJ gave them a quick tour of Anchorage.

June 28
– The Beatles continued their flight to Tokyo.

June 30
– The Beatles arrived at Haneda airport, Tokyo at 3:40 am (having lost a day by crossing the date line). They stayed at the Tokyo Hilton where they had their own floor.
– *Nippon Budokan Hall, Tokyo,* with Yuya Uchida and Isao Bitoh. The Beatles played one concert to 10,000 fans. There was considerable right-wing opposition - including death threats - to The Beatles playing at Nippon Budokan Hall (Martial Arts Hall), because the building was regarded as a national

The Manila Incident

On July 4 The Beatles were exhausted and slept late. Unfortunately, Imelda Marcos had organised a lunch party for 300 sons and daughters of top army officers and businessmen at the Malacanang Palace to introduce them to The Beatles. The group were still asleep after the previous night's debacle when officials came looking for them. Brian Epstein claimed to know nothing of the invitation and refused to allow any further indignities to be perpetrated upon them. Naturally this was taken as a grave insult, with

potentially dangerous repercussions.

That afternoon they played the Rizal Memorial Football Stadium, before 30,000 fans, and again in the evening to 50,000 fans.

The next day the hotel provided no room service. They found that their front man, Vic Lewis, had been questioned by high ranking military officials until dawn, and all military security had been withdrawn. The Beatles and their entourage had to run the gauntlet to get to their plane. They were spat at, insulted and jostled.

At the airport Alf Bicknell was thrown to the floor and kicked by military security men and the escalator was turned off so that they had to struggle up with all their equipment. Mal Evans and Brian Epstein had to get off the plane again to sort out a passport and tax problem which officials suddenly invented before KLM flight 862 was finally allowed to leave Manila at 4:45 pm.

George summed up The Beatles' feelings succinctly: "The only way I'd ever return to the Philippines would be to drop an atom bomb on it."

Two army battalions in full combat gear met The Beatles and took them to navy headquarters before transferring them to a private yacht where a wealthy Filipino, Don Manolo Elizalde, showed them off to a party of rich friends. It was not until 4 am that Brian Epstein was able to regain control of the situation and The Beatles finally reached their suite at the Hotel Manila.

Paul lights up during the Heathrow press conference.

July 6
– Returning home, there was a refuelling stop in Bangkok after which The Beatles arrived in New Delhi, India, where they hoped to take a peaceful three day break. Unfortunately, 600 fans were already waiting at the airport when they landed and their hotel was soon under siege. They managed to sneak out the back way and do some shopping and sightseeing. They all bought Indian instruments.

July 8
– The Beatles arrived back in London at 6 am. There was a short press

conference when they landed and George and Ringo appeared on the morning edition of the BBC Home Service's radio show *Today*.
– The EP **Nowhere Man** was released in the UK as PARLOPHONE GEP 8952 (mono).
   SIDE A: **'Nowhere Man', 'Drive My Car';**
   SIDE B: **'Michelle', 'You Won't See Me'.**

July 12
– The Beatles were awarded Ivor Novello Awards for 'We Can Work It Out' (top selling single of 1965), 'Yesterday' (most outstanding song of the year) and 'Help!' (second best selling single of 1965).

July 23
– *The Cavern Club* reopened in Liverpool under new ownership. The Beatles sent a telegram and the opening ceremony was attended by Prime Minister Harold Wilson, whose constituency was in Liverpool.

July 29
– The American magazine *Datebook* published Maureen Cleave's interview with John in which he said "We're bigger than Jesus now." American Christian fundamentalists reacted with outrage.

July 30
– The album Yesterday... and Today reached number one on the *Billboard* Hot 100 charts where it stayed for five weeks.

July 31
– Zealots in Birmingham, Alabama, were shown on BBC television news burning Beatles records just as the Nazis burned books.

August 1
– Paul recorded an interview for the BBC Light Programme's *David Frost At The Phonograph*.

August 2
– George and Patti drive to Stoodleigh in Devon for a few days holiday with Patti's mother, Diana Jones, in her 18th century farmhouse.

August 5
– **'Yellow Submarine'/'Eleanor Rigby'** was released in the UK as Parlophone R 5493.
– The album REVOLVER was released in the UK as PARLOPHONE PMC 7009 (mono) and PCS 7009 (stereo).

   SIDE A: **'Taxman', 'Eleanor Rigby', 'I'm Only Sleeping', 'Love You To', 'Here There And Everywhere', 'Yellow Submarine', 'She Said She Said';**
   SIDE B: **'Good Day Sunshine', 'And Your Bird Can Sing', 'For No One', 'Dr Robert', 'I Want To Tell You', 'Got To Get You Into My Life', 'Tomorrow Never Knows'.**

August 6
– Brian Epstein flew to the US to try and sort out the problems caused by John's remarks about Jesus. There were fears that the entire American tour might have to be cancelled. By August 6 a total of 30 American radio stations had banned Beatles records.
– Paul and John recorded an hour-long interview about songwriting for the BBC Light Programme at Paul's new house in Cavendish Avenue. It was broadcast as *The Lennon And McCartney Songbook*.
– Paul's interview with David Frost was broadcast on the BBC Light Programme's *David Frost At The Phonograph*.

August 8
– Beatles records were banned by the South African Broadcasting Corporation after John's supposedly irreligious remarks offended the apartheid regime. The ban lasted five years, until after The Beatles broke up. After that Paul, George and Ringo's solo albums were allowed, but not John's.
– The single **'Eleanor Rigby'/'Yellow Submarine'** was released in the US as CAPITOL 5715.
– The album REVOLVER was released in the US as CAPITOL T-2576 (mono) and ST-2576 (stereo). As usual it had fewer tracks than the UK release.
   SIDE A: **'Taxman', 'Eleanor Rigby', 'Love You To', 'Here There And Everywhere', 'Yellow Submarine', 'She Said She Said';**
   SIDE B: **'Good Day Sunshine', 'For No One', 'Doctor Robert', 'I Want To Tell You', 'Got To Get You Into My Life', 'Tomorrow Never Knows'.**

August 11
– The Beatles flew to the US, landing first at Boston, then at Chicago, where they arrived at 4:18 pm.

"We are inviting local **teenagers** to bring in their **records** and **other symbols** of the group's popularity **to be burned** at a public bonfire on Friday night, August 13."

August 12
– *International Amphitheater, Chicago,* with The Remains, Bobby Hebb, The Cyrkle and The Ronettes. They played two sets, each to 13,000 people. They played the same set on this US tour as on their European and Japanese tour: 'Rock And Roll Music', 'She's A Woman', 'If I Needed Someone', 'Day Tripper', 'Baby's In Black', 'I Feel Fine', 'Yesterday', 'I Wanna Be Your Man', 'Nowhere Man',

'Paperback Writer' and 'I'm Down', sometimes adding 'Long Tall Sally'.
August 13
– *Olympic Stadium, Detroit.* Two sets.
– Station KLUE in Longview, Texas, getting on the bandwagon a bit late, organised a public burning of Beatles' records. The station manager said,
– The Grand Dragon of the South Carolina Ku Klux Klan attached a Beatles record to the large wooden

cross which he then set on fire as part of their ritual.
– Spanish Radio was reported to have banned the airplay of Beatles records "forever" because of John's "blasphemous remark" and in Holland there were moves to ban The Beatles from playing in the country and to have their records banned from the airwaves.
George: "They've got to buy them before they can burn them."

John: "When they started **burning our records...** that was a real shock, the **physical** burning. I couldn't go away knowing I'd created another little piece of **hate** in the world so I apologised."

John and Jesus

The press and all three television networks were waiting in Chicago and talked of nothing but John's remarks about Jesus. The Beatles had to do a live press conference (above) from the 27th floor of the Astor Towers Hotel where they were staying. John was obviously very uncomfortable, being forced to apologise for something which the Americans had taken out of context.

John: "Look, I wasn't saying The Beatles are better than God or Jesus. I said 'Beatles' because it's easy for me to talk about Beatles. I could have said 'TV' or 'the cinema', 'motorcars' or anything popular and I would have got away with it...
"I'm not anti-God, anti-Christ or anti-religion. I was not saying we are greater or better. I believe

in God, but not as one thing, not as an old man in the sky. I believe that what people call God is something in all of us. I believe that what Jesus, Mohammed, Buddha and all the rest said was right. It's just the translations have gone wrong.
"I wasn't saying whatever they're saying I was saying. I'm sorry I said it, really. I never

meant it to be a lousy anti-religious thing. From what I've read, or observed, Christianity just seems to me to be shrinking, to be losing contact."
Reporter: "A disc jockey in Birmingham, Alabama, who actually started most of the repercussions, has demanded an apology from you."
John: "He can have it, I apologise to him."

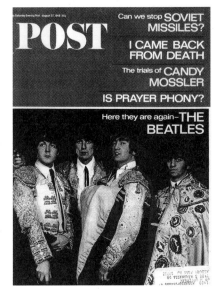

221

Los Angeles, August 28.

I tried to avoid the depression of the change of life by leaping into the movie.

– The album Revolver entered the UK charts at number one, and remained there for nine weeks.
– After the second set in Detroit they left by bus for Cleveland, Ohio, arriving at 2 am.

August 14
– Radio station KLUE in Longview, Texas, was taken off the air the day after their Beatles records bonfire when a lightning bolt struck their transmission tower, destroying electronic equipment and knocking their news director unconscious.
– *Municipal Stadium, Cleveland, Ohio.* Two sets to 20,000 fans. When 2,500 fans got into the arena area, the show was stopped and The Beatles retired backstage for about 20 minutes until order was restored.

August 15
– *DC Stadium, Washington, DC* to 32,000 fans. The Beatles flew into the capital that afternoon and travelled to Philadelphia by coach as soon as their one show was over.
– The album THIS IS WHERE IT STARTED by Tony Sheridan and The Beatles was released in the US.

August 16
– *Philadelphia Stadium, Philadelphia.* One evening show held amid the beginnings of an electric storm with almost continuous lightning. The rain did not start until just after their set had finished. They flew straight to Canada after the show.

August 17
– *Maple Leaf Gardens, Toronto, Canada.* The Beatles did two shows and stayed overnight before flying to Boston.

August 18
– *Suffolk Downs Racetrack, Boston.* The bleachers were filled by 25,000 fans.

August 19
– *Mid South Coliseum, Memphis.* Six Ku Klux Klansmen picketed the stadium in their costumes. A small number of fanatics threw rubbish on stage and exploded a firecracker. Outside The Beatles' coach was surrounded by hordes of Christian demonstrators screaming abuse.

August 20
– *Crosley Field, Cincinnati.* This show was postponed because of heavy rain and re-scheduled for the next day.

August 21
– *Crosley Field, Cincinnati.* A midday concert, after which they flew 350 miles to St. Louis.
– *Busch Stadium, St. Louis, Missouri.* The Beatles played at 8:30 pm during a heavy rain-storm to a very wet audience of 23,000 fans. The group were protected by a flimsy tarpaulin which dripped water on the amps. It was this gig which finally convinced Paul McCartney that The Beatles should stop live performances. The other Beatles had decided this long before.

August 23
– *Shea Stadium, New York.* There were 44,000 fans at the show. The Beatles flew straight to Los Angeles after they left the stage.

August 24
– The Beatles arrived in Los Angeles in the early hours of the morning and rested up at 7655 Carson Road, the private house in Beverly Hills that Brian Epstein had rented for them.

August 25
– *Seattle Coliseum, Seattle.* The Beatles flew in that morning and stayed at the Edgewater Inn. Their flight back to Los Angeles from Seattle was delayed for five hours because one of the plane's wheels was discovered to be worn right down to the canvas and had to be replaced.

August 28
– *Dodger Stadium, Los Angeles.* There were 45,000 fans for this show and only 102 security men. Dozens of fans were injured and 25 people detained during clashes between police and fans. The Beatles's limousine was besieged by fans and had to turn back. They eventually made their escape in an armoured van.

August 29
– *Candlestick Park, San Francisco.*
– The radio show *The Lennon and McCartney Songbook* was transmitted by the BBC Light Programme.

August 30
– The Beatles left Los Angeles for London.

August 31
– The Beatles arrived back in London from Los Angeles.

CANDLESTICK PARK

Paul: "They were zealots. It was horrible to see the hatred on their faces."

September 5
– John flew to Hanover, Germany, to begin filming his part in *How I Won The War* with director Richard Lester on a NATO tank range in Celle, outside Hanover. **John: "There were many reasons for doing it: a) it was Dick Lester and he asked me; b) it was anti-war; and c) I didn't know what to do because The Beatles had stopped touring and I thought if I stopped and thought about it I was going to have a big bum trip for nine months so The thing I remember is that Dick Lester had more fun than I did."**

September 6
– John had his hair cut short for his role as Private Gripweed. The momentous event occurred in the breakfast room of the bar The Inn On The Heath in Celle. In addition to an army haircut, he wore small round "granny" glasses, which his use made fashionable.

September 10
– The album Revolver reached number one on the *Billboard* Hot 100 charts, where it remained for six weeks.

September 14
– George and Patti flew to Bombay, India, for George to take sitar lessons with Ravi Shankar and study yoga. They checked into the Taj Mahal, Bombay, under the names Mr and Mrs Sam Wells.

September 15
– Paul attended a performance of free-form music given by AMM with Cornelius Cardew at the Royal College of Art. The audience of a dozen or so people was invited to join in and Paul made occasional sounds on the radiator and a beer mug. **Paul: "You don't have to like something to be influenced by it."**

The last ever Beatles concert

August 29 was the last time The Beatles performed before a paying audience. It was seen by 25,000 fans. Their last number on stage was 'Long Tall Sally', one of their Hamburg show-stoppers.
John: "On our last tour people kept bringing blind, crippled and deformed children into our dressing room and this boy's mother would say, 'Go on, kiss him, maybe you'll bring back his sight.' We're not cruel. We've seen enough tragedy in Merseyside, but when a mother shrieks, 'Just touch him and maybe he'll walk again', we want to run, cry, empty our pockets. We're going to remain normal if it kills us."

Left: Ringo visits John in Spain, on location for How I Won The War; Below: Private Gripweed, John's character in the film.

– John and Neil Aspinall took the train to Paris.

September 16

– Paul and Brian Epstein joined John and Neil Aspinall for a weekend break in Paris.

September 18

– John and Neil Aspinall went to Spain where the filming for *How I Won The War* was due to continue the next day in Carboneras, Spain. John and Cynthia shared a villa in Almera - owned by Sam Spiegal - with the actor Michael Crawford and his family.

September 19

– Location filming began again. John had to get up at 6 each morning for his driver to take him to the film set in his black Rolls.

– The press discovered that George and Patti were staying in India and George had to give a press conference at the Taj Mahal in which he explained he had come to India to study and get some peace and quiet.

October 4

– Ringo and Maureen flew to Almeria to spend a few days visiting John on the film set of *How I Won The War*.

October 21

– George did an interview with the BBC correspondent in Bombay, Donald Milner, about his reasons for spending five weeks in India.

October 22

– George and Patti returned to London from Bombay.

October 26

– When Ravi Shankar arrived at London Airport from India, George was there to meet him, dressed in Indian clothes. Ravi Shankar, European educated, was wearing a Western suit.

October 27

– Penguin Books published *The Penguin John Lennon*, a double volume of John's two books.

October 31

– Donovan arrived to spend a week at George's house in Esher.

Yoko

The day before the opening of her show, Unfinished Paintings and Objects, Yoko was introduced to John by the co-owner of the Indica gallery, John Dunbar. John: "I got the word that this amazing woman was putting on a show next week and there was going to be something about people in bags, black bags, and it was going to be a bit of a happening and all that. So I went down to a preview of the show, I got there the night before it opened. I went in – she didn't know who I was or anything – I was wandering around, there was a couple of artsy type students that had been helping lying around there in the gallery, and I was looking at it and I was astounded. There was an apple on sale there for 200 quid, I thought it was fantastic – I got the humour in her work immediately. I didn't have to have much knowledge about avant-garde or underground art, but the humour got me straight away. There was a fresh apple on a stand, this was before Apple – and it was 200 quid to watch the apple decompose.

"But there was another piece which really decided me for-or-against the artist, a ladder which led to a painting which was hung on the ceiling. It looked like a blank canvas with a chain with a spyglass hanging on the end of it. This was near the door where you went in. I climbed the ladder, you look through the spyglass and in tiny little letters it says 'yes'.

"So it was positive. I felt relieved. It's a great relief when you get up the ladder and you look through the spyglass and it doesn't say 'no' or 'fuck you' or something. It said 'yes' I was very impressed and John Dunbar sort of introduced us – neither of us knew who the hell we were, she didn't know who I was, she'd only heard of Ringo I think, it means apple in Japanese. And she came up and handed me a card which said 'Breathe' on it, one of her instructions, so I just went (pant). That was our meeting."

In fact Yoko knew very well who The Beatles were. She had approached Paul several weeks before, hoping to solicit some original Lennon and McCartney manuscripts to give to John Cage for his 50th birthday celebrations as Cage collected original scores of modern music. Paul said no but told her that John might let her have one.

November 4

– NEMS finally vacated 13 Monmouth Street, Brian Epstein's first London office. Most of the operation had been in Argyll Street since 1964.

November 6

– Paul put his Aston Martin on the plane-ferry at Lydd, Kent, and flew to France. Wearing a disguise, he spent a week driving slowly through the chateaux of the Loire, before he met up with Beatles roadie Mal Evans under the grand clock in Bordeaux.

November 9

– John met Yoko Ono for the first time at the Indica Gallery, Mason's Yard, London.

November 11

– John and Cynthia saw Ben E. King play the Scotch St James's.

November 12

– Paul and Mal drove from Bordeaux to Spain, making home movies enroute. Paul originally intended to meet John in Almeria but John finished shooting his part early and was already home. Paul decided on a safari instead and arranged to meet Jane in Africa. Paul and Mal drove to Seville and organised someone to drive the Aston back to London. They flew to Madrid and from there to Nairobi. They had a ten-hour stopover in Rome which they spent sightseeing at St Peter's and the usual sights.

November 13

– The Four Tops played the Saville Theatre with a backdrop supposedly designed by Paul.

November 18

– The single 'From Head To Toe'/

'Night Time' by The Escorts, produced by Paul McCartney, was released in the UK as COLUMBIA DB 8061.

November 19

– Paul, Jane and Mal flew back to London from Kenya.

November 20

– Brian Epstein gave a party for The Four Tops in his home in Chapel Street. John and George attended.

November 24

– Abbey Road. The Beatles reconvened to start work on a new album, beginning with John's 'Strawberry Fields Forever'.

November 25

– The Beatles' fourth Christmas record Pantomime: Everywhere It's Christmas was recorded in the demo studio in the basement of the New Oxford Street offices of Dick James, their music publisher.

November 27

– John made a filmed appearance in Peter Cook and Dudley Moore's BBC Television show Not Only... But Also in which he played a uniformed nightclub doorman. The filmed location for the club was the underground gentlemen's lavatory on Broadwick Street, near Berwick Street market, Soho. John was shown wearing his new "granny" glasses.

November 28

– Abbey Road. The group recorded three more takes of 'Strawberry Fields Forever'.

November 29

– Abbey Road. More work on 'Strawberry Fields Forever'.

John: "The awareness apparently trying to be **expressed** is – let's say in one way I was **always hip.** I was hip in kindergarten. I was **different from the others.** I was different all my life. The second verse goes, 'No one I think is in my tree.' Well I was too shy and **self-doubting.** Nobody seems to be as hip as me is what I was saying. Therefore, I must be **crazy** or a **genius** – 'I mean it must be **high** or **low**,' the next line. There was **something wrong** with me, I thought, because I seemed to see things other people didn't see. I thought I was crazy or an **egomaniac** for claiming to **see things** other people didn't see."

December 1

– Paul saw The Young Rascals make their UK debut at the Scotch St James's.

December 2

– Paul was so impressed by The Young Rascals that he saw them a second time, this time at Blaises.

December 6

– Abbey Road. Work began on 'When I'm Sixty Four'. The Beatles also taped Christmas greetings for the pirate stations Radio London and Radio Caroline.

December 8

– Abbey Road. Paul added his vocal to 'When I'm Sixty Four' in the afternoon and all four Beatles arrived for an evening session working on 'Strawberry Fields Forever' again.

December 9

– Abbey Road. The Beatles continued to work on 'Strawberry Fields Forever'.

December 10

– The album A COLLECTION OF BEATLES OLDIES was released in the UK as PARLOPHONE PMC 7016 (mono) and PCS 7016 (stereo).

SIDE A: 'She Loves You', 'From Me To You', 'We Can Work It Out', 'Help!', 'Michelle', 'Yesterday', 'I Feel Fine', 'Yellow Submarine';

SIDE B: 'Can't Buy Me Love', 'Bad Boy', 'Day Tripper', 'A Hard Day's Night', 'Ticket To Ride', 'Paperback Writer', 'Eleanor Rigby', 'I Want To Hold Your Hand'.

December 11

– The BBC Home Service programme The Lively Arts broadcast an interview done with George in India in which he discussed philosophy and Indian music.

December 15

– *Abbey Road.* The Beatles continued work on 'Strawberry Fields Forever'.

December 16

– Members of The Beatles fan club were sent copies of The Beatles' fourth Christmas flexi-disc called **Pantomime: Everywhere It's Christmas**.

SIDE ONE: 'Song; Everywhere It's Christmas', 'Orowanyna', 'Corsican Choir And Small Choir', 'A Rare Cheese', 'Two Elderly Scotsmen', 'The Feast', 'The Loyal Toast'; SIDE TWO: 'Podgy The Bear And Jasper', 'Count Balder And Butler', 'Felpin Mansions (Part Two)', 'The Count And The Pianist', 'Song; Please Don't Bring Your Banjo Back', 'Everywhere It's Christmas', 'Mal Evans', 'Reprise: Everywhere It's Christmas'.

Ringo: "We worked it out between us. Paul did most of the work on it. He thought up the 'Pantomime' title and the two song things."

Paul: "I drew the cover myself. There's a sort of funny pantomime horse in the design if you look closely. Well I can see one there if you can't."

December 18

– Paul and Jane attended the premiere of the film *The Family Way* at the Warner Theatre which had an incidental soundtrack written by Paul and arranged by George Martin.

John: "I copped money for *The Family Way*, the film music that Paul wrote when I was out of the country filming *How I Won The War*. I said, 'You'd better keep that.' He said, 'Don't be soft.' It's the concept. We inspired each other so much in the early days. We write how we write now because of each other."

December 19

– Binder, Edwards and Vaughan announced that Paul had made an experimental electronic tape to be played at the Carnival of Light to

Above: John with Peter Cook, filming his appearance in Not Only ... But Also, November 27; Below: Paul (right) at the Indica Gallery with Miles, John Dunbar, Marianne Faithfull and Peter Asher.

be held at the Roundhouse, Chalk Farm, in January.

December 20

– *Abbey Road.* More vocals were added to 'When I'm Sixty Four.'
– The Beatles recorded interviews with John Edwards for the ITN (Independent Television News) programme *Reporting '66* and were filmed arriving at Abbey Road and working on a song together.

December 21

– *Abbey Road.* Woodwind was added to 'When I'm Sixty Four' and John added more vocals to 'Strawberry Fields Forever'.
– The single **'Love In The Open Air'/'Theme From The Family Way'** by The George Martin Orchestra and written by Paul McCartney was released in the UK as UNITED ARTISTS UP 1165.

December 25

– All four Beatles remained in London and the Home Counties for Christmas.

December 26

– John's appearance on Peter Cook and Dudley Moore's BBC Television show, *Not Only... But Also*, was screened.

December 29

– *Abbey Road.* Paul working alone in the studio recorded the backing track to his 'Penny Lane', finishing up at 2:15 am. **Paul: "'Penny Lane' is a bus roundabout in Liverpool and there is a barber's shop... There's a bank on the corner so we made up the bit about the banker in his motor car. It's part fact, part nostalgia for a place which is a great place – blue suburban skies as we remember it, and it's still there."**

December 30

– *Abbey Road.* Further work done on 'When I'm Sixty Four' and 'Penny Lane'.

December 31

– George and Patti, Brian Epstein, Eric Clapton and others were refused admittance to Annabel's Night Club because George was not wearing a tie. He refused the one offered to him by the doorman. They saw in the New Year at the Lyon's Corner House Restaurant on Coventry Street.

19**67**

January
– <u>Paul</u> asked his housekeepers, the Kellys, to leave after he found that they had written an article about his home life for an Australian magazine.

Paul: "Mr and Mrs Kelly are looking for another place and I'm getting another couple to replace them. There have been disagreements over the running of the household. I haven't asked them to leave instantly because that would be unreasonable."

They were replaced by Mr and Mrs Mills. ("She still hasn't given me a tune yet," quipped <u>Paul</u>, referring to popular pianist Mrs Mills.)

January 4
– *Abbey Road*. Sgt Pepper sessions. Continued work on 'Penny Lane'.

January 5
– *Abbey Road*. Sgt Pepper sessions. <u>Paul</u>'s vocal track on 'Penny Lane' was followed by a free-form, "Freak Out", The Beatles' only combined effort at producing "a bit of random". David Vaughan, of the design team Binder, Edwards and Vaughan, asked <u>Paul</u> for some music for a sound and light rave to be held at the *Roundhouse, Chalk Farm*. <u>Paul</u> obliged, and at 13 minutes, 14 seconds, produced the longest Beatles track ever recorded. There was no rhythm track, just heavily echoed bursts of percussion, shouts and random bits of piano and guitar. <u>George</u> refused to allow it onto the Anthology series of CDs in 1996.

January 6
– *Abbey Road*. Sgt Pepper sessions. More work on 'Penny Lane'.
– The album THE FAMILY WAY (Original Soundtrack Album) by The

Above: John and Ringo take a working lunch during the Sgt Pepper sessions at Abbey Road. Opposite: George in Newquay during the filming of Magical Mystery Tour.

George Martin Orchestra and written by <u>Paul McCartney</u> was released in the UK as Decca SKL 4847.
  SIDE ONE: **'Love In The Open Air'** (cuts one to six);
  SIDE TWO: **'Love In The Open Air'** (cuts one to seven).

January 8
– <u>Paul</u> and <u>John</u> attended a fancy-dress party thrown by Georgie Fame at the Cromwellian Club.

January 9
– *Abbey Road*. Sgt Pepper sessions. Wind instruments added to 'Penny Lane.'

January 10
– *Abbey Road*. Sgt Pepper sessions. More work on 'Penny Lane'.
– American ABC TV broadcast the 1965 recording of *The Beatles At Shea Stadium*.

January 11
– <u>Paul</u> saw the BBC2 programme *Masterworks*, on which David Mason played piccolo trumpet on Bach's Brandenburg Concerto No 2 in F Major with the English Chamber Orchestra from Guildford Cathedral. <u>Paul</u> realised that this was the sound he wanted on 'Penny Lane'.

January 12
– George Martin telephoned David Mason and booked him for a session on the 17th to play piccolo trumpet on 'Penny Lane'.
– *Abbey Road*. Sgt Pepper sessions. More work on 'Penny Lane'.
– Afterwards <u>Paul</u> and Jane had a "candlelit dinner" at <u>Paul</u>'s house in Cavendish Avenue before Jane left to tour the US with the Bristol Old Vic Repertory Company.

January 13
– <u>Paul</u> and <u>Ringo</u> went to the Bag O'Nails on Kingly Street to see The Jimi Hendrix Experience.

January 14
– It was reported in the London press that <u>Paul</u> had turned down an offer from the National Theatre to write music for the songs in Shakespeare's *As You Like It* which would have been produced at the Old Vic and starred Sir Laurence Olivier. <u>Paul</u> told them that he could not write contemporary music

to go with Elizabethan words, but he would write 'The Larry O Stomp' if they wanted.

January 15
– John had a minor car accident but was not hurt.
– Paul and George saw Donovan at the Royal Albert Hall.

January 17
– *Abbey Road.* Sgt Pepper sessions. David Mason added his famous piccolo trumpet solo to 'Penny Lane'. Paul improvised the part by singing it to George Martin, who then wrote it out on score paper for Mason to play.

Paul: "I got the idea of using trumpets in that pizzicato way on 'Penny Lane' from seeing a programme on television. I didn't know whether it would work, so I got the arranger for the session into the studio, played the tune on the piano and sang how I wanted the brass to sound. That's the way I always work with arrangers." The song was now complete.

January 18
– Paul was interviewed in London by Jo Durden-Smith for a Granada Television documentary on the London underground scene, of which Paul was

part. The film, for the *Scene Special* programme, was subtitled *It's So Far Out, It's Straight Down* (whatever that meant).

January 19
– *Abbey Road.* Sgt Pepper sessions. The basic track for 'A Day In The Life' was recorded with Mal Evans counting off the 24 empty bars in the middle and marking the end with an alarm clock.

January 20
– *Abbey Road.* Sgt Pepper sessions. Vocal tracks added to 'A Day In The Life'.

January 21
– Paul attended a party given by Julie Felix at her flat in Old Church Street, Chelsea.
– George gave Donovan his first lesson on the sitar.

January 25
– *Abbey Road.* Sgt Pepper sessions. Paul supervised a new mix of 'Penny Lane' because he was not satisfied with the old one.
– Brian Epstein signed a deal allowing *Sunday Times* newspaper journalist Hunter Davies to write an authorised biography of The Beatles, granting their co-operation in exchange for a percentage of the royalties.

January 27
– The Beatles and Brian Epstein signed a new nine-year worldwide recording contract with EMI records.

January 28
– Paul and George went to see The Four Tops, presented by Brian Epstein, at the Royal Albert Hall.

January 29
– John and Paul saw The Jimi Hendrix Experience and The Who at Brian Epstein's Saville Theatre.

January 30
– EMI were desperate to release a new Beatles single, so Brian Epstein asked George Martin for two tracks from the Sgt Pepper sessions. George reluctantly gave him 'Penny Lane' and 'Strawberry Fields'.
– The Beatles began filming the promotional films for 'Strawberry Fields Forever' and 'Penny Lane' at Knole Park, Sevenoaks in Kent where director Peter Goldmann filmed them next to a dead oak tree in the park.

John: "Well, it was a peak. Paul and I were definitely working together, especially on 'A Day In The Life' that was real... The way we wrote a lot of the time: you'd **write** the **good bit,** the part that was **easy,** like 'I read the news today', or whatever it was, then when you got stuck or whenever it got hard, instead of carrying on, you just drop it; then we would meet each other, and I would **sing half,** and he would be inspired to write the next bit and vice versa. He was a bit shy about it because I think he thought it's already a good song. Sometimes we wouldn't let each other interfere with a song either, because you tend to be a bit lax with someone else's stuff, you experiment a bit. So we were doing it in his room with the piano. He said 'Should we do this?' Yeah, let's do that. But **Pepper** was a **peak** all right."

John on location for the 'Strawberry Fields'/ 'Penny Lane' promo film at Sevenoaks.

Below Right: By the time Sgt Pepper was being recorded, The Beatles had carte blanche to use Abbey Road's Studio 2 whenever they wanted.
Bottom: Paul with Micky Dolenz of the Monkees, February 7.

January 31
– Pirate station Radio London became the first station to play 'Penny Lane' on the air.
– John bought an 1843 circus poster in an antique shop in Sevenoaks, near where they were filming. The poster provided him and Paul with almost the complete lyrics for 'Being For The Benefit Of Mister Kite', which they wrote together at Kenwood, where John had hung the poster on the wall of his den.
– Filming was completed for the 'Strawberry Fields' promo at Knole Park.

February 1
– *Abbey Road.* Sgt Pepper sessions. The 'Sgt Pepper's Lonely Hearts Club' theme was recorded.

February 2
– *Abbey Road.* Sgt Pepper sessions. Further work on 'Sgt Pepper's Lonely Hearts Club Band'.

February 3
– *Abbey Road.* Sgt Pepper sessions. Work on 'A Day In The Life'. Ringo added his wonderful drum track, replacing the previous one.

February 5
– Part of the horse-riding scene for the 'Penny Lane' promotional film was made at Angel Lane in Stratford, East London.

February 7
– The Beatles returned to Knole Park, Sevenoaks, Kent, to shoot more horse-riding and the candelabra scenes for their 'Penny Lane' promotional film.
– Monkee Micky Dolenz and his road-manager, Ric Klein, spent an evening at Paul's house in Cavendish Avenue.

February 8
– *Abbey Road.* Sgt Pepper sessions. Work began on John's 'Good Morning, Good Morning'.

February 9
– The Beatles recorded three takes of 'Fixing A Hole' at *Regent Sound Studios, Tottenham Court Road,* instead of at *Abbey Road.* It was their first time away from EMI's own studio facility.

February 10
– *Abbey Road.* Sgt Pepper sessions. The famous orchestral chord on 'A Day In The Life' was recorded.

Paul: "I had come to the conclusion that The Beatles were getting **a little bit safe,** and we were a little **intimidated** by the idea of making 'the new Beatles album'. It was quite a big thing: **'Wow, follow that!'** So to relieve the pressure I got the idea, maybe from some friends or something I'd read, that we shouldn't record it as The Beatles. Mentally we should approach it as another group of people and totally give ourselves **alter egos."**

Studio guests included Mick Jagger and Marianne Faithfull, Keith Richards, Donovan, Micky Dolenz, Patti Harrison, clothes designers Simon Postuma and Marijke Koger of The Fool, and various friends.

Paul: "Once we'd written the main bit of the music, we thought, now look, there's a little gap there and we said oh, how about an orchestra? Yes, that'll be nice. And if we do have an orchestra, are we going to write them a pseudo-classical thing, which has been done better by people who know how to make it sound like that – or are we going to do it like we write songs? Take a guess and use instinct. So we said, right, what we'll do to save all the arranging, we'll take the whole orchestra as one instrument. And we just wrote it down like a cooking recipe: 24 bars; on the ninth bar, the orchestra will take off, and it will go from its lowest note to its highest note."

February 11
– BBC's *Juke Box Jury* showed part of the 'Penny Lane' promotional film.

February 13
– *Abbey Road.* Sgt Pepper sessions.

George's 'Only A Northern Song' was begun. (Not used on Sgt. Pepper, but finally released on the Yellow Submarine soundtrack album.)
– The single **'Penny Lane'/'Strawberry Fields Forever'** was released in the USA as CAPITOL 5810.

February 14
– *Abbey Road.* Sgt Pepper sessions. More work on 'Only A Northern Song'.

February 16
– *Abbey Road.* Sgt Pepper sessions. Work on 'Good Morning, Good Morning'.
– BBC Television's *Top Of The Pops* showed the 'Penny Lane' and 'Strawberry Fields Forever' promotional clips.

February 17
– *Abbey Road.* Sgt Pepper sessions. Work on 'Being For The Benefit Of Mister Kite.'
– The single **'Penny Lane'/'Strawberry Fields Forever'** was released in the UK as PARLOPHONE R 5570.

John: "We don't often write entirely on our own – I mean, I did bits of 'Penny Lane' and Paul wrote some of 'Strawberry Fields'."
– Paul played Mellotron on the opening of 'Strawberry Fields' using the flute setting and getting it in one take. George and Paul played timpani and bongo drums while Ringo played electronic drums.

No-one I think is in my tree... John during the Sgt Pepper sessions.

February 19
– Another Brian Epstein presentation at the Saville Theatre: John and Ringo saw Chuck Berry and Del Shannon perform.

– George and Patti spent the evening at Keith Richards' house in Sussex with Christopher Gibbs, Marianne Faithfull and others, but left before the police arrived and arrested Mick Jagger, Keith Richards and Robert Fraser for drug possession. It is said that the police waited for George and Patti to leave in order not to bust the holder of an MBE.

February 20
– *Abbey Road.* Sgt Pepper sessions. Fairground sounds were added to 'Being For The Benefit Of Mister Kite'. George Martin: **"'For The Benefit Of Mr Kite' was an attempt to create atmosphere. John wanted a circus fairground atmosphere and said he wanted to hear sawdust on the floor, so we had to try and provide that! I wanted a backwash, a general melange of sound, the kind you would hear at a fairground if you closed your eyes. To achieve this we found a load of old steam organ tapes which played things like 'Stars And Stripes Forever'. I chopped them up into foot-long sections and joined them together, sometimes back to front. The whole thing was to create a sound that was unmistakably a steam organ, but which had no particular tune at all."**

February 21
– *Abbey Road.* Sgt Pepper sessions. 'Fixing A Hole' was completed.

February 22
– *Abbey Road.* Sgt Pepper sessions. The giant piano chord was added to 'A Day In The Life'. Paul, John, Ringo and Mal Evans, seated at three pianos, all played E major. After overdubbing the chord lasted for 53 seconds. The recording levels were turned up so high in the mix that the sound of Abbey Road's air conditioning system could be heard.

John: "I **never** took it in the studio. **Once I did,** actually. I thought I was **taking some uppers,** and I was not in the state of handling it... I suddenly got **so scared** on the mike. I said, '**What is it? I feel ill...**'"

February 23
– *Abbey Road.* Sgt Pepper sessions. Work began on Paul's 'Lovely Rita'.
February 24
– *Abbey Road.* Sgt Pepper sessions. More work on 'Lovely Rita'.
February 26
– Brian Epstein bought Rushlake Green Mansion in Sussex. It was always a great joke with Brian that in order to get to his country house he had to drive through the village of Black Boys.
February 28
– *Abbey Road.* Sgt Pepper sessions. The day was spent in studio two rehearsing 'Lucy In The Sky With Diamonds'. Three-year-old Julian had brought home a drawing from school showing a schoolmate and some diamond shaped stars in the sky. Julian's teacher had asked him what it was, and was told "Lucy In The Sky With Diamonds". The teacher then carefully wrote the title across the top of the drawing, which is where John found the title for his song.

Paul: "So we had a nice title. We did the whole thing like an Alice in Wonderland idea, being in a boat on the river, slowly drifting downstream and those great Cellophane flowers towering over your head. Every so often it broke off and you saw Lucy in the Sky, with Diamonds all over the sky. This Lucy was God, the big figure, the white rabbit. You can just write a song with imagination on words and that's what we did.

"It's like modern poetry, but neither John nor I have read much. The last time I approached it I was thinking 'This is strange and far out', and I did not dig it all that much, except Dylan Thomas who I suddenly started getting, and I was quite pleased with myself because I got it, but I hadn't realised he was going to be saying exactly the same things.

"It's just that we've at last stopped trying to be clever, and we just write what we like to write. If it comes out clever, OK 'Love Me Do' was our greatest philosophical song. For it to be simple and true means that it's incredibly simple."
March 1
– *Abbey Road.* Sgt Pepper sessions. Work on 'Lucy In The Sky With Diamonds'.
March 2
– *Abbey Road.* Sgt Pepper sessions. Work on 'Lucy In The Sky With Diamonds'.
March 3
– *Abbey Road.* Sgt Pepper sessions: four French horns were added to the 'Sgt. Pepper's Lonely Heart's Club Band' track. As usual, Paul hummed the melody, George Martin transcribed it and the session musicians played it. Afterwards they mixed 'Lucy In The Sky With Diamonds'.
March 6
– *Abbey Road.* Sgt Pepper sessions. Sound effects of audience laughter and applause were added to the title track.
March 7
– *Abbey Road.* Sgt Pepper sessions. More work on 'Lovely Rita'.
– Peter Blake and Jann Howarth had supper with Paul and Jane at Cavendish Avenue and Paul played them an acetate of 'Lovely Rita'.
– Granada Television transmitted *It's So Far Out, It's Straight Down* in their *Scene Special* programme.
March 9
– *Abbey Road.* Sgt Pepper sessions. Work began on Paul's 'Getting Better'.
March 10
– *Abbey Road.* Sgt Pepper sessions. More work on 'Getting Better.'
March 13
– *Abbey Road.* Sgt Pepper sessions. The brass section was added to 'Good Morning Good Morning.'
March 15
– *Abbey Road.* Sgt Pepper sessions. Work began on George's 'Within You Without You' using four Indian musicians on tabla, dilruba, swordmandel and tamboura. The other Beatles did not play on this track but were there.
Afterwards Peter Blake and Jann

Ringo and Maureen.

Howarth had dinner with John and Paul.
March 17
– *Abbey Road.* Sgt Pepper sessions. The orchestral track for Paul's 'She's Leaving Home' was recorded. George Martin had been unavailable to orchestrate it (he was producing a Cilla Black record), so Paul used Mike Leander as an arranger instead, something which upset George Martin considerably.
March 20
– *Abbey Road.* Sgt Pepper sessions. John and Paul recorded the vocal track for 'She's Leaving Home'.
– While at the studio, Brian Matthew interviewed the group for the BBC Transcription Service programme *Top Of The Pops* (no relation), and recorded acceptance speeches for three 1966 Ivor Novello Awards to be edited into the BBC Light Programme's *The Ivor Novello Awards For 1966* programme which John and Paul did not want to attend in person.
March 21
– *Abbey Road.* Sgt Pepper sessions. The piano solo was added to 'Lovely Rita' but vocals on 'Getting Better' were interrupted when John found himself on an accidental acid trip.
– Because so many fans were gathered outside the studios, George Martin took John up onto the flat roof to get some air. When Paul and George realised what was happening they ran up the stairs after them. They knew that the studio roof had just a low parapet and were worried that John might try to fly. Paul and Mal Evans took John back to nearby Cavendish Avenue and Paul decided to keep him company on the trip – Paul's second.
March 22
– Abbey Road. Sgt Pepper sessions. George continued work on 'Within You Without You' while the others listened to playbacks.
March 23
– *Abbey Road.* Sgt Pepper sessions. Further work on 'Getting Better'.
March 25
– It was announced that The Beatles had won two Ivor Novello Awards for 1966.

John plays up to the cameras at the Sgt Pepper launch party at Brian Epstein's house, May 19.

The Pepper sleeve

The sleeve for Sgt Pepper was shot at Michael Cooper's photographic studio at 4 Chelsea Manor Studios, Flood Street, off the King's Road, with a number of friends present.

Paul: "I came up with the title and went to Robert with some drawings for the idea of the cover."

Robert Fraser: "The whole concept of the cover was Paul McCartney's. He asked me if I knew anybody who could execute this idea. It was my suggestion to put it through Peter Blake and his wife and Michael Cooper, as I knew they were the only people who would understand. It was built in Michael's studio in Flood Street and everybody came up with ideas – all The Beatles, all of us – it became a collaboration."

Peter Blake: "We had an original meeting with all four Beatles, Robert Fraser and Brian Epstein; most of the subsequent talking was done with Paul at his house and with John there sometimes."

Paul: "The original idea was to be a presentation from the mayor and corporation, like a Northern thing. There'd be a floral clock and there'd be us, and then on a wall or something, we'd have photos of all the band's heroes – they were going to be on a photo. So I said to everyone, 'Who are your favourites? Make a list.' Marlon Brando was one of the first choices, Brigitte Bardot, Monroe, James Dean – all obvious ones. Then George came up with a list of gurus, and all sorts of other things came in."

The original list of "Heroes" made by The Beatles before the Sgt Pepper sleeve was given to Robert Fraser and Peter Blake was as follows (sic throughout): "Yoga's; Marquis de Sade; Hitler; Neitch; Lenny Bruce; Lord Buckley; Alistair Crowley; Dylan Thomas; James Joyce; Oscar Wilde; William Burroughs; Robert Peel; Stockhausen; Auldus Huxley; H.G.Wells; Izis Bon; Einstein; Carl Jung; Beardsley; Alfred Jarry; Tom Mix; Johnny Weissmuller; Magritte; Tyrone Power; Carl Marx; Richard Crompton; Tommy Hanley; Albert Stubbins; Fred Astaire". In addition, Paul's original sketch for the sleeve featured Brigitte Bardot six times larger than anyone else.

Paul "I took the idea of the floral clock, and the heroes and the presentation by a mayor to Robert and he and I went to Peter Blake and Peter developed it all from there. The lists were his idea, and all the cut-outs instead of using real people, and the floral clock got changed around; but basically it was the original theme."

The list grew enormously, with Robert adding in his favourite LA painters, and Peter and Jann adding their favourites. The final line-up on the sleeve was: Stuart Sutcliffe; Aubrey Beardsley; five gurus; two anonymous women; drawings of three girls; Sonny Liston; George (in wax); John (in wax); Ringo (in wax); Paul (in wax); "Cheeky" Max Miller; Sir Robert Peel; Aleister Crowley; Mae West; Lenny Bruce; Aldous Huxley; Dylan Thomas; Marlon Brando; Tom Mix; Terry Southern; Karlheinze Stockhausen; W.C. Fields; Dion; Tony Curtis; Oscar Wilde; Wallace Berman; C.G. Jung; Tyrone Power; Edgar Allan Poe; Tommy Handley; Marilyn Monroe; Dr Livingstone (in wax); Larry Bell; Johnny Weismuller; Fred Astaire; William Burroughs; Stephen Crane; Issy Bonn; Merkin; Stan Laurel; George Bernard Shaw (in wax); Richard Lindner; Oliver Hardy; Albert Stubbins (footballer); Karl Marx; Huntz Hall (of The Bowery Boys); H.G. Wells; Einstein; Bobby Breen (singing prodigy); Marlene Deitrich; Simon Rodia (creator of Watts-Towers); Robert Allen Zimmerman; Lawrence of Arabia; Lewis Carroll; an American legionnaire; Diana Dors and Shirley Temple.

Paul: "Jesus and Hitler were on John's favourites list but they had to be taken off. John was that kind of guy but you couldn't very well have Hitler and so he had to go. Gandhi also had to go because the head of EMI, Sir Joe Lockwood, said that in India they wouldn't allow the record to be printed. There were a few people who just went by the wayside."

March 28
– *Abbey Road.* Sgt Pepper sessions. John added the lead vocal to 'Good Morning Good Morning'. The animal noises were added to it, and further work was done on 'Being For The Benefit Of Mister Kite'.

March 29
– *Abbey Road.* Sgt Pepper sessions. Work began on 'With A Little Help From My Friends'.
– The title of The Beatles' next album was announced as Sgt. Pepper's Lonely Hearts Club Band, a name which Paul and Mal Evans came up with on a plane flight, when Mal asked Paul what the "P" on the paper packet with the in-flight meal meant.

March 30
– *Abbey Road.* Sgt Pepper sessions. Further work was done on 'With A Little Help From My Friends'.

April 1
– *Abbey Road.* Sgt Pepper sessions. The 'Sgt Pepper's Lonely Hearts Club Band (Reprise)' was recorded and mixed all in one session.

April 3
– Paul flew to Los Angeles with Mal Evans. Shortly after midnight, Mal Evans took his bags around to Paul's house in Cavendish Avenue.

Paul: "I was just thinking nice words like Sergeant Pepper and Lonely Hearts Club, and they came together for no reason. But after you have written that down you start to think, 'There's this **Sergeant Pepper** who has taught a band to play, and got them going so that at least they found one number. They're a **bit of a brass band** in a way, but also a rock band because they've got the San Francisco thing. We went into it just like that; just us doing a **good show.**"

Paul went to bed at 3:30 am but was up early because decorators arrived to begin working on the house. Two Air France officials arrived to collect Paul and Mal and not long afterwards they flew into Paris-Orly Airport. From there they took a flight to Los Angeles. Paul had intended to bring a copy of the photograph for the front of Sgt Pepper to show Jane when he met up with her in Denver but he forgot. Paul's American visa turned out to have expired but American customs and immigration at Los Angeles sorted it out in 30 minutes. Then a private Lear jet, hired from Frank Sinatra, took them to San Francisco.
– *Abbey Road.* Sgt Pepper sessions. George added his lead vocal to 'Within You Without You'.

April 4
– Paul and Mal Evans flew in to San Francisco which had had its first snow in 42 years and was much colder than they had been expecting. They did the sights, photographed the Golden Gate Bridge and bought records. They stopped by the Fillmore Auditorium and found Jefferson Airplane rehearsing there. They returned to their house and Paul jammed with them. Paul smoked pot with them but declined the DMT he was offered, despite the stories to the contrary still circulating in San Francisco.

April 5
– Paul flew into Denver, Colorado, where Jane Asher was playing Shakespeare with the Bristol Old Vic company, to pay a surprise visit on her 21st birthday.

Paul's Lear jet covered the journey from San Francisco to Denver quickly: 650 mph at 41,000 feet. At Denver Airport Paul was met by Bert Rosenthal who had lent Paul his house. Mal booked into the Driftwood Motel. Later in the day, Paul and Jane were collected by Rosenthal and taken to the hotel where Jane's 21st was to be held. The Bristol Old Vic people laid on a wonderful party.

April 6
– Mal hired a Hertz rental car and drove Paul and Jane up into the Rockies. They parked off the road among the trees and walked down a rocky gorge to the river where they ended up paddling in the cold water. They walked barefoot in the drifts of snow in the crisp air. That evening they demolished a huge meal and fell asleep in front of Rosenthal's colour television.

"i think i'm going to fall over,"

April 7
– Mal took Paul's camera to be fixed, then went to the park to see the Greek Theatre. Paul filmed Jane walking among the trees and it was then that Paul thought of the Magical Mystery Tour as an idea for a TV special.

April 8
– Jane had a matinée performance, so Paul and Mal drove into the mountains, past Central City to the old Boodle Mine, complete with its own graveyard. Both Paul and Mal got stuck in snow and mud and finished up looking pretty scruffy. Back in Central City they found "Paul's Cafe" and went in to refresh themselves and eat. Across the street, in the Gilded Garter bar, they had a few drinks and listened to a local country singer. The singer approached them and asked if they were folk singers because he was sure he knew their faces. They returned to Denver in time to see Jane in Romeo and Juliet.
– In Chertsey, Surrey, John visited the workshops of coach builders J.P. Fallon Limited to discuss the possibility of having his Rolls Royce repainted in a psychedelic pattern. They were happy to

Below: John with George Martin.

oblige and the car was driven to the workshop a few days later.

April 9
– The Old Vic company flew out of Denver to continue their tour of America. In the afternoon, Paul and Mal went to see the Red Rocks Stadium, scene of a memorable Beatles concert three years before. Paul signed a lot of autographs and really enjoyed himself. Then Bert Rosenthal drove them to the airport. The Lear Jet was late in arriving but they were soon in Los Angeles and ensconced in the home of Mr and Mrs Derek Taylor.

April 10
– Paul and Mal spent the day shopping at Century Plaza, surprising the locals. Mal bought a talking pillow. Afterwards they visited John and Michelle Phillips of The Mamas and Papas and sat around watching the rain. It was a very friendly visit but Paul also wanted to visit The Beach Boys, and drove off leaving Mal beside the Phillips' log fire.

Brian Wilson was producing the track 'Vegetables' released on The Beach Boys' Pet Sounds album. Paul is said to have had a hand in its production.

April 11
– After playing guitar on 'On Top Of Old Smokey' at The Beach Boys session, Paul arrived back at John and Michelle Phillips' house at midnight, bringing Brian Wilson and his wife with him. John and Michelle got out their collection of instruments. At Paul's request, John brought out a tray of glasses, filled with different amounts of water, which he demonstrated how to play. Paul played cello and even flugelhorn. The jam session lasted most of the night. They arrived at Derek Taylor's house in time for breakfast and to pack. Paul spent the flight back to London working on new songs and on the idea of a Magical Mystery Tour film.

April 12
– Paul and Mal arrived at Heathrow airport.

April 19
– The Beatles' tax lawyers had suggested that they form an umbrella company controlling all their subsidiary interests. This company, later known as Apple, would have them under an exclusive contract. The Beatles themselves would become a legal partnership, sharing all their income, whether from group, live or solo work (except songwriting) and The Beatles & Co. was created to bind them together legally for ten years on a goodwill share issue of £1 million.

April 20
– *Abbey Road.* Sgt Pepper sessions. Standing around a single microphone, The Beatles recorded several minutes of gibberish which was then overdubbed, reversed and edited to make the final run-out groove on the album. While recording this, Ringo felt faint. He said and toppled backwards, to be caught by the ever resourceful Mal Evans.
– John also suggested that a high-pitched note, beyond the range of the human ear, be added especially for dogs and considerable time was spent with all The Beatles, several friends, and George Martin, seeing how high they could hear. All of them still had good hearing, due in part to the fact that stage foldback had not yet been introduced, so the volume at their

concerts was low by modern standards. Also, mixing and playback was then conducted at relatively low levels compared to the practice in the Seventies and Eighties.

April 24
– The single **'Love In The Open Air'** by George Martin & His Orchestra, written by Paul McCartney, was released in the US as UNITED ARTISTS UA 50148.
– All four Beatles attended the first night of Donovan's week-long engagement at the Saville Theatre.

April 25
– *Abbey Road.* Work began on the 'Magical Mystery Tour' theme song. Despite the fact that Sgt Pepper was not yet released, The Beatles moved straight on to another project: Paul's idea for Magical Mystery Tour which Brian Epstein thought was a fine vehicle for all four Beatles.

John: "*Magical Mystery Tour* was something Paul had worked out with Mal and he showed me what his idea was and this is how it went, it went round like this, the story and how he had it all... the production and everything. Paul had a tendency to come along and say well he's written these ten songs, let's record now. And I'd say, 'well, give us a few days and I'll knock a few off', or something like that."

April 26
– *Abbey Road.* Further work on 'Magical Mystery Tour'.

April 27
– *Abbey Road.* Vocals were added to 'Magical Mystery Tour'.

April 29
– The 14 Hour Technicolour Dream benefit party for the underground newspaper *International Times* was held at Alexandra Palace – The Ally Pally. John Lennon and John Dunbar saw a news clip about it on the television at John's house in Weybridge while they were on an acid trip, and John immediately called his driver and had them driven there. John was filmed at the event. Coincidentally, Yoko Ono was one of the 41 performers.

May 1
– The single 'I Don't Want To See You Again' (Lennon & McCartney) /'Woman' (Paul McCartney) by Peter & Gordon was released in the US as CAPITOL STARLINE 6155.

May 3
– *Abbey Road.* The trumpets were added to 'Magical Mystery Tour'.

May 4
– *Abbey Road.* A mixing session for 'Magical Mystery Tour' which Paul and possibly other Beatles attended.

May 7
– Ringo saw The Jimi Hendrix Experience at *the Saville Theatre.*

May 9
– *Abbey Road.* The Beatles recorded an instrumental jam which was probably intended for the film of *Magical Mystery Tour,* but was never completed or used.

May 11
– 'Baby You're A Rich Man' session held at Olympic Sound Studios in Barnes, intended for the cartoon film *Yellow Submarine* but in fact used on their next single. Mick Jagger was among their guests at the session.

May 12
– Pirate station Radio London became the first station to play Sgt Pepper in its entirety – before copies had even been pressed.
– *Abbey Road.* 'All Together Now', for the *Yellow Submarine* film, was recorded and mixed all in one session. The Beatles were committed to providing three exclusive new songs for the film.

May 15
– Paul went to see Georgie Fame at the Bag O'Nails nightclub on Kingly Street, Soho. There he met Linda Eastman, who was there with Chas Chandler and The Animals. Afterwards they went on to The Speakeasy Club, on Margaret Street, where Procol Harum's 'A Whiter Shade Of Pale' was being played for the first time.

May 17
– *Abbey Road.* Work began on 'You Know My Name, Look Up The Number', the lyrics to which John had found written on the front of the London Telephone Directory while visiting Paul at Cavendish Avenue.

Above: John at the Sgt Pepper launch.

("You know their name, look up the number".)
– John Lennon and John Dunbar made a brief appearance on BBC2's *Man Alive*, a television documentary about the 14 Hour Technicolour Dream.

May 18
– Photo session in Hyde Park with Marvin Lichtner from *Time* magazine.
– Paul and John sang backing vocals on The Rolling Stones' single 'We Love You' at Decca Studios. Allen Ginsberg attended the recording session and described them as "two young princes in their finery".

Paul: "We recorded Sgt Pepper to alter our **egos, free ourselves** and have a **lot** of **fun.**"

May 19
– Sgt Pepper's Lonely Hearts Club Band was launched with a small press party held at Brian Epstein's house at 24 Chapel Street. Linda Eastman was invited to the party as a press photographer and met Paul again.

George Martin: **"Obviously Paul and John were the prime movers of Sgt Pepper, Paul probably more than John. But their inspiration, their creation of original ideas was absolutely paramount, it was fundamental to the whole thing. I was merely serving them in helping them to get those ideas down, so my role had become that of interpreter. In John's case, his ideas weren't all that concise so I had to try to realise what he wanted and how to effect it, and I would do this either by means of an orchestra or sound effects or a combination of both. This role was an interesting one because it presented many challenges for me. I would come up to new problems every day because the songs themselves presented those problems. The songs in the early days were straight-forward and you couldn't play around with them too much. Here we were building sound pictures."**

Paul: **"Whereas we'd just been The Beatles and song writers, I now started to sort of nudge with the avant-garde and said, 'Hell, we could do this'. The whole idea of taking on a new identity came out of all this. The idea that we didn't have to be The Beatles any more. We could be The Enlightened Beatles or we could be somebody altogether different – Sgt Pepper's Band.**

"It seemed obvious to us that peace, love and justice

Below: Paul with Linda Eastman at the Sgt Pepper launch party. This was only the second time that Paul had met Linda, the first being four days previously, on May 15, at the Bag O'Nails nightclub.

ought to happen. We were opening ourselves to millions of peoples' influences, things that arrived in the form of, say, 'A Day In The Life'."
May 20
– Ringo invited John, Cynthia, George, Patti and Brian Epstein to take afternoon tea with Maureen, Zak and himself at "Sunny Heights".
– DJ Kenny Everett officially previewed Sgt Pepper on his BBC Light Programme show *Where It's At*. He was unable to play the final track, however, because BBC censors had banned 'A Day In The Life' on the grounds that it advocated the use of drugs. The show also featured a pre-recorded interview with John, Paul and Ringo about the album.
May 24
– All four Beatles went to the Speakeasy to see Procol Harum.
May 25
– The Beatles recorded 'It's All Too Much' at the *De Lane Lea* recording studio on Kingsway.
– John took delivery of his Rolls Royce, now painted with psychedelic fairground patterns like a gypsy

caravan. Rolls Royce launched a formal objection.
May 28
– All four Beatles attended a party at Brian Epstein's new country house near Heathfield in Surrey.
May 31
– Further work was done on 'It's All Too Much' at the *De Lane Lea* recording studios.
June 1
– An unstructured instrumental jam was recorded at *De Lane Lea* studios in Kingsway.
– The album SGT PEPPER'S LONELY HEARTS CLUB BAND was released in the UK as Parlophone PMC 7027 (mono) and PCS 7027 (stereo).
SIDE A: 'Sgt Pepper's Lonely Hearts Club Band', 'With A Little Help From My Friends', 'Lucy In The Sky With Diamonds', 'Getting Better', 'Fixing A Hole', 'She's Leaving Home', 'Being For The Benefit Of Mr Kite'; SIDE B: 'Within You Without You', 'When I'm Sixty Four', 'Lovely Rita', 'Good Morning Good Morning', 'Sgt Pepper's Lonely Hearts Club Band (reprise)', 'A Day In The Life'.

"You **can't** just **go off the cuff.** We've got to **prepare something."**

– The amazing thing was that Sgt Pepper was recorded on an antique Studer J37 4-track. In 1981 it was auctioned by Jackson Music Ltd. for £500.

June 2
– Work on 'It's All Too Much' at *De Lane Lea*.
– The album SGT PEPPER'S LONELY HEARTS CLUB BAND was released in the US as CAPITOL MAS 2653 (mono) and SMAS 2653 (stereo) with the same track list as the UK release.

June 4
– Paul and Jane, George and Patti were in the audience at Brian Epstein's Saville Theatre to see The Jimi Hendrix Experience headline a bill which included Denny Lane And His Electric String Band, The Chiffons and Procol Harum. Jimi Hendrix opened his set with the title track from Sgt Pepper. Paul described it as among the greatest honours he had ever had bestowed upon him, particularly as Jimi had only three days to rehearse the piece.

June 7
– *Abbey Road*. Another take of 'You Know My Name, Look Up The Number' was made.
– The animated *Yellow Submarine* film was announced.

June 8
– *Abbey Road*. Paul invited Brian Jones from The Rolling Stones to attend the recording session, thinking he might bring along a guitar and play some rhythm. Brian arrived with an alto saxophone, which used to be his instrument in the pre-Rolling Stones Ramrods. He played a sax solo for them on 'You Know My Name, Look Up The Number' which remains one of Paul McCartney's favourite Beatles' numbers.

June 9
– *Abbey Road*. 'You Know My Name, Look Up The Number' was mixed.

June 12
– The album THE FAMILY WAY (Original Soundtrack Album) by The George Martin Orchestra and written by Paul McCartney was released in the USA as LONDON MS 82007 with the same tracks as the UK release.

Right: On the steps of Brian Epstein's house, May 19.

June 14
– The backing track for 'All You Need Is Love' was recorded at *Olympic Studios, Barnes*, for use on the first live worldwide satellite link-up which was expected to be seen by 200 million people. George Martin pleaded with them; John came back with 'All You Need Is Love' and Martin orchestrated it.

George Martin: **"When it came to the end of their fade-away as the song closed, I asked them: 'How do you want to get out of it?' 'Write absolutely anything you like, George,' they said. 'Put together any tunes you fancy, and just play it out like that.'"** Martin came up with the Marseillaise, a Bach two-part invention, Greensleeves and a short quote from 'In The Mood' (which EMI ultimately had to pay copyright on).

June 17
– *Life* magazine ran an interview with Paul McCartney in which he revealed that he had taken acid.

June 19
– *Abbey Road*. Further work done on 'All You Need Is Love'.

June 21
– *Abbey Road*. 'All You Need Is Love' was mixed.

June 23
– *Abbey Road*. The orchestral track was added to 'All You Need Is Love'.

June 24
– *Abbey Road*, preparing for the satellite link-up. The Beatles, the 13-man orchestra and their conductor did a full run-through for the BBC cameramen. More than 100 journalists and photographers were allowed into the studio for a late-morning photocall.

Paul and LSD

After Paul's admission in *Life* magazine, the British press besieged him to make a statement. Paul gave an interview to Independent Television News for broadcast on the 9 pm news that evening.

Reporter: "How often have you taken LSD?"

Paul: "Um, four times."

Reporter: "And where did you get it from?"

Paul: "Well, you know, I mean, if I was to say where I got it from, you know, it's illegal and everything, it's silly to say that so I'd rather not say it."

Reporter: "Don't you believe that this was a matter which you should have kept private?"

Paul: "Well the thing is, you know, that I was asked a question by a newspaper and the decision was whether to tell a lie or to tell the truth, you know. I decided to tell him the truth but I really didn't want to say anything because if I'd had my way I wouldn't have told anyone because I'm not trying to spread the word about this but the man from the newspaper is the man from the mass medium. I'll keep it a personal thing if he does too, you know, if he keeps it quiet. But he wanted to spread it so it's his responsibility for spreading it. Not mine."

Reporter: "But you're a public figure and you said it in the first place. You must have known that it would make the newspapers."

Paul: "Yes, but to say it, you know, is only to tell the truth. I'm telling the truth. I don't know what everyone is so angry about."

Reporter: "Well, do you think you have encouraged your fans to take drugs?"

Paul: "I don't think it will make any difference. You know, I don't think my fans are going to take drugs just because I did. But the thing is, that's not the point anyway. I was asked whether I had or not and from then on the whole bit about how far its going to go and how many people it's going to encourage is up to the newspapers and up to you, you know, on television. I mean, you're spreading this now, at this moment. This is going into all the homes in Britain and I'd rather it didn't, you know. But you're asking me the question and if you want me to be honest I'll be honest."

Reporter: "But as a public figure, surely you've got a responsibility to not say any..."

Paul: "No, it's you've got the responsibility. You've got the responsibility not to spread this now. You know, I'm quite prepared to keep it as a very personal thing if you will too. If you'll shut up about it, I will!"

June 25

– The Beatles performed 'All You Need Is Love' on the BBC *Our World Live* worldwide TV link-up live from EMI's massive studio one.

The studio was filled with potted flowers and The Beatles wore uniforms of green, pink and orange, similar to the Sgt Pepper cover. Waist-long flowing scarves wafted from their necks but the slightly medieval look was marred slightly by the headphones they all wore, as well as the usual studio clutter of microphones, headphone leads, instruments and music stands. Among the guests were Keith Richards, Eric Clapton, Graham Nash and Gary Leeds. Keith Moon fooled around on the drums with Ringo during the long wait before transmission. Simon, Marijka and Joshi, from The Fool, wore the flowing patchwork patterns and headscarves they would shortly market through the Apple boutique. The Small Faces sat close to each other in new Granny Takes A Trip clothes. Mick Jagger sat on the floor with Marianne Faithfull, close by Paul's high stool, wearing

a silk jacket with a pair of psychedelic eyes painted on it, smoking a very fat joint in front of the 200 million viewers, the day before he was to be busted for drugs. "All You Need Is Love!" streamers and balloons floated down from the ceiling and the audience all sang along. Placards with the message ALL YOU NEED IS LOVE written large in many languages were paraded before the cameras. The vocals, Paul's bass, Ringo's drums, George's solo and the orchestra were all mixed live on the air. In the control room afterwards George Martin played back the tape.

June 26

– *Abbey Road.* Ringo added the opening drum roll to 'All You Need Is Love' and the record was mixed, ready for instant release.

June 28

– George was fined £6 at South Western Court, London, for speeding in Roehampton Lane, Putney in his black Mini Cooper.

June 29

– The *Beatles' Book Monthly* photographer, Leslie Bryce,

Paul: "Another **big hit!**"

photographed John at Kenwood, his mock-Tudor mansion in Weybridge, for an "at home" session.

July 1

– The BBC Light Programme show, *Where It's At* broadcast a pre-recorded interview with Paul talking about 'All You Need Is Love'.

July 3

– Vic Lewis gave a private party for The Monkees at the Speakeasy. The guests included John and Cynthia, George and Patti, Paul and Jane, The Who, Eric Clapton, the Manfred Mann group, Lulu, Procol Harum, The Fool, Micky Most, Vicki Wickham, Dusty Springfield, and Monkees Peter Tork, Mike Nesmith and Micky Dolenz (Davy Jones and Ringo were both away).

July 5

– John and Cynthia saw Marmalade at the Speakeasy.

July 7

– The single **'All You Need Is Love'/'Baby You're A Rich Man'** was released in the UK as PARLOPHONE R 5620. It was only decided 24 hours before the TV show that 'All You Need Is Love' should be their next single, based on the demand that the world-wide viewing would cause.

– 'Baby You're A Rich Man' was originally intended for the soundtrack of the full-length Beatles cartoon, *Yellow Submarine.* It was originally called One Of The Beautiful People.

July 17

– The single **'All You Need Is Love'/'Baby You're A Rich Man'** was released in the USA as CAPITOL 5964.

July 20

– Paul and Jane attended a Chris Barber recording session at the Chappell Recording Studios to see him record Paul's instrumental 'Catcall'. Paul played piano, along with Brian Auger, and can be heard yelling in the chorus at the end.

– John had long had the idea that The Beatles should all live together on an island with a recording studio/ entertainment complex in the middle, surrounded by four separate villas. Beyond that would be housing for their friends and the staff. Alex Mardas, a TV repairman whom John had dubbed "Magic Alex", had

"Once on a **trip** to a hill village, we came round a corner of the **peaceful road** only to find **hundreds** of photographers **clicking** away at us."

friends in the Greek Military Junta, and arranged for The Beatles to island-seek there. Though the authorities had already banned both long hair and rock'n'roll, they felt that The Beatles visiting Greece might help prop up their tourist industry and undermine some of the bad press they had been getting for torturing dissidents. Alex flew to Greece and came up with the island of John's dreams: the island of Leslo, about 80 acres surrounded by four habitable islands, one for each Beatle. The island was for sale for £90,000, including a small fishing village, four ideal beaches and 16 acres of olive groves.

– George and Patti, Ringo and Neil Aspinall flew to Athens where they were met by Alex and his father, who was in the military police. They stayed at the Mardas house in suburban Athens until the remaining members of the party arrived.

July 22

– John and Cynthia with Julian, Paul and Jane, Patti's 16-year-old sister Paula, Mal Evans and Alistair Taylor from the NEMS office, who was in charge of buying the island, set off for Greece. Their hired yacht, the M.V. Arvi, was stuck near Crete in high winds and did not get to Athens until the 25th, so they all stayed in Athens.

July 23

– In a convoy of a Mercedes and two huge American taxis, the party went out into the country. Paul, Jane and Neil's taxi caught fire in the extreme heat and when the others turned back to look for them they were found walking along the road, back towards the village where the party had eaten lunch.
– Alex arranged a few sightseeing trips to prevent them from getting bored, but he also kept the Greek tourist authorities informed of their timetable so wherever they went there were crowds of people following. Alistair Taylor wrote:

July 24

– The Oxford University drama company invited The Beatles to attend a performance of *Agamemnon* by Aeschylus, at the theatre at Delphi, but Alex had informed the tourist authorities who broadcast the fact

Jane Asher, her sister Paula, Paul, John's son Julian and John arrive in Athens, July 22.

they would be there on Athens Radio. They arrived in Delphi to an enormous crowd of fans and pushy journalists. They climbed back into their Mercedes and headed straight back to Athens.

July 25

– George and Paul stayed in, playing guitars and relaxing while John, Ringo and the others went shopping for instruments, attracting a large crowd of sightseers and fans.
– The yacht finally arrived. It had 24 berths and a crew of eight including the captain, a chef and two stewards.

July 26

– Ringo and Neil Aspinall flew back to London from Athens. Maureen was pregnant and with the baby nearly due Ringo did not want to be away too long.
The others boarded the yacht. The first few days were spent swimming,

sun-bathing, and taking LSD. Then they set off to inspect Leslo, where they were to build their commune. After a full day of exploring the island, planning where the recording studio would be located and who would live on which island, Alistair Taylor was instructed to fly straight back to London and make the arrangements to buy it.

Export controls meant that The Beatles had to buy special export dollars and then apply to the government for permission to spend them. Taylor eventually got the clearance but by then no-one was interested in the idea anymore and he was told to sell the property dollars back to the government. In the meantime, their value had increased so The Beatles made £11,400 profit on the deal.

July 29

– George, Patti and Mal Evans returned from Greece to prepare for a trip to Los Angeles.

July 31

– Paul, Jane, John, Cynthia, Julian, Paula and Alex flew back to London from Athens.
– Ringo recorded a farewell message at pirate station Radio London, broadcast on their last day on the air before the government stamped them out and replaced them with their own anodyne version of pop radio.

August 1

– George, Patti, "Magic" Alex Mardas and Neil Aspinall flew from London to Los Angeles where they had rented a house on Blue Jay Way. George and Patti flew as Mr and Mrs Weiss, taken from Nat Weiss, the director of Nemperor Artists in New York, who was to meet them at the airport and look after them.
– That evening George called Derek Taylor and gave him directions to get there but Derek got lost in the LA fog trying to find their house. While he was waiting, George wrote a song with the street name as the title.

August 2

– George, Patti, Neil and Alex visited Ravi Shankar's Music School and watched him teach. Afterwards they had a meal with Shankar on Sunset Strip.

The 'pot' ad

On July 24 *The Times* ran a full-page advertisement headed, "The law against marijuana is immoral in principle and unworkable in practice" which was signed by, among others, all four Beatles and Brian Epstein. The petition's arguments included the following: that the smoking of cannabis on private premises should no longer constitute an offence; cannabis should be taken off the dangerous drugs list and controlled, rather than prohibited; possession of cannabis should either be legally permitted or at most be considered a misdemeanour and that all persons now imprisoned for possession of cannabis or for allowing cannabis to be smoked on private premises should have their sentences commuted.

It was signed by 65 eminent names including Francis Crick, the co-discoverer of the DNA molecule and a Nobel laureate, novelist Graham Greene, and MPs Brian Walden and Tom Driberg, as well as future MP Jonathan Aitken, but the four MBEs caused the most press concern. Questions were asked in the House, and a chain of events set off, which did actually result in the liberalisation of the laws against pot in Britain. The £1,800 advertisement was paid for by The Beatles at Paul McCartney's instigation.

Below Right: Ringo with baby Jason.

August 3
– George, Alex and Neil went to Ravi Shankar's Music School where George and Ravi Shankar held a press conference to promote Shankar's Hollywood Bowl concert set for the following day. Patti and her sister Jenny, who flew down from San Francisco to join them, went sightseeing.
– That evening they attended a Mamas And Papas recording session with Derek Taylor.

August 4
– George and his party attended Ravi Shankar's concert at the Hollywood Bowl.

August 5
– George and company attended a recording session by Alla Rahka, after which they went for a meal in Alvira Street with Derek Taylor and his entire family.

August 6
– George visited Ashish, Ali Akbar Khan's son, the sarod player, while the others visited Disneyland. That evening they dined at Ravi Shankar's house.

August 7
– George, Patti, Jenny, Derek Taylor and Neil Aspinall walked around the Haight-Ashbury district of San Francisco, attracting a huge crowd of hippies and beggars.

August 9
– Neil, Alex, George and Patti flew back to London.

August 11
– The Beatles were photographed by Richard Avedon at the penthouse photographic studio in Thompson House. Avedon used the images for a series of four psychedelic posters which appeared first in *Look* magazine before being published separately and adorning thousands of student bedrooms around the world.

August 18
– The single 'We Love You' by The Rolling Stones, with backing vocals by John Lennon and Paul McCartney, was released in the UK as DECCA F 12654.

August 19
– Maureen Starkey gave birth to a second son, Jason, at Queen Charlotte's Hospital, London.

but **I've had** a lot of people **die** around me and the other **feeling** is, 'What the **fuck?** What can I **do?**'

August 22
– The Beatles began work on 'Your Mother Should Know' at *Chappell Recording Studios, London.*

August 23
– The Beatles finished work on 'Your Mother Should Know' at Chappell.

August 24
– John and Cynthia, Paul and Jane, George and Patti attended a lecture by the Maharishi Mahesh Yogi at the London Hilton on Park Lane. After the lecture they had a private audience with the Maharishi and arranged to attend his seminar which was to be held in Bangor that weekend.

August 27
– Brian Epstein was found dead in his London house.

Jane Asher received the telephone call which brought them the news in Wales, and gave the receiver to Paul. Saddened, worried and confused, The Beatles gave a brief press conference then departed for London.

John: "We were in Wales with the Maharishi. We had just gone down after seeing his lecture first night. We heard it then. I was stunned, we all were, I suppose, and the Maharishi, we went in to him. 'What, he's dead' and all that, and he was sort of saying oh, forget it, be happy, like an idiot, like parents, smile, that's what the Maharishi said. And we did.

"I had that feeling that anybody has when somebody close to them dies: there is a sort of little hysterical, sort of hee, hee, I'm glad it's not me or something in it, the funny feeling when somebody close to you dies. I don't know whether you've had it,

"I knew we were in trouble then. I didn't really have any misconceptions about our ability to do anything other than play music and I was scared. I thought, 'We've fuckin' had it.'

"I liked Brian and I had a very close relationship with him for years, because I'm not gonna have some stranger runnin' things, that's all. I like to work with friends. I was the closest with Brian, as close as you can get to somebody who lives a sort of 'fag' life, and you don't really know what they're doin' on the side. But in the group I was closest to him and I did like him.

"We had complete faith in him when he was runnin' us. To us, he was the expert. I mean originally he had a shop. Anybody who's got a shop must be all right. He went round smarmin' and charmin' everybody. He had hellish tempers and fits and lock-outs and y'know he'd vanish for days. He'd come to a crisis every now and then and the whole business would fuckin'

Opposite: Paul and Ringo en route to Bangor, August 25.
Above: Paul, George and John at the London Hilton, August 24.

stop cause he'd go on sleepin' pills for days on end and wouldn't wake up. Or he'd be missin' y'know, beaten up by some old docker down the Old Kent Road. But we weren't too aware of it. It was later on we started findin' out about those things.

"We'd never have made it without him and vice versa. Brian contributed as much as us in the early days, although we were the talent and he was the hustler. He wasn't strong enough to overbear us. Brian could never make us do what we didn't really want to do."

Enter the Maharishi

On August 25 The Beatles, their wives and girlfriends, Mick Jagger and Marianne Faithfull took the train from Euston Station to Bangor to attend the Maharishi's teaching seminar. Cynthia Lennon got caught in the crush and a policeman refused to let her through the barrier onto the platform until it was too late and the train pulled away without her. Neil Aspinall drove her there.

John: "Bangor was incredible, you know, Maharishi reckons the message will get through if we can put it across. What he says about life and the universe is the same message that Jesus, Buddha and Krishna and all the big boys were putting over. Mick came up there and he got a sniff and he was on the phone saying:

'Keith, send Brian, send them all down'. You just get a sniff and you're hooked.

"There's none of this sitting in the lotus position or standing on your head. You just do it as long as you like. (In a heavy accent) Tventy minutes a day is prescribed for ze workers. Tventy minutes a morning and tventy minutes after verk. Makes you happy, intelligent and more energy. I mean look how it all started. I believe he just landed in Hawaii in his nightshirt, all on his own, nobody with him, in 1958.

"The main thing is not to think about the future or the past, the main thing is to just get on with now. We want to help people to do that with these academies. We'll make a donation and we'll ask for money from anyone we know with money, anyone that's interested, anyone in the so-called establishment who's worried about kids going wild and drugs and all that. Another groovy thing: Everybody gives one week's wages when they join. I think it's the fairest thing I've heard of. And that's all you ever pay, just the once.

"Even if you go into the meditation bit just curious or cynical, once you go into it, you see. We weren't so much sceptical because we'd been through that phase in the middle of all the Beatlemania like, so we came out of being sceptics a bit. But you've still got to have a questioning attitude to all that goes on. The only thing you can do is judge on your own experience and that's what this is about."

August 28
– The single 'We Love You' by The Rolling Stones (John Lennon and Paul McCartney on backing vocals) was released in the US as LONDON 905.

August 29
– Brian Epstein's funeral was a strictly family affair with none of his groups, not even The Beatles, in attendance.

September 1
– The Beatles met at Paul's house on Cavendish Avenue to discuss their future. They decided to continue with the Magical Mystery Tour project and put everything else on hold.

September 5
– *Abbey Road*. Magical Mystery Tour sessions. Work began on John's 'I Am The Walrus.'

September 6
– *Abbey Road*. Magical Mystery Tour sessions. Further work done on 'I Am The Walrus', including John's vocal. Paul recorded a demo version of 'The Fool On The Hill' and the basic tracks were recorded for George's 'Blue Jay Way'.

September 7
– *Abbey Road*. Magical Mystery Tour sessions. Work on 'Blue Jay Way'.

September 8
– *Abbey Road*. Magical Mystery Tour sessions. The instrumental 'Flying' was recorded. At this time the track was called 'Aerial Tour Instrumental' and was meant for a flying sequence in which The Beatles intended to have the coach actually fly, using special effects.

September 11
– The coach for the Magical Mystery

Tour was still being painted with its psychedelic livery and was delayed for two hours in leaving Allsop Place, where rock'n'roll package tours always started. Paul went in search of a cup of tea in the nearby London Transport canteen above Baker Street station. There he signed a few autographs and chatted until the bus arrived. The other three Beatles were picked up in Virginia Water, Surrey, near their homes. All 43 seats in the coach were filled with technicians, Beatles, Mal, Neil and even a few fan club secretaries. They drove to Teignmouth, Devon, stopping for lunch at the Pied Piper restaurant in Winchester en route. In Teignmouth the entire party stayed at The Royal Hotel where 400 local fans were waiting for them in the pouring rain. Paul gave a short press conference about the film.

September 12
– The coach got stuck on a bridge on its way to Widecombe Fair, blocking the road, and had to back half a mile up the road to turn around. The AA redirected traffic. John was filmed losing his temper but the footage was not used. They abandoned plans to

visit the fair and stopped at the Grand Hotel in Plymouth for lunch. John and Paul gave an interview to Hugh Scully for the local BBC1 news magazine programme *Spotlight South West* and posed for a photo call.
– The coach continued to Newquay, Cornwall, with several stops to film en route. In Newquay they stayed at the Atlantic Hotel.

September 13
– John directed a film sequence in which Scottish "funny walks" specialist Nat Jackley chased bikini-clad girls around the Atlantic Hotel swimming pool.
– Spencer Davis was staying in Cornwall and saw a news item showing the AA and local police trying to push The Beatles' bus round the narrow bend and off the bridge. He phoned the Atlantic Hotel and spoke with Mal Evans who invited him over.
– George was interviewed by Miranda Ward for the BBC's new Radio One programme *Scene and Heard*.
– BBC TV's *Spotlight South West* aired their interview with John and Paul.

September 14
– Filming in various locations.

John: "Paul made an attempt to **carry on** as if **Brian** hadn't **died** by saying, 'Now, now, boys, we're going to make a record.' Being the kind of person I am, I thought well, we're going to make a record all right, so I'll go along, so we went and made a record. And that's when we made *Magical Mystery Tour*.

"Paul said, 'Well, here's the segment, you write a little piece for that,' and I thought **'Bloody hell,'** so I ran off and I wrote the dream sequence for the **fat woman** and all the things with the spaghetti. Then George and I were sort of **grumbling** about the fuckin' **movie** and we thought we'd better do it and we had the feeling that we **owed** it to the **public** to do these things."

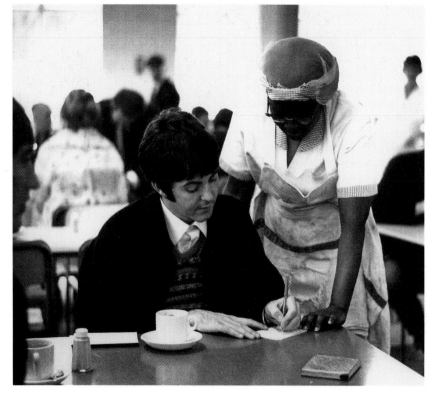

Top Left: Brian Epstein, whose death threw The Beatles into turmoil and ultimate disintegration. Left: Paul takes tea near Allsop Place while awaiting the Magical Mystery Tour coach, September 11.

– Miranda Ward joined The Beatles' party and interviewed <u>Ringo</u> for *Scene And Heard*.

– Spencer Davis returned The Beatles' hospitality of the previous evening and invited them over to Perranporth where he and his family were on holiday. <u>Ringo</u>, <u>Paul</u>, Neil and Miranda Ward went with several other coach passengers. Spencer Davis: **"I invited some of them back to the pub in the evening and Ringo and Paul came, but George and John were doing something else. There was a piano in the corner and Paul stuck a pint of beer on the top and started playing and**

John directs the bikini clad girls at the Atlantic Hotel, Newquay, September 13.

people hadn't even noticed that he was in there. There was one girl who looked and said, 'The piano player, look who it is!' It was so funny to see the reaction on their faces."

<u>Paul</u> led the sing-song around the pub piano until 2 am but refused to play the pub standard, 'Yellow Submarine'.

September 15

– Filming in front of the hotel and various locations en route to London. They stopped for lunch at a small fish and chip shop in Taunton (in Somerset) and filmed there.

September 16

– *Abbey Road.* Magical Mystery

Tour sessions More work done on 'Your Mother Should Know'.

September 18

– The Beatles filmed at *the Raymond Revue Bar in Soho* with the Bonzo Dog Doo-Dah Band and stripper Jan Carson whose bare breasts were covered in the film with a superimposed CENSORED sign.

September 19

– The Beatles filmed at West Malling Air Station, Maidstone, Kent, when they found that you needed to book film studios ahead of time.

September 20

– Filming at West Malling Air Station, Maidstone, Kent.

Left: On the sea front in Plymouth, September 15. Below: John at Newquay. Opposite: George at Plymouth.

September 21
– Filming at West Malling Air Station, Maidstone, Kent.
September 22
– Filming at West Malling Air Station, Maidstone, Kent.
September 23
– Filming at West Malling Air Station, Maidstone, Kent.
September 24
– Filming at West Malling Air Station, Maidstone, Kent. The grand finale, with The Beatles trooping down the staircase singing 'Your Mother Should Know', was filmed with the aid of the 160 members of The Peggy Spencer Formation Dancing Team and two dozen Women's Royal Air Force cadets.
Paul: "That was the shot that used most of the budget."
September 25
– The Beatles had allowed two weeks for editing, but in the end it took eleven. Editing began immediately and was done by Roy Benson in a rented Soho editing suite: Norman's Film Productions at the corner of Old Compton Street and Wardour Street. Paul was present throughout all 11 weeks, unless he was recording, and the others appeared to a lesser degree.
– *Abbey Road.* Magical Mystery Tour sessions. Work began on Paul's 'The Fool On The Hill'.
September 26
– *Abbey Road.* Magical Mystery Tour sessions. More work on 'The Fool On The Hill'.

September 27
– *Abbey Road.* Magical Mystery Tour sessions. The orchestra and the Mike Sammes Singers' parts were added to 'I Am The Walrus'. Paul added a new vocal to 'The Fool On The Hill'.
September 28
– *Abbey Road.* Magical Mystery Tour sessions. Work done on 'I Am The Walrus' and 'Flying'.
September 29
– John and George appeared on Rediffusion Television's *The Frost Programme*, discussing transcendental meditation with David Frost.
– *Abbey Road.* Magical Mystery Tour sessions. The sound effects were added to 'I Am The Walrus' including the fragment of Shakespeare's *King Lear*. Paul's 'Your Mother Should Know' was also finished.
September 30
– The first edition of BBC Radio 1's *Scene And Heard* broadcast its interview with George.
October 1
– A further one-day shoot at West Malling.
October 2
– *Abbey Road.* Work began on The Beatles' next single, Paul's 'Hello, Goodbye'.
October 4
– John and George made a follow-up appearance on *The Frost Programme* continuing their discussion of transcendental meditation.

October 6
– *Abbey Road.* Magical Mystery Tour sessions. 'Blue Jay Way' completed.
October 7
– The Beatles turned down New York promoter Sid Bernstein's offer of $1 million for a single concert.
October 11
– Yoko's one-woman show, Yoko Plus Me, opened at the Lisson Gallery in London. Me was the anonymous John Lennon, who also underwrote the cost of the exhibition.
John: "She gave me her *Grapefruit* book and I used to read it and sometimes I'd get very annoyed by it; it would say things like 'Paint until you drop' or 'bleed' and then sometimes I'd be very enlightened by it and I went through all the changes that people go through with her work – sometimes I'd have it by the bed and I'd open it and it would say something nice and it would be alright and then it would say something heavy and I wouldn't like it.

"There was all that and then she came to me to get some backing for a show and it was half a wind show. I gave her the money to back it and the show was, this was a place called Lisson Gallery, another one of those underground places. For this whole show everything was in half; there was half a bed, half a room, half of everything, all beautifully cut in half and painted white. And I said to her 'why don't you sell the other half in bottles?' having caught on by then what the game was and she did that – this was still before we had the nuptials – and we still have the bottles from the show, it's my first. It was presented as Yoko Plus Me – that was our first public appearance. I didn't even go to see the show, I was too uptight."

October 12
– George's 'It's All Too Much' was mixed at *De Lane Lea Studios,* where it was recorded.
– *Abbey Road.* Magical Mystery Tour sessions. Mixing 'Blue Jay Way' followed by John producing a recording of 'Shirley's Wild Accordion', a Lennon and McCartney composition played by Shirley Evans (accordion) and Reg Wale (percussion), for use in the film. (Not in fact used.)

October 13
– The single **'How I Won The War'**, by Musketeer Gripweed (John Lennon) and The Third Troop (Ken Thorne, voice: John) was released in the UK as UNITED ARTISTS UP 1196.

Above: George and Patti arriving at Brian Epstein's memorial service, October 17.

October 14
– Miranda Ward's interview with Ringo was broadcast on Radio 1's *Scene And Heard.*

October 17
– The Beatles attended a memorial service for Brian Epstein held at 6 pm at the New London Synagogue, Abbey Road, London.
– Mick Jagger revealed that he and Paul had had talks about The Rolling Stones and The Beatles setting up a jointly owned recording studio.

October 18
– John and Cynthia attended the Motor Show, held at the Earl's Court Exhibition Hall.

That evening all four Beatles, their wives and girlfriends attended the première of Richard Lester's film *How I Won The War,* starring John Lennon, held at the London Pavilion.

Afterwards they went to Cilla Black's flat at 9b Portland Place for a celebration party.

October 19
– George and Ringo flew to Sweden, via Copenhagen, to visit the Maharishi Mahesh Yogi at his Transcendental Meditation Academy in the coastal resort of Falsterbohus. They flew back to London the same day.
– *Abbey Road.* Magical Mystery Tour sessions. Further work on 'Hello, Goodbye'.

October 20
– *Abbey Road.* Magical Mystery Tour sessions. The flute passage was added to 'The Fool On The Hill' and the viola to 'Hello, Goodbye'.
– The single 'Catcall' by The Chris Barber Band, written by Paul McCartney, was released in the UK as MARMALADE 598005.

October 29
– Paul and Mal Evans flew to Nice with cameraman Aubrey Dewar and engaged a taxi driver to wake them and take them to the mountains overlooking Nice before the break of dawn.
– Ringo filmed the getting-on-the-bus sequence for *Magical Mystery Tour* in Lavender Hill, London.

October 30
– Paul and Aubrey Dewar filmed the sunrise in the mountains behind Nice,

and Paul mimed 'Fool On The Hill' for the *Magical Mystery Tour* film. They stayed on the mountain for most of the day, though only the dawn footage was eventually used.

November 1
– Paul flew back to London from Nice.
– George and John attended a reception for the group Family at Sybilla's.

November 2
– *Abbey Road.* Paul added an extra bass line to 'Hello, Goodbye'.

November 3
– George's 'Blue Jay Way' sequence was filmed at Ringo's house, "Sunny Heights", in Weybridge, Surrey.

November 6
– *Abbey Road.* Mixing session which The Beatles probably attended.

November 7
– *Abbey Road.* Paul added a new vocal to 'Magical Mystery Tour'.

November 10
– Paul directed the promotional film for 'Hello, Goodbye' on stage at the *Saville Theatre, Shaftesbury Avenue,* complete with dancing girls in grass skirts.

November 17
– The Beatles Limited changed its name to Apple Music Limited, and Apple Music Limited became The Beatles Limited.
– Neil Aspinall flew to New York to personally deliver copies of the 'Hello, Goodbye' promotional film to the producers of such television programmes as the *Ed Sullivan Show* and *Hollywood Palace.*

November 19
– Paul and Jane went to see The Bee Gees, The Bonzo Dog Doo-Dah Band, The Flowerpot Men and Tony Rivers & The Castaways at the Saville Theatre.

November 20
– 'I Am The Walrus' was banned by both BBC Television and BBC Radio, although no announcement was made. The BBC clearly felt that there must be a drug reference there somewhere, and anyway the reference to knickers was obscene.

November 21
– The Musicians' Union closed shop prohibited miming, so The Beatles' promotional films for 'Hello, Goodbye' were not shown in Britain. An attempt

The Beatles in animated form as they appeared in Yellow Submarine.

was made to include the promo clip as a piece of footage being edited by The Beatles in the Soho cutting room, but it didn't work and was scrapped.

November 22
– <u>George</u> worked on his solo *Wonderwall* film project at *Abbey Road,* with two flautists and a tabla player.

November 23
– <u>George</u> continued work on the *Wonderwall* soundtrack at *Abbey Road.*
– ITV also banned The Beatles' film and a plan to screen one of the three films in colour on BBC2's *Late Night Line Up,* was also abandoned. Instead, *Top Of The Pops* showed 'Hello, Goodbye', with a clip from *A Hard Day's Night,* much to The Beatles' annoyance.

November 24
– The single **'Hello Goodbye'/'I Am The Walrus'** was released in the UK as Parlophone R 5655.
– <u>John</u> and <u>Paul</u> attended the first recording session by Apple's new signing, Grapefruit, held at the IBC Recording Studio on Portland Place.
– <u>John</u> worked on a compilation of his home tapes at *Abbey Road.*

November 25
– Radio 1's *Where It's At* programme transmitted an interview done with <u>John Lennon</u> by Kenny Everett and Chris Denning. The whole of the Magical Mystery Tour double EP was played, the only time 'I Am The Walrus' was broadcast by the BBC, which had unofficially banned it.

November 27
– The single **'Hello Goodbye'/'I Am The Walrus'** was released in the USA as Capitol 2056.
– The album MAGICAL MYSTERY TOUR was released in the US as Capitol MAL 2835 (mono) and SMAL 2835 (stereo).
> SIDE A: **'Magical Mystery Tour', 'The Fool On The Hill', 'Flying', 'Blue Jay Way', 'Your Mother Should Know', 'I Am The Walrus';**
> SIDE B: **'Hello Goodbye', 'Strawberry Fields Forever', 'Penny Lane', 'Baby You're A Rich Man', 'All You Need Is Love'.**

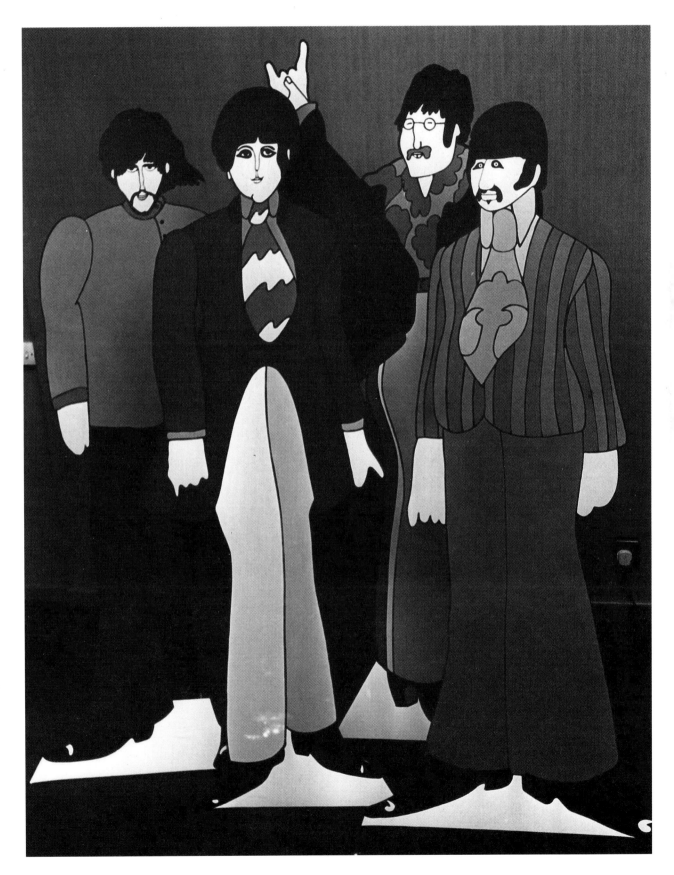

Above: Paul, at home with his father Jim McCartney. Below: Ringo with boxer Sugar Ray Robinson.

November 28
– *Abbey Road.* The Beatles recorded Christmas Time (Is Here Again), their fifth Christmas record to be sent out to members of their fan club.
– Afterwards John worked on sound effects tapes for his upcoming stage version of *The Lennon Play: In His Own Write.*

December 3
– Ringo flew to Rome to begin work on his cameo role in the movie, *Candy,* directed by Christian Marquand and based on the Olympia Press novel by

Terry Southern and Mason Hoffenberg. Ringo played the Mexican gardener.
– Paul and Jane drove to Paul's farm in Campbeltown, Scotland, for a break.

December 5
– John and George represented The Beatles at a party to celebrate the impending opening of the Apple Boutique at 94 Baker Street, London.

December 7
– Ringo's first day before the cameras in Rome filming *Candy.*
– The Apple Boutique opened its doors to the public.

December 8
– The EP **Magical Mystery Tour** was released in the UK as PARLOPHONE MMT I (mono) and SMMT1 (stereo).
SIDE A: ‘Magical Mystery Tour’, ‘Your Mother Should Know’;
SIDE B: ‘I Am The Walrus’;
SIDE C: ‘The Fool On The Hill’, ‘Flying’;
SIDE D: ‘Blue Jay Way’.

December 9
– Ringo filmed with Ewa Aulin, the former Miss Teen Sweden, who was playing Candy.

December 11
– Ringo filmed with Ewa Aulin
– Apple Music signed its first group. John named them Grapefruit, coincidentally the name of Yoko's book. Most of the group were former members of Tony Rivers & The Castaways, one of Brian Epstein's groups.

December 12
– Ringo filmed with Ewa Aulin

December 13
– Ringo filmed his sex scene with Ewa.
– Speaking on behalf of The Beatles, a NEMS Enterprises spokesman dismissed as “guesswork” the idea that The Beatles would form their own record label in 1968 under the aegis of their new Apple organisation.

December 14
– Ringo filmed more of his sex scene with Ewa.

December 15
– The Beatles' fan club flexi-disc **Christmas Time (Is Here Again)** was released.

The Apple Boutique

John: “Clive Epstein or some other such business freak came up to us and said you've got to spend so much money, or the tax will take you. We were thinking of opening a chain of retail clothes shops or some barmy thing like that... and we were all thinking that if we are going to open a shop let's open something we're interested in, and we went through all these different ideas about this, that and the other. Paul had a nice idea about opening up white houses, where we would sell white china and things like that, everything white, because you can never get anything white, you know, which was pretty groovy, and it didn't end up with that, it ended up with Apple and all this junk and The Fool and all those stupid clothes and all that.”

– Ringo filmed at a "love-in".

December 16

– John and George flew to Paris to attend a UNICEF gala at the Palais de Chailloy with Maharishi Mahesh Yogi.

– Ringo's last day of filming.

December 17

– Ringo flew back to London from Rome, his role in the film *Candy* completed.

– John and George flew back to London where they acted as hosts at the *Magical Mystery Tour* party for the area secretaries of the Official Beatles Fan Club, at the Hanover Grand Film and Art Theatre, London. An advance copy of *Magical Mystery Tour* was shown as well as *The Beatles At Shea Stadium*.

December 19

– Seven investment companies were registered and formed in London on behalf of The Beatles: Apricot

Below: Ringo, John and Paul, together with Maureen and Jane Asher, in fancy dress for the Magical Mystery Tour launch party, December 21.

Investments Ltd., Blackberry Investments Ltd., Cornflower Investments Ltd., Daffodil Investments Ltd., Edelweiss Investments Ltd., Foxglove Investments Ltd. and Greengage Investments Ltd.

December 20

– Paul and Jane returned to London from Campbeltown.

December 21

– A fancy dress party was held for the complete crew of *Magical Mystery Tour* including all the technical staff, plus relatives and a few friends. Robert Morley was Father Christmas. The Bonzo Dog Doo-Dah Band played. Paul and Jane arrived as a cockney pearly king and queen and John dressed as a teddy boy.

December 25

– Paul and Jane announced that they were engaged to be married.

December 26

– *Magical Mystery Tour* was given its world première in monochrome on BBC Television.

December 27

– In order to answer and counter the adverse press criticism of *Magical Mystery Tour* Paul appeared live on Rediffusion's *The Frost Programme* where he discussed the film and wider issues with David Frost.

December 29

– John and his friend, the actor Victor Spinetti, were talking about Morocco. John suggested that they go there immediately and they collected their passports and took the next flight from London Airport that day.

December 31

– The Beatles saw in the New Year at Cilla Black's flat on Portland Place.

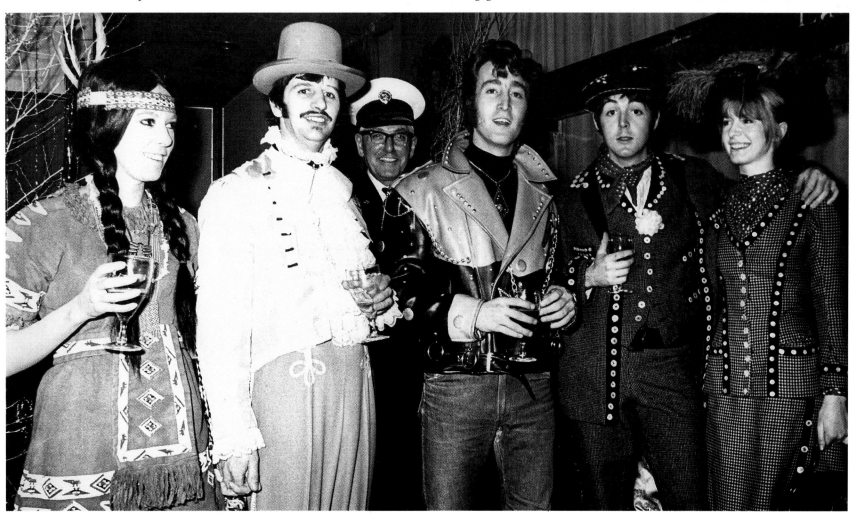

1968

January 5
– John got together with his father Freddie once more, this time at Kenwood, John's House in Weybridge. Freddie had been washing dishes in a nearby hotel. John told the *Daily Mirror* that he had ended his feud with his father: **"From now on I hope we'll be in close contact all the time."**
– George worked on the soundtrack to the film *Wonderwall* at Abbey Road.
– *Magical Mystery Tour* was repeated on BBC2, this time in colour.

January 6
– *The Daily Telegraph* reported that Brian Epstein had left £486,032 (£266,032 net) and that his mother was to control the estate.

January 7
– George flew from London to Bombay, with stopovers in Paris, Frankfurt and Teheran, to record the *Wonderwall* film soundtrack using local Indian musicians.

January 9
– George began work at EMI's Bombay recording studios.

January 12
– The Beatles Film Productions Limited changed its name to Apple Film Limited and Apple Music Limited changed its name to Apple Corps Limited.
– George completed the recordings needed for *Wonderwall* and began recording ragas and other traditional pieces of music for possible use on Beatles records, one of which was the basic track for 'The Inner Light'.

January 17
– John, Ringo and Paul attended a press reception organised by RCA Records to celebrate the release of 'Dear Delilah', the first single by the Apple-managed group Grapefruit.

January 18
– George flew back to London from Bombay with the *Wonderwall* tapes.

January 19
– The single 'Dear Delilah' by Grapefruit was released in the UK. The press were informed that John and Paul helped produce the session.

January 22
– Apple opened offices at 95 Wigmore St, London.

January 25
– *Twickenham Film Studio.* The Beatles filmed their cameo appearance in the animated cartoon *Yellow Submarine.* Afterwards John and George attended Ossie Clark's fashion show in London.

January 27
– John was interviewed by Kenny Everett at Kenwood, Weybridge, for BBC Radio 1's *The Kenny Everett Show.*

Below: Ringo, John and Paul at a party welcoming the group Grapefruit to the Apple label, January 28. Standing, left to right: Brian Jones, Donovan, Ringo, John, Cilla Black and Paul; Grapefruit – George Alexander, Pete and Geoff Swettenham and John Perry – are seated at the table.

January 30
– Cilla Black's television series *Cilla* went on the air using Paul's 'Step Inside Love', sung by Cilla, as its signature tune.
– George completed work on the soundtrack for the film *Wonderwall* at Abbey Road.

February 1
– Ringo attended rehearsals at the BBC Rehearsal Rooms in North Acton, London, for his live appearance on Cilla Black's new television show, *Cilla.*

February 2
– Ringo attended a second day of rehearsals for *Cilla.*

February 3
– *Abbey Road.* Work began on Paul's 'Lady Madonna'.

February 4
– *Abbey Road.* Work began on John's 'Across The Universe'. Two fans, waiting outside, were brought into the studio to provide the high falsetto harmonies needed.
– John's interview on BBC Radio 1's *The Kenny Everett Show* was broadcast.

February 5
– Ringo attended camera position rehearsals for his appearance on *Cilla* at the BBC Television Theatre, Shepherd's Bush, London.
– Paul appeared at a press conference held at the Royal Garden Hotel, London to publicise the Leicester Arts Festival. He was persuaded to do it by a student who managed to talk his way into Paul's Cavendish Avenue house.

February 6
– Ringo appeared live on BBC Television's *Cilla*, taking part in sketches, singing and even tap dancing.
– *Abbey Road.* The other three Beatles worked on 'The Inner Light'

Previous Spread: The Beatles, their wives and girlfriends, and others at the Maharishi's ashram. Below Left: Paul with Mal Evans arriving in India.

and completed 'Lady Madonna' (taking a break to watch Ringo's appearance on *Cilla*). 'Lady Madonna' featured the saxophone talents of Ronnie Scott, Harry Klein, Bill Povey and Bill Jackman. Paul played all the piano, and the comb and paper routine was actually just him singing through cupped hands.

February 8
– *Abbey Road*. 'The Inner Light' was completed and most of the session was spent working on 'Across The Universe'. John remained unsatisfied with the results. Spike Milligan, who watched the session as George Martin's guest, asked if he could use 'Across The Universe' on a wildlife charity record he was organising and The Beatles agreed.

February 10
– Paul and Jane saw Paul's brother Michael in a Scaffold concert at *Queen Elizabeth Hall, London.*

February 11
– *Abbey Road*. The Beatles intended to shoot footage of the recording of 'Lady Madonna', their next single, as a promotional film, but chose instead to record a new song, 'Hey Bulldog'. The filming was directed by Tony Bramwell, head of Apple Films.

February 14
– Mal Evans collected luggage belonging to George and Patti, her sister Jenny, John and Cynthia, and

took Quantas flight 754 to Delhi. The excess baggage charge was £195.19.6d. He went a day early in order to organise transport for John and George when they arrived on the 16th to begin their much delayed study of transcendental meditation with Maharishi Mahesh Yogi.

February 15
– George, Patti, John and Cynthia flew from London Airport to India.

February 16
– George, Patti, John and Cynthia arrived in Delhi at 8:15 am, on the overnight flight. Mal met them at the airport with Mia Farrow, who had already decided that she was part of The Beatles' entourage. Mal had organised three cars for the 150-mile drive from Delhi to Rishikesh.

February 19
– Paul, Jane, Ringo and Maureen flew from London Airport to India. Paul,

Jane, Ringo and Maureen arrived in Delhi, attracting much more press attention as the media were now alterted to what was going on. A film crew was on hand as they stepped from the plane after the exhausting 20-hour flight, jet-lagged from the five time zones. Mal Evans and Raghvendra, from the ashram, placed garlands of red and yellow flowers around their necks as a traditional token of greeting. Ringo's arm was giving him pain from the required injections so they set off to find a hospital. Their driver lost his way and finished up in a dead end, followed by a whole convoy of press cars, one of which came to the rescue and led them to the hospital.

February 24
– *The London Evening Standard* ran an interview with Paul in which he said, "Instead of trying to amass money for the sake of it, we're setting up a business concern at Apple – rather like a Western Communism... we've got all the money we need. I've got the house and the cars and all the things that money can buy."

March 1
– Ringo and Maureen left Rishikesh much earlier than anticipated. They were unhappy away from their children and did not like the food. Ringo told the press it was like a Butlin's holiday camp.

March 8
– The single 'Step Inside Love' by Cilla Black, written for her by Paul McCartney, was released in the UK as Parlophone R 5674.
– The single 'And The Sun Will Shine' by Paul Jones, featuring Paul on drums, was released in the UK as Columbia DB 8379.

March 9
– Sgt Pepper's Lonely Hearts Club

Band won four Grammy awards: Best Album of the Year, Best Contemporary Album, Best Engineered Record and Best Album Cover.

March 14
– Tony Bramwell's promotional film for 'Lady Madonna' (which actually showed them recording 'Hey Bulldog') was shown on BBC TV's *Top Of The Pops*.

March 15
– The single **'Lady Madonna'/'Inner Light'** was released in the UK as Parlophone R 5675.
– The promotional film for 'Lady Madonna' was shown on BBC Television's *All Systems Freeman* presented by Alan Freeman.

March 18
– The single **'Lady Madonna'/'The Inner Light'** was released in the USA as Capitol 2138.

March 26
– Paul, Jane and Neil Aspinall returned to England from Rishikesh, leaving George and Patti, John and Cynthia and "Magic" Alex who had come out to join them.

April
– Paul spent several weeks at his farm in Scotland.

April 2
– A new Beatles music publishing company, Python Music Limited, was formed.

April 12
– John and Cynthia, George and Patti and "Magic" Alex returned to London in a hurry from Rishikesh, India, after "Magic" Alex convinced John and George that the Maharishi was using his position to gain sexual favours from at least one of the female meditators. The Maharishi had never claimed to be celibate, and since he was not given

India

The Academy of Transcendental Meditation was built 150 feet above the Ganges surrounded on three sides by jungle-covered mountains. The students lived in six stone cottages. Each room had twin beds and modern bathroom facilities though the water supply sometimes broke down.

Breakfast from 7 until 11 am consisted of porridge, puffed wheat or cornflakes; fruit juice, tea or coffee, toast, marmalade or jam. Breakfast was followed by meditation practice, with no rules or timetable. Lunch and dinner both consisted of soup followed by a vegetarian main dish,

tomato and lettuce salads, turnips, carrots with rice and potatoes on the side. John and George were already vegetarians so the diet was nothing strange, but Ringo found the spices too hot for his taste. Mal assembled a stock of eggs so that he could cook Ringo fried, boiled, poached or scrambled eggs.

The Beatles were three weeks behind the other students so the Maharishi gave them extra tuition and lectures in the afternoons. These took place in the open air, sometimes on his flat sun roof. If it was a cool day, they would go to his bungalow and sit on cushions. Mal had his own chair because he was

unable to cross his legs comfortably.

The Beatles were on a TM teachers' course: there were 90-minute lectures at 3:30 and 8:30 pm with questions and answers, and progressively longer meditation sessions. Other students included Paul Horn, Mike Love and Donovan.

John: "The **aim** of the company isn't a **stack** of **gold teeth** in the bank. We've **done** that bit. It's more of a trick to see if we can't get **artistic freedom** within a **business** structure; to see if we can **create** things and **sell** them without charging **three** times our cost. "

a chance to explain or deny the charge, the reasons for their departure remain unclear. Alex Mardas certainly did not want to relinquish his claim to be John's "guru" and it would appear that he engineered the whole thing. At Delhi Airport, John wrote 'Sexy Sadie', at that time called 'Maharishi'.

John: "There was this big hullaballoo about him trying to rape Mia Farrow or somebody and trying to get off with a few other women and things like that. We went to see him after we stayed up all night discussing was it true or not true. When George started thinking it might be true, I thought well, it must be true; because if George started thinking it might be true there must be something in it.

"So we went to see Maharishi, the whole gang of us, the next day, charged down to his hut, his bungalow, and as usual, when the dirty work came, I was the spokesman – whenever the dirty work came, I actually had to be leader – and I said, 'We're leaving'.

"'Why?' he asked, and all that shit and I said, 'Well, if you're so cosmic, you'll know why.' He was always intimating, and there were all these right-hand men always intimating, that he did miracles. And I said 'You know why,' and he said, 'I don't know why, you must tell me,' and I just kept saying 'You ought to know' and he gave me a look like, 'I'll kill you, you bastard,' and he gave me such a look. I knew then. I had called his bluff and I was a bit rough to him."

April 16
– Apple Publicity Limited was formed.
April 18
– John and Ringo went to the launch party of Bell Records at *the Revolution Club, London*.
April 20
– Apple Music published an advertisement soliciting tapes from unknown artists. Apple was promptly inundated and only a tiny percentage of them were actually played.
May 5
– Twiggy saw Mary Hopkin on the television talent show *Opportunity Knocks* and telephoned Paul to suggest she would be a good person for Apple to sign.
May 6
– The single 'Step Inside Love' by Cilla

Above: John and Paul arrive in New York to launch Apple.
Below: George photographs the Maharishi.

Black and written by Lennon and McCartney was released in the US as BELL 726.
May 9
– John and Ringo held a meeting at Apple with various members of staff to discuss the possibility of an Apple children's school, which would be run by John's former schoolfriend Ivan "Ivy" Vaughan, now a qualified teacher.
May 11
– John and Paul, accompanied by "Magic" Alex, flew to New York to launch Apple in the US. They stayed with their lawyer, Nat Weiss, at his apartment at 181 East 73rd Street but conducted most of their interviews from hotels.
May 12
– John and Paul had an Apple "business meeting" while cruising round the Statue of Liberty in a Chinese junk.
May 13
– John and Paul conducted interviews with *The New York Times* and other newspapers all day from a suite at the St. Regis Hotel.
May 14
– John and Paul gave a press conference at the Americana Hotel on Central Park West.
– At the Americana press conference Paul met up with Linda Eastman once again, who wrote her telephone number on an unused cheque and gave it to him.
– The Beatles taped an interview with Mitchell Krause for WNDT, the non-commercial Channel 13's programme *Newsfront*.
– That evening they appeared on NBC's *The Tonight Show* where they were interviewed by Joe Garagiola as Johnny Carson was away. As well as discussing their plans for Apple, John used the opportunity to denounce the Maharishi.
May 15
– Accompanied by Linda, Nat Weiss drove John, Paul and "Magic" Alex to the airport for their flight back to London.
– George, Patti, Ringo and Maureen flew to Cannes, in the south of France to attend the premiere of *Wonderwall* at the Cannes Film Festival.

John & Yoko

John: "I'd never known love like this before, and it hit me so hard that I had to halt my marriage to Cyn. And don't think that was a reckless decision, because I felt very deeply about it and all the implications that would be involved. When we are free – and we hope that will be within a year – we shall marry. There is no need to marry – as Mick and Marianne say – but there's nothing lost in marrying either.

"Some say my decision was selfish. Well, I don't think it is. Are your children going to thank you when they're 18? There is something else to consider, too – isn't it better to avoid rearing children in a strained relationship?

"My marriage to Cyn was not unhappy. But it was just a normal marital state where nothing happened and which we continued to sustain. You sustain it until you meet somebody who suddenly sets you alight.

"With Yoko I really knew love for the first time. Our attraction was a mental one, but it happened physically too. Both are essential in the union – but I never thought I would marry again. Now the thought of it seems so easy.

"When we got back from India we were talking to each other on the phone. I called her over, it was the middle of the night and Cyn was away, and I thought well now's the time if I'm gonna get to know her any more. She came to the house and I didn't know what to do; so we went upstairs to my studio and I played her all the tapes that I'd made, all this far out stuff, some comedy stuff, and some electronic music. She was suitably impressed and then she said well let's make one ourselves so we made 'Two Virgins'. It was midnight when we started 'Two Virgins', and it was dawn when we finished, and then we made love at dawn. It was very beautiful."

– Channel 13 in New York screened their interview with John and Paul.

May 16
– John, Paul and "Magic" Alex arrived in London on TWA's early flight.
– Apple Management Limited was incorporated.

May 17
– The album McGough & McGear by Roger McGough and Mike McGear, produced by Paul McCartney, was released in the UK as PARLOPHONE PCS 7047. The album was launched with a small lunch party, and the copies given to those attending had a typed (multiple carbons) press release enclosed written by Derek Taylor in very stoned mode, which has become very collectable. It read:
HELLOW.
Thank you for coming to lunch.
    It is very nice of you and we are your friends.
    Now then, what do you want to know about it all?
    "Oh well of course" you may say "How do we know what we want to know; surely you would be the best judge of that. After all is said and done, what is there to know?"
    It is so much a case of guessing, for there's no knowing what anyone would want to know.
    No.
    Let us guess.
    Eyes down.
    "Our father, all the eights, 88 ......"
We are already confusing the issue.
This approach is what the psychiatrists call "maze making" or "problem posing" or "crisis creating" brought about in order

to find a solution, or an exit line.
    Now .... some names ....
    Jane and Mrs. Asher... William I Bennet (WIB)... Spencer Davies (is)... Barry Fantoni... Mike Hart... Jimi Hendrix... Vera Kantrovitch... Gary Leeds... Dave Mason and Carol... MIKE McGEAR... ROGER McGOUGH... John Mayall... Paul McCartney... John Mitchell... Zoot... Graham Nash... Viv Prince (yes)... Andy Roberts... Prince "Stash" de Rola... Paul Samwell-Smith... Martin Wilkinson...
    What have they in common? What have they not? They are all beautiful. The two in capital letters are here today. They made the album. You have in your hand or adjacent. They are in the Scaffold. (The capital letters were mine not theirs. McGear and McGough have no egos).
    The other people are friends. Friends. Friends who all contributed to the album in one way or many or all or a little.
    At any rate they all went into the recording session and sang or played or beat some tangible thing or simply waved their arms to create in the air some benign (we mean, of course, benign) turbulence.
    McGear and McGough are from Liverpool poetic and funny, concerned and open....
    Well listen, we are all here together now aren't we? In circumstances such as these, who needs a press release?
    Have we not tongues to speak.
    You are kind.
    Thank you.
    Derek.
– The World premiere of Wonderwall was given at the Cannes Film Festival, France with George, Patti, Ringo and Maureen in attendance.

May 19
– With Cynthia taking a short holiday, John called Yoko Ono and invited her out to Kenwood. They made a random sound tape, which was later issued as Two Virgins with the notorious sleeve showing them both naked. When Cynthia returned, she found Yoko ensconced in the bedroom, wearing Cynthia's dressing gown.
– George, Patti, Ringo and Maureen returned to London from Cannes.

May 21
– Paul and Jane had lunch with Andy Williams and his French wife Claudine Longet. That evening they attended his final Royal Albert Hall show and the end of the show party afterwards.

May 22
– George and John, accompanied by Yoko, attended the press launch and press conference for Apple's second boutique, Apple Tailoring (Civil and Theatrical) housed at 161 New King's Road, London.

May 23
– Apple Tailoring opened its doors to the public.
– Paul and Ringo were interviewed at Abbey Road for Tony Palmer's BBC Television Omnibus documentary on pop music called All My Loving.

May 26
– Paul directed a promotional film for Grapefruit's new single, 'Elevator', at the Albert Memorial in Hyde Park, London.
– Towards the end of May, The Beatles gathered at George's American-style bungalow "Kinfauns" in Esher, to record a demo tape of songs from

which they would choose what to put on their next album. Most of the songs had been written during their visit to India. They first recorded John's songs: 'Cry Baby Cry', 'Child Of Nature', 'The Continuing Story of Bungalow Bill', 'I'm So Tired', 'Yer Blues', 'Everybody's Got Something To Hide Except Me And My Monkey', 'What's The New Mary Jane' and 'Revolution'. Then came George's new compositions: 'While My Guitar Gently Weeps', 'Circles', 'Sour Milk Sea', 'Not Guilty' and 'Piggies'. They returned to John's notebook for 'Julia', then came Paul's songs: 'Blackbird', 'Rocky Racoon', 'Back In The USSR', 'Honey Pie', 'Mother Nature's Son', 'Ob-La-Di, Ob-La-Da' and 'Junk'. They finished with two more of John's: 'Dear Prudence' and 'Sexy Sadie'.

May 30
– Abbey Road. Work began on what was to become the double album The Beatles, usually known as The White Album. The first song worked on was John's 'Revolution 1'.

May 31
– Abbey Road. The White Album sessions. Work continued on 'Revolution 1' and the last six minutes was removed to form the basis of the chaotic 'Revolution 9'. Yoko screamed on the track, her first appearance on a Beatles recording.

June 4
– Abbey Road. The White Album sessions. Further work on 'Revolution 1'.
– Paul began seeing Francie Schwartz.

June 5
– Abbey Road. The White Album sessions. Recording began on Ringo's 'Don't Pass Me By', his first composition used on a Beatles record.

June 6
– Abbey Road. The White Album sessions. Further work on 'Don't Pass Me By'.
– Kenny Everett visited the studio to record an interview for his BBC Radio 1 programme The Kenny Everett Show.
– John and Victor Spinetti were filmed for the BBC2 arts programme Release discussing The John Lennon Play: In His Own Write, directed by Victor Spinetti, which was due to open in London on the 18th.

June 7
– George, Patti, Ringo and Maureen flew to California to enable George to film a guest appearance in Ravi Shankar's film *Raga*.

June 8
– Paul was the best man at his brother Michael's wedding to hair stylist Angela Fishwick, held in Carrog, Merioneth, North Wales.

June 9
– BBC Radio 1 broadcast The Beatles' interview on *The Kenny Everett Show*.

June 10
– *Abbey Road.* The White Album sessions. John worked on 'Revolution 9', adding more sound effects.

June 11
– *Abbey Road.* The White Album sessions. John did further work on 'Revolution 9', while Paul, in a separate studio, recorded and mixed 'Blackbird', without the aid of the other Beatles.
– Tony Bramwell from Apple Films shot a colour promotional film of Paul with Mary Hopkin, to help in the launch of her record.
– In California, George and Ravi Shankar were filmed walking along the coast-cliffs in Big Sur, and taking part in a "teach-in".

June 15
– John and Yoko held their first public event by planting an acorn for peace at Coventry Cathedral.

June 16
– Intertel TV Studios, Wembley. David Frost interviewed Paul before a live audience for an all-British Frost programme taped for transmission in America. The programme was called *David Frost Presents... Frankie Howerd*, and on it, Howerd interviewed Paul about Apple, then Paul introduced Mary Hopkin and she sang two songs.

June 18
– George, Patti, Ringo and Maureen flew back to London from California.
– The National Theatre production of *The John Lennon Play: In His Own Write*, directed by Victor Spinetti, opened at the Old Vic Theatre, London. John and Yoko's arrival together at the theatre was seized upon by the press.

June 20
– Paul, Tony Bramwell and Ivan Vaughan flew to Los Angeles where

Paul was due to address the Capitol Records Sales Conference (Capitol were the American distributors of Apple records). He contacted Linda Eastman who flew out from New York the next day to join him.
– *Abbey Road.* The White Album sessions. John and Yoko utilised three studios to continue the assembly of loop tapes for 'Revolution 9'. One was made from a Royal Academy of Music examination tape in which an anonymous man, asking question number nine, had his voice turned into an endless loop which John and Yoko faded in and out at will.

June 21
– *Abbey Road.* The White Album sessions. 'Revolution 1' was finished with the addition of the horn section and guitar solo.
– In Los Angeles, Paul addressed a Capitol Records Sales Conference and announced that in future all Beatles records would appear on the Apple label, although the group technically was still on EMI/Capitol.

June 22
– John and Victor Spinetti appeared on the BBC2 arts programme *Release*.

– Apple paid half a million pounds for a new headquarters building at 3 Savile Row, the former home of Nelson's Lady Hamilton.

June 24
– *Abbey Road.* George began work as a producer, recording 'Sour Milk Sea' with new Apple signing, Jackie Lomax, an old friend from Liverpool.
– The White Album sessions. John and Yoko worked on the stereo mixes of 'Revolution 9'.

June 25
– *Abbey Road.* George continued work with Jackie Lomax on 'Sour Milk Sea'.
– The White Album sessions: John and Yoko cut one minute from 'Revolution 9', though it was to remain the public's least favourite "Beatles" track.
– Paul, Tony Bramwell and Ivan Vaughan returned to London from Los Angeles.

June 26
– *Abbey Road.* The White Album sessions: work on John's 'Everybody's Got Something To Hide Except Me And My Monkey.'

June 27
– *Abbey Road.* The White Album sessions. Further work on John's 'Everybody's Got Something To Hide Except Me And My Monkey'.

June 28
– *Abbey Road.* The White Album sessions. Recording began on 'Good Night', John's lullaby for five-year-old Julian. John sang it through in the studio several times so that Ringo would get the phrasing but declined to record himself, thinking it was too "soft" for his hard image. Unfortunately no recording of John's acoustic version was made.

June 30
– Paul recorded The Black Dyke Mills Band in Saltaire, near Bradford, playing one of his own compositions, 'Thingumybob' (which he wrote as the theme tune for a London Weekend Television comedy series of the same name) and 'Yellow Submarine' as a B-side.
– While in Saltaire he was interviewed by Tony Cliff for the local BBC Television programme *Look North*.
– On the way home Paul, with Derek

John: "I declare these balloons high."

Taylor and Peter Asher, stopped in Harrold, a small Bedfordshire village, where Paul entertained the locals at the piano in the village pub.

July 1
– *Abbey Road.* The White Album sessions. John added the lead vocal to 'Everybody's Got Something To Hide Except Me And My Monkey'.
– Before the session, John and Yoko arrived dressed in white at the opening of John's first full art exhibition, *You Are Here*, at the Robert Fraser Gallery, London, which consisted mostly of charity collecting boxes. John marked the opening by releasing 365 helium-filled balloons over London.
– BBC1's Yorkshire local news programme *Look North* broadcast the interview with Paul.

July 2
– *Abbey Road.* The White Album sessions. Ringo recorded more vocals for 'Good Night'.
– Paul had lunch with Sir Joseph Lockwood, chairman of EMI, and Lord Poole at Lazards, the City merchant bank, to discuss Apple.

July 3
– *Abbey Road.* The White Album sessions. Work on Paul's 'Ob-La-Di, Ob-La-Da'.

July 4
– *Abbey Road.* The White Album

sessions. More work on 'Ob-La-Di, Ob-La-Da'.

July 5
– *Abbey Road.* The White Album sessions. Horns added to 'Ob-La-Di, Ob-La-Da'.

July 8
– *Abbey Road.* The White Album sessions. Paul did not like the results so far on 'Ob-La-Di, Ob-La-Da' and started afresh.
    Rehearsals began for 'Revolution', intended by John as an A-side for the next single (but ultimately used as the B-side).
– The actor David Peel approached Paul about Apple paying for a children's beach show at Brighton. David Peel: **"He agreed to help straight away, as well as suggesting our title."** The Punch and Judy puppet shows were called Apple Peel.

July 10
– *Abbey Road.* The White Album sessions. More work on John's 'Revolution'.

July 11
– *Abbey Road.* The White Album sessions. Piano and bass added to 'Revolution' and horns added to 'Ob-La-Di, Ob-La-Da'.

July 12
– *Abbey Road.* The White Album

Above: Yoko, John and Paul arrive at the London Pavilion Cinema in Piccadilly Circus for the premiere of Yellow Submarine; *Below: George and Patti arrive, accompanied by Neil Aspinall.*

sessions: 'Don't Pass Me By' was virtually completed and from midnight on, a new bass and guitar part was added to 'Revolution'.

July 15
– *Abbey Road.* The White Album sessions. Paul added a new vocal to 'Ob-La-Di, Ob-La-Da' and John remixed 'Revolution'. After this they rehearsed 'Cry Baby Cry'.

July 16
– *Abbey Road.* The White Album sessions. More work done on 'Cry Baby Cry'.
– Balance engineer Geoff Emerick finally quit working with the group. He could no longer tolerate the swearing and ill-mannered attitude shown towards the engineers (particularly from John), and the tense atmosphere in the studio.

July 17
– The world premiere of the animated *Yellow Submarine* film was held at the *London Pavilion in Piccadilly Circus.* Fans as usual brought traffic to a standstill and blocked the streets. Ringo and Maureen, John and Yoko were present but Paul attended alone.
– Afterwards they attended the celebration party at the Royal Lancaster Hotel, where the discotheque had been re-named *Yellow Submarine* for the occasion (and was to remain so for several years after).

July 18
– *Abbey Road.* The White Album sessions. More work on 'Cry Baby Cry' and rehearsals for Paul's 'Helter Skelter'.

July 19
– *Abbey Road.* The White Album sessions. Work began on John's send-up of the Maharishi, 'Sexy Sadie'.

July 20
– Jane Asher, appearing on Simon Dee's BBC Television show *Dee Time*, said that her engagement to Paul was off – but that it was not she that had broken it. She told Dee that they had been engaged for seven months, after knowing each other for five years. (She had arrived back at Cavendish Avenue one day to find Paul in bed with a girl named Francie Schwartz.)

July 22
– *Abbey Road.* The White Album

Now **everything** that is left is for the **public.**"

sessions. 'Don't Pass Me By' was completed, then a new version of 'Good Night' was recorded with the orchestra and Mike Sammes Singers. Ringo did his vocal track just after midnight.

July 23
– *Abbey Road.* The White Album sessions. 'Everybody's Got Something To Hide Except Me And My Monkey' was completed.

July 24
– *Abbey Road.* The White Album sessions. More work on John's 'Sexy Sadie'.

July 25
– *Abbey Road.* The White Album sessions. Work began on George's 'While My Guitar Gently Weeps'.

July 28
– The Beatles spent almost the entire day in and around London on various promotional photographic assignments.

July 29
– *Abbey Road.* Work began on Paul's 'Hey Jude', destined to become the next single.

July 30
– *Abbey Road.* More work done preparing 'Hey Jude' for final recording which was to take place in an independent studio.
– The Beatles were filmed at work by James Archibald for a documentary film intended for cinematic exhibition called Music.
– The Apple Boutique closed down.

Paul: "We decided to close down the shop last Saturday – not because it wasn't making any money, but because we thought the retail business wasn't our particular scene. So we went along, chose all the stuff we wanted – I got a smashing overcoat – and then told our friends."

July 31
– *Trident Studios, Soho.* The backing track for 'Hey Jude' was laid down.
– Queues formed all night around the block for a chance to grab free clothing from the Apple Boutique. The shop was completely stripped, with people taking away shop fittings and even the carpet. Apple gave the other boutique at 161 King's Road to the store manager.

Above: Paul's ad for The Beatles' new single traced on the windows of the closed Apple boutique. Opposite: John on the floor of Abbey Road studio two during the sessions for The White Album.

August 1
– *Trident Studios, Soho.* The orchestra, bass and lead vocals were added to 'Hey Jude' using Trident's eight-track facility (EMI still used 4-track). There were fierce arguments between John and Paul about who was to get the A-side of the new single, their first on the Apple label, but Paul eventually won and 'Hey Jude' became the first Apple release (and the biggest selling Beatles single of all time).

August 2
– *Trident Studios.* 'Hey Jude' was completed with overdubs and mixed.
– The London Weekend Television series *Thingumybob*, starring Stanley Holloway and with Paul's title tune, began transmission.

August 3
– Paul and Francie Schwartz spent an evening at the Revolution Club. She later wrote a kiss-and-tell biography about her brief relationship with him called *Body Count*.

August 6
– *Trident Studios.* 'Hey Jude' was

mixed from stereo to mono.
– John, Patti Harrison and fashion editor Suzy Menkes attended a fashion show at Revolution. John was interviewed by Matthew Robinson for that evening's edition of the BBC Radio programme *Late Night Extra*.

August 7
– *Abbey Road.* The White Album sessions. Work continued on George's 'Not Guilty'.

The session didn't end until 5:30 am, after which Paul went with Francie Schwartz to the now empty Apple Boutique and traced the name of The Beatles' new single on the whitewashed windows: 'Hey Jude' and 'Revolution'. When local Jewish traders misunderstood the title 'Hey Jude' and complained, Paul said he was sorry if he offended them, it was nothing to do with Jews and told the *Evening Standard*: "We thought we'd paint the windows for a gas. What would you do if your shop had just closed?"

August 8
– *Abbey Road.* The White Album

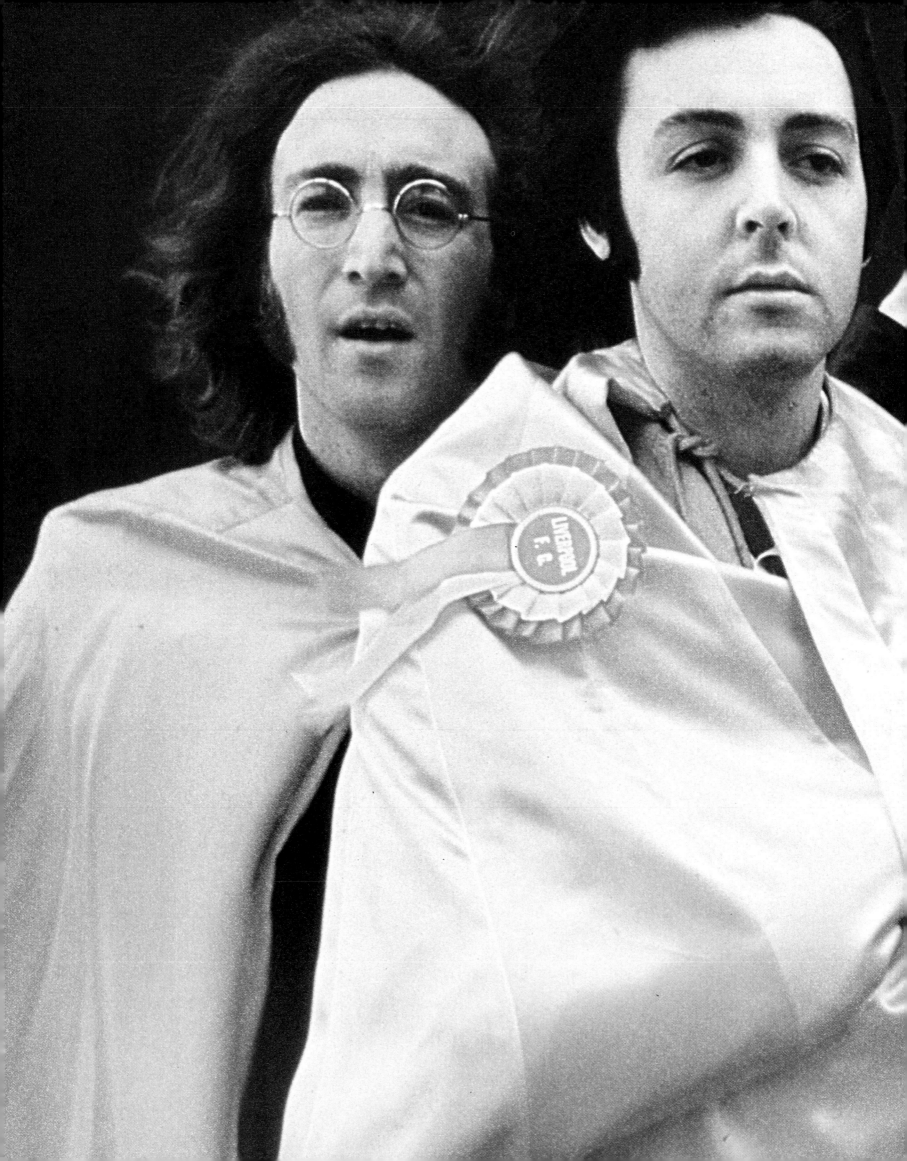

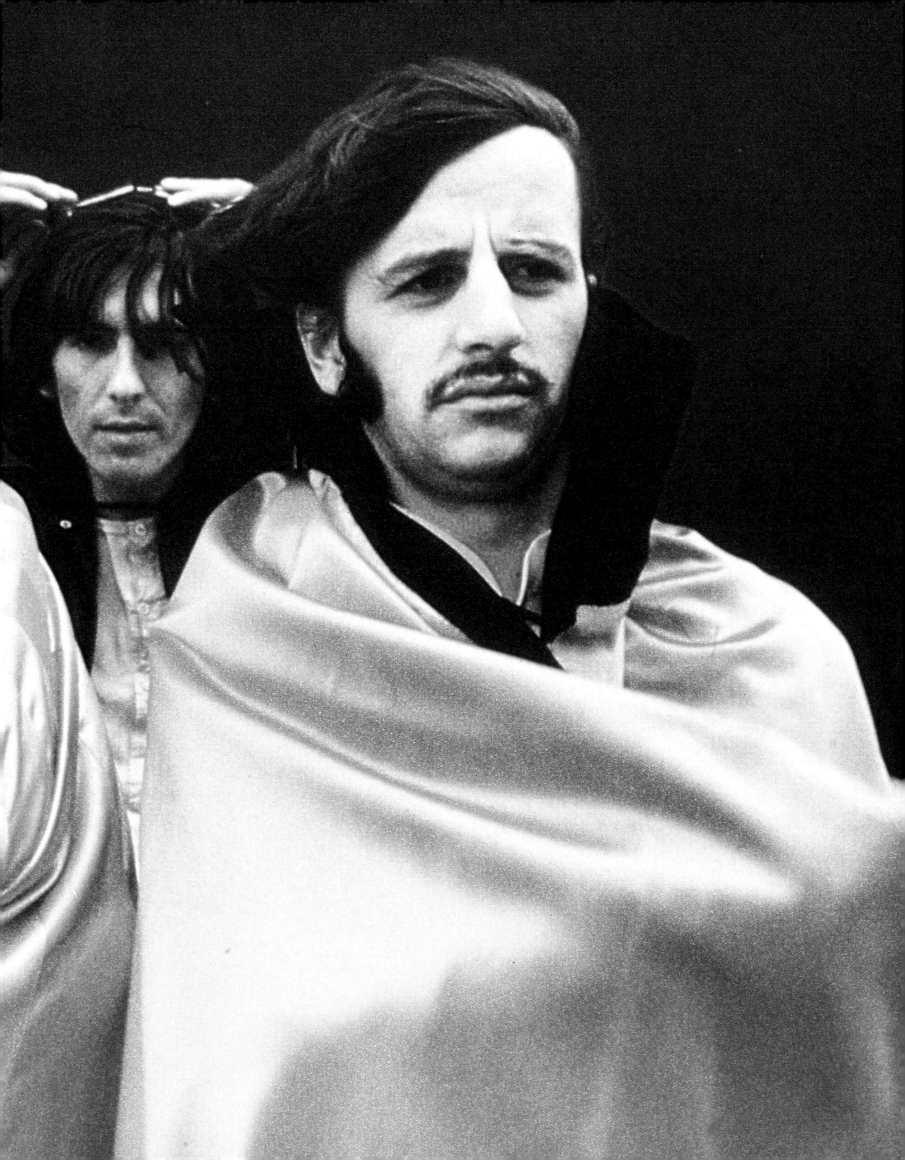

sessions. George's 'Not Guilty' reached take 101. It was not included on the final album.

August 9
– *Abbey Road.* The White Album sessions. More work on 'Not Guilty'.

After the session, Paul alone recorded 'Mother Nature's Son' which the other Beatles did not play on.

August 11
– Apple Records was officially launched with "National Apple Week". The press received a special pack, labelled "Our First Four", containing copies of 'Hey Jude' by The Beatles, 'Sour Milk Sea' by Jackie Lomax, 'Thingumybob' by The Black Dyke Mills Band and Mary Hopkin's 'Those Were The Days.' 'Hey Jude' became the biggest selling Beatles single ever, selling six million copies in four months, (ultimately eight million worldwide). In addition, Mary Hopkin's 'Those Were The Days' sold four million copies worldwide in four months, getting Apple Records off to a good start.

August 12
– *Abbey Road.* The White Album sessions: George's vocal on 'Not Guilty' was taped in the control booth, with the microphone plugged straight into the board.

– John and Yoko attended an Ossie Clark fashion show in Chelsea.

August 13
– *Abbey Road.* The White Album sessions. 'Sexy Sadie' was remade and John's 'Yer Blues' begun. The group crowded into a small tape room off the main studio to try and re-create the cramped Cavern feeling for 'Yer Blues' and were very pleased with the acoustics there. Worries about leakage proved unfounded.

Ringo quits ...

August 20: The bad feelings between the group reached crisis point and Ringo announced he was quitting. He left to consider his future. The actual incident that caused him to storm out was a fluffed tom-tom fill. Ringo flew to the Mediterranean to spend a fortnight on Peter Sellers' yacht. It was there, after refusing to eat the squid served to him, that Ringo wrote 'Octopus's Garden'. Work began on Paul's 'Back In The USSR' with Paul playing drums.

August 14
– *Abbey Road.* The White Album sessions. 'Yer Blues' was virtually finished, then, after Paul and Ringo left, John and George recorded 'What's The New Mary Jane', one of John's "experimental", Yoko-influenced numbers.

August 15
– *Abbey Road.* The White Album sessions. Paul's 'Rocky Racoon' recorded.

August 16
– *Abbey Road.* The White Album sessions. new version of George's 'While My Guitar Gently Weeps'.

August 17
– George and Patti flew to Greece for a short break.

August 20
– *Abbey Road.* The White Album sessions. 'Yer Blues' finished off.

Paul added the brass overdubs to 'Mother Nature's Son'. After this he recorded the short 'Wild Honey Pie' and 'Etcetera' (for use as a demo by Marianne Faithfull – she declined to record it). The tension in the studio between the members of the group was reported as being very bad at this point.

August 21
– *Abbey Road.* The White Album sessions. John added a new lead vocal to 'Sexy Sadie.'

– George and Patti returned to London from Greece.

August 22
– *Abbey Road.* The White Album sessions.

– Cynthia filed for divorce, citing John's adultery with Yoko as the reason. John did not contest the order.

August 23
– *Abbey Road.* The White Album sessions. 'Back In The USSR' was finished.

August 24
– John and Yoko appeared live, talking about art, happenings and peace, on David Frost's London Weekend Television programme *Frost On Saturday*, broadcast from Wembley.

– Ronan O'Rahilly, the former head of Radio Caroline (before the government closed the pirate ships down), joined Apple as a "business

Ringo returns

September 3: Ringo returned to the studio, having decided to remain in the group, to find his drum kit smothered in flowers. In fact he did not record that day; the time was spent "liberating" EMI's new eight-track machine which was still being "evaluated" by EMI technical experts. Ringo: "I felt tired and discouraged... took a week's holiday, and when I came back to work everything was all right again."

However, he added, "Paul is the greatest bass guitar player in the world. But he is also very determined; he goes on and on to see if he can get his own way. While that may be a virtue, it did mean that musical disagreements inevitably arose from time to time."

adviser". Derek Taylor's press release said "John admires him very much for what he did with Radio Caroline".

August 26

– The single **'Hey Jude'/'Revolution'** was released in the US as APPLE (CAPITOL) 2276.
– The single **'Thingumybob'/'Yellow Submarine'** by John Foster & Sons Ltd. Black Dyke Mills Band, written and produced by Paul McCartney, was released in the US as APPLE 1800.
– The single 'Those Were The Days'/'Turn! Turn! Turn! (To Everything There Is A Season)' by Mary Hopkin, and produced by Paul McCartney, was released in the US as APPLE 1801.
– The single 'Sour Milk Sea' by Jackie Lomax and written and produced by George Harrison was released in the US as APPLE 1802.

August 27

– While visiting his family, Paul went to a Liverpool v. Everton football match.

August 28

– *Trident Studios, Soho*. The White Album sessions. The Beatles, minus Ringo, began work on John's 'Dear Prudence'.

August 29

– *Trident Studios, Soho*. The White Album sessions. Overdubs were added to 'Dear Prudence'.

August 30

– *Trident Studios, Soho*. The White Album sessions. The completed 'Dear Prudence' was mixed.
– The single **'Hey Jude'/'Revolution'** was released in the UK as APPLE (PARLOPHONE) R 5722.
– The single 'Those Were The Days'/'Turn! Turn! Turn! (To Everything There Is A Season)' by Mary Hopkin and produced by Paul McCartney was released in the UK as APPLE 2.

– The single 'Sour Milk Sea' by Jackie Lomax and written and produced by George Harrison was released in the UK as APPLE 3.
– Neil Aspinall married Susan Ornstein at Chelsea Register Office. The Beatles gave them a house as a wedding present.

August 31

– *Private Eye* announced that John and Yoko's forthcoming album would have a full-frontal nude cover.

September 3

– *Abbey Road*. The White Album sessions.

September 4

– *Twickenham Film Studios*. Promotional films, directed by Michael Lindsay-Hogg, were made for both 'Hey Jude' and 'Revolution'. While at the film studios, David Frost taped an introduction to the clips to use on his *Frost On Sunday* programme, giving the viewers the illusion that The Beatles were playing live on his show and fooling the Musicians' Union into believing that no miming was involved. On the promotional films, an orchestra was present and The Beatles had their instruments, but it was only Paul's voice that was actually live.

September 5

– *Abbey Road*. The White Album sessions. More work done on George's 'While My Guitar Gently Weeps'.

September 6

– Thames Television filmed Paul and Mary Hopkin at the Apple Building, 3 Savile Row, for their new children's series, *Magpie*.
– *Abbey Road*. The White Album sessions. Eric Clapton added his famous solo to George's 'While My Guitar Gentle Weeps' with Ringo on percussion and Paul playing fuzz bass and doing vocal harmonies as George recorded his lead vocal.

– The single **'Thingumybob'/'Yellow Submarine'** by John Foster & Sons Ltd., The Black Dyke Mills Band, written by Lennon & McCartney and produced by Paul McCartney was released in the UK as APPLE 4.

September 8

– The film clip of 'Hey Jude' was given its premiere performance on London Weekend Television's *Frost On Sunday*.

September 9

– *Abbey Road*. The White Album sessions. A new version of Paul's 'Helter Skelter' recorded.

September 10

– *Abbey Road*. The White Album sessions. Overdubs added to 'Helter Skelter'.
– Thames Television's children's programme *Magpie*, showing Paul and Mary Hopkin with the show's presenter Pete Brady, was broadcast.

September 11

– *Abbey Road*. The White Album sessions. Work began on John's 'Glass Onion'.

September 12

– *Abbey Road*. The White Album sessions. More work on 'Glass Onion'.

September 13

– *Abbey Road*. The White Album sessions. Drums and piano for 'Glass Onion'.

September 16

– *Abbey Road*. The White Album sessions. Recording began on Paul's 'I Will' and overdubs were added to 'Glass Onion'.

September 17

– *Abbey Road*. The White Album sessions. Paul's 'I Will' was completed.

September 18

– *Abbey Road*. The White Album sessions. Paul arrived at the session early and had already blocked out 'Birthday' before the others arrived. By mid-evening most of it was finished. All of The Beatles, plus Yoko, Patti Harrison, acting producer Chris Thomas and others, walked round the corner to Paul's house to see *The Girl Can't Help It*, Jayne Mansfield's first film, featuring Little Richard, Fats Domino, The Platters, Gene Vincent and Eddie Cochran which was screened on BBC2 at 9:05 pm. Afterwards they returned to the studio and by 5 am they had finished and mixed the song.
– George was interviewed by Alan Smith for BBC Radio 1's *Scene And Heard* .

September 19

– *Abbey Road*. The White Album sessions. George's 'Piggies' was recorded, with producer Chris Thomas on harpsichord.

September 20

– *Abbey Road*. The White Album sessions. 'Piggies' was completed.

September 23

– *Abbey Road*. The White Album sessions. Work began on John's 'Happiness Is A Warm Gun'.

September 24
– *Abbey Road.* The White Album sessions. More work was done on the rhythm track for 'Happiness Is A Warm Gun'.

September 25
– *Abbey Road.* The White Album sessions. Recording of 'Happiness Is A Warm Gun' was completed.

September 26
– *Abbey Road.* The White Album sessions. 'Happiness Is A Warm Gun' was mixed and John spent most of the session making a sound effects tape for 'Glass Onion' which went unused.

September 28
– George's interview for *Scene And Heard* was broadcast by BBC Radio 1.

September 30
– Hunter Davies's authorised biography of The Beatles, *The Beatles*, was published in the UK by William Heinemann Limited.
– Throughout September Paul's father, James, was ill in hospital. Paul visited Liverpool frequently to see him.

October 1
– *Trident Studios, Soho.* The White Album sessions. Paul's 'Honey Pie' was virtually completed.

October 2
– *Trident Studios, Soho.* The White Album sessions. Paul added the lead vocal and guitar to 'Honey Pie'.

October 3
– *Trident Studios, Soho.* The White Album sessions. George's 'Savoy Truffle' was begun. It was inspired by the contents of a box of Mackintosh's Good News chocolates – Eric Clapton's favourite.

October 4
– *Trident Studios, Soho.* The White Album sessions: Paul and a 14-piece orchestra recorded 'Martha My Dear' and added the finishing touches to 'Honey Pie'.

October 5
– *Trident Studios, Soho.* The White Album sessions. George added the lead vocal, and Paul the bass and drums to 'Savoy Truffle'.

October 7
– *Abbey Road.* The White Album sessions. A long session, from 2:30 pm until 7 the next morning, was spent on the rhythm track for George's 'Long

Long Long'. John was not there.

October 8
– *Abbey Road.* The White Album sessions. Another long session, 4 pm until 8 am the following morning, during which John's 'I'm So Tired' and 'The Continuing Story Of Bungalow Bill' were both recorded and finished, and more work was done on George's 'Long Long Long'.

October 9
– *Abbey Road.* The White Album sessions. Final work was done on 'The Continuing Story of Bungalow Bill' and 'Long Long Long'. While this was going on, Paul quickly recorded 'Why Don't We Do It In The Road' in the next door studio.

October 10
– *Abbey Road.* The White Album sessions. 'Piggies' and 'Glass Onion' were completed, and Paul again slipped away, this time with Ringo, and the two of them completed 'Why Don't We Do It In The Road'.
– George Harrison formed a new music publishing company, Singsong Limited.

October 11
– *Abbey Road.* The White Album sessions. Six saxophones were added to 'Savoy Truffle'.
– The single 'I'm The Urban

Spaceman' by The Bonzo Dog Doo-Dah Band, produced by Paul McCartney as Apollo C. Vermouth, was released in the UK as LIBERTY LBF 15144.

October 12
– *Abbey Road.* The White Album sessions. The whole evening was spent mixing various tracks.
– Jane Asher told the *London Evening Standard*: "I know it sounds corny but we're still very close friends. We really are. We see each other and we love each other, but it hasn't worked out. That's all there is to it. Perhaps we'll be childhood sweethearts and meet and get married when we're about seventy."

October 13
– *Abbey Road.* The White Album sessions. John recorded and mixed his ballad, 'Julia', without the aid of the other Beatles.

October 14
– *Abbey Road.* The White Album sessions. Overdubs were added to 'Savoy Truffle' and the rest of the session was spent mixing the tracks for the now complete double album.
– No longer needed for the final mixing and sequencing of the album, Ringo went for a holiday in Sardinia with Maureen.

October 15
– *Abbey Road.* The White Album sessions. Mono and stereo mixing sessions.

October 16
– *Abbey Road.* The White Album sessions. Paul, John and George Martin held a 24 hour session, beginning at 5 pm and ending at 5 pm the following day, choosing the songs and working out the sequencing of the four sides of the double album. They were up against a tight deadline, and every studio and listening room at Abbey Road was used for this marathon task: studios one, two and three as well as listening rooms 41 and 42. In the end 30 songs were presented to the public as The Beatles (and, as usual, the two sides of their new single was not included).

George was not involved in the final selection and sequencing because he flew to Los Angeles that day to continue working with Jackie Lomax on his forthcoming Apple album.

October 18: John busted

The Drugs Squad raided John and Yoko who were living at 34 Montagu Square, London, on loan to them from Ringo. They found 219 grains of cannabis resin and took the couple to Paddington Green police station where they also charged them with obstructing the police in execution of a search warrant.

John: "So all of a sudden like, there was this knock on the door and a woman's voice outside and I look around and there is a policeman standing in the window wanting to be let in. We'd been in bed and our lower regions were uncovered like. Yoko ran into the bathroom to get dressed with her head poking out so they wouldn't think she was hiding anything. And then I said 'Ring the lawyer, quick', but she went and rang Apple, I'll never know why. So then they got us for obstruction which was ridiculous because we only wanted to get our clothes on."

"Why don't you do it yourself?
You don't need me.
I'm the wrong sort of artist for you."

October 19
– John and Yoko appeared at Marylebone Magistrates' Court. They were remanded on bail and their case was adjourned until November 28.

October 25
– The single 'Quelli Erand Giorni'/ 'Turn! Turn! Turn! (To Everything There Is A Season)' by Mary Hopkin and produced by Paul McCartney was released in Italy as Apple 2.
– John and Yoko announced that Yoko was pregnant and they were expecting a baby in February 1969.

October 28
– Cynthia Lennon's divorce petition was officially listed.

October 31
– Linda Eastman moved to London to live with Paul, bringing her daughter Heather with her and enrolling her in a local private school.
– Tony Palmer's BBC Television documentary on pop music, called *All My Loving*, was screened.

November
– George spent nearly seven weeks in Los Angeles recording six more tracks with Jackie Lomax for the album *Is This What You Want?* At Sound Recorders Studio, using the best of the Los Angeles session men including Hal Blaine on drums, Larry Knechtel on keyboards and Joe Osborn on bass.

November 1
– The album WONDERWALL MUSIC (Original Soundtrack Album) by George Harrison & Band/Indian Orchestra, written and produced by George Harrison, was released in the UK by Apple as SAPCOR 1.
SIDE ONE: 'Microbes', 'Red Lady', 'Medley', 'Tabla and Pakavaj', 'In The Park', 'Medley', 'Greasy Legs', 'Ski-ing and Gat Kirwani', 'Dream Scene';
SIDE TWO: 'Party Seacombe', 'Medley', 'Love Scene', 'Crying', 'Cowboy Museum', 'Fantasy Sequins', 'Glass Box', 'On The Bed', 'Wonderwall To Be Here', 'Singing Ohm'.

November 5
– Paul and Linda drove to Scotland for a long rest on his farm.

November 8
– Cynthia was granted decree nisi in the London Divorce Court because of John's admitted adultery with Yoko.

Cynthia Lennon arrives to begin divorce proceedings against John at the Royal Courts of Justice in the Strand.

She retained custody of her son, Julian.
– It was reported that George's five-year songwriting contract with *Northern Songs Limited* had expired in March and not been renewed.

November 11
– The album UNFINISHED MUSIC NO.1 – TWO VIRGINS by John Lennon and Yoko Ono and written and produced by John and Yoko was released in the US as APPLE T 5001.
SIDE ONE: 'Two Virgins No.1', 'Together', 'Two Virgins (numbers 2 to 6)'.
SIDE TWO: 'Two Virgins', 'Hushabye Hushabye', 'Two Virgins (numbers 7 to 10)'.
– The photograph of the two of them in the nude on the sleeve caused offence in some quarters, and EMI refused to distribute it. Track Records did the job instead. In the US, Capitol also refused to have anything to do with it, for fear that the Bible Belt would react with their customary prurience. A small label called Tetragrammaton, mostly known for spoken word records, took up the challenge but even they felt obliged to put the record into a brown paper sleeve, with a cut-away allowing John and Yoko's faces to peer through.

November 15
– While in Los Angeles, George made a short, unannounced appearance on the CBS TV show *The Smothers Brothers' Comedy Hour* before a live audience in Hollywood.

November 17
– George's appearance on *The Smothers Brothers' Comedy Hour* was broadcast on the CBS network in the US.

November 19
– Ringo, Maureen and their children moved from "Sunny Heights" in Weybridge to a new home, "Brookfields" near Elstead.

November 20
– Paul was interviewed at his home in Cavendish Avenue, St John's Wood, by Tony MacArthur for a two-hour Radio Luxembourg special, *The Beatles*.

November 21
– Yoko suffered a miscarriage of her baby at Queen Charlotte's Hospital, London, caused almost certainly by the stress of being arrested. John stayed at her side, sleeping overnight in a spare hospital bed. When the bed was needed for a patient, John slept on the floor.

November 22
– The album THE BEATLES (known as The White Album) was released in the UK as APPLE (PARLOPHONE) PMC 7067-7068 (mono) and PCS 70677068 (stereo).
SIDE ONE: 'Back In The USSR', 'Dear Prudence', 'Glass Onion', 'Ob-La-Di, Ob-La-Da', 'Wild Honey Pie', 'The Continuing Story Of Bungalow Bill', 'While My Guitar Gently Weeps', 'Happiness Is A Warm Gun';
SIDE TWO: 'Martha My Dear', 'I'm So Tired', 'Blackbird', 'Piggies', 'Rocky Racoon', 'Don't Pass Me By', 'Why Don't We Do It In The Road', 'I Will', 'Julia';
SIDE THREE: 'Birthday', 'Yer Blues', 'Mother Nature's Son', 'Everybody's Got Something To Hide Except Me And My Monkey', 'Sexy Sadie', 'Helter Skelter', 'Long Long Long';
SIDE FOUR: 'Revolution 1', 'Honey Pie', 'Savoy Truffle', 'Cry Baby Cry', 'Revolution 9', 'Good Night'.
– Robert Fraser proposed that, since Peter Blake had art directed Sgt Pepper, Richard Hamilton, another leading figure in British Pop Art, should do the next. He was asked to meet The Beatles at the Apple office in Savile Row, and after being kept waiting for an hour or more he was ushered in. By then Hamilton was having second thoughts about getting involved with the pop music business and asked Paul, He said that as Sgt Pepper was so over the top, he would be inclined to do a very prissy thing, almost like a limited edition, and went on to propose a plain white album. He also suggested that they number each copy, a joke numbered edition of something like five million copies. Paul thought this was an amusing idea and agreed.
Richard Hamilton: "Then I began to feel a bit guilty at putting their double album under plain wrappers; I suggested it could be jazzed up with a large edition print, an insert that would be even more glamorous than a normal sleeve.
"That's why the album ended up the way it did. Most

Bottom Right: John and Yoko working on their movie Rape with editor Tony Trow.

"Can I just ask a question? As this stuff is all mine, will it be me only who is involved"

people, among them Yoko, think it was Yoko's idea. I've no doubt that she would have been very supportive – from what I knew of her work and Fluxus background, the approach would have been right up her street. It was at the time when Yoko was really moving into the Beatle business and putting her oar in strongly. But my contact with the project was only through Paul – even EMI was held off."

– Paul: "Richard and I worked together on the collage for The Beatles' White Album. Richard and I sat down all week while he did the collage from childhood photos of us all. The thing that impressed me at the end of the week was that after he'd filled the whole board with pictures and got his composition right, his final move was to take pieces of white paper and place them strategically to give space through the whole thing so that it wasn't just crammed with pictures. It was beautiful and I remember being very impressed with the way he put this negative space on – it was the first time that I'd ever seen that idea."

November 24
– The group Grapefruit left Apple. Their manager, Terry Doran, told *The People*: "I like The Beatles as friends, but not bosses... there's too much driftwood at Apple."

November 25
– The album THE BEATLES (White Album) was released in the US as APPLE (CAPITOL) SWBO 101 (stereo only) with the same tracks as the UK release.

November 28
– John pleaded guilty to the charge of unauthorised possession of cannabis resin at Marylebone Magistrates' Court. In an effort to gain sympathy for the couple, John's solicitor told the court that after the raid, Yoko had lost her baby and that this had been a terrible blow to them. John was fined £150 and

ordered to pay cost 20 of guineas. He and Yoko were found not guilty on the charge of obstructing the police in execution of a search warrant. In court it was reported that while being questioned after the raid, in an effort to protect Yoko, whom he feared might be deported because she was not a British citizen, John asked, This drug conviction was to haunt John for years and was used by the Nixon administration to deny him a Green Card for residence in the US.

November 29
– The album UNFINISHED MUSIC NO.1 – TWO VIRGINS by John Lennon and Yoko Ono and written and produced by John and Yoko was released in the UK as APPLE SAPCOR 2 with the same tracks as the USA release.

November 30
– *New Musical Express* reported that 'Hey Jude' was approaching sales of six million worldwide.

December
– During December and January, John and Yoko made the film *Rape* for Australian television. A camera team hounded a young woman until she was near to tears. **John: "We are showing how all of us are exposed and under pressure in our contemporary world... what is happening to this girl on the screen is happening in Biafra, Vietnam, everywhere."**

December 2
– The album WONDERWALL MUSIC (Original Soundtrack Album) by George Harrison & Band/Indian Orchestra, written and produced by George Harrison, was released in the US as APPLE ST 3350 with the same tracks as the UK release.

December 4
– George circulated a memo to the staff of Apple warning them that he had invited a group of Californian Hell's Angels over to stay at 3 Savile Row: "Hell's Angels will be in London within the next week, on the way to straighten out Czechoslovakia. There will be 12 in number complete with black leather jackets and motor cycles. They will undoubtedly arrive at Apple and I have heard they may try to make full use of Apple's facilities. They may look as though they are going to do

you in but are very straight and do good things, so don't fear them or uptight them. Try to assist them without neglecting your Apple business and without letting them take control of Savile Row."

December 6
– The album James Taylor by James Taylor and featuring Paul McCartney on bass guitar (first track side two: 'Carolina On My Mind') was released in the UK as APPLE SAPCOR 3.

December 7
– The American correspondent for *Disc and Music Echo* reported that Paul had been going out with New York photographer Linda Eastman.

December 10
– "Kenwood", John and Cynthia's house in the St George's Hill Estate in Weybridge, was put up for sale.
– John and Yoko attended rehearsals at Wembley Studios for the next day's filming of The Rolling Stones' extravaganza: *Rock And Roll Circus*. John sang 'Yer Blues'.

December 11
– On the spur of the moment, Paul and Linda with Linda's daughter, Heather, flew to Praia da Luz in the Algarve, Portugal, to stay with Hunter Davies who had casually sent a postcard inviting them. They decided too late for a commercial flight, so Neil Aspinall hired a private jet. They arrived at Davies's rented villa at night and banged on the door, waking him up. They had no Portuguese currency so Davies had to pay the taxi.
– John and Yoko, with John's son, Julian, spent the day and most of the

night at Wembley Studios filming the all-star jam session: *The Rolling Stones' Rock And Roll Circus*. In the event, Jagger thought The Stones were outperformed by The Who and the project was shelved until 1997 when it was released on video. Around midnight John and Yoko drove back to central London to appear live on BBC Radio's *Night Ride* where they talked about their *Two Virgins* album and played a few minutes of the new The Beatles album.

December 12
– The arrival of a private jet at tiny, newly opened Faro Airport had attracted press attention and Paul had to conduct a press conference on the beach.

December 18
– The single 'I'm The Urban Spaceman' by The Bonzo Dog Doo-Dah Band (Paul as Apollo C. Vermouth) and produced by Paul McCartney was released in the US as IMPERIAL 66345.
– John and Yoko appeared onstage in a large white bag as part of a Christmas party happening at the *Royal Albert Hall.*

December 20
– The fan club flexi-disc, **The Beatles' 1968 Christmas Record**, was released.

December 23
– Apple's first Christmas party was held at 3 Savile Row, complete with Hell's Angels, and members of a visiting Californian hippie commune. John and Yoko, who had hardly been seen at Apple since it opened its new headquarters, dressed up as Father and Mother Christmas and handed out presents to all the children attending.

1969

January 2

– Filming *Get Back* at Twickenham Studios.

Under pressure from Paul to return to live performance, the other Beatles had reluctantly agreed to make an appearance before a live audience, which would be filmed and released as a one-hour television show. However, it proved impossible to agree upon a venue: The Roundhouse in Chalk Farm was booked and cancelled, the idea of a Roman amphitheatre in Tunisia, filmed at dawn, empty of people, and slowly filling up with all races and creeds for the concert, was given serious consideration before Ringo vetoed it on the grounds that he wouldn't like the food.

Since they all agreed on the idea of the television film, Apple Films producer Denis O'Dell proposed that they begin rehearsing and suggested that they film the rehearsals for inclusion in the proposed film.

He had Twickenham Film Studios booked from February 3 for use on Ringo's *Magic Christian* film, and he proposed they use the time until then to film on the sound stage in full 16mm. It was a disaster. They were still exhausted from the marathon The Beatles sessions. Paul bossed George around; George was moody and resentful. John would not even go to the bathroom without Yoko at his side and for her part Yoko made sure she was in every shot. The tension was palpable, and it was all being caught on film.

– They worked on 'Don't Let Me Down' and 'Everybody Had A Hard Year'.

January 3

– Filming *Get Back* at Twickenham Studios. The Beatles worked on George's 'All Things Must Pass' and their own oldie 'One After 909'.

– Police in New Jersey, US, impounded 30,000 copies of John and Yoko's Two Virgins album on the grounds that the cover was pornographic.

John: "We were both a bit embarrassed when we peeled off for the picture – so I took it myself with a delayed action shutter. The picture was to prove that we are not a couple of demented freaks, that we are not deformed in any way and that our minds are healthy. If we can make society accept these kind of things without offence, without sniggering then we shall be achieving our purpose. There has got to be law and order; but that doesn't mean we should suffer bad, out of date laws. If laws weren't changed they would still be jumping on queers and putting them away. So there is a case for us all to put society right – and that is basically why there is unrest all over the world; because revolution must come."

January 6

– Filming *Get Back* at Twickenham Studios. Some work done on 'Don't Let Me Down' and 'Two Of Us'. John, strung out on heroin, was mostly silent and withdrawn, leaving Yoko to do most of the talking.

January 7

– Filming *Get Back* at Twickenham Studios. Poor rehearsals of 'Maxwell's

Patti Harrison and Yoko.

Silver Hammer' and John's 'Across The Universe', during which John forgot his own words. In an argument between George and Paul, George suggested that The Beatles should break up.

January 8

– Filming *Get Back* at Twickenham Studios. The main feature of this day was an argument between John and George, with John putting down George's songwriting.

January 9

– Filming *Get Back* at Twickenham Studios. Jam session on 'Suzy Parker'.

January 10

– Filming *Get Back* at Twickenham Studios.

January 12

– The *Wonderwall* film opened at the Cinecenta cinema.

– The Beatles met at Ringo's house to try and iron out their difficulties but the feud between John and George remained intractable.

January 13

– Filming *Get Back* at Twickenham Studios. Paul and Ringo were the only Beatles to attend and spent the session discussing what to do about John's decision to let Yoko do all his talking for him. John made a brief appearance in the late afternoon, but no work was done.

George quits

George's feeling that Paul was treating him as an inferior, combined with the tension he felt at always having Yoko present, reached breaking point during the Get Back sessions on January 10. After a fierce argument with John, criticising him for contributing nothing to the sessions and showing no interest in the project, George walked off the set from the studio canteen telling the others he'd "see them round the clubs", and drove to Liverpool to see his parents. George therefore became the second Beatle to leave the group.

The Beatles finished their lunch. On return to the studio, Yoko took up position on George's blue cushion and finally got the remaining Beatles to back her on an extended "wailing" session.

Twickenham Studios: Let It Be would offer a depressing glimpse of The Beatles on the verge of meltdown.

to the group was to cancel plans for a live concert, and end the filming at Twickenham. The *Get Back* film project was switched to Apple's new basement recording studios at 3 Savile Row where John's guru, "Magic" Alex, had supposedly built them a 72-track recording facility. Unfortunately, Alex did not have the slightest idea how a recording studio actually worked and had not even provided a conduit connecting the studio with the control room so microphone leads and instruments could be connected to the desk. Confronted with an unusable studio, The Beatles called on George Martin to rescue them. He borrowed a pair of four-track machines from EMI, the leads were trailed in through the control room door, and The Beatles began work.

January 21
– Ringo was interviewed by David Wigg for the BBC Radio 1 programme *Scene And Heard*. In 1976 Wigg released all of his BBC interviews with The Beatles on a double album, *The Beatles Tapes*. Legal moves by The Beatles failed to prevent its release.

January 22
– *Get Back* sessions. With cameras and tapes rolling, The Beatles began work on the album and film which would have broken up any normal group. On the first day they ran through 'All I Want Is You' (later called 'Dig A Pony'), 'I've Got A Feeling', 'Don't Let Me Down', 'She Came In Through The Bathroom Window' and a few cover versions including The Drifters' 'Save The Last Dance For Me' and Canned Heat's 'Going Up The Country'.
– Billy Preston, a friend of The Beatles since Hamburg days, was visiting Apple and was recruited by George to play on The Beatles' sessions and in the film in order to help ease the tension between the four of them.

January 23
– *Get Back* sessions. Work on Paul's 'Get Back'.

January 24
– *Get Back* sessions. Work on Paul's 'On Our Way Home' (later called 'Two Of Us'), 'Teddy Boy', 'Maggie Mae', John's 'Dig It', 'Dig A Pony' and 'I've Got A feeling'.

– The album YELLOW SUBMARINE was released in the US as APPLE (CAPITOL) SW 385 (stereo only).
**SIDE A: 'Yellow Submarine', 'Only A Northern Song', 'All Together Now', 'Hey Bulldog', 'It's All Too Much', 'All You Need Is Love';
SIDE B: Seven soundtrack instrumental cuts by The George Martin Orchestra.**

January 14
– Filming *Get Back* at Twickenham Studios. John showed up but complained that he had been up all night on drugs and wasn't feeling well. They played 'Madman' and 'Watching Rainbows'.

January 15
– Filming *Get Back* at Twickenham Studios. George returned from Liverpool, and during a five-hour meeting, made up his difficulties with John. He told the others that he would leave the group unless the idea of

a live performance was dropped. He was prepared, however, to be filmed making an album, but for that he suggested they use their own state-of-the-art 72-track recording studio that "Magic" Alex was supposed to be building for them at Savile Row.

January 17
– The album YELLOW SUBMARINE was released in the UK as APPLE (PARLOPHONE) PMC 7070 (mono) and PCS 7070 (stereo) with the same tracks as the US release.

January 18
– In an off-the-record remark on the stairs at Apple, John told the editor of *Disc And Music Echo*, Ray Coleman, "Apple is losing money every week... if it carries on like this, all of us will be broke in the next six months." Coleman printed the quote, causing consternation among Apple's bankers and The Beatles' tax advisers.

January 20
– Part of George's terms for returning

Apple A&R chief Peter Asher listens in as George and John have a frank exchange of opinions.

Enter Allen Klein

On January 29 Allen Klein had a meeting with all four Beatles. Acting on the advice of John Eastman, Linda's brother, they had been about to buy NEMS for £1m, which EMI was prepared to lend them as an advance against royalties. (NEMS was entitled to take 25% of their record royalties for a further nine years even though Brian Epstein's management contract had expired, something that Epstein slipped into his renewal contract with EMI that The Beatles had not read or noticed.) Klein pointed out that royalties were subject to a high rate of tax, and they would have to earn £2 million to repay the debt. He said that until he had a chance to examine John's financial situation he wouldn't recommend buying NEMS. George and Ringo asked him to examine theirs too. Paul left the meeting.

January 25
– *Get Back* sessions. After jamming on the Everly Brothers' 'Bye Bye Love' they worked on Paul's 'Let It Be' and 'George's Blues' (later retitled 'For You Blue').
– David Wigg's interview with Ringo was broadcast by BBC Radio 1's *Scene And Heard*.

January 26
– *Get Back* sessions. Work on 'Dig It' was followed by a long rock'n'roll jam to loosen themselves up: 'Shake Rattle And Roll', 'Kansas City', 'Miss Ann', 'Lawdy Miss Clawdy', 'Blue Suede Shoes', 'You Really Got A Hold On Me' and 'Tracks Of My Tears'. Then they were ready to work on Paul's 'Long And Winding Road' and a song of George's which eventually appeared as 'Isn't It A Pity' on his All Things Must Pass triple album.
– With the filmed live concert cancelled, the director of the film side of the project, Michael Lindsay-Hogg, realised that he might have months of filming ahead of him, judging by how long it took The Beatles to record an album. At a meeting in the board room at Apple, he proposed that they give a live concert, but all they would have to do was walk up one flight of stairs to the roof of their own building. Even this met with resistance, with George reluctant and Ringo determined not to do it. This time John and Paul combined persuaded the others, albeit only minutes before the actual event.

January 27
– *Get Back* sessions. Work on 'Get Back', 'Oh! Darling', 'I've Got A Feeling' and a jammed version of Jimmy McCracklin's 'The Walk'. John's 'Sweet Loretta Fart she thought she was a cleaner...' parody of 'Get Back' was also recorded during this session.
– Lennon Books Limited changed its name to Lennon Productions Limited.

January 28
– *Get Back* sessions. The Beatles recorded both sides of their next single, 'Get Back' and 'Don't Let Me Down', as well as working on a remake of 'Love Me Do', 'The One After 909', 'Dig A Pony', 'I've Got A Feeling' and 'Teddy Boy'.
– Derek Taylor gave Allen Klein John's telephone number and John and Yoko met with Klein in the Harlequin suite of the Dorchester Hotel, London. They were very impressed with him, and John decided on the spot to make him his personal adviser. There and then he wrote to Sir Joseph Lockwood, the chairman of EMI: "Dear Sir Joe: From now on Allen Klein handles all my stuff."

January 29
– *Get Back* sessions. Work on versions of 'Teddy Boy', 'The One After 909', 'I Want You', Buddy Holly's 'Not Fade Away', 'Mailman, Bring Me No More Blues' as well as the old Hamburg and Cavern days standard 'Besame Mucho'.

January 31
– The last of filming the *Get Back* sessions. Several of Paul's songs ('The Long And Winding Road', 'Let It Be' and 'Two Of Us') were unsuitable for the rooftop concert because they featured a piano or acoustic guitar. These were filmed at this session. A version of 'Lady Madonna' was also recorded. With the project in the can, The Beatles now put it on the shelf, where it would stay for more than a year.
– EMI got their tape recorders back and workmen moved in to tear out "Magic" Alex's non-functioning studio.

Below: Allen Klein and Neil Aspinall.

February 2
– The divorce of Yoko and her husband Anthony Cox in the Virgin Islands was ratified and Yoko was granted custody of their child Kyoko even though Cox had essentially been the one who brought her up. Cox objected to the settlement terms which were obtained by the powerful lawyers that John's money provided, and continued to look after Kyoko. John and Yoko were both now free to remarry.

February 3
– Ringo began an intense filming schedule at Twickenham Film Studios, playing support to Peter Sellers in Joe McGrath's *The Magic Christian*, based on the book by Terry Southern (as *Candy* also was). Filming went on from Monday to Friday for 13 weeks and Ringo was at the studio most days.
– The Beatles, Allen Klein and John Eastman held a meeting. Allen Klein was appointed as The Beatles' business manager, charged with examining their finances and finding a way to stop NEMS from bleeding them of a quarter of their income.

February 4
– As a compromise to Paul, Eastman and Eastman, Linda's father and brother, were appointed as Apple's General Council, to keep an eye on Allen Klein's activities.

January 30: The rooftop concert

Mal and Neil set up the instruments, as of old, and The Beatles, with Billy Preston, took up position on the flat roof of their Savile Row headquarters. Traffic was brought to a halt as the lunchtime crowds gathered on the pavement below and all the windows and roofs nearby quickly filled with West End office workers, getting a privileged view of the last ever Beatles live concert. The police tried put a stop to it, but the combined Apple door security, and reluctance on the part of the police to actually pull the plug on such an extraordinary scene, meant that they played for 42 minutes. They began with a rehearsal of 'Get Back', 'Don't Let Me Down', 'I've Got A feeling', 'The One After 909', 'Dig A Pony' (for this, an assistant had to kneel in front of John holding the words on a clipboard), 'God Save The Queen', 'I've Got A Feeling' (again), 'Don't Let Me Down' (again) and 'Get Back' (again). This final version of 'Get Back' was interrupted by the police and Paul ad-libbed, "You've been playing on the roofs again and you know your momma doesn't like it, she's gonna have you arrested!" At the end of the song, Maureen Starkey burst into loud applause and cheers, causing Paul to return to the microphone and acknowledge her, "Thanks, Mo!"

John ended the set, and The Beatles' live career, with "I'd like to say 'thank you' on behalf of the group and ourselves and I hope we passed the audition."

February 5
– The album Goodbye by Cream (featuring George Harrison on 'Badge') was released in the US as ATCO SD 7001.

February 7
– George entered University College Hospital, London, to have his tonsils removed.

February 8
– In a press report of the news that Klein had joined Apple as a financial adviser, John was quoted as saying: **"We know him through Mick Jagger and we trust him - as much as we trust any businessman."** In fact Jagger had been lukewarm about the idea, having had very bad experiences with Klein himself. He sent Paul a personal note warning him against using Klein, but when summoned to the board room of Apple, and faced by all four Beatles, he caved in to Lennon's obvious enthusiasm for Klein and simply said, Klein was to get control of the copyrights of all of Mick Jagger and Keith Richards' early songs.

February 11
– *Abbey Road.* John and Yoko did a mixing session of some of their experimental tapes.

February 12
– Paul was made sole director of a new

"He's **all right,** if you **like** that kind of **thing.**"

Mary Hopkin is the centre of attention in the Apple Press office. Beatles PR guru Derek Taylor, whose wicker peacock chair was a gift from Herb Alpert, looks on.

off-the-shelf company, Adagrose Limited, which was later renamed McCartney Productions Limited.

February 13
– Mary Hopkin's first album, Postcard, produced by Paul, with a sleeve designed by Paul and photographed by Linda, was launched by Apple at a party held in the restaurant on the top of the Post Office Tower in Bloomsbury. Jimi Hendrix and Donovan were among the guests, and Paul and Linda stayed until the end to show support for their new act.

February 14
– John Eastman wrote to Clive Epstein, who was now running NEMS after his brother's death: "As you know, Mr Allen Klein is doing an audit of The Beatles affairs vis-à-vis NEMS and Nemperor Holdings Ltd. When this has been completed I suggest we meet to discuss the results of Mr Klein's audit as well as the propriety of the negotiations surrounding the nine-year agreement between EMI, The Beatles and NEMS."

February 15
– Clive Epstein replied to John Eastman: "Before any meeting takes place, please be good enough to let me know precisely what you mean by the phrase 'the propriety of the negotiations surrounding the nine-year agreement between EMI, The Beatles and NEMS'."
– George, his tonsils successfully removed, left University College Hospital.

February 17
– Leonard Richenberg of Triumph Investment Trust, a city merchant bank, acquired a 70 per cent stake in NEMS and Nemperor Holdings. The Beatles were horrified at the idea of merchant bankers collecting their income for them and wrote a letter to EMI, signed by all four Beatles, saying: "We hereby irrevocably instruct you to pay Henry Ansbacher & Co. all royalties payable by you directly or indirectly to Beatles and Co. or Apple Corps." (Henry Ansbacher & Co was their merchant banker and considered OK.) EMI didn't know what to do so they froze the money – £1.3m in royalties – and put it into the nearest branch of Lloyds Bank.
– The album James Taylor by James

Taylor (produced by Peter Asher and featuring Paul McCartney's bass playing on 'Carolina In My Mind') was released in the US as APPLE SKAO 3352.

February 19
– Ringo was served a writ to quit the premises by Bryman Estates, landlords of 34 Montagu Square, for breaking the terms of his lease by allowing John and Yoko to use drugs there.

February 20
– Ringo attended the world premiere of *Candy* at the Odeon Cinema, Kensington, London.

February 21
– The album Postcard by Mary Hopkin, produced by Paul McCartney, was released in the UK as APPLE SAPCOR 5.
– The single 'Rosetta' by The Fourmost, produced by Paul McCartney, was released as CBS 4041.

February 22
– *Trident Studios, Soho.* Further work done on John's 'I Want You' (with Billy Preston).

February 23
– *Trident Studios, Soho.* John mixed 'I Want You.'

February 24
– It was announced that The Triumph Investment group of companies had gained control of NEMS Enterprises.

February 25
– *Abbey Road.* George, working by himself, cut three demo tapes of his latest songs: 'Old Brown Shoe', 'Something' and 'All Things Must Pass'. The recordings were mixed and he was able to take home acetates after a good day's work.

February 28
– The album Goodbye by Cream (featuring George Harrison on 'Badge') was released in the UK as POLYDOR 583053.
– The eviction action against Ringo by Bryman Estates was settled out of court, allowing Ringo to sell his leasehold on 34 Montagu Square.

March
– Dick James and Charles Silver sold their shares in Northern Songs to Lew Grade's ATV, who then announced that they wanted to buy a controlling interest.

"I'm a **tidy** person.
I keep my **socks** in the **sock drawer**
and my **hash** in the hash box.
It's not **mine.**"

Left: Paul and Linda, exhausted after the events of March 12, with Heather, Linda's daughter from her earlier marriage to John See.
Below Right: George and Patti outside Esher and Walton Magistrates Court, March 18.

March 1
– Paul produced both sides of Mary Hopkin's new single, 'Goodbye' and 'Sparrow', at *Morgan Studios in Willesden.*
– Ringo began work on *The Magic Christian*, at Twickenham Film Studios.

March 2
– John and Yoko made an unscheduled appearance, together with John Tchikai and John Stevens, at an evening of avant-garde jazz and experimental music at Lady Mitchell Hall, Cambridge University.
– Paul did more work on Mary Hopkin's new single at Morgan Studios.

March 3
– The album Post Card by Mary Hopkin, produced by Paul McCartney, was released in the US as APPLE ST 3351 with the fourth track of side two ('Someone To Watch Over Me' on the UK release) replaced by her number one hit, 'Those Were The Days'.

March 4
– Princess Margaret met Ringo when she visited the set of *The Magic Christian* at Twickenham Film Studios to see her friend Peter Sellers. Paul and Linda were also there.
– George was interviewed by David

Wigg for the BBC Radio 1 programme *Scene And Heard*.

March 8
– Part of George's interview with David Wigg was broadcast on BBC Radio 1's *Scene And Heard*.

March 11
– Paul produced Jackie Lomax singing 'Thumbin' A Ride', a Lieber and Stoller Coasters B-side that he found in his record collection. Paul played drums, George played guitar and Billy Preston played keyboards.

March 12
– Paul and Linda were married at Marylebone Register Office, with his brother Michael and roadie Mal Evans as witnesses. Afterwards they went to St John's Wood Church where their marriage was blessed by the Rev. Noel Perry-Gore. There was a luncheon reception afterwards at the Ritz Hotel given by Rory McKeown. Princess Margaret and Lord Snowdon were there and Patti's sister Paula tried to hand Margaret a joint in full view of everyone.
   None of the other Beatles attended the wedding, though George and Patti went to the reception. They arrived very late because the notorious Sergeant Pilcher chose

Paul's wedding day to raid George's house for drugs, bringing a large piece of hashish with them (in case they didn't find anything) which they "found" on the floor. George commented, They were taken to Esher Police Station and formally charged with possession of cannabis resin. Pilcher was later found guilty in the police corruption trials of the early Seventies.
– After the reception Paul returned to the studio to continue work on 'Thumbin' A Ride'.
– *Abbey Road.* John and Yoko recorded 'Peace Song.'

March 13
– Ringo shot a grouse-hunting scene on Chobham Common, Surrey, for *The Magic Christian.*

March 16
– Paul and Linda with Heather, Linda's daughter by a previous marriage, flew to New York to spend three weeks with her family.
– John and Yoko flew to Paris, intending to get married. They booked into the Plaza Athenée but were unable to get married in France because they had not been in residence long enough.

March 17
– The single 'Badge' by Cream, written by George Harrison and Eric Clapton, was released in the US as ATCO 6668.
– The single 'Carolina In My Mind' by James Taylor, with Paul McCartney on bass, was released in the US as APPLE 1805.

March 18
– Ringo and Spike Milligan shot the traffic warden scene outside the Star and Garter, in Putney, for *The Magic Christian*.

March 20
– John and Yoko, still in Paris, had tried to get married on the cross-channel ferry but were refused permission to board The Dragon at Southampton because of "inconsistencies in their passports". Peter Brown at Apple found that they could get married on the British-governed island of Gibraltar. John, Yoko, Peter Brown and David Nutter flew to Gibraltar by private jet. They arrived at 8:30 am and were at the British Consulate when it opened at 9 am. There, registrar Cecil Wheeler married them with Peter Brown and David Nutter as their witnesses. They remained in Gibraltar for just 70 minutes before flying straight back to Paris and their luxury suite.
John: "We chose Gibraltar because it is quiet, British and friendly. We tried everywhere else first. I set out to get married on the car ferry and we would have arrived in France married, but they wouldn't do it. We were no more successful

John and Yoko are married in Gibralter under the watchful eye of Beatles assistant Peter Brown, March 20.
Opposite: Christ you know it ain't easy: The Amsterdam Hilton, March 29.

with cruise ships. We tried embassies, but three weeks' residence in Germany or two weeks' in France were required."
March 21
– Allen Klein was appointed business manager of Apple. His first task was to sort out the mess caused by Dick James selling his Northern Songs shares without first offering them to The Beatles. Klein told the *Daily Telegraph* that under a three year contract he would receive 20 per cent of all the money collected by Apple but no money from existing recording contracts. He would, however, receive 20 per cent of any increase he negotiated on those contracts. He began firing the staff.
– The album Is This What You Want? by Jackie Lomax, produced by George Harrison, was released in the UK as Apple SAPCOR 6.
March 24
– John and Yoko had lunch with Salvador Dali in Paris.
March 25
– John and Yoko flew to Amsterdam to begin a seven-day peace bed-in in room 902 of the Hilton Hotel.
March 28
– John was in bed for peace when he read in the newspaper that Dick James, the man they had made into a multi-millionaire, had sold his shares in Northern Songs to ATV without first offering them to The Beatles. John was furious: **"I won't sell. They are my shares and my songs and I want to keep a bit of the end product. I don't have to ring Paul. I know damn well he feels the same as I do."**
– The single 'Goodbye' (Lennon & McCartney)/'Sparrow' by Mary Hopkin, produced by Paul McCartney, was released in the UK as Apple 10.
March 31
– The last day of John and Yoko's seven-day bed-in. John and Yoko then flew to Vienna where they held a press conference from inside a white bag at the Hotel Sacher. It received worldwide coverage which a normal press conference would not, despite the fact

that no-one was sure it really was them. They were in Vienna for the world television premiere of *Rape*, which they produced.
– George and Patti were found guilty of possession of cannabis at Esher and Walton Magistrates' Court and were fined £250 each with ten guineas' costs each. **George: "I hope the police will leave us alone now."**
April
– John and Yoko sent out "Acorns For Peace": every world leader was sent an acorn and asked to plant it for peace. The idea was John and Yoko's but Apple had to do the work. It took the staff of the press office weeks to find enough acorns, as it was the wrong season, and they finished up digging holes in the London parks trying to find where the squirrels had hidden them. An offer of acorns at £1 each was turned down. Months later some of the boxes had still not been addressed and sent out, as promoting 'Get Back' and Mary Hopkin's new single took precedence.
April 1
– Ringo and Laurence Harvey filmed a Hamlet striptease scene at the Theatre Royal, in Stratford, East London, for *The Magic Christian*.
– John and Yoko returned to London and gave a press conference at Heathrow. Later they appeared live on Thames Television's *Today* programme where they attempted to explain "Bagism" to Eamonn Andrews.
– *The Daily Express* reported John as saying: "I am back to work, recording with The Beatles – I need the money... I'm scratching the deck, to my way of thinking. Right now, in cash, I have about £50,000."
April 2
– John and Paul, together with Allen Klein, visited The Beatles' merchant bankers, Henry Ansbacher and Company, to plot a strategy to try and get back Northern Songs for themselves. Their adviser was Mr Bruce Ormrod. It looked an evenly matched fight with ATV and The Beatles controlling about the same number of shares: ATV had acquired 1,604,750 shares from Silver and

John's bed-in

John: "Can you think of a better way to spend seven days? It's the best idea we've had." They were ridiculed by the world's media but by reporting the event at all, the press was passing on a message about the need for peace, so John and Yoko felt satisfied.

"I'm not going to be **fucked** around by men in **suits sitting** on their **fat arses** in the City."

James, and already held 137,000, giving them nearly 35 per cent of the company. The Beatles between them controlled 29.7 per cent: Paul had the most at 751,000, John had 644,000 and held another 50,000 on trust and Ringo had 40,000. George had sold his but Patti had 1,000. Apple controlled another 30,000 through Subafilms. John called it.

April 3
– John and Yoko appeared on *The Eamonn Andrews Show* live from the Café Royal in Regent Street, where they tried to get Andrews to climb into a white bag with them. Fellow guests Jack Benny and Yehudi Menuhin were not amused.

– George was interviewed by Sue McGregor for the lunchtime BBC Radio 1 programme *World At One* in which he discussed Ravi Shankar.

– The single 'Badge' by Cream, written by George Harrison and Eric Clapton, was released in the UK as POLYDOR 2058 285

April 5
– *The Financial Times* reported: "It appears that Dick James, managing director of Northern Songs, has failed to persuade Beatles John Lennon and Paul McCartney to accept the £9 million bid for Northern from ATV."

April 7
– The single 'Goodbye' (Lennon & McCartney)/'Sparrow' by Mary Hopkin, produced by Paul McCartney, was released in the US as APPLE 1806.

April 9
– Ringo filmed a boat race scene at Barclays Bank Rowing Club on the Thames Embankment for *The Magic Christian*.

April 10
– The Beatles rejected ATV's offer of £9 million for their shares in Northern Songs and announced that they were considering a counter bid (though where they would have obtained the £9.5 million required in real cash is hard to imagine). Lew Grade told *the Daily Telegraph*: "We have 35 per cent of the shares and will not let go of that for anything." The publicity caused market speculators to get in on the act and soon a powerful syndicate of holders of Northern Songs shares

"**Monopoly** with **real money**,"

John and Yoko with Eamonn Andrews on Thames Television's Today programme, April 1.

was formed known as The Consortium. Between them they had 14 per cent of the shares, enough to swing the outcome, and they met in secret to discuss their strategy.

April 11
– The single **'Get Back'/'Don't Let Me Down'** by The Beatles, with Billy Preston, was released in the UK as APPLE (PARLOPHONE) R 5777.

April 12
– John and Yoko had a meeting at Ansbachers in the City to work out the complicated financing necessary for The Beatles' counter bid for Northern Songs.

– The second part of George's interview with David Wigg was broadcast on BBC Radio 1's *Scene And Heard*.

April 14
– John and Yoko arrived at Paul's house in Cavendish Avenue so that

Paul could go over 'The Ballad Of John And Yoko' with John. Despite their business problems, the Lennon and McCartney songwriting partnership was always held in very high regard by both partners, and was a major source of income for both of them. Once the song was complete, they went over to nearby Abbey Road and recorded it, without the aid of the other Beatles (George was abroad and Ringo was filming). Paul played drums, bass, piano and percussion. John did lead vocals and lead guitar.

April 15
– More meetings at Ansbachers. At one point Mr Ormrod had persuaded a number of City institutions who owned Northern Songs shares to go in with The Beatles in a deal that would have given The Beatles control but, with the papers all drawn up and waiting for John, Paul, George and Ringo's signature, John announced. The City businessmen decided that they would be better off siding with ATV.

April 16
– *Abbey Road.* The group recorded George's 'Old Brown Shoe' and began work on his 'Something'.

April 18
– *Abbey Road.* George's 'Old Brown Shoe' completed and further work done on 'I Want You'.

– The Beatles, advised by Henry Ansbacher, surprised the City by saying they were bidding for control of Northern Songs only, which caused Northern's share price to drop. Lew Grade announced that he was not considering raising his bid.

April 19
– The press found out more details of The Beatles' offer and reported that it was being mounted by three Beatles companies: Apple Corps, Subafilms and John and Paul's Maclen (Music).

April 20
– There was a massive row at Ansbacher's because Paul, on Eastman's advice, refused to commit his shares in Northern Songs as part of the collateral required for the loan from Ansbacher's to finance The Beatles' bid. Their offer amounted to £2.1 million of which Ansbacher was lending them about £1.2 million

against collateral. John and Paul together could just about manage it, but Paul refused to put up his shares. John's shares in Northern Songs were worth about £1.1 million, Maclen Music was worth just over half a million and Subafilms – which owned rights to *A Hard Day's Night, Help!* and *Yellow Submarine* – was worth about £350,000. Allen Klein had to put in all his shares in MGM: 45,000 shares worth about £650,000. The Beatles were now in a position to finance their bid.

– *Abbey Road.* Work done on 'I Want You' and 'Oh! Darling!'.

April 21
– John and Yoko formed Bag Productions Limited.
– In the City, the Consortium declared its hand and staged a blocking operation.

April 22
– In a short formal ceremony on the roof of the Apple building at 3 Savile Row, John changed his middle name from Winston to Ono by deed poll before Commissioner of Oaths Bueno de Mesquita. **John: "Yoko changed her name for me, I've changed mine for her. One for both, both for each other. She has a ring, I have a ring. It gives us nine 'O's between us, which is good luck. Ten would not be good luck."** Unfortunately for John, he technically became John Winston Ono Lennon (ten 'O's) as one can never fully revoke a name given at birth.
– *Abbey Road.* John and Yoko taped the heartbeats used on The Wedding Album.

April 24
– Paul denied a rumour started by an American DJ that he was dead: he told *Life* reporters.
– In a deal hammered out between Klein and Richenberg, NEMS surrendered its claim to 25 per cent of The Beatles royalties for the next nine years. Instead Triumph received £750,000 cash, 25 per cent of the royalties already frozen by EMI (over £300,000). Triumph received £50,000 for the 23 per cent that NEMS held in The Beatles' film company Subafilms and received 5 per cent of the gross record royalties from 1972 until 1976.

This had been a sticking point but in the end Richenberg was satisfied because he knew that Klein would next turn his attention on EMI and obtain a substantial royalty rate increase. The Beatles also received an option on the 4.5 per cent of Northern Songs shares owned by NEMS, useful in the forthcoming battle for Northern Songs, and received 266,000 shares in Triumph (valued at £420,00) in exchange for The Beatles' 10 per cent share in NEMS. Everyone was satisfied with the outcome.

– On this same day, The Beatles offered 42s 6d per share for the 20 per cent of Northern Songs shares they needed to gain control. This would have cost them £2,100,000. They also said they would extend their contracts with Northern Songs for a further two years and would add other valuable assets to the company if they gained control. They added that they "would not be happy to continue, let alone renew, their existing contracts with Northern under the aegis of ATV".

– BBC1's *Top Of The Pops* showed a clip of The Beatles singing 'Get Back' on the roof of the Apple building.

April 25
– John and Yoko attended a showing of their film *Rape* at the Montreux Television Festival in Switzerland.

April 26
– *Abbey Road.* Paul added a lead vocal to 'Oh! Darling!' and work began on Ringo's 'Octopus's Garden'.
– Dr Richard Asher, Jane Asher's father, was found dead in his Wimpole Street home.

April 27
– *Abbey Road.* John and Yoko made another recording of their heartbeats for use on The Wedding Album.

April 29
– *Abbey Road.* Ringo added his lead vocal to 'Octopus's Garden'.

April 30
– *Abbey Road.* New guitar added to 'Let It Be' and the rest of the session spent adding vocals and overdubs to 'You Know My Name (Look Up The Number)'.
– The Beatles paid for quarter-page ads in four national newspapers, promising to extend their songwriting services

Paul with Neil Aspinall.

"I'm as fit as a fiddle"

and saying they would not interfere in Northern Songs' management.

May 1
– *Abbey Road.* A mixing session for 'Oh! Darling!' and John and Yoko's heartbeat track 'John And Yoko'.

May 2
– *Abbey Road.* The Beatles worked on George's 'Something'.
– John and Yoko were interviewed earlier by Michael Wale at BBC's Lime Grove Studios for the BBC1 television arts programme *How Late It Is*, discussing their film *Rape*. It was broadcast that evening.
– ATV claimed that they had support from shareholders holding 45 per cent of the Northern Songs shares and extended their offer until May 15.

May 4
– John and Yoko bought a new home, a Georgian mansion in 72 acres of land called "Tittenhurst Park" in Sunninghill in Berkshire, once owned by the tycoon Peter Cadbury. It cost £145,000.
– John and Yoko, Paul and Linda, joined Ringo and Maureen at Les Ambassadeurs club in London for a party hosted by Ringo and Peter Sellers to celebrate the completion of the UK filming of *The Magic Christian*. Other guests included Richard Harris, Sean Connery, Stanley Baker, Spike Milligan, George Peppard, Roger Moore and Christopher Lee.

May 5
– *Olympic Sound Studios, Barnes, London.* New bass and guitar added to 'Something.'
– The single **'Get Back'/'Don't Let Me Down'** by The Beatles with Billy Preston was released in the US as APPLE (CAPITOL) 2490.

May 6
– *Olympic Sound Studios, Barnes, London.* Work began on 'You Never Give Me Your Money', Paul's response to the financial problems at Apple.

May 7
– *Olympic Studios:* The session was spent mixing and listening to playbacks.

May 8
– John and Yoko were interviewed by David Wigg for the BBC Radio 1 programme *Scene and Heard.*
– As part of Klein's draconian restructuring of Apple, he sacked Alistair Taylor, the general manager of Apple who had previously been Brian Epstein's personal assistant and who witnessed The Beatles first contract with Epstein. Taylor:
"It was a hell of a blow."
– John, George and Ringo signed a management contract with Allen Klein, in effect making him their manager. Paul held out.

May 9
– *Olympic Sound Studios, Barnes, London.* The Beatles had a very stormy meeting in which Paul continued to hold out against the other three who wanted Allen Klein to manage them for a 20 per cent cut of their earnings. Paul thought 15 per cent would be sufficient. When Paul refused to sign the relevant documents until he had consulted his lawyer, the others stormed out of the studio, cancelling the planned recording session.
– Allen Klein's ABKCO Industries (Allen and Betty Klein Corporation) was duly appointed business manager of The Beatles' companies but Paul all along refused to sign the contract and remained opposed to Klein's involvement in Apple or The Beatles, preferring his own in-laws, The Eastmans.
– Paul stayed behind in the studio and after a long talk with Steve Miller, recorded 'My Dark Hour' with him,

on which Paul played drums, bass and did backing vocals. He was credited on the record as "Paul Ramon".
– BBC1's *Top Of The Pops* showed a clip of The Beatles singing 'Get Back' on the roof of the Apple building.

May 9
– Zapple, Apple Records' new experimental and avant-garde label, was launched with the release of two experimental Beatles solo albums.
– The album UNFINISHED MUSIC NO.2: LIFE WITH THE LIONS by John Lennon and Yoko Ono, written and produced by John and Yoko, was released in the UK as ZAPPLE 01.
  SIDE ONE: **'Cambridge 1969 ('Song For John', 'Cambridge', 'Lets Go On Flying', 'Snow Is Falling All The Time', 'Mummy's Only Looking For Her Hand In The Snow')';**
  SIDE TWO: **'No Bed For Beatle John', 'Baby's Heartbeat', 'Two Minutes Silence', 'Radio Play'.**
– The album ELECTRONIC SOUND, performed and produced by George Harrison was released in the UK as ZAPPLE 02.
  SIDE ONE: **'Under The Mersey Wall';**
  SIDE TWO: **'No Time Or Space'.**
– The single 'I Fall Inside Your Eyes' by Jackie Lomax, produced by George Harrison, was released in the UK as APPLE 11. (Side A, produced by Jackie Lomax and Mal Evans, featured Ringo on drums).

May 11
– John and Yoko's interview with David Wigg was transmitted by BBC Radio 1's *Scene And Heard* programme.

May 15
– Paul was interviewed by Roy Corlett for BBC Radio Merseyside's *Light And Local* programme at his father's house, "Rembrandt", in Heswell, Cheshire.
– BBC1's *Top Of The Pops* showed a clip of The Beatles singing 'Get Back' on the roof of the Apple building.

May 16
– Ringo and Maureen, Peter Sellers and his wife, director Joe McGrath and producer Denis O'Dell and their wives were given a free trip to New York on the newly launched Queen Elizabeth II by Commonwealth United, the backers of *The Magic Christian*, as a reward for bringing in the film on time and under budget.
– John and Yoko intended to travel with them but were prevented by the US immigration authorities, who refused to grant John a visitor's visa because of his November 28 1968 drug conviction.
– Paul and Linda flew to Corfu for a holiday.
– BBC Radio Merseyside's *Light And Local* programme transmitted their interview with Paul.

May 18
– The second part of John and Yoko's interview with David Wigg was broadcast by BBC Radio 1's *Scene And Heard* programme.

Paul: "It is **not possible** to be **nice** about giving someone the **sack.**"

("We're a **big** act. He'll **take 15 per cent**")

Below: L to R Peter Asher, John and Ron Kass at Apple.

May 19

– The album Is This What You Want? by Jackie Lomax and produced by George Harrison (except for the third track, 'New Day', with Ringo on drums, which was produced by Jackie Lomax and Mal Evans and replaced the third track, 'How Can You Say Goodbye', on the UK version) was released in the US as APPLE ST 3354. All the tracks except the third were the same as the UK release.

May 20

– John and George had a meeting at Ansbacher's.

May 22

– Ringo, Maureen, Peter Sellers and company arrived in New York then flew to the Bahamas for a two-week holiday to celebrate the end of filming.

– Hey Jude won the 1968 Ivor Novello award for top selling British song.

– BBC1's *Top Of The Pops* showed a clip of The Beatles singing 'Get Back' on the roof of the Apple building.

May 23

– It was announced that Dick James would continue as MD of Northern Songs and Charles Silver would remain chairman of the board. The Beatles were invited to nominate a board member but declined.

May 24

– John and Yoko flew from London to the Bahamas to hold another bed-in for peace at the Sheraton Oceanus Hotel. His choice of the Bahamas was not because Ringo was there, or the pleasant weather, but because it was just off the coast of the US and therefore the American press would be able to cover the event.

May 25

– John and Yoko found that the Bahamas were further from the US than they thought, and that 86 degrees Fahrenheit was not the ideal temperature in which to spend a week in bed. They flew instead to Toronto. They were held at the airport for two and a half hours by the immigration authorities but were eventually allowed to enter the country where they spent the night in a Toronto motel.

May 26

– The album UNFINISHED MUSIC NO.2: LIFE WITH THE LIONS performed, written and produced by John Lennon and Yoko Ono, was released in the US as ZAPPLE ST 3357 with the same tracks as the UK release.

– The album ELECTRONIC SOUND, performed and produced by George Harrison was released in the US as ZAPPLE ST 3358 with the same tracks as the UK release.

– John and Yoko flew from Toronto to Montreal where they began an eight-day bed-in for peace in room 1742 of the Queen Elizabeth Hotel, handily located for the New York press corps.

May 30

– The single **'The Ballad Of John And Yoko'/'Old Brown Shoe'** was released in the UK as APPLE (PARLOPHONE) R 5786.

June

– Apple head of A & R, Peter Asher, resigned. He told the press:

June 1

– John and Yoko's bed-in continued. John, Yoko and a roomful of visitors, including Allen Ginsberg, Phil Spector

"When I joined Apple the idea was that it would be **different** from the other companies in the record business.

Its policy was to **help** people and be **generous.** It didn't mean actually I had a tremendous amount of freedom; I was always in danger of one Beatle saying: **'Yes, that's a great idea, go ahead,'** and then another coming in and saying he didn't know anything about it. But it did mean that it was a nice company to work for. **Now that's all changed.** There's a new concentrative policy from what I can see and it's **lost** a great deal of its **original feeling.**"

and Timothy Leary, recorded the peace anthem 'Give Peace A Chance'.

– George and Patti flew to Sardinia for a holiday.

June 2

– The single 'A New Day'/'Thumbin' A Ride' by Jackie Lomax with Ringo on drums on side A, and side B, produced by Paul McCartney, was released in the US as APPLE 1807.

– The last day of John and Yoko's bed-in ended in the afternoon when John and Yoko went to Ottawa for a university conference on peace. In the evening they flew back to London

June 4

– The single **'The Ballad Of John And Yoko'/'Old Brown Shoe'** was released in the US as APPLE (CAPITOL) 2531.

June 14

– John and Yoko recorded an appearance for the US edition of *The David Frost Show* recorded with a studio audience at *InterTel Studios*, Wembley.

June 16

The single 'My Dark Hour' by The Steve Miller Band with Paul McCartney (as Paul Ramon) on bass guitar, drums and backing vocals, was released in the US as CAPITOL 2520.

June 17

– Paul and Linda returned from their holiday in Corfu.

June 23

– George and Patti returned from their holiday in Sardinia.

Losing Northern Songs

On May 19 Lew Grade's ATV gained control of Northern Songs Limited after a long and bitter battle. John had become disillusioned by the terms of the deal worked out by Ormrod and the Consortium in which the new board would have three representatives from each side with David Platz as the MD. John said he didn't see why The Beatles should bother to take over a company and then be told that they couldn't do what they liked with it. He said that he would rather let Grade have it than be dictated to like this. The company would not have been theirs to play with, of course, since all they were buying was control, and other shareholders were nervous that Klein might finish up running it. The Consortium sided with ATV who got the majority they needed a mere 15 minutes before The Beatles' offer expired. ATV now controlled virtually all of John and Paul's songs, and all future songs until 1973. The Beatles finished up owing Ansbacher's £5,000 for their services.

– Ringo shot a scene near the National Film Theatre on the South Bank in which paper money was thrown into a huge tank full of slaughterhouse offal and manure.

June 27
– Ringo and Maureen flew to the south of France for a holiday.
– The single 'That's The Way God Planned It'/'What About You?' by Billy Preston and produced by George Harrison was released in the UK as APPLE 12.

June 29
– John, Yoko, Kyoko and John's son Julian began a motoring holiday in Scotland.

July 1
– *Abbey Road*. Abbey Road sessions. Paul added a new lead vocal to 'You Never Give Me Your Money'.
– John and Yoko were involved in a car crash in Golspie, in the north of Scotland, when John let the car go out of control. They were taken to the Lawson Memorial Hospital where John had 17 stitches in a facial wound, Yoko 14 stitches and Kyoko four. John's son Julian was suffering from shock and they were all detained in hospital.

July 2
– *Abbey Road*. Abbey Road sessions. Paul recorded the 'Her Majesty' fragment which was to end Abbey Road. When George and Ringo arrived they all worked on 'Golden Slumbers'/'Carry That Weight'.
– Cynthia Lennon arrived in Scotland to tell John what she thought of him and to take Julian back to London.

July 3
– *Abbey Road*. Abbey Road sessions. More work done on 'Golden Slumbers' /'Carry That Weight'.
– With John and Yoko still in hospital, Ringo and Maureen substitute for them at the launch party for The Plastic Ono Band's 'Give Peace A Chance' single at the Chelsea Town Hall, London.

July 4
– *Abbey Road*. Abbey Road sessions. More work on 'Golden Slumbers' /'Carry That Weight.'
– The single **'Give Peace A Chance'** (Lennon & McCartney)/**'Remember**

Love' (Yoko Ono) by The Plastic Ono Band and produced by John and Yoko was released in the UK as APPLE 13.

July 6
– John and Yoko chartered a helicopter to transfer them to a private jet for the flight back to London. The helicopter left from the lawn of the Lawson Memorial Hospital with the staff waving goodbye. Their smashed car was crushed into a cube and exhibited on the lawn of Tittenhurst Park.

July 7
– *Abbey Road*. Abbey Road sessions. The three Beatles, John at home recovering from his car crash, worked on 'Here Comes The Sun'.
– The single 'That's The Way God Planned It'/'How About You?' by Billy Preston and produced by George Harrison was released in the US as APPLE 1808.
– The single **'Give Peace A Chance'** (Lennon & McCartney)/**'Remember Love'** (Ono) was released in the US as APPLE 1809.

July 8
– *Abbey Road*. Abbey Road sessions. More work on 'Here Comes The Sun'.

July 9
– *Abbey Road*. Abbey Road sessions. John arrived back in the studio and worked on Paul's 'Maxwell's Silver Hammer'. Yoko, more seriously injured than John, accompanied him as usual. A double bed was delivered to the studio by Harrods and Yoko lay in it, a microphone suspended above her mouth in case she wanted to add her thoughts.

July 10
– *Abbey Road*. Abbey Road sessions. Overdubs added to 'Maxwell's Silver Hammer'.

July 11
– *Abbey Road*. Abbey Road sessions. More overdubs added to 'Maxwell's Silver Hammer' (Ringo played anvil), and work done on 'Something' and 'You Never Give Me Your Money'.

July 15
– *Abbey Road*. Abbey Road sessions. The vocals and chimes were overdubbed and added to 'You Never Give Me Your Money'.

July 16
– *Abbey Road*. Abbey Road sessions.

John and Yoko at Heathrow Airport, July 6.

More work on 'Here Comes The Sun' and 'Something'.

July 17
– *Abbey Road*. Abbey Road sessions. Paul added his lead vocal to 'Oh! Darling!' followed by all The Beatles working on Ringo's 'Octopus's Garden.'

July 18
– *Abbey Road*. Abbey Road sessions. Paul had another try at the lead vocal to 'Oh! Darling!' followed by Ringo's vocal on 'Octopus's Garden.'
– The single 'My Dark Hour' by The Steve Miller Band, with Paul McCartney as Paul Ramon, was released in the UK as CAPITOL CL 15604.

In the dying days of The Beatles' collective career, Paul often preferred to drum on his tracks.

– The EP Wall's Ice Cream with 'Little Yellow Pills' by Jackie Lomax, produced by George Harrison, and 'Happiness Runs (Pebble And The Man)' by Mary Hopkin, produced by Paul McCartney, was released in the UK as APPLE CT I, as an Apple special business promotion.

July 21
– *Abbey Road.* Abbey Road sessions, Work began on John's 'Come Together'.

July 22
– *Abbey Road.* Abbey Road sessions. Paul had another try at the vocal on 'Oh! Darling!' then the group worked on John's 'Come Together'.

July 23
– *Abbey Road.* Abbey Road sessions. Rehearsals and recording of 'The End'.

July 24
– *Abbey Road.* Abbey Road sessions. First Paul cut a demo of 'Come And Get It' for Apple band, the Iveys, soon to change their name to Badfinger. Then The Beatles recorded 'Sun King'/'Mean Mister Mustard'.

July 25
– *Abbey Road.* Abbey Road sessions. More work on 'Sun King'/'Mean Mister Mustard' and 'Sun King'. Then they began work on John's 'Polythene Pam' and Paul's 'She Came In Through The

Bathroom Window', recording them as one continuous number.

July 28
– *Abbey Road.* Abbey Road sessions. More work on 'Polythene Pam'/'She Came In Through The Bathroom Window'.

July 29
– *Abbey Road.* Abbey Road sessions. Guitar was added to 'Come Together' and work done on 'Sun King'/'Mean Mister Mustard'.

July 30
– *Abbey Road.* Abbey Road sessions. An overdub day working on 'Come Together', 'Polythene Pam'/'She Came In Through The Bathroom Window', 'You Never Give Me Your Money' and 'Golden Slumbers'/'Carry That Weight'. After this they worked on a trial order for the medley, and Paul rejected 'Her Majesty' from the set, asking the tape operator John Kurlander to edit it out and throw it away. EMI threw away nothing so he attached it to the end of the master tape on a long piece of leader tape. When an acetate was cut, the long gap, followed by 'Her Majesty' remained and Paul liked it that way, so it stayed.

July 31
– *Abbey Road.* Abbey Road sessions.

'You Never Give Me Your Money' was completed and overdubs added to 'Golden Slumbers'/'Carry That Weight'.

August 1
– *Abbey Road.* Abbey Road sessions. Work began on John's ballad 'Because'.

August 4
– *Abbey Road.* Abbey Road sessions. The three part harmonies on 'Because' were recorded.

August 5
– *Abbey Road.* Abbey Road sessions. Paul put the loop tapes for the crossfade from 'You Never Give Me Your Money' to 'Sun King' onto four-track. 'Because' was completed by George playing the Moog synthesiser and vocals were added to 'The End'.

August 6
– *Abbey Road.* Abbey Road sessions. George added guitar to 'Here Comes The Sun' and Paul added synthesiser to 'Maxwell's Silver Hammer'.

August 7
– *Abbey Road.* Abbey Road sessions. Work on 'The End'. First vocals were added then a guitar track with Paul, George and John trading solos.

August 8
– *Abbey Road.* Abbey Road sessions: After lunch, in the studio, new drums and bass were added to 'The End', work was done on 'I Want You' and Paul added lead guitar to 'Oh! Darling!'.

August 11
– *Abbey Road.* Abbey Road sessions. Further work on 'I Want You', to which 'She's So Heavy' was added. More work was done on 'Oh! Darling!' and 'Here Comes The Sun'.
– John and Yoko moved into their new mansion at Tittenhurst Park, Ascot.

August 12
– *Abbey Road.* Abbey Road sessions. Mixing session.

August 13
– *Abbey Road.* Abbey Road sessions. Mixing session.

The Abbey Road sleeve

On August 8 at 11:35 am, with a policeman holding up the traffic, photographer Iain Macmillan climbed up a stepladder in the middle of Abbey Road and shot the now famous photograph of The Beatles walking across the zebra crossing near the recording studio. It was a hot day so Paul was not wearing shoes. The cover had been Paul's idea – he drew a sketch of how he wanted the photograph to look – and when the transparencies were developed, he was the one who chose which shot to use.

August 14
– *Abbey Road.* Abbey Road sessions.
Editing work done on the medley.
John was interviewed at the studio
by Kenny Everett for his BBC Radio 1
show *Everett Is Here.*

August 15
– *Abbey Road.* Abbey Road sessions.
Orchestral overdubs were added to
'Golden Slumbers'/'Carry That
Weight', 'The End', 'Something'
and 'Here Comes The Sun'.

August 18
– *Abbey Road.* Abbey Road sessions.
Paul added piano to 'The End'.

August 19
– *Abbey Road.* Abbey Road sessions.

*The Beatles at their
last ever photo shoot
at Tittenhurst Park.*

'Here Comes The Sun' and 'Something'
were completed.

August 20
– *Abbey Road.* Abbey Road sessions.
John's 'I Want You (She's So Heavy)'
was completed, with its abrupt ending,
made by literally cutting the tape.
After this The Beatles listened to the
tracks in the proposed running order
for the album. This was the last time
that all four Beatles were together
in Abbey Road.

August 21
– *Abbey Road.* Abbey Road sessions.
A mixing and editing session.
– Apple Corps' first annual general
meeting was held at 3 Savile Row with

all four Beatles in attendance.
– Adagrose Ltd. changed its name
to McCartney Productions Limited.

August 22
– The Beatles posed together for
a photo session in the grounds of
Tittenhurst Park. It was the last
ever Beatles photo shoot.
– The single 'Hare Krishna Mantra'
/'Prayer To The Spiritual Masters'
by Radha Krishna Temple, produced
by George Harrison, was released in
the US as APPLE 1810.
– The album That's The Way God
Planned It by Billy Preston and
produced by George Harrison was
released in the UK as Apple SAPCOR 9.

August 25
– *Abbey Road.* Abbey Road sessions. Final editing on tracks for the medley.

August 27
– As part of the deal struck on April 24, The Beatles sold Triumph their shares in NEMS Enterprises Limited.

August 28
– Paul and Linda's daughter Mary was born at Avenue Clinic, London.
– George and several bus loads of journalists attended the Apple press release of the Radha Krishna Temple's first recording 'Hare Krishna Mantra', in the gardens of a large country house in Sydenham, south London. Indian food was served but no alcohol.

August 29
– The single 'Hare Krishna Mantra'/'Prayer To The Spiritual Masters' by Radha Krishna Temple and produced by George Harrison was released in the UK as Apple 15.
– The album Songs For A Tailor by Jack Bruce and featuring George Harrison (as L'Angelo Misterioso) on track one, 'Never Tell Your Mother She's Out Of Time', was released in the UK as POLYDOR 583-058.

August 31
– George and Patti, Ringo and Maureen, John and Yoko all travelled to the Isle of Wight for the next day's Dylan concert.

September 1
– All The Beatles, except Paul, saw

Dylan headline at the Isle of Wight outdoor festival. Dylan returned to Tittenhurst Park with John and Yoko but refused to join in a recording session.

September 5
– John and George resigned as directors of Hayling Supermarkets Limited.

September 8
– Ringo was taken to the Middlesex Hospital, central London, suffering from an intestinal complaint and kept in for observation.

September 10
– The album That's The Way God Planned It by Billy Preston and produced by George Harrison was released in the US as APPLE ST 3359 with the same tracks as the UK release.
– *The Institute of Contemporary Arts* held an evening of John and Yoko's avant-garde films. John and Yoko sent a couple to sit in a white bag on stage beneath the screen throughout the screening, thought by many people to be the Lennons themselves.

September 12
– Rock promoter John Brower telephoned John and Yoko to invite them to attend the Toronto Rock'n'Roll Revival concert the next day to hear Little Richard, Chuck Berry and Jerry Lee Lewis, offering eight first-class tickets for them and six friends. John immediately agreed provided he and

Plastic Ono Band Live in Toronto

On September 13, John woke up and wanted to back out of the Toronto concert but Clapton said he was keen to play. John just made the plane and during the flight he made a half-hearted attempt to rehearse a few songs with The Plastic Ono Band, as he dubbed them. Meanwhile the Canadian radio stations were going wild and there were several hundred fans waiting at the airport, reminiscent of the old days.

They hastily rehearsed a few songs and before going on stage at the Varsity Stadium of Toronto University, John was so nervous he threw up. The Plastic Ono Band stuck to classics: 'Blue Suede Shoes', 'Money', 'Dizzy Miss Lizzy', 'Yer Blues', 'Cold Turkey' and 'Give Peace A Chance'.

John: "The ridiculous thing was that I didn't know any of the lyrics. When we did 'Money' and 'Dizzy' I just made up the words as I went along. The band was bashing it out like hell behind me. Yoko came up on stage with us, but she wasn't going to do her bit until we'd done our five songs. Then after 'Money' there was a stop, and I turned to Eric and said 'What's next?' He just shrugged, so I screamed 'C'mon!' and started into something else. We did 'Yer Blues' because I've done that with Eric before. It blew our minds. Meanwhile Yoko had whipped offstage to get some lyrics out of her white bag. Then we went into 'Give Peace A Chance' which was just unbelievable. I was making up the words as we went along. I didn't have a clue."

his band could play live. The astonished promoter accepted at once and, since John had no band – The Beatles had not played live in three years – he had to form one quick. He quickly summoned together Eric Clapton, Klaus Voormann and session drummer Alan White. Mal Evans was informed that he was handling the gear. Brower dealt with visas and immigration, still unable to believe that he had attracted a Beatle to his festival.

September 16
– Maclen (Music) Limited instigated legal proceedings against Northern Songs Limited requesting a re-audit of royalty statements from February 11 1965 onwards. This was an area that Klein specialised in, and nearly always came up trumps.

September 19
– The single 'Que Sera Sera'/'Fields Of St Etienne' by Mary Hopkin and produced by Paul McCartney was released in France as APPLE 16.
– Paul was interviewed by David Wigg for the BBC Radio 1 *Scene And Heard* programme.
– BBC2's *Late Night Line-Up* previewed the entire Abbey Road album.
– Lew Grade's ATV bought sufficient shares in Northern Songs from the Consortium to give it just under 50 per cent. The Beatles had lost control of their publishing but Klein and Grade got on extremely well and got together to work out a new deal to bring The Beatles back into the Northern Songs stable. ATV would buy all their

Ringo, Linda, Paul, Yoko and John: an uneasy truce at Apple.

Below: John and Yoko with their symbolic doves.

Everett Is Here broadcast the first part of its interview with John.

September 21
– The first part of David Wigg's interview with Paul for the BBC Radio 1 *Scene And Heard* programme was broadcast.
– The single 'Badge' by Cream and written by George Harrison and Eric Clapton was reissued in the UK (POLYDOR 2058-285).

September 25
– *Abbey Road.* John and Yoko supervised stereo mixes of their Toronto concert for release: 'Blue Suede Shoes', 'Money (That's What I Want)', 'Dizzy Miss Lizzy', |'Yer Blues', 'Cold Turkey', 'Give Peace A Chance', 'Don't Worry Kyoko (Mummy's Only Looking For Her Hand In The Snow)' and 'John, John (Let's Hope For Peace)'.
– John and Yoko attended a lunch time press reception at Apple Studios for the launch of Trash's new single 'Golden Slumbers', a Lennon & McCartney song taken from Abbey Road.
  Afterwards John and Yoko, with The Plastic Ono Band (John on guitar and vocals, Yoko on whatever, Eric Clapton on guitar, Klaus Voormann on bass and Ringo on drums) returned to Abbey Road where they recorded 'Cold Turkey'.

September 26
– The album ABBEY ROAD was released in the UK as APPLE (PARLOPHONE) PCS 7088 (stereo only).
  SIDE A: 'Come Together', 'Something', 'Maxwell's Silver Hammer', 'Oh! Darling', 'Octopus's Garden', 'I Want You (She's So Heavy)';
  SIDE B: 'Here Comes The Sun', 'Because', 'You Never Give Me Your Money', 'Sun King'/'Mean Mr. Mustard', 'Polythene Pam'/'She Came In Through The Bathroom Window', 'Golden Slumbers'/'Carry That Weight', 'The End', 'Her Majesty'.
– Radio Luxembourg broadcast an interview with Ringo by Kid Jensen, talking about Abbey Road.

September 27
– Kenny Everett's BBC Radio 1 show *Everett Is Here* broadcast the second part of its interview with John.

Northern Songs shares in exchange for stock and cash – so they would have stock in ATV, which controlled their songs. They would resign as songwriters until 1976. Maclen would be sold back to John and Paul and Apple would get the lucrative sub-publishing rights for the US. It was a very good deal but because The Eastmans would have nothing to do with Klein, it too fell through.

September 20
– Allen Klein negotiated a tough new contract for The Beatles with EMI/Capitol giving them an increased royalty rate. Though their contract was not due to expire until 1976, the group had virtually fulfilled the minimum provision of five long-playing records and five singles and so Klein was in a strong bargaining position. Their previous deal with Capitol was already very good: 17.5 per cent of

wholesale in the US, but Klein managed to get them 25 per cent. Paul gave credit where it was due and signed the contract along with Ringo and John. George was in Cheshire visiting his sick mother but he returned a few days later and added his.
  At the meeting John and Yoko made Klein the business manager of their company, Bag Productions.
– Kenny Everett's BBC Radio 1 show

John quits

John used the September 20 meeting to finally tell the other Beatles that he was leaving the group:
  John: "I said to Paul, 'I'm leaving.' I knew on the flight over to Toronto or before we went to Toronto: I told Allen I was leaving, I told Eric Clapton and Klaus that I was leaving then, but that I would probably like to use them as a group. I hadn't decided how to do it – to have a permanent new group or what – then later on, I thought fuck, I'm not going

to get stuck with another set of people, whoever they are.
  "I announced it to myself and the people around me on the way to Toronto a few days before. And on the plane – Klein came with me – I told Allen, 'It's all over.' When I got back, there were a few meetings, and Allen said well, cool it, cool it, there was a lot to do, business-wise you know, and it would not have been suitable at the time.
  "Then we were discussing something in the office with

Paul, and Paul said something or other about The Beatles doing something, and I kept saying 'No, no, no,' to everything he said. So it came to a point where I had to say something, of course, and Paul said 'What do you mean?'
  "I said, 'I mean the group is over, I'm leaving.' Allen was saying don't tell. He didn't want me to tell Paul even. So I said 'It's out.' I couldn't stop it, it came out. Paul and Allen both said that they were glad that I wasn't going to announce it, that I wasn't going to make an event

out of it. I don't know whether Paul said don't tell anybody, but he was darned pleased that I wasn't going to. He said 'Oh, that means nothing's really happened if you're not going to say anything.'
  "So that's what happened. So, like anybody when you say divorce, their face goes all sorts of colours. It's like he knew really that this was the final thing; and six months later he comes out with whatever. I was a fool not to do it, not to do what Paul did, which was use it to sell a record."

– An interview with John by Kid Jensen was broadcast on Radio Luxembourg.

September 28
– *Trident Studios, Soho.* The Plastic Ono Band, with the same line-up as on September 25, re-cut 'Cold Turkey'.
– The second part of David Wigg's interview with Paul for the BBC Radio 1 *Scene And Heard* programme was broadcast.

September 29
– *Abbey Road.* John supervised the mixing of 'Cold Turkey'.

October 1
– The album ABBEY ROAD was released in the US as APPLE (CAPITOL) SO 383 (stereo only), with the same tracks as the UK release.

October 3
– *Lansdowne Studios, London.* A studio version of Yoko's 'Don't Worry Kyoko (Mummy's Only Looking For Her Hand In The Snow)' was recorded by The Plastic Ono Band as the B-side of 'Cold Turkey'.

October 5
– *Abbey Road.* Overdubs put on The Plastic Ono Band's 'Cold Turkey'.

October 6
– The single **'Something'/'Come Together'** was released in the US as APPLE (CAPITOL) 2654.
– The album Songs For A Tailor by Jack Bruce, featuring George Harrison as L'Angelo Misterioso on 'Never Tell Your Mother She's Out Of Time', was released in the US as ATCO SD-306.

October 8
– George recorded an interview with David Wigg at Apple for the BBC Radio 1 programme *Scene And Heard.*

October 9
– Yoko was taken to King's College Hospital, London, for emergency blood transfusions when it seemed she might loose another baby. John stayed at her bedside throughout. She and John had not long gone through a cold turkey withdrawal from heroin addiction.

October 12
– After four days in hospital, with John still at her side, Yoko miscarried her expected baby.
– The first part of David Wigg's interview with George for the BBC Radio 1 programme *Scene And Heard* was broadcast.

Paul at the Apple offices.

October 13
– Paul and Linda, Ringo and Maureen attended the opening night of Mary Hopkin's cabaret season at the Savoy Hotel, London.

October 15
– Ringo and Maureen flew from London to Los Angeles.

October 17
– The single 'Everything's All Right' by Billy Preston and produced by George Harrison was released in the UK as APPLE 19.

October 19
– The second part of David Wigg's interview with George for the BBC Radio 1 programme *Scene And Heard* was broadcast.

October 20
– *Abbey Road.* John and Yoko did a new mix of the tapes of the Toronto Plastic Ono Band concert.
– The single **'Cold Turkey'** (Lennon)/**'Mummy's Only Looking For A Hand In The Snow'** (Ono) by The Plastic Ono Band and produced by John and Yoko was released in the US as APPLE 1813.
– The album WEDDING ALBUM by John Ono Lennon and Yoko Ono Lennon, written and produced by John and Yoko, was released in the US as APPLE SMAX 3361.
　SIDE ONE: **John And Yoko;**
　SIDE TWO: **Amsterdam.**
– George attended a Ravi Shankar concert at the Royal Albert Hall.

October 21
– John was interviewed by David Wigg for the BBC Radio 1 programme *Scene And Heard.*

October 22
– Paul and Linda went to Paul's farm in Scotland.
– Ringo and Maureen returned home to London from LA.

October 24
– Paul was interviewed on his Scottish farm by BBC journalist Chris Drake who had travelled to Scotland, determined to put an end to the absurd "Paul is dead" rumours coming from the States.
– The single 'Everything's All Right' by Billy Preston and produced by George Harrison was released in the US as APPLE 1814.

– The single **'Cold Turkey'** (Lennon)/ **'Mummy's Only Looking For A Hand In The Snow'** (Ono) by The Plastic Ono Band and produced by John and Yoko was released in the UK as APPLE 1001.

October 26
– John's interview with David Wigg for the BBC Radio 1 programme *Scene And Heard* was broadcast.
– Part of Chris Drake's interview with Paul was broadcast on BBC Radio 4's *The World This Weekend.*

October 27
– *Abbey Road.* Ringo began work on Sentimental Journey which, discounting soundtracks and experimental work, made him the first Beatle to produce a solo album. Ringo and a 17-piece orchestra recorded 'Night And Day'.
– Part of Chris Drake's interview with Paul was broadcast on BBC Radio 4's *The World At One.*
– Another extract from Chris Drake's interview with Paul was broadcast on BBC Radio 2's *Late Night Extra.*
– Contractors began work installing a recording studio at Tittenhurst Park for John and Yoko.

October 31
– The single **'Something'/'Come Together'** was released in the UK as APPLE (PARLOPHONE) R 5814.
– George was reported to have recorded with Eric Clapton, Ric Grech and Denny Laine at *Olympic Sound Studios, Barnes, London.*

November
– Journalist and documentary film-maker Tony Palmer was commissioned by John and Yoko to write their authorised biography but given only six days to do it. He knocked out 75,000 words and met the deadline, only to be told that they had changed their mind and no longer wanted the book.
– Early in the month, John and Yoko took a Mediterranean cruise with "Magic" Alex, intending to free themselves completely from heroin use – the probable cause of Yoko's miscarriages.

November 3
– *The ICA* screened another evening of John and Yoko's experimental films.

November 6
– *Abbey Road.* Ringo's Sentimental

"Your **Majesty**,
I am **returning** my MBE as a **protest**
against Britain's involvement in the Nigeria – Biafra thing,
against our support of **America** in **Vietnam**
and against 'Cold Turkey'
slipping down the charts.
With Love,
John Lennon"

*John, about to go on stage
at London's Lyceum
Ballroom, December 15.*

Journey sessions. <u>Ringo</u> recorded
Lena Horne's 'Stormy Weather' with an
18-piece orchestra. It was not included
on the final album.

November 7
– *Abbey Road.* <u>Ringo</u>'s Sentimental
Journey sessions. Orchestral tracks
were recorded for 'Stardust'. (<u>Paul</u> was
credited on the sleeve for the
arrangement.)
– The album WEDDING ALBUM
by <u>John Ono Lennon</u> and Yoko Ono
Lennon, written and produced by <u>John</u>

and Yoko, was released in the UK as
APPLE SAPCOR 11 with the same tracks
as the US release.

November 10
– A third programme of <u>John</u> and Yoko's
short films was presented at the *ICA.*

November 13
– Back in 1966, <u>John</u> bought Dorinish,
an uninhabited island off the coast of
county Mayo, Ireland, which he only
visited once, on a week-long acid trip.
Now he offered free use of it to hippies
wishing to establish a commune.

November 14
– *Abbey Road.* <u>Ringo</u>'s Sentimental
Journey sessions. <u>Ringo</u> added his vocal
to 'Stardust' and began work on
'Dream'.

November 15
– *Melody Maker* journalist Richard
Williams mistakenly reviewed all four
sides of the advance pressing he had
been sent of <u>John</u> and Yoko's latest
experimental offering, The Wedding
Album. In fact it was a double album
and the other two sides consisted of
studio EQ test tones. Richard found the
infinitesimal variances in pitch of sides
two and four interesting.

November 25
– <u>John</u> returned his MBE to the Queen.
It was delivered by his chauffeur in the
morning. He attached the following
note:
– <u>John</u> was interviewed by David Bellan
from BBC Radio 4.

November 26
– *Abbey Road.* <u>John</u> and Yoko
supervised the remix of 'What's The
New Mary Jane' and 'You Know My
Name (Look Up The Number)' for
release as a Plastic Ono Band single
because it seemed that The Beatles
were not going to release them.
– <u>John</u>'s interview with David Bellan
was broadcast on BBC Radio Four's
Today programme.

November 28
– *Abbey Road.* <u>Ringo</u>'s Sentimental
Journey sessions. <u>Ringo</u> recorded 'Blue
Turning Grey Over You'.
– Apple announced the December 5
release of 'You Know My Name (Look
Up The Number)' by The Plastic Ono
Band. It was quickly withdrawn,
possibly because it was one of <u>Paul</u>'s
favourite Beatles tracks and he wanted
it out under their name. It finally
appeared as the B-side of 'Let It Be' in
March 1970.

December 1
– <u>Ringo</u> was filmed in various London
locations talking with Tony Bilbow for a
full-length BBC2 documentary on him
for an edition of *Late Night Line-Up* to
be broadcast on the day of the world
premiére of Ringo's new film, *The
Magic Christian.*
– <u>John</u> and Yoko, moved by the
persecution of gypsies, offered to buy

a 32-foot caravan for use as a school for gypsy children at an unofficial site in Caddington, Bedfordshire.

– The 77th and last issue of *The Beatles Book* monthly magazine was published. (It was revived in May 1976 and passed issue 250 in 1997.)

– George and Patti, Ringo and Maureen went to the first night of the Delaney & Bonnie & Friends tour which opened at the Royal Albert Hall, London. George enjoyed the show so much that he decided to join the tour and played two sets each night with them, standing unobtrusively at the back of the stage.

December 2

– John was interviewed by anthropologist Desmond Morris, best known for his BBC Children's Television programme *Zoo Time*, for a programme called *Man Of The Decade*. ATV had asked Alistair Cooke, Mary McCarthy and Morris to choose the Man of the Decade. Cooke chose JFK, McCarthy chose Ho Chi Minh and Morris went for John. The 20-minute section devoted to John also used archive footage, chosen by John.

– The same day, BBC1 began filming John and Yoko – including him being filmed by ATV – for their own *The World of John and Yoko* documentary for the 24 Hours series, presented by David Dimbleby.

– George joined Delaney & Bonnie & Friends on stage at the *Colston Hall, Bristol.*

December 3

– Tim Rice and Andrew Lloyd Webber asked John if he would play the role of Christ in the new musical they had written called *Jesus Christ, Superstar.*

– BBC1 filmed John and Yoko for *The World of John and Yoko.*

– John was interviewed by American journalist Gloria Emerson. They argued furiously when she questioned his sincerity. BBC Radio 2 broadcast the result two weeks later.

– George joined Delaney & Bonnie & Friends on stage at the *Town Hall, Birmingham.*

December 4

– *Abbey Road.* Ringo's Sentimental Journey sessions. Ringo and a 17-piece orchestra completed 'Blue Turning Grey Over You'.

– *Abbey Road.* John and Yoko, Mal Evans, Eddie Klein, Anthony Fawcett, Geoff Emerick and many others recorded two experimental tapes. The first was a track on which everyone laughed uproariously and shouted out things which was later given a percussion and chanting backing track. In the second all the participants approached the microphone and whispered a message. John and Yoko announced that this would be the fourth in the series Two Virgins, Life With The Lions and The Wedding Album but it was never released. BBC1 filmed the entire thing for *The World of John and Yoko.*

– George joined Delaney & Bonnie & Friends on stage at *City Hall, Sheffield.*

December 5

– BBC1 filmed John and Yoko for *The World of John and Yoko* in the snow-covered Suffolk countryside. John and Yoko, and the BBC 24 Hours film crew spent the night at The Bull in Long Melford, Suffolk.

– George joined Delaney & Bonnie & Friends on the stage at the *City Hall, Newcastle Upon Tyne.*

– The single 'Come And Get It' by Badfinger, written and produced by Paul McCartney, was released in the US as APPLE 1815.

December 6

– The final day of filming for *The World of John and Yoko.*

– The three stars of *The Magic Christian* – Ringo, Peter Sellers and Spike Milligan – appeared together on *Frost On Saturday* to plug the film. The programme was taped earlier that day at the London Weekend Television studios in Wembley.

– The BBC1 crew finished their filming for *The World of John and Yoko* with some footage of John and Yoko in their hotel room at The Bull in Long Melford.

– George joined Delaney & Bonnie & Friends on stage at the *Empire Theatre, Liverpool.*

December 7

– John and Yoko appeared on BBC1's religious programme *The Question Why*, in a debate chaired by Malcolm Muggeridge. It was broadcast live

from the BBC's Lime Grove Studios.

– George joined Delaney & Bonnie & Friends on the stage at the Fairfield Hall, Croydon, for the final night of their tour. Both sets were recorded and released in May 1970 as the live album Delaney & Bonnie On Tour With Eric Clapton.

December 8

– *Abbey Road.* A new vocal track for Ringo's 'Octopus's Garden' was recorded so that he could mime it on George Martin's *With A Little Help From My Friends* television show without the Musicians' Union knowing.

December 9

– John and Yoko announced through Apple that they intended to make a film about James Hanratty who was hanged for murder. It was described as a gesture of support for Hanratty's parents' campaign to prove their son's innocence. Apple said that the Lennons' film would reveal new evidence to prove his innocence.

John: "We spent many hours with the parents. They convinced us that there was a miscarriage of justice without a shadow of a doubt."
(The film, called *Hanratty*, financed by John and Yoko, was shown only once, in London.)

December 10

– Ringo and Maureen, accompanied by John and Yoko, attended the royal

Above: James Hanratty; Below John and Yoko with Hanratty's father.

world premiére of *The Magic Christian* at the Odeon Cinema, Kensington, London. John and Yoko startled the queues outside by slowly marching past them carrying a banner proclaiming "Britain Murdered Hanratty".

– BBC 2's arts programme, *Late Night Line-Up* – this edition just called *Line-Up* – broadcast their full-length documentary on Ringo.

– George appeared with Delaney & Bonnie & Friends for all three nights of their residence at *the Falkoner Theatre, Copenhagen, Denmark.*

December 11

– George appeared with Delaney & Bonnie & Friends for their second night at *the Falkoner Theatre, Copenhagen, Denmark.*

December 12

– George appeared with Delaney & Bonnie & Friends for the final night at *the Falkoner Theatre, Copenhagen, Denmark.*

– The album THE PLASTIC ONO BAND – LIVE PEACE IN TORONTO by The Plastic Ono Band, produced by John and Yoko, was released in the UK as APPLE CORE 2001.

SIDE ONE: **'Introduction Of The Band', 'Blue Suede Shoes', 'Money (That's What I Want)', 'Dizzy Miss Lizzy', 'Yer Blues', 'Cold Turkey', 'Give Peace A Chance'**

SIDE TWO: **Don't Worry Kyoko (Mummy's Only Looking For Her Hand In The Snow), 'John, John (Let's Hope For Peace)'.**

– The album THE PLASTIC ONO BAND – LIVE PEACE IN TORONTO by The Plastic Ono Band was released in the US as APPLE SW 3362 with the same tracks as the UK release.

– The album NO ONE'S GONNA CHANGE OUR WORLD by various artists with the first track 'Across The Universe' by The Beatles was released in the UK as EMI STAR LINE SRS 5013.

December 14

– Ringo taped his contribution to George Martin's *With A Little Help From My Friends* spectacular, alongside The Hollies, Dudley Moore, Lulu, Spike Milligan and the 40-piece George Martin Orchestra at the Talk Of The Town near Leicester Square.

– A white bag, labelled "A Silent Protest For James Hanratty" containing two wriggling occupants – possibly John and Yoko but more likely not – was delivered to Speakers' Corner in Hyde Park, London where Hanratty's father called for a public enquiry into his son's murder conviction. Later that day a petition was handed in at 10 Downing Street.

December 15

– Ringo taped a two-minute appeal on behalf of the British Wireless for the Blind Fund, to be broadcast by the BBC on Christmas Day.

– John and Yoko's Plastic Ono Supergroup played at the Peace For Christmas concert at *the Lyceum Ballroom, Covent Garden, London,* in aid of UNICEF. George Harrison was among the musicians in the hastily assembled group: the first time he and John had appeared together in concert since August 1966. The other members of the line-up were Eric Clapton, Delaney and Bonnie, Alan White, Bobby Keys, Keith Moon, Klaus Voormann, Jim Gordon and Billy Preston. They performed extended versions of 'Cold Turkey' and 'Don't Worry Kyoko (Mummy's Only Looking For Her Hand In The Snow)'. The entire show was recorded and part of their set was released on John and Yoko's 1972 double album Sometime in New York City.

– The BBC 24 Hours documentary *The World of John and Yoko* was transmitted.

December 16

– Huge posters and billboards were erected in 11 cities across the world proclaiming "War Is Over! If You Want It. Happy Christmas from John and Yoko." In some countries the message was translated into the native language.

– John and Yoko flew to Toronto, Canada, for their third visit this year. They stayed on Ronnie Hawkins' ranch, where they telephoned radio stations all over the world, giving them a peace message to broadcast. Hawkins got stuck with the phone bill.

December 17

– In Toronto, John and Yoko announced plans for a three-day Peace Festival, to be held there from July 3 – 5 1970.

December 19

– The fan club album, **The Beatles Seventh Christmas Record**, was released.

December 20

– CBS TV (Columbia Broadcasting Corporation) filmed a conversation between John and Marshall McLuhan, author of *The Medium Is The Message*, at his office in the University of Toronto.

– John was interviewed live on the CBC (Canadian Broadcasting

George on stage with Delaney and Bonnie, Copenhagen, December 11.

Corporation) programme Weekend by Lloyd Robertson.

December 22

– At a press conference at the Château Champlain Hotel in Montreal, John said: **"We think this was a positive decade, not a depressing one. This is just the beginning. What we've got to do is keep hope alive, because without it we'll sink."**

December 23

– John and Yoko had a 51-minute meeting with the Canadian Prime Minister, Pierre Trudeau, in Ottawa. Afterwards John said: **"If all politicians were like Trudeau there would be world peace."**

December 24

– John and Yoko arrived back in England where they headed for Rochester Cathedral, Kent, to join a sit-in and fast calling for peace and to spotlight world poverty.

December 25

– BBC1's *Top Of The Pops '69* showed a clip of The Beatles singing 'Get Back' on the roof of the Apple building, the first time it had been televised in Britain in colour.

– Ringo appeared in a BBC Radio 1 charity appeal on behalf of the British Wireless for the Blind Fund.

December 29

– John and Yoko flew to the small village of Ålborg in Denmark where they spent the New year with Yoko's previous husband, Anthony Cox, his new wife Melinda, and Kyoko, his daughter by Yoko.

At a press conference they performed a Danish folk song called 'Kristelighed' and pledged to donate all their further record royalties to the peace movement. (Something which was later discreetly forgotten.)

December 30

– ATV broadcast *Man of the Decade*, the last 20 minutes of which were devoted to John Lennon, including an interview filmed at Tittenhurst Park.

– December 31

– George and Patti, Paul and Linda were among the among the guests at Ringo and Maureen's New Year's party in Highgate, London.

– John and Yoko issued a statement:

"We **believe** that the **last** decade was the **end** of the **old machine crumbling** to pieces. And we **think** we can get it **together,** with your **help.** We have great **hopes** for the new year."

John, Yoko and George with the cast of the Peace for Christmas Concert, Lyceum, December 15. Back row, left to right: Jim Price, Bobby Keyes, Jim Gordon, Klaus Voorman, Bonny and Delaney Bramlett; centre: George, Allan White, Keith Moon, Neil Boland, Eric Barrett, Billy Preston, Eric Clapton; front: Tony Ashton, John and Yoko.

1970

January 3
– *Abbey Road.* Paul, George and Ringo worked on overdubs to George's 'I Me Mine' for use on the *Let It Be* soundtrack album (as the Get Back film and soundtrack were now called).

January 4
– *Abbey Road.* Further overdubs to 'Let It Be'.

January 8
– *Olympic Sound Studios, Barnes, London.* George added a vocal overdub to the Glyn Johns production of 'For You Blue'.

January 12
– The single 'Come And Get It' by Badfinger and produced by Paul McCartney was released in the US as Apple 1815.

January 14
– *Olympic Sound Studios, Barnes, London.* Ringo's Sentimental Journey sessions. Ringo added his vocals to 'Love Is A Many Splendoured Thing' and 'Sentimental Journey'.

January 15
– A two-week exhibition of John Lennon's "Bag One" lithographs opened at the *London Arts Gallery in New Bond Street.*

January 16
– Police detectives raided *the London Arts Gallery* and confiscated the eight erotic lithographs. The exhibition continued with just six exhibits. On April 27, the gallery got the prints back, having argued in court that Picasso's erotic lithographs had been shown in Britain and not deemed obscene.

January 17
– 'Come And Get It' by Badfinger entered the *New Musical Express* charts.

January 20
– John and Yoko had their hair cropped

Below: John and Yoko began to resemble one another at the turn of the decade.
Opposite: John performing Instant Karma on Top Of The Pops, February 11.

short in Denmark, described by the *Daily Mirror* as "the most sensational scalpings since the Red Indians went out of business".

January 22
– John's "Bag One" lithographs were exhibited at the *London Gallery in Detroit, Michigan.* There were no confiscations.

January 25
– John and Yoko flew back to London from Denmark.

January 26
– Ringo and Maureen flew to Los Angeles.

January 27
– *Abbey Road.* John and The Plastic Ono Band cut a new single: 'Instant Karma!' produced by Phil Spector, working with John for the first time.

John took the vocals and played acoustic guitar, with Alan White on drums, Klaus Voormann on bass, Billy Preston on electric piano and George playing lead guitar. By 4 am it was finished and mixed.
– In Los Angeles, Ringo taped an appearance before a live audience for the NBC-TV show, *Rowan and Martin's Laugh In.*

January 28
– *The London Arts Gallery* exhibition of John's "Bag One" lithographs closed.

January 29
– Ringo and Maureen attended the American premiere of *The Magic Christian* in Los Angeles.
– Allen Klein was convicted of ten tax offences in the New York Federal District Court.

January 30
– Ringo and Maureen went to Las Vegas to see Elvis Presley in concert.
– The single 'All That I've Got I'm Gonna Give It To You' by Billy Preston, produced by George Harrison, was released in the UK as Apple 21.

January 30
– *Rolling Stone* read between the lines in various John Lennon interviews and published a story under the headline "Beatles Splitting? Maybe, Says John".

January 31
– Ringo and Maureen returned to Los Angeles from Las Vegas.

February 1
– Ringo and Maureen flew to New York from Los Angeles.

February 2
– Ringo and Maureen returned to London from New York.

February 3
– *Abbey Road.* Ringo's Sentimental

Journey sessions. A 16-piece orchestra recorded the backing track for a remake of 'Love Is A Many Spendoured Thing' and Ringo added his vocal track.

February 4
– In another rooftop ceremony, this time with London Black Power leader Michael X (Michael Abdul Malik), John and Yoko swapped their shorn hair – brought back in a bag from Denmark – for a pair of Muhammad Ali's blood stained boxing shorts at the Black House in north London. John and Yoko said they intended to auction the boxing trunks to raise money for peace. The proceeds from their hair were to go to "the Black community".

February 5
– Abbey Road. Ringo's Sentimental Journey sessions. Ringo recorded a new vocal for 'Love Is A Many Splendoured Thing'.

February 6
– John and Yoko were interviewed at Apple by John Bellan for BBC Radio 1's Scene And Heard.

– The single 'How The Web Was Woven'/'Thumbin' A Ride' by Jackie Lomax produced by George Harrison (A-side) and Paul McCartney (B-side) was released in the UK as APPLE 23.
– The single **'Instant Karma! (We All Shine On)'** by The Plastic Ono Band/**'Who Has Seen The Wind?'** by Yoko Ono Lennon (side B produced by John Lennon) was released in the UK as APPLE 1003.

February 7
– Short-haired John and Yoko were interviewed for London Weekend Television's The Simon Dee Show. They brought with them Michael Abdul Malik – Michael X, the Black community leader to whom they had given their hair the previous week.

February 8
– The Simon Dee Show transmitted its interview with John, Yoko and Michael X.

February 9
– Abbey Road. Ringo's Sentimental Journey sessions. Ringo added vocals

Below: John and Yoko with Michael X, February 4.

to 'Have I Told You Lately That I Love You?'.

February 11
– John and The Plastic Ono Band taped a live appearance before an audience for BBC1's Top Of The Pops to promote 'Instant Karma!'. The line-up consisted of John on vocals and electric piano, Klaus Voormann on bass, Alan White on drums, Mal Evans on tambourine, and Yoko holding cards and knitting while blindfolded. In fact John's vocal was the only thing recorded as the entire backing track was the one from the actual single, which had been specially mixed at Abbey Road the day before for the occasion. This was John's second time on TOTP – The Beatles had only appeared on the show once, back in June 1966.
– John paid outstanding fines amounting to £1,344 imposed on 96 anti-Apartheid protesters demonstrating against a South African rugby team which played a match in Scotland in December 1969.
– Abbey Road. Ringo's Sentimental Journey sessions. Klaus Voormann conducted a 15-piece orchestra in his own arrangement of 'I'm A Fool To Care' then Ringo added his vocal track.
– The album The Magic Christian (Original Soundtrack Album) by Ken Thorne & Orchestra (additional tracks by Badfinger) and produced by Paul McCartney, Ringo Starr and Peter Sellers was released in the US as COMMONWEALTH UNITED CU 6004.

February 12
– Abbey Road. Ringo's Sentimental Journey sessions. A 31-piece orchestra plus nine singers recorded an arrangement of 'Let The Rest Of The World Go By', then Ringo added his vocal track.
– Paul had been working on his own solo album since the end of 1969, using a Studer four-track at his home in Cavendish Avenue. He tested the machine by recording 'The Lovely Linda', then recorded 'That Would Be Something', 'Valentine Day', 'Momma Miss America (Rock'n'Roll Springtime)', 'Glasses', 'Oo You', 'Teddy Boy', 'Junk' and an instrumental of the same tune called 'Singalong Junk'. He had to make guesses about

the levels because the machine had no properly functioning VU meters so he continued work at Morgan Studios, booking himself in under the name Billy Martin. There he cut 'Hot As Sun' and, on this day, 'Kreen-Akore'. He went on to make eight-track copies of his four-track masters so that he could overdub onto them.
– *Top Of The Pops* screened The Plastic Ono Band playing 'Instant Karma!'.

February 13
– The single 'Ain't That Cute' (Harrison/Troy), produced by George Harrison/'Vaya Con Dios' (Russell/Starkey/James/Hoff – with George Harrison on guitar) by Doris Troy was released in the UK as Apple 24.

February 15
– John and Yoko's interview was broadcast by BBC Radio 1's *Scene And Heard*.

February 16
– John and Yoko began editing a film of their Montreal bed-in for peace.

February 18
– *Abbey Road*. Ringo's Sentimental Journey sessions. Ringo recorded new vocals for 'Have I Told You Lately That I Love You' and 'Let The Rest Of The World Go By'. This was followed by a midnight recording session for Ringo's composition 'It Don't Come Easy'. George Martin produced the track, George Harrison conducted the musicians: George on acoustic guitar, Klaus Voormann on bass, Ringo on drums and Stephen Stills on piano. Ringo added his vocals to the best take and by 4:40 am it was mixed.

February 19
– *Abbey Road*. Ringo recorded another vocal track for 'It Don't Come Easy'.

February 20
– The single 'Instant Karma! (We All Shine On)' by The Plastic Ono Band/ **'Who Has Seen The Wind?'** by Yoko Ono Lennon (side B produced by John) was released in the US as Apple 1818.

February 21
– *Abbey Road*. Paul's McCartney sessions. Once again booked in as Billy Martin, Paul began mixing his eight-track masters.

February 22
– *Abbey Road*. Paul's McCartney sessions. More mixing, then Paul recorded 'Every Night' and 'Maybe I'm Amazed'.

February 23
– NBC broadcast the edition of *Rowan And Martin's Laugh In* in which Ringo appeared.

February 24
– *Abbey Road*. Paul's McCartney sessions. Paul had a mixing session in studio two.
– *Abbey Road*. Ringo's Sentimental Journey sessions. In studio one, Ringo added a new vocal to 'Blue Turning Grey Over You'.

February 25
– *Abbey Road*. Paul's McCartney sessions. Paul recorded 'Man We Was Lonely', completing it and mixing it into stereo. As on all the tracks on the album, Paul played all the instruments.
– Ringo switched his sessions to De Lane Lee's new studio in Soho, where Johnny Dankworth conducted a 20-piece orchestra playing 'You Always Hurt The One You Love' and Ringo added his vocals.
– John and Yoko disassociated themselves from the Toronto Peace Festival, planned for July 3 – 5, when they found out that there was to be an admission charge. The festival didn't happen.

February 26
– The album HEY JUDE was released in the US as Apple (Capitol) SW 385 (stereo only).
   SIDE A: **'Can't Buy Me Love', 'I Should Have Known Better', 'Paperback Writer', 'Rain', 'Lady Madonna', 'Revolution';**
   SIDE B: **'Hey Jude', 'Old Brown Shoe', 'Don't Let Me Down', 'The Ballad Of John And Yoko'.**

March 5
– Yoko once more entered the London Clinic for observation. John stayed at her bedside throughout.
– On Paul's recommendation, Ringo tried out Morgan Sound Studios, where he completed Sentimental Journey. On this day he recorded 'Whispering Grass' and 'Bye Bye Blackbird' with a 36-piece orchestra.
– BBC1's *Top Of The Pops* showed

Paul and Linda stepping out in London.

a January 1969 film of The Beatles recording 'Let It Be'.

March 6

– Ringo completed his Sentimental Journey album at Morgan: drums, piano and sax, played by Johnny Dankworth were added to 'You Always Hurt The One You Love' and four other tracks were mixed. The album was now ready for release.

– The single **'Let It Be'/'You Know My Name (Look Up The Number)'** was released in the UK as APPLE (PARLOPHONE) R 5833.

– The single 'Govinda'/'Govinda Jai Jai' by Radha Krishna Temple and produced by George Harrison was released in the UK as APPLE 25.

March 7

– An interview with Ringo, done while he was in the States, was screened by American ABC TV's show Get It Together.

March 8

– Trident Studios, Soho. Ringo did another remake of 'It Don't Come Easy' with George helping in the studio.

March 9

– George was interviewed by Johnny Moran for a BBC Radio 1 Easter Monday special called The Beatles Today, which they recorded at the BBC's Aeolian Hall in New Bond Street.

– That evening, George assisted Ringo in the studio for more work on 'It Don't Come Easy' which for some reason was not released until April 1971.

– The single 'How The Web Was Woven'/'I Fall Inside Your Eyes' by Jackie Lomax, produced by George Harrison, was released in the US as APPLE 1819.

– Yoko, with John, was discharged from the London Clinic.

March 11

– The single **'Let It Be'/'You Know My Name (Look Up The Number)'** was released in the US as APPLE (CAPITOL) 2764.

March 12

– George and Patti moved out of "Kinfauns", their bungalow in Esher, Surrey, and moved to Friar Park, a huge Victorian mansion in Henley-on-Thames, Oxfordshire, which had turrets, an underground boating lake

As The Beatles disintigrated, George discovered his own identity as a songwriter and supporter of all things Indian.

and a scaled down reconstruction of Mont Blanc in its extensive gardens.

March 14

– John's "Bag One" lithographs opened at the Denise René Hans Mayer Gallery in Düsseldorf. No pictures were seized. The show also opened without problems at the Lee Nordness Gallery in New York.

March 15

– At Talk of The Town, Ringo shot a promotional film of himself singing the title song from Sentimental Journey to promote the album. The shoot was directed by Neil Aspinall before an invited audience and featured the Talk Of The Town Orchestra, conducted by George Martin.

– BBC Radio 1's Scene And Heard, broadcast part of Johnny Moran's interview with George.

March 16

– Abbey Road. Paul's McCartney sessions. Paul attended a playback session of his tapes.

– The single 'Ain't That Cute' (Harrison/Troy), produced by George Harrison with 'Vaya Con Dios' (Russell/Starkey/James/Hoff – with George Harrison on guitar) by Doris Troy was released in the US as APPLE 1820.

March 17

– Ringo and Maureen attend Patti's birthday party at Friar Park.

March 19

– BBC1's Top Of The Pops showed a January 1969 film clip of The Beatles recording 'Let It Be'.

March 22

– The French magazine L'Express carried an interview with John in which he claimed that The Beatles smoked marijuana in the toilets at Buckingham Palace before receiving their MBEs on October 26 1965. He was exaggerating: what really happened was that they slipped away for a cigarette.

March 23

– Abbey Road. Paul's McCartney sessions. Paul finished off the master tapes of McCartney to his satisfaction and took them away.

– In room four at Abbey Road, at John and Allen Klein's request, Phil Spector was just beginning his remixing of the Let It Be tapes. Paul

didn't know about this.

– The album Leon Russell by Leon Russell with George Harrison on guitar and Ringo Starr on drums was released in the US as SHELTER SHE 1001.

March 24

– The single 'Govinda'/'Govinda Jai Jai' by Radha Krishna Temple, produced by George Harrison was released in the US as APPLE 1821.

March 25

– Abbey Road. Phil Spector remixed 'Two Of Us' and Paul's 'Teddy Boy'.

– Ringo was interviewed at Apple by David Wigg for BBC Radio 1's Scene And Heard.

March 26

– Abbey Road. Phil Spector continued his remix of Let It Be.

March 27

– Abbey Road. Phil Spector continued his remix of Let It Be.

– The album SENTIMENTAL JOURNEY by Ringo Starr was released in the UK as APPLE PCS 7101.

SIDE ONE: **'Sentimental Journey', 'Night And Day', 'Whispering Grass (Don't Tell The Trees)', 'Bye Bye Blackbird', 'I'm A Fool To Care', 'Star Dust';**
SIDE TWO: **'Blue Turning Grey Over You', 'Love Is A Many Splendoured Thing', 'Dream', 'You Always Hurt The One You Love', 'Have I Told You Lately That I Love You', 'Let The Rest Of The World Go By'.**

March 28

– Five of John's "Bag One" lithographs were confiscated by police from the Merrill Chase Gallery in Oak Brook, near Chicago, Ill.

March 29

– Ringo appeared live on David Frost's London Weekend Television show Frost On Sunday to promote his new album and show the film clip made at the Talk Of The Town.

– John telephoned a message of support to a CND gathering in east London. In it he revealed that Yoko was pregnant again, but she later miscarried once more.

– Ringo's interview with David Wigg was broadcast on BBC Radio 1's Scene And Heard.

March 30

– Abbey Road. Phil Spector continued his remix of Let It Be,

On the day the Beatles came apart after Paul said 'quit'

GEORGE SITS ALONE... WITH MEMORIES

As the Beatles sing their swan song...

How they changed and how they changed us

By PEARSON PHILLIPS

BEFORE them there was God Save the Queen at the cinema and a password to conformity which went: 'Just a short back and sides, please.'

After them there were Union Jack shopping bags and a quarter of a million people at a pop music concert in Hyde Park.

Heaven knows what they meant, what they symbolised or whether they were anything more than children of their times. Future historians will explain that in a footnote.

Fashion

From here all we know is that when they arrived things changed. Music changed, show business changed, society changed.

Didn't love change? That word lurv. Before them there were things called Romance and Glamour. They injected sincerity, realism, sex. They picked up a pass from D. H. Lawrence, and they ran the whole length of the field. They put the sugar on The Pill.

Your Royal Familee changed. The Middle Class got hip. The working classes disappeared in a flurry of silk neckerchiefs.

Footballers changed. The collar-stud industry collapsed. The Times changed. Liverpool arrived. The North invaded the South. Youth crystallised into an entity of its own. Nobody wanted to be grown up any more, even the grown-ups. Especially not the grown-ups. Votes came at 18.

Possibly it would have all happened without them. Discotheques would have pounded into the King's Road, Carnaby Street. But it would not, could not, have happened with the same style.

They brought irreverence, humour, carefully nurtured individuality to it all. They pricked many wrinkled balloons.

And now, in the way of all the best meteorites, they have disintegrated.

By BRIAN DEAN and RICHARD HERD

PAUL McCARTNEY'S break with the Beatles may not be for ever.

He said yesterday: 'Temporary or permanent? I don't know.' But of one thing he is sure - he wants to build a solo career.

Yesterday he listed his reasons for quitting 'Personal differences, business differences, musical differences.'

He added: 'But most of all because I have a better time with my family.'

The 27-year-old millionaire guitarist made it quite clear that he does not get on with American Alen Klein, the 'show business doctor' brought in to run Apple, the Beatles' business organisation.

Paul said: 'I am not in contact with him and he does not represent me in any way.

'Apple? It is the office of a company which I part-own with the three other Beatles.'

RUMOURS become fact

Paul is bringing out his first solo LP next week. That was the first sign that rumoured rift had become a fact.

His songwriting partner, John Lennon, has already gone it along and made LPs with his wife, Yoko Ono.

Paul could not see the Lennon - McCartney songwriting team starting again. 'I love John, and respect what he does—but it doesn't give me any pleasure.'

Paul warned John Lennon of his decision on Thursday night in a phone call from his home in St John's Wood, London, where he lives with photographer wife, Linda, her daughter, Heather, and their own baby, Mary.

All day yesterday there were top-level conferences at Apple headquarters—Georgian house in Savile Row, London, W.

There Alen Klein admitted : 'It's never pleasant when someone appears not to like you. Paul's reasons are his own personal problem.

'Unfortunately, he is committed to Apple for a number of years. (The Beatles are under contract with Apple until 1977). His dissociation from me has no effect.'

FEAR of going solo

It was Paul's open dislike for Mr Klein that helped bring matters to a head.

The Beatles decided to appoint a 'business adviser.' Eventually they settled on Klein.

His appointment was strongly resisted by Paul, who suggested that the job should go to his father-in-law, American attorney Lee Eastman.

But he was outvoted by the other Beatles.

Mr Klein, 37-year-old New Yorker and president of the company which runs Apple, said : 'This is Paul's decision. He wants to do it himself. He wanted his in-laws in, I don't dislike him.'

Derek Taylor, head of Apple publicity, said : 'There is no argument about money — there never has been.

'It is probably something to do with growing up. Once they were four boys. Now they're four, men with wives and children.'

'One of the reasons for the split is that John has been going it alone for a long time and that has left Paul out on a limb. They have to work out a way of going solo after being collective.

'There is no jealousy between them — but there may be fear of going it alone.'

MALCOLM STUART

GEORGE HARRISON took a lonely trip down Memory Lane last night ... to recall an old British institution called The Beatles.

The "quiet one" sat alone watching newsreel after newsreel about the Beatles as they were before Paul McCartney's "I go it alone" statement yesterday.

In a room at the Apple Organisation offices in Savile-row, Mayfair, George watched silently and impassively the filmed record of the group's phenomenal eight-year existence.

He lived again the early heady days of success. Screaming teenagers... the Royal Command performance... Variety Club awards... meeting Harold Wilson... that incredible first tour of America... the MBE awards.

NO SECRET

But he would not be drawn into the present. One of the Apple men said: "George doesn't want to talk about it. He just wants to be left alone."

And it was left to Alan Klein, the American accountant John Lennon called in to manage the Beatles a year ago, and their Press officer, ex-Army sergeant, ex-Liverpool reporter Derek Taylor, to talk about the McCartney split.

Taylor said: "It is no secret that Klein and Paul have never hit it off. He has been into this building just twice since Klein came here. He opposed the appointment of Klein and wanted to make his father-in-law John Eastman, a New York lawyer, manager."

The crisis of independence has come over a one-man long playing record "McCartney," entirely composed and performed by Paul.

'DIVORCED'

He told the other Beatles nothing of what he was doing and even issued his own Press handouts, but since the four are contracted to be with each other until 1977 he had to issue the record under the Apple label.

McCartney and John Lennon were the closest Beatles, the original musical wonders. Each has now married an intelligent, independently-minded wife.

"It is," says Taylor, "almost as if they have divorced each other."

John Lennon said enigmatically: "You can say I said jokingly he didn't quit, he was fired."

Ringo Starr said: "This is all news to me."

ANNE NIGHTINGALE

McCartney with his wife Linda

Beatle Paul decides to quit

By Daily Mail Reporter

PAUL McCARTNEY wants to quit the Beatles. He is expected to give his reasons, in a statement today.

But early today a friend of the three other Beatles said: 'Paul is under contract until 1977 and no one can see how he can leave.'

The threatened break comes after months of friction within the Beatles organisation Apple.

A year ago John Lennon, George Harrison and Ringo Starr outvoted Paul and engaged American 'whiz kid' Allen Klein to manage their business affairs.

Paul, 28, who married photographer Linda Eastman, made it known that he would have liked his American father-in-law lawyer Lee Eastman to have been given a job in the organisation.

A friend said last night : 'Paul's cut up about this, but he felt there was no other way. It's all very sad...'

Paul plans to go solo—his first enterprise is a record of his own songs and music under the title McCartney.

DAILY Mirror

5d.　Friday, April 10, 1970　No. 20,616

Lennon-McCartney song team splits up

PAUL IS QUITTING THE BEATLES

Swing to Labour .. but Tories are still in command

LABOUR scored morale-boosting gains in the Greater London Council elections early today—but the swing was not nearly enough to wrest control from the Tories.

They captured three seats from the Tories at Camden—and one at Greenwich.

First results showed an average swing to Labour of just over 3 per cent. compared with 1967, when the seats were last contested.

At 2 a.m. it was still doubtful whether Labour would be able to gain the eleven seats needed to win control of the Inner London Education Authority.

But there was no doubt that they would not be able to gain the 32 seats necessary to control the Greater London Council itself.

Hampered

Labour held their seats at Barking, Tower Hamlets, Hackney and Newham.

The Tories held Harrow, Havering, Hillingdon, Kingston, Sutton, Waltham Forest, Merton, Bexley, Redbridge and Richmond.

Labour's recovery was hampered by the low turnout in many areas.

Bad weather played a significant part in discouraging people from voting.

With half the results declared, the average turnout was 33 per cent.

Outside London, the Tories were consolidating their hold on the counties.

With results from twenty-eight counties in, the Tories were showing 40 gains in seats and Labour 28.

The Tories gained control of one county, East Suffolk, where previously Independents held sway.

One of Labour's biggest

By VICTOR KNIGHT

disappointments was in Northumberland, where they had high hopes of regaining control.

They lost three seats to the Tories—though they picked up one from an Independent.

Union Movement candidates come bottom of the poll in several London boroughs.

Labour did well in Buckinghamshire, gaining six seats from the Tories.

The "Homes Before Roads" candidates made very little impression.

In Lancashire there was a swing of 6 per cent. to Labour in Premier Harold Wilson's constituency of Huyton.

Counts

The voting in London was for 97 seats on the Greater London Council. Three more—in Hammersmith—are to be contested on April 27.

A record total of 491 candidates contested the 100 seats.

Only 26 of the London constituencies did their counts last night.

Five—Ealing, Westminster, Barnet, Croydon and Kensington and Chelsea—declare today.

Mrs. Lena Townsend,

leader of the Inner London Education Authority, lost her seat at Camden.

A significant feature of the London poll was the large number of Independents standing under varying descriptions.

All of them were annihilated.

The Liberals, though not doing as badly as the Independents, also made a poor showing.

Date

Labour also did well in London by successfully fighting off a Tory challenge at marginal Islington.

It is unlikely that this week's council results will help Premier Harold Wilson to decide the date of the General Election.

Labour leaders can point to some modest gains.

But the low polls in many areas make it extremely difficult to reach hard-and-fast conclusions.

It is still possible that Mr. Wilson will call a General Election in May or June—particularly if there is a good reaction to next week's Budget.

But most M.P.s are forecasting that the Prime Minister will wait at least until October.

BY DON SHORT

McCartney ... a policy deadlock.

PAUL McCARTNEY has quit the Beatles. The shock news must mean the end of Britain's most famous pop group, which has been idolised by millions the world over for nearly ten years.

Today 27-year-old McCartney will announce his decision, and the reasons for it, in a no-holds-barred statement.

It follows months of strife over policy in Apple, the Beatles' controlling organisation, and an ever-growing rift between McCartney and his song-writing partner, John Lennon.

In his statement, which consists of a series of answers to questions, McCartney says:

"I have no future plans to record or appear with the Beatles again. Or to write any more music with John."

Last night the statement was locked up in a safe at Apple headquarters in Saville-row, Mayfair—in the very rooms where the Beatles' break-up began.

The Beatles decided to appoint a "business adviser." Eventually they settled for American Allen Klein.

His appointment was strongly resisted by Paul, who sought the job for his father-in-law, American attorney Lee Eastman.

After a meeting in London Paul was out-voted 3-1 by John, and the other Beatles, George Harrison and Ringo Starr.

Since the Klein appointment, Paul has refused to go to the Apple offices to work daily.

He kept silent and stayed at his St. John's Wood home with his photo-

grapher wife, Linda, her daughter Heather, and their own baby, Mary.

Close friends tried to pacify John and Paul. But August last year was the last time they were to work together — when they collaborated on the "Abbey Road" album.

Clash over the running of Apple

Films

There were other elements that hastened Paul's decision to quit. John Lennon, on his marriage to Yoko Ono, set out on projects of his own. Ringo went into films, and George stepped in as a record producer.

Today McCartney will reveal his own plans for a solo programme.

Early today an Apple spokesman denied that Paul McCartney had left the Beatles.

But he said that there were no plans "at the moment" for any more recordings.

adding fragments of dialogue from the film footage, none of which made it onto the finished album.

March 31

– Ringo appeared live on the BBC Radio Two programme *Open House.* where he was interviewed by Pete Murray.

April 1

– *Abbey Road.* Spector recorded a 50-piece orchestra and chorus to create a "wall of sound" backing track for 'Across The Universe', 'The Long And Winding Road' and 'I Me Mine'. Spector was his usual temperamental self, and managed to anger and upset everyone involved with the session: the musicians downed instruments – but eventually picked them up again – the conductors and technical staff were all annoyed and Pete Brown, the balance engineer, stormed out of the building and went home. Spector had to call him and apologise before he would return. Ringo – the only Beatle there – had to order Spector to calm down and eventually the session was completed.

– John and Yoko issued a hoax press release for April Fool's Day stating they had both entered the London Clinic for a dual sex-change operation.

– In the London Arts Gallery prosecution, defence lawyers compared John's lithographs with the later work of Picasso.

April 2

– *Abbey Road.* Spector mixed three orchestral tracks from the previous day and the Let It Be album was finished – at least as far as he was concerned.

April 10

– Paul had his solo album, McCartney, ready for release on April 17, but did not want to do any interviews for it.

– The final press release for The Beatles, written by Derek Taylor, typed by Mavis Smith, read as folows:

– April 10, 1970

Spring is here and Leeds play Chelsea tomorrow and Ringo and John and George and Paul are alive and well and full of hope.

The world is still spinning and so are we and so are you.

When the spinning stops – that'll be the time to worry. Not before.

Until then, The Beatles are alive and well and the Beat goes on, the Beat goes on.

May 8

– The album LET IT BE was released in the UK as APPLE (PARLOPHONE) PCS 7096 (stereo only);

SIDE A: 'Two Of Us', 'Dig A Pony', 'Across The Universe', 'I Me Mine', 'Dig It', 'Let It Be', 'Maggie May'; **SIDE B:** 'I've Got A Feeling', 'The One After 909', 'The Long And Winding Road', 'For You Blue', 'Get Back'.

– Glyn Johns had edited and mixed a completed album on January 5 but none of The Beatles were entirely happy with it, nor could John understand why Glyn Johns wanted credit as producer, even though he produced most of it.

John: "Phil Spector came in and listened to every take. He changed the takes originally used. He listened

to about one thousand million miles of tape, none of which had been marked or catalogued. Which is why The Beatles couldn't face the album, because there was too much shit and nobody was interested enough to pull it together. And Phil pulled it together, remixed it, added a string or two here and there. I couldn't be bothered because it was such a tough one making it. We were really miserable then. Spector has redone the whole thing and it's beautiful."

– In an interview published in the *Evening Standard* on April 21 and 22 Paul said: "The album was finished a year ago, but a few months ago American record producer Phil Spector was called in by John Lennon to tidy up some of the tracks. But a few weeks ago, I was sent a re-mixed version of my song 'The Long And Winding Road', with harps, horns, an orchestra and women's choir added. No one had asked me what I thought. I couldn't believe it. I would never have female voices on a Beatles record. The record came with a note from Allen Klein saying he thought the changes were necessary. I don't blame Phil Spector for doing it but it just goes to show that it's no good me sitting here thinking I'm in control because obviously I'm not. Anyway I've sent Klein a letter asking for some of the things to be altered, but I haven't received an answer yet."

May 11

– The single **'The Long And Winding Road'/'For You Blue'** was released in the US as APPLE (CAPITOL) 2832.

May 13

– The film *Let It Be* was premiered in New York.

May 18

– The album LET IT BE was released in the US as APPLE (CAPITOL) AR 34001 with the same tracks as the UK release.

May 20

– The film *Let It Be* was premiered in Liverpool and London, but none of The Beatles turned up to see it.

George Martin: "It was always understood that the album would be like **nothing** The Beatles had done before. It would be **honest**, no overdubbing, no editing, **truly live...** almost amateurish. When John brought in Phil Spector he contradicted everything he had said before. When I heard the final **sounds** I was **shaken.** They were so uncharacteristic of the clean sounds The Beatles had always used. At the time Spector was John's buddy, **mate** and **pal...** still is, I don't know. I was astonished because I knew Paul would **never** have **agreed** to it. In fact I contacted him and he said **nobody** was more **surprised** than **he** was."

Paul quits

Paul asked Peter Brown at Apple to write a questionnaire with the usual sort of things that journalists would want to know and he would answer it. Naturally Peter Brown slipped in the question that journalists had been clamouring to ask for six months: Brown opened up with fairly standard press questions but at question 28 he asked:

Is this album a rest away from Beatles or start of solo career?

Paul: Time will tell. Being a solo album means "the start of a solo career"... and not being done with The Beatles means it's a rest. So it's both.

Peter Brown: Have you any plans for live appearances

Paul: No

Peter Brown: Is your break with The Beatles temporary or permanent, due to personal differences or musical ones?

Paul: Personal differences, business differences, but most of all because I have

a better time with my family. Temporary or permanent? I don't know.

Peter Brown: Do you foresee a time when Lennon-McCartney becomes an active songwriting partnership again?

Paul: No.

The press release was printed and enclosed with advance copies of the album. The media went wild: "The Beatles Break Up!" was headline news around the world.

*George with a company
of Indian singers and
instrumentalists, including
Ravi Shankar, at the Royal
Festival Hall, September 17.*

The End of The Beatles

Paul's press release attracted headlines around the world. The greatest group in history was no more. Even Derek Taylor's whimsical optimism failed to disguise the awful truth: The Beatles had split into two camps with John, George and Ringo on one side and Paul on the other. The rift was irreversible and The Beatles were no more.

Not much was heard from them for the rest of the year. John, Paul and George all worked on solo albums, while Ringo's second solo effort 'Beaucoups Of Blues', was issued in October. In September George appeared at a press conference at the Royal Festival Hall, welcoming a group of Indian musicians to a celebration of Indian art. Like Paul, he'd grown a scruffy beard and like all his former colleagues he looked desperately tired, as if the trials and tribulations of the past 12 months had aged them prematurely.

In America a single of 'The Long And Winding Road' (Apple 2832) topped the charts in June, as did Let It Be, the album from which it was taken. Paul was horrified at the way in which Phil Spector had added lush strings to his ballad and would cite this interference with his work as a key element in his forthcoming lawsuit to formally disband the group.

There were, of course, plenty of speculative newspaper stories suggesting Beatle activity and, it has to be said, these were not discouraged by those who worked at Apple and whose jobs were on the line in the event of a total meltdown. One tradition that Apple did maintain was The Beatles annual Christmas album, and on December 18 The Beatles' US Fan Club album, The Beatles' Christmas Album, was released in the US as Apple SBC 100 consisting of a compilation of their previous Christmas flexi-discs. Side One: 'The Beatles' Christmas Record' (Dec. 1963), 'Another Beatles' Christmas Record' (Dec. 1964), 'The Beatles' Third Christmas Record' (Dec, 1965), 'The Beatles' Fourth Christmas Record' (Dec. 1966); Side Two: 'Christmas Time Is Here Again!' (Dec. 1967), 'The Beatles' 1968 Christmas Record' (Dec. 1968), 'The Beatles' Seventh Christmas Record' (Dec. 1969).The Beatles' UK Fan Club album From Them To Us, was released in the UK as Apple LYN 2154 featuring the same tracks as the US The Beatles' Christmas Album.

On December 31 Paul began proceedings in the High Court of Justice in London to wind up The Beatles.

Paul: "I for one am very proud of the Beatle thing. It was great and I can go along with all the people you meet on the street who say you gave so much happiness to many people. I don't think that's corny... I believe that we did bring a real lot of happiness to the times."

And... in the end

Regardless of how many rock and pop musicians stand up each year to receive their Grammys, Brits and platinum albums, The Beatles remain the yardstick by which their success is measured. Thanks to the ever increasing size of the global music industry they established in the first place, many of the statistical sales records that The Beatles once held have now been eclipsed, but no-one has ever really become "bigger than The Beatles" or even the "new Beatles", nor are they ever likely to because becoming "bigger than The Beatles" is simply unattainable. Their achievements will forever remain unique because of the context and the manner in which they were accomplished.

As this book was being prepared, the latest act whose success was likened in the popular press to that of The Beatles was The Spice Girls, five sassy young women whose début album and concurrent singles sold in their millions in many territories of the world. They were but the latest in a long line of performers who never asked for this comparison to be made and, with just the single album recorded at the time, it was wholly inappropriate even to consider them at all. "Bigger than The Beatles", of course, is the kind of emotive phrase that helps to sell tabloid newspapers (while its perpetual usage only adds to The Beatles' impregnable status).

Most of those compared briefly to The Beatles begin and end their careers as what are today referred to as 'boy bands', but many of these acts don't even play musical instruments, let alone write all their own material. Nowadays their stage shows are often limited to displays of athletic dancing while they sing along to pre-recorded tapes, and there is tendency for their back catalogues to stagnate within 12 months of their demise. What price today the back catalogues of The Monkees, The Osmonds, The Bay City Rollers, Duran Duran, Kajagoogoo, Wham!, A-Ha, Bros, New Kids On The Block, Brother Beyond or even Take That?

It is equally inconclusive to compare the success of The Beatles with serious stadium filler artists of the calibre of R.E.M., U2 or even Bruce Springsteen, none of whom were actually compared to The Beatles because their careers developed slowly and big success arrived only after several years of hard graft. Although all three have now produced around as many albums as The Beatles and their record sales (and concert ticket sales) certainly measure up, it has taken them at least three times as long to achieve this. Regardless of their integrity in an increasingly profit motivated industry, R.E.M., U2 and Springsteen never really changed anything, or even attract more than a few dozen fans whenever they land at Heathrow Airport.

As the millennium approaches, it seems that any act who becomes very popular very quickly are tagged "the new Beatles", but this overlooks the fact that The Beatles, or at least three of them, played together for almost four years before they saw the inside of a real recording studio. In the meantime, somehow, they scratched a living by performing live. In the modern era it's unlikely that any group, including R.E.M. or U2, would stick it out together for four years from formation to recording, though Springsteen certainly paid his dues on the New Jersey shore. Among The Beatles' near contemporaries, only The Who, again just three of them, made a living playing live for four years before recording. But The Who made only four albums in the Sixties, against The Beatles' twelve. By comparison, less than six months elapsed between the formation of The Beatles' biggest rivals, The Rolling Stones, and the recording session that produced their first single.

Of course, the sedulous conditions under which The Beatles produced their work are unlikely ever to be repeated. It seems extra-ordinary to say it, but for all their modern-day sophistication, today's multi-national record companies are simply not equipped to handle two albums a year from the same artist, nor are they likely to welcome non-album singles which won't act as promotional tools for the triennial album. Perhaps there's a lesson to be learned here: today's Top Five singles often sell less than 100,000; in their heyday The Beatles' singles sold over a million on advance orders alone and that's just in the UK!

At present the Manchester band Oasis are enjoying great success, but it is unlikely that more than 2,000 other artists will record a cover version of any of their songs. Nor do more recent bands have the widespread appeal of The Beatles. Again, looking at the cover versions of their songs, they have been covered by everyone from Ella Fitzgerald, Sinatra, Ray Charles, Fats Domino and Peggy Lee at one end of the scale, to Laibach's thrash metal version of the entire *Let It Be* album on the other, to say nothing of Cathy Berberian's *Beatles' Arias*, an entire album of Beatles songs given operatic treatment, or the many brass band, string quartet and even steam organ versions of their songs.

The Beatles cast a giant shadow, a shadow so huge that many bands don't even realise they sit within its umbra. At the height of their fame, in the mid-Sixties, they influenced a huge number of their contemporaries: from Brian Jones period Rolling Stones (particularly Jones's use of sitar, and the whole of *Satanic Majesties* which was a *Sgt Pepper* imitation), through Donovan, The Kinks to all the other pop acts who went on to produce more complex, lasting work, spurred on by the advances and experiments of The Beatles. Before the end of the Sixties their vocal harmonies were influencing everyone from The Hollies to The Bee Gees and by the end of the decade their impact was spreading out through ELO who took mid-period psychedelic Beatles songs as a blue print for almost everything they did. Another strand of their work, notably the guitar heavy *White Album*, was developed by Led Zeppelin, much more of a Beatles band than most people think; and Syd Barrett took much from The Beatles for the whimsical early Pink Floyd. Their influence was all encompassing. In the US, one only has to look at the work of The Byrds, The Beach Boys and Buffalo Springfield – to name just those groups whose name also begins with "B" – to see how the Americans coped with the British Invasion.

Interest in their work remains far higher than any of their contemporaries, so much so that their complete repertoire remains in print at full price, and fans still clamour for more. They have become the most collected group of all time and the most bootlegged. In the years since The Beatles disbanded lawyers and managers representing their interests have increased their tight stranglehold on the group's product. Although Paul and John's heir Yoko Ono have lost control of their song publishing, they (and George and Ringo) have effectively turned around the slave and master situation that existed with EMI in the Sixties, i.e. The Beatles are now the very much the masters.

All of which probably explains why the three volume *Anthology* series of rarities and outtakes, released in 1996, sold as well as it did and, together with the accompanying eight volume video collection, raised a sum not unadjacent to $400 million for the three surviving Beatles and Yoko. This made them, in 1996, almost 40 years after John first encountered Paul at the Woolton village fete, the third highest paid entertainers in the world, after Oprah Winfrey and Steven Spielberg.

Their musical accomplishments aside, this cold cash statistic alone explains why The Beatles remain the yardstick by which others are and always will be measured – and why no-one will ever become 'bigger than The Beatles'.

Picture Credits

Front cover: John Wengard/Life Magazine ©Time Inc/Katz; Advertising Archives: 86, 116r, 134b, 221r, 224; Associated Press: 1 x flap, 84, 102, 106, 113b, 123, 126, 132b, 136, 141t, 146, 149, 155t, 158t, 162, 163t, 175t, 218, 221l, 225r, 244; Jane Bown/Camera Press: 64, 65, 74b, 77, 202, 230, 232/233, 275; Tony Bramwell: 268; Peter Bruckman/Redferns: 22, 117; Leslie Bryce: 234, 243; AlecByrne: 1 x flap, 309; Cambridge Newspapers Ltd: 75; Camera Press: 2 x flap, 107b, 108, 112t, 132t, 170, 174, 235, 245, 284, 301; Christie's Images: 185, 190b, 191, 192t, 198; Clive Donald/Camera Press: 169; Robert Freeman/Camera Press: 152, 166; Harry Goodwin: 125, 312; Philip Gotlop/Camera Press: 66; Ray Green/Camera Press: 208; Ray Green/ Redferns: 178/179; Wolf-Hinrich Groeneveld/Camera Press: 217b; Tom Hanley/Camera Press: 11, 14, 288, 302, 303; Tom Hanley/Redferns: 188/189, 285, 295, 296, 298; Frank Hermann/Camera Press: 1 x flap, 228, 231t, 238; Hulton Getty: 3 x flap, 10, 12/13, 15, 25t&b, 33, 35, 41, 43, 47, 48, 57, 71t, 73, 76, 81, 85, 89r, 93, 95, 97, 98, 99r, 100, 101, 103, 104/105, 107, 112t, 117t, 119, 122b, 124t, 127, 128, 131t&b, 134l, 137t&b, 138/139, 140, 141b, 150, 155b, 157, 159, 160, 167t&b, 171t&b, 172t, 173t&b, 175b, 194/195, 200/201, 210, 213r, 214, 215, 219, 210, 225l, 227t, 229, 237, 239, 240, 241, 247, 248b, 249, 250t, 251, 252/253, 254, 255, 256t&b, 257, 260/261, 263t&b, 267t&b, 276/277, 278, 289b, 292, 305t&b, 306, 308, 310, 317, 319; David Hurn/ Magnum: 1 x flap, 114/115, 116l, 118; Mail Newspapers plc: 314 by permission of The British Library; Jewish Chronicle: 70b; Philip Jones Griffiths/Magnum: 51, 52/53, 54, 55; Graham Keen: 227b; John Kelly/ Camera Press: 248t, 272b, 289t, 293; Astrid Kirchherr/Redferns: 1 x flap, 21, 26/27, 29, 30, 36, 37, 46; K&K Studios/Redferns: 28, 186/187; Kobal Collection: 20; LFI: 3 x flap, 6, 18, 45, 50, 58, 60, 63, 70t, 82, 109, 142, 145, 148, 153, 184, 193, 196/197, 216, 222/223, 242, 262, 269, 294, 304, 307, 311; Bruce McBroom/Camera Press: 206/207, 299, 300;

Don McCullin/Magnum: 1 x flap, 204/205, 259, 265, 270/271, 272t, 273, 274; Albert Marrion: 42; Mirror Syndication International: 1 x flap, 67, 71b, 74t, 88, 89l, 112b, 154b, 211, 212, 213l, 231b, 246, 250b, 266, 282/283, 286/287, 315 by permission of The British Library; David Nutter/Camera Press: 290; PA News: 2 x flap, 59, 83, 87, 92, 94, 96t&b, 120/121, 122l&t, 124b, 133, 134t, 154t, 161, 163b, 168, 172b, 217t, 258, 297; Thomas Picton/Camera Press: 156; Pictorial Press: 34, 38, 143; Harry Prytherch: 17, 40; Ellen Piel/Redferns: 23, 31; David Redfern: 199, 313; Rex Features: 49, 99l, 113t, 117b, 158b, 226; S&G/Redferns: 182/183; Tony Robbins/Camera Press: 280; Sotheby's: 192r; Terence Spencer/Camera Press: 2 x flap, 61t&b, 68/69, 72, 78/79, 90/91, 130, 135, 151, 164/165; David Steen/Camera Press: 62; Joseph Tandl/ Camera Press: 279; Tracks: 180/181, 190t, 203; Stefan Tyszko/Camera Press: 281; Laurens Van Houten: 1 x flap, 291.